**Fodor's** 4th Editi

# Miami and Miami Beach

The Guide for All Budgets

Completely Updated

Where to Stay, Eat, and Explore

On and Off the Beaten Path

When to Go, What to Pack

Maps, Travel Tips, and Web Sites

Fodor's Travel Publications • New York, Toronto, London, Sydney, Auckland

**www.fodors.com**

## Fodor's Miami and Miami Beach

**EDITOR:** Melisse J. Gelula

**Editorial Contributors:** Kathy Foster, Jennifer Karetnick, Karen Schlesinger, Gretchen Schmidt, Matthew Windsor
**Editorial Production:** Taryn Luciani
**Maps:** David Lindroth, Inc., Mapping Specialists, Ltd., *cartographers*; Rebecca Baer and Bob Blake, *map editors*
**Design:** Fabrizio La Rocca, *creative director*; Guido Caroti, *art director*; Jolie Novak, *senior picture editor*; Melanie Marin, *photo editor*
**Cover Design:** Pentagram
**Production/Manufacturing:** Angela L. McLean
**Cover Photo (Art Deco on South Beach):** Annie Griffiths Belt/Corbis

## Copyright



Fourth Edition

ISBN 1-4000-1048-9

ISSN 1070-6399

## Important Tip

Although all prices, opening times, and other details in this book are based on information supplied to us at press time, changes occur all the time in the travel world, and Fodor's cannot accept responsibility for facts that become outdated or for inadvertent errors or omissions. So **always confirm information when it matters,** especially if you're making a detour to visit a specific place.

## Special Sales

Fodor's Travel Publications are available at special discounts for bulk purchases for sales promotions or premiums. Special editions, including personalized covers, excerpts of existing guides, and corporate imprints, can be created in large quantities for special needs. For more information, contact your local bookseller or write to Special Markets, Fodor's Travel Publications, 280 Park Avenue, New York, NY 10017. Inquiries from Canada should be directed to your local Canadian bookseller or sent to Random House of Canada, Ltd., Marketing Department, 2775 Matheson Boulevard East, Mississauga, Ontario L4W 4P7. Inquiries from the United Kingdom should be sent to Fodor's Travel Publications, 20 Vauxhall Bridge Road, London SW1V 2SA, England.

PRINTED IN THE UNITED STATES OF AMERICA

10 9 8 7 6 5 4 3 2 1

# CONTENTS

## Maps

# ON THE ROAD WITH FODOR'S

The more you know before you go, the better your trip will be. Miami's most fascinating small museum (or its hottest new restaurant) could be just around the corner from your hotel, but if you don't know it's there, it might as well be on the other side of the globe. That's where this book comes in. It's a great step toward making sure your next trip lives up to your expectations. As you plan, check out the Web as well. Guidebooks have been helping smart travelers find the special places for years; the Web is one more tool. Whatever reference you consult, be savvy about what you read, and always consider the source. Images and language can be massaged to make places appear better than they are. And one traveler's quaint is another's grimy. Here at Fodor's, and at our on-line arm, Fodors.com, our focus is on providing you with information that's not only useful but accurate and on target. Every day Fodor's editors put enormous effort into getting things right, beginning with the search for the right contributors—people who have objective judgment, broad travel experience, and the writing ability to put their insights into words. There's no substitute for advice from a like-minded friend who has just come back from where you're going, but our writers, having seen all corners of Miami and Miami Beach, are the next best thing. They're the kind of people you'd poll for tips yourself if you knew them.

Travel writer **Kathy Foster,** who has explored almost every spot from Miami to the Keys via bicycle, updated the Essential Information, Exploring, and Outdoor Activities and Sports chapter. When not biking, she's at work as an editor for the *Miami Herald*'s feature section.

**Jen Karetnick** is a restaurant critic and columnist for the *Miami New Times* and *New Times Broward/Palm Beach* weekly newspapers. She is the author of *Around Miami with Kids* (Fodor's) and the forthcoming cookbook *Miami Restaurant Recipes* (Tierra Publications).

As a writer for travel and trade publications, longtime Miamian **Gretchen Schmidt** loves visiting exotic places. But she's always happy to return to South Florida's cacophony of languages, the perfume of gardenias and frangipani in the air, and the indescribable splendor of the full moon rising over Miami. She contributed to the Nightlife and the Arts chapter.

Freelance writer **Karen Schlesinger** has been exploring South Florida shopping for more than a decade. A local expert and regular contributor to newspapers, magazines, and such books as *Cash in the City: Affording Manolos, Martinis and Manicures on a Working Girl's Salary,* Karen recently developed a Web site (theysay.cc)—a source for what's hip and haute in South Florida shopping and fashion. She currently lives in Ocean Ridge, Florida, with her husband and more than 200 pairs of shoes.

As an editor with Miami Lakes–based travel trade publication *Recommend,* **Matt Windsor** has had plenty of time to ponder the byzantine complexities of the South Florida hotel scene and bring this knowledge to bear in updating the Lodging chapter. He didn't chafe at the idea of writing up the city's hotel day spas either.

## Don't Forget to Write

Your experiences—positive and negative—matter to us. If we have missed or misstated something, we want to hear about it. We follow up on all suggestions. Contact the Miami editor at editors@fodors.com or c/o Fodor's, 280 Park Avenue, New York, New York 10017. And have a fabulous trip!

Karen Cure
*Editorial Director*

## Greater Miami

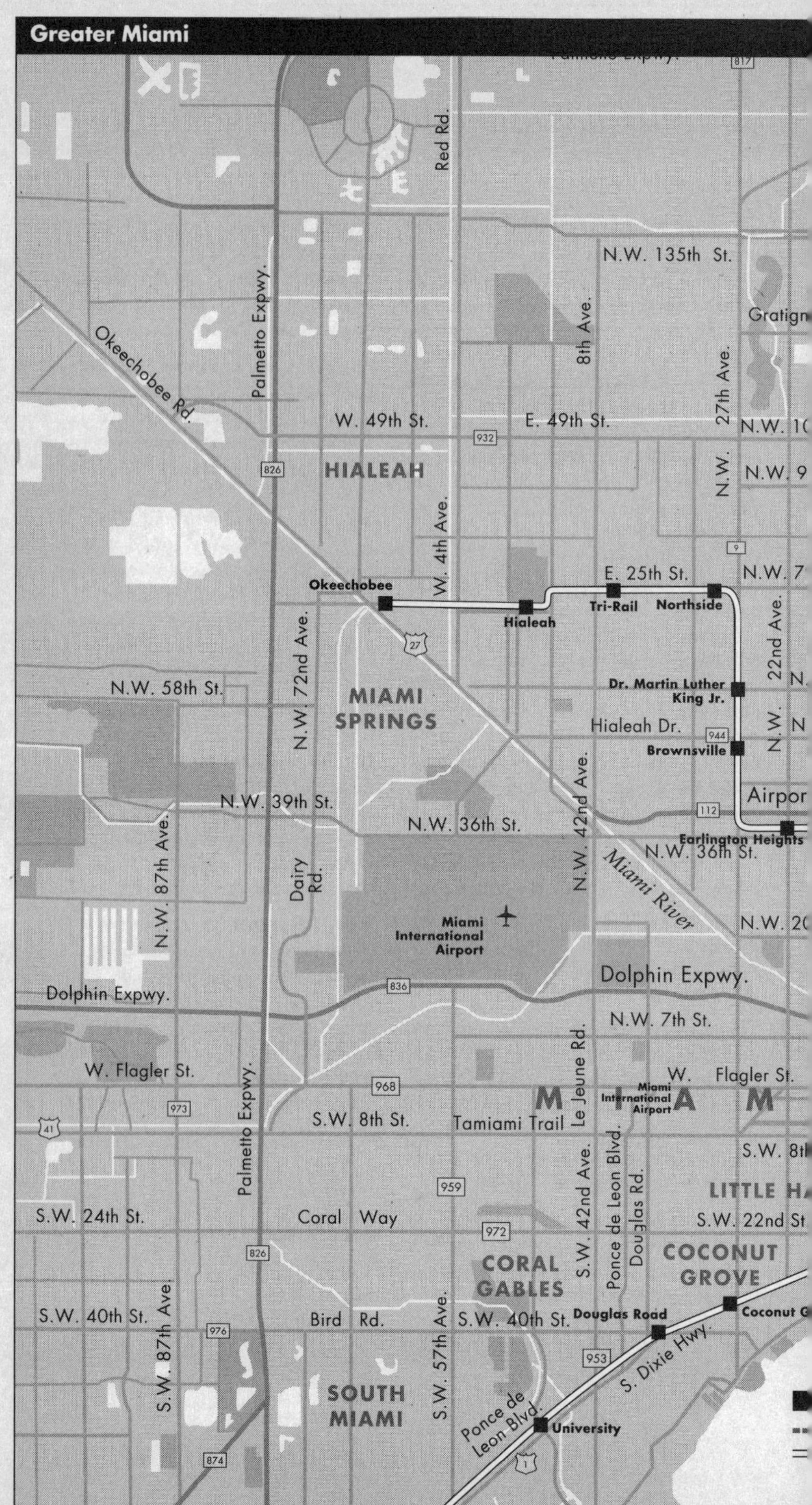

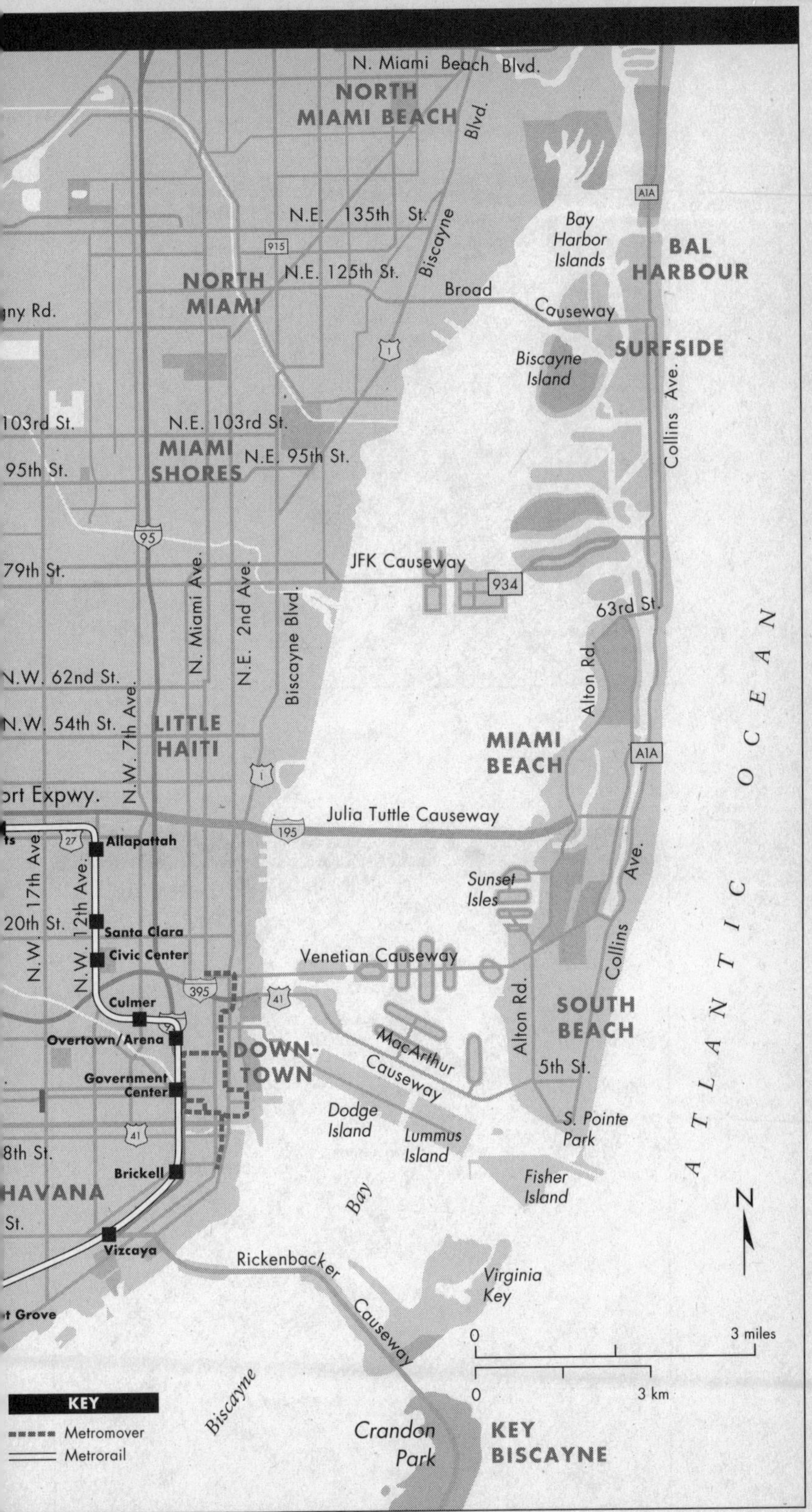

N. Miami Beach Blvd.
NORTH MIAMI BEACH
Biscayne Blvd.
N.E. 135th St.
915
N.E. 125th St.
NORTH MIAMI
Broad Causeway
Bay Harbor Islands
BAL HARBOUR
A1A
SURFSIDE
Biscayne Island
Collins Ave.
1
N.E. 103rd St.
103rd St.
MIAMI SHORES
N.E. 95th St.
95th St.
95
79th St.
JFK Causeway
934
63rd St.
N. Miami Ave.
N.E. 2nd Ave.
Biscayne Blvd.
Alton Rd.
N.W. 62nd St.
N.W. 54th St.
N.W. 7th Ave.
LITTLE HAITI
MIAMI BEACH
A1A
ATLANTIC OCEAN
Julia Tuttle Causeway
195
27
Allapattah
N.W. 17th Ave.
N.W. 12th Ave.
20th St.
Santa Clara
Civic Center
Sunset Isles
Collins Ave.
Venetian Causeway
395
41
Culmer
Overtown/Arena
DOWNTOWN
Government Center
MacArthur Causeway
Alton Rd.
SOUTH BEACH
5th St.
Dodge Island
Lummus Island
S. Pointe Park
8th St.
Brickell
HAVANA
Fisher Island
Bay
Vizcaya
Rickenbacker Causeway
Virginia Key
N
0
3 miles
0
3 km
KEY
Metromover
Metrorail
Biscayne
Crandon Park
KEY BISCAYNE

## Metrorail

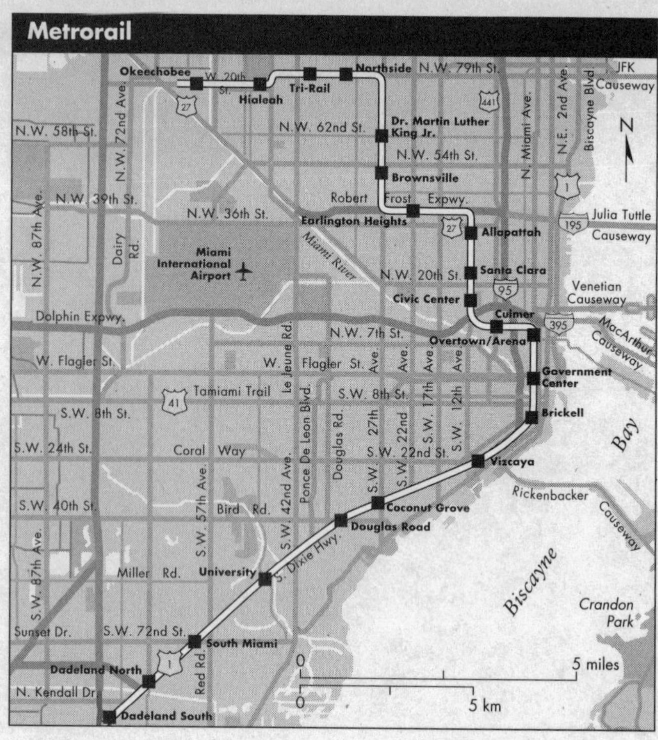


## South Florida

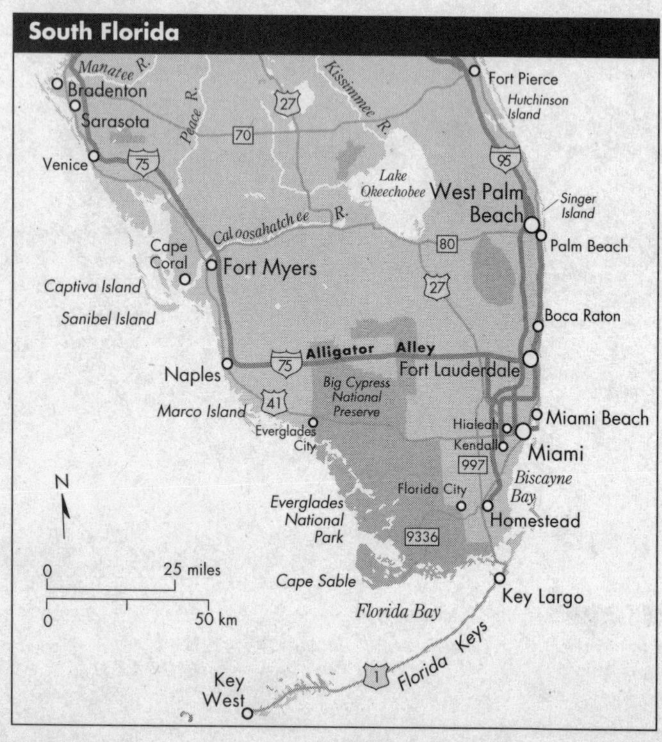

# ESSENTIAL INFORMATION

## ADDRESSES

Greater Miami is made up of more than 30 municipalities, although vacation favorites Miami and Miami Beach are only two of the cities which make up Miami-Dade County. Throughout this guide you'll see references to Miami-Dade, Dade County, or Greater Miami—all are used interchangeably.

Within Greater Miami, addresses fall into four quadrants: NW, NE, SW, and SE. The north–south dividing line is Flagler Street, and the east–west dividing line is Miami Avenue. Numbering starts from these axes and gets higher the farther away an address is from them. Avenues run north–south and streets east–west. Some municipalities, including Miami Beach, Coral Gables, Coconut Grove, and Key Biscayne, have their own street naming and numbering systems, so a map is a good idea. In South Beach, all north–south roads are named and the main drags are Ocean Drive, Collins and Washington avenues, and Alton Road. Streets are numbered and run east–west; 1st Street is at the beach's southernmost point and numbers get higher as you head north.

## AIR TRAVEL TO AND FROM MIAMI

### BOOKING

When you book **look for nonstop flights** and **remember that "direct" flights stop at least once.** Try to avoid connecting flights, which require a change of plane. For more booking tips and to check prices and make online flight reservations, log on to www.fodors.com.

Consider, too, whether other major airports in the area might be more convenient to your final destination, e.g., Fort Lauderdale International Airport.

### CARRIERS

➤ MAJOR AIRLINES: **AirTran** (☎ 800/825–8538). **America West** (☎ 800/235–9292). **American** (☎ 800/433–7300). **American Transair** (☎ 800/225–2995). **Continental** (☎ 800/525–0280). **Delta** (☎ 800/221–1212). **Midway** (☎ 800/446–4392). **National** (☎ 888/757–5387). **Northwest** (☎ 800/225–2525). **Southwest** (☎ 800/435–9792). **TWA** (☎ 800/221–2000). **United** (☎ 800/241–6522). **US Airways** (☎ 800/428–4322).

➤ FOREIGN CARRIERS: **ACES** (☎ 800/846–2237). **Aeroflot** (☎ 888/340–6400). **Aerolineas Argentina** (☎ 800/333–0276). **Aeromexico** (☎ 800/237–6639). **Aeropostal** (☎ 888/912–8466). **Air Aruba** (☎ 800/882–7822). **Air Canada** (☎ 888/247–2262). **Air France** (☎ 800/237–2747). **Air Jamaica** (☎ 800/523–5585). **Alitalia** (☎ 800/223–5730). **ALM** (☎ 800/327–7230). **Avensa** (☎ 800/428–3672). **Avianca** (☎ 800/284–2622). **Aviateca** (☎ 800/535–8780). **Bahamasair** (☎ 800/222–4262). **British Airways** (☎ 800/247–9297). **BWIA** (☎ 800/538–2942). **Canadian Airlines** (☎ 888/247–2262). **Cayman Airways** (☎ 800/422–9626). **City Bird** (☎ 888/248–9247). **Copa** (☎ 800/359–2672). **El Al** (☎ 800/223–6700). **LAB** (☎ 800/327–7407). **Lacsa** (☎ 800/225–2272). **Lan Chile** (☎ 800/735–5526). **Lan Peru** (☎ 800/735–5590). **LOT Polish Airlines** (☎ 800/223–0593). **LTU** (☎ 800/888–0200). **Lufthansa** (☎ 800/645–3880). **Martinair Holland** (☎ 800/366–4655). **Mexicana** (☎ 800/531–7921). **Nica** (☎ 800/831–6422). **Northwest/KLM** (☎ 800/225–2525). **Qantas** (☎ 800/227–4500). **Surinam** (☎ 800/327–6864). **Swissair** (☎ 800/221–4750). **Taca** (☎ 800/535–8780). **Transbrasil** (☎ 800/872–3153). **Varig** (☎ 800/468–2744). **VASP** (☎ 800/732–8277). **Virgin Atlantic** (☎ 800/862–8621).

➤ REGIONAL AIRLINES: **American Eagle** (☎ 800/433–7300). **Comair**

(☎ 800/221–1212). **Delta Express** (☎ 800/325–5205). **Gulfstream International** (☎ 800/992–8532). **Jet Blue** (☎ 800/538–2583) to Fort Lauderdale. **US Air Express** (☎ 800/428–4322).

➤ SEAPLANE: **Chalk's Ocean Airways** (☎ 800/424–2557) offers daily service from Watson Island in Miami and Ft. Lauderdale International Airport to Bimini and Paradise Island.

## CHECK-IN AND BOARDING

Assuming that not everyone with a ticket will show up, airlines routinely overbook planes. When everyone does, airlines ask for volunteers to give up their seats. In return, these volunteers usually get a certificate for a free flight and are rebooked on the next flight out. If there are not enough volunteers, the airline must choose who will be denied boarding. The first to get bumped are passengers who checked in late and those flying on discounted tickets, so **get to the gate and check in as early as possible,** especially during peak periods.

Always **bring a government-issued photo ID to the airport;** a passport is best. You will be required to show it before you are allowed to check in and board.

## CUTTING COSTS

The least expensive airfares to Greater Miami must usually be purchased in advance and are nonrefundable. The Internet offers a whole new way to travel and compare prices. If you're willing to travel at the last minute or learn to navigate on-line travel auctions, you can save even more. Many airline sites offer Internet-only fares, which are substantially cheaper than if you call the airline directly. Some of the best booking sites are www.expedia.com; www.orbitz.com; www.priceline.com; www.travelocity.com; and www.hotwire.com. The www.smarterliving.com site allows you to plug in your departure airport(s) and then sends you weekly e-mail alerts with the best available domestic and international fares from all the major airlines. Even if you don't buy a ticket on-line, it's best to **check on-line rates first** to get a ballpark ticket rate and then consult a travel agent or the airlines directly.

It's smart to **call a number of airlines, and when you are quoted a good price, book it on the spot**—the same fare may not be available the next day. Travel agents, especially low-fare specialists, are helpful.

Always **check different routings** and look into using different airports. If you're destined for the north side of Miami-Dade County, consider flying into Fort Lauderdale International Airport; you may find cheaper fares. Miami's airport has a wider selection of international flights and quicker access to South Beach and the county's southern environs. Airline fares to South Florida are most often discounted in Miami's shoulder seasons—late fall–early winter, and after Easter but before summer family vacations. Also price off-peak flights, which may be significantly less expensive.

Consolidators are another good source. They buy tickets for scheduled international flights at reduced rates from the airlines, then sell them at prices that beat the best fare available directly from the airlines, usually without restrictions. Sometimes you can even get your money back if you need to return the ticket. Carefully read the fine print detailing penalties for changes and cancellations, and **confirm your consolidator reservation with the airline.**

➤ CONSOLIDATORS: **Cheap Tickets** (☎ 800/377–1000). **Discount Airline Ticket Service** (☎ 800/576–1600). **Unitravel** (☎ 800/325–2222). **Up & Away Travel** (☎ 212/889–2345). **World Travel Network** (☎ 800/409–6753).

## ENJOYING THE FLIGHT

For more legroom, **request an emergency-aisle seat.** Don't sit in the row in front of the emergency aisle or in front of a bulkhead, where seats may not recline. If you have dietary concerns, **ask for special meals when booking.** These can be vegetarian, low-cholesterol, or kosher, for example. On long flights, try to maintain a normal routine, to help fight jet lag. At night, **get some sleep.** By day, **eat light meals, drink water** (not alcohol), and **move around the cabin** to stretch your legs. For additional jet-lag tips consult *Fodor's FYI: Travel Fit & Healthy* (available at bookstores everywhere).

### FLYING TIMES

Approximate flying times to Miami are 3 hours from Chicago, 5 hours from Los Angeles, 6 hours from London, 3 hours 20 minutes from Montreal, 2 hours 50 minutes from New York, and 3 hours 5 minutes from Toronto.

### HOW TO COMPLAIN

If your baggage goes astray or your flight goes awry, complain right away. Most carriers require that you **file a claim immediately.**

➤ AIRLINE COMPLAINTS: U.S. Department of Transportation **Aviation Consumer Protection Division** (✉ C-75, Room 4107, Washington, DC 20590, ☎ 202/366–2220, WEB www.dot.gov/airconsumer). **Federal Aviation Administration Consumer Hotline** (☎ 800/322–7873).

## AIRPORTS AND TRANSFERS

Miami International Airport (MIA), 7 mi west of downtown Miami, is the only airport in Greater Miami that provides scheduled service. If you're destined for the north side of Miami-Dade County, though, consider flying into Fort Lauderdale International Airport. Less crowded and more user friendly, you may also find greatly reduced fares on airlines that don't serve MIA. More than 1,400 daily flights make MIA the ninth busiest passenger airport in the world. Approximately 34 million visitors pass through annually, more than half of them international travelers. Altogether, more than 100 airlines serve nearly 150 cities and five continents with nonstop or one-stop service from here, more than any other airport in the Western Hemisphere.

The airport is undergoing a $5.4 billion expansion program that is expected to be finished within the next six to eight years. If local politics don't muddy the waters, ambitious plans will provide a much needed boost to retail facilities, and expanded gate and public areas are expected to reduce congestion. For the time being, gridlock in and out of the airport—especially during holidays and peak periods—is the rule and not the exception. The airport has already added additional parking garages with easy-to-follow color designations. Long-term parking is $4 per hour for the first and second hour, $2 for the third hour, and a maximum of $10 per 24-hour period. Short-term parking is $2.50 per half hour, with a maximum of $25 per day.

Getting around MIA is easy if you envision a horseshoe or U-shape terminal. Eight concourses extend out from the terminal; Concourse A is on the right or north side, E is in the center, and H is on the left or south side (a map of the airport is available on the MIA Web site). If you're headed from one concourse to another, **take the Moving Walkway** on the skywalk (third) level; it links all eight concourses and the parking garages. Skycaps are available for hire throughout the airport, but on busy days be prepared to wait. Within Customs, portage is free only from baggage claim to the inspection line. A better bet: **grab a luggage cart**—they're free within Customs and $2 elsewhere.

A Tourist Information Center, open 6:30 AM–10:30 PM, is on Level 2, Concourse E; free brochures here tell you everything you'd want to know about the airport. Services for travelers include multilingual information and paging phones, a full-service bank and post office on Level 4 of Concourse B, myriad ATMs and currency exchange booths (the booth at Concourse E operates 24 hours a day), two 24-hour drugstores (although only the Concourse F location dispenses prescription drugs, 10–5 Monday–Friday), a barbershop and hairstyling salon, and countless food and retail outlets. MIA has 14 duty-free shops that carry liquor, perfume, electronics, and various designer goods; international airline tickets and passports are required to enter. Lighted airport directories are located on columns throughout Level 2 of the terminal building and beside the elevators on Level 3.

International flights arrive at concourses A, B, D, E, and F, as well as at the International Satellite Terminal located ¼ mi west of the main terminal. International passengers can be met outside U.S. Customs exits on the lower level of Concourse E or on the third level of Concourse B.

Also available on-site is the 260 soundproof-room **Miami International Airport Hotel** (✉ Concourse E, upper level, ☎ 305/871–4100). If you have a layover (or an ambitious hour or two), their health club has a pool, jogging track, and sun deck.

➤ AIRPORT INFORMATION: **Miami International Airport** (☎ 305/876–7000, WEB www.miami-airport.com). **Fort Lauderdale–Hollywood International Airport** (☎ 954/359–1200, WEB www.co.broward.fl.us/fll.htm).

## AIRPORT TRANSFERS

Shuttle and limousine service are available outside baggage claim areas on Level 1. Taxis can be found on both the arrival (1) and departure (2) levels; **look for a uniformed county dispatcher** to hail a cab for you. On the mainland (i.e., west of Biscayne Bay) cabs cost $1.50 for the first ¼ mile and $1.75 each mile thereafter (plus a $1 surcharge for trips originating at MIA or the Port of Miami); the fare from the airport to downtown Miami averages $15–$18, and the Port is a flat fare of $18.

Flat-rate fares are set for five zones along the barrier island generally referred to as Miami Beach. The long, thin stretch of beachfront actually encompasses not only Miami Beach proper but Indian Creek Village, Surfside, Bay Harbor Islands, Bal Harbour, Sunny Isles, Golden Beach, the Village of Key Biscayne and adjacent unincorporated areas. The fare zones comprise five east–west bands bound on the east by the Atlantic Ocean and on the west by the mainland. Flat-rate fares run $24 (South Beach)–$41 (north Dade, Sunny Isles) per trip, not passenger; they include tolls and the airport surcharge, but no gratuity.

For taxi service to destinations in the immediate vicinity of the airport, **ask the dispatcher to call an ARTS (Airport Region Taxi Service) cab** for you. These blue cars offer a short-haul flat fare in two zones. An inner-zone ride costs $7; the outer-zone fare is $10. The area of service runs north to 36th Street, west to the Palmetto Expressway (77th Avenue), south to Northwest 7th Street, and east to Douglas Road (37th Avenue). Maps are posted in cab windows on both sides.

Limo service is available through prior arrangement only, but SuperShuttle vans transport passengers on demand between MIA and local hotels, the Port of Miami, and even individual residences on a 24-hour basis. Shuttles are available throughout the lower level of the terminal outside baggage claim areas. Service extends from Palm Beach to Monroe County (including the Lower Keys). It's best to **make reservations 24 hours in advance for the return,** although the firm will try to arrange pickups within Miami-Dade County on as little as four hours' notice. Per-person rates average $9–$19; additional members of a party pay a lower rate for many destinations, and children under three ride free with their parents. There's a pet transport fee of $5 for a cat and $8 for a dog under 50 pounds in kennels.

Public transportation may not be the most user-friendly option, but it's definitely cheaper. For long hauls as far north as Palm Beach County, TriRail is the best bet and offers free shuttle service to and from MIA. Metrobus service is also available with routes connecting to both Metrorail and TriRail. Both are on Level 1, across Airport Drive from Concourse E. From the airport you can take Bus 7 to downtown, Bus 37 south to Coral Gables and South Miami or north to Hialeah, Bus J east to Miami Beach, and Bus 42 to Coconut Grove. For South Beach, take Bus J to 41st Street in Miami Beach and transfer to a southbound Bus H, which goes all the way to the South Point Drive. Some routes change after 7:00 PM and on weekends—although an Airport Owl line, running hourly from 11:50 PM to 5:40 AM, makes a loop to South Beach and back. If sticking to a budget is your priority, the bus is the best deal at around $1.25. **Grab a bus schedule at the airport tourist information center** or visit the Miami Dade Transit Web site before you go for the latest schedule—and be prepared to wait.

➤ AIRPORT TRANSFER CONTACTS: Miami-Dade Transit, **Metrobus** (☎ 305/770–3131, WEB www.co.miami-dade.fl.us/transit). **SuperShuttle** (☎ 305/871–2000 from MIA; 954/764–1700 from Fort Lauderdale; 800/874–8885 elsewhere, WEB www.supershuttle.com). **TriRail** (☎ 800/874–7245, WEB www.tri-rail.com).

## BIKE TRAVEL

Great weather and flat terrain make Miami great for cycling, but as a general method of transportation, it shouldn't be your first choice given traffic and limited bike paths. You can opt for Miami-Dade Transit's "Bike and Ride" program, which lets permitted cyclists take single-seat two-wheelers on Metrorail and select bus routes. Bicycles are allowed on Metrorail weekdays before 6:30 AM, from 9 to 4, and after 6 PM, and anytime on weekends and major holidays. You can also store your bicycle in lockers at most Metrorail stations; leases are available for 3, 6, or 12 months.

➤ BIKE INFORMATION: **Miami-Dade Bicycle–Pedestrian Coordinator** (☎ 305/375–4507) has details on permits, bike maps, and lockers, and is open weekdays 8–5.

## BOAT AND FERRY TRAVEL

If you enter the United States in a private vessel along the Atlantic Coast south of Sebastian Inlet, you must **call the U.S. Customs Service.** Customs clears most boats of less than 5 tons by phone, but you may be directed to a marina for inspection.

In Greater Miami all boats with motors, regardless of size, must be properly registered. Always obey "No Wake" signs; slow zones are strictly monitored and many serve to protect Florida's endangered manatees. **Watch for personal watercraft:** they're everywhere and their drivers don't always practice safe boating. For boating emergencies or environmental concerns, call the Florida Marine Patrol or the U.S. Coast Guard.

### FARES AND SCHEDULES

➤ BOAT AND FERRY INFORMATION: **Florida Marine Patrol** (☎ 800/342–5367). **U.S. Coast Guard** (☎ 305/535–4368 in Greater Miami; 800/432–1216 elsewhere). **U.S. Customs Service** (☎ 800/432–1216 for small vessel arrival near Miami; 305/536–5263 for Port of Miami office).

## BUS TRAVEL AROUND MIAMI

Metrobus stops are marked with blue-and-green signs with a bus logo and route information. If you want to get around by bus or rapid transit, **call Miami-Dade Transit for exact bus routes.** It's staffed with people who can give you specific information and route schedules. If you call from your hometown, they can also mail you a map of Miami-Dade showing all the bus routes and their numbers.

### FARES AND SCHEDULES

The frequency of service varies widely from route to route, depending on the demand, so call in advance to **obtain specific bus schedules.** Buses on the most popular routes run every 10 to 15 minutes. The fare is $1.25 (exact change only); 60¢ for seniors (65 and older) and students. Transfers cost 25¢ and 10¢, respectively. Some express routes carry surcharges of $1.50.

➤ BUS SERVICE INFORMATION: Miami-Dade Transit, **Metrobus** (☎ 305/770–3131, WEB www.co.miami-dade.fl.us/transit).

## BUS TRAVEL TO AND FROM GREATER MIAMI

Most motor coaches that stop in the Miami area are chartered tour buses. One company, Bus One, offers daily round-trip service to Orlando only; $98 includes meals on board and free pick-up at select area hotels. Regularly scheduled, interstate Greyhound buses stop at five terminals in Greater Miami; the airport terminal is 24-hour. There is no service to Miami Beach.

➤ BUS INFORMATION: **Bus One** (☎ 305/870–0919 in Greater Miami; 888/287–1669 elsewhere). **Greyhound** (☎ 800/231–2222).

➤ BUS TERMINAL INFORMATION: **Homestead:** 5 N.E. 3rd Rd., ☎ 305/247–2040. **Miami Bayside–Downtown:** ✉ 100 N.W. 6th St., ☎ 305/374–6160. **Miami South:** ✉ 20505 S. Dixie Hwy., ☎ 305/296–9072. **Miami West–Airport:** ✉ 4111 N.W. 27th St., ☎ 305/871–1810. **North Miami:** ✉ 16560 N.E. 6th Ave., ☎ 305/945–0801.

## BUSINESS HOURS

Most Greater Miami businesses are open weekdays 9–5; banks usually close sometime between 4 and 5, although larger branches have drive-through windows that are open until 6 and for a few hours Saturday mornings. ATMs are everywhere for quick money, deposits, even cash advances 24 hours a day.

### MUSEUMS AND SIGHTS

Operating hours for sights and museums vary, but most are open daily, rain or shine. It's always best to check, though, since some have seasonal hours. For the most part, parks and beaches operate sunrise to sunset.

### PHARMACIES

For late-night pharmacies, *see* Health.

### RESTAURANTS AND CLUBS

Miamians dine and party late. Restaurants in high-traffic areas stay open until at least midnight and there are a few 24-hour spots. Reservations are always a good idea since some places take a break on Monday or may close for lunch—there are even a few seasonal restaurants. No one goes to a club before 11 PM and on South Beach many stay open 'til 5 AM.

### SHOPS

Most stores are open daily 10–6, but those in malls close as late as 9 PM Mon–Sat. Shops in complexes with movie theaters, restaurants, and other attractions, and those in South Beach, generally stay open until 11. Some of the larger grocery chains operate a limited number of 24-hour stores, but most close at 9 or 10.

## CAMERAS AND PHOTOGRAPHY

The *Kodak Guide to Shooting Great Travel Pictures* (available at bookstores everywhere) is loaded with tips.

➤ PHOTO HELP: **Kodak Information Center** (☏ 800/242–2424).

### EQUIPMENT PRECAUTIONS

**Don't pack film and equipment in checked luggage,** where it is much more susceptible to damage. X-ray machines used to view checked luggage are becoming much more powerful and therefore are much more likely to ruin your film. Always **keep film and tape out of the sun.** Carry an extra supply of batteries, and **be prepared to turn on your camera or camcorder** to prove to security personnel that the device is real. Always **ask for hand inspection of film,** which becomes clouded after repeated exposure to airport X-ray machines, and **keep videotapes away from metal detectors.**

## CAR RENTAL

If your vacation is South Beach–based, you may prefer not to rent a car because parking is difficult and taxis are ubiquitous here. If you want to take side trips or explore Greater Miami, consider renting a car for the day. **If you're not staying in South Beach, rent a car.** If your day-trip is last minute, ask your hotel concierge about arranging for a car rental; otherwise **book in advance for cheaper rental rates.**

Florida is a bazaar of car rental companies, with more discounts and fine print than any other state. Rates in Greater Miami average $25 a day and $150 a week for an economy car with air-conditioning, automatic transmission, and unlimited mileage. For a convertible—one of South Florida's great winter pleasures—add 15–20%. Bear in mind that rates fluctuate tremendously depending on demand and season, and you'll find the best deal on a weekly or weekend rental. Rental cars are more expensive—and harder to find—during peak holidays.

Avis, Budget, Dollar, Globetrotters, Hertz, National, and Royal all have counters on the lower level of MIA, although no one has actual cars on the premises. Just about everybody offers free shuttles to nearby lots though, as is evidenced by the gridlock of minivans and buses in and out of the airport. Simply **flag a courtesy shuttle outside baggage claim** for your preferred company. You can also price local companies for even lower rates. Either way, check on availability, whether service is 24 hours, and hidden costs. Prices are usually best during off-peak periods.

Miami's TOP (Tourist Oriented Police) officers heavily patrol the airport triangle where most car rental lots are located. Despite this and the absence of tags and stickers identifying a car as a rental, to avoid being targeted as a tourist **make sure you know where you're going before you set off.** Local legislation requires that all rental companies provide area maps. You can also rent cellular phones and many of the larger companies offer computerized navigation systems.

➤ AIRPORT CAR RENTAL AGENCIES: **Avis** (☎ 800/331–1212; 800/879–2847 in Canada; 02/9353–9000 in Australia; 09/525–1982 in New Zealand). **Budget** (☎ 800/527–0700; 0144/227–6266 in the U.K.).**Dollar** (☎ 800/800–4000; 0181/897–0811 in the U.K., where it is known as Eurodollar; 02/9223–1444 in Australia). **Globetrotters** (☎ 800/899–3204). **Hertz** (☎ 800/654–3131; 800/263–0600 in Canada; 0181/897–2072 in the U.K.; 02/9669–2444 in Australia; 03/358–6777 in New Zealand). **National InterRent** (☎ 800/227–7368; 0345/222525 in the U.K., where it is known as Europcar InterRent). **Royal Rent A Car** (☎ 800/314–8616).

## CUTTING COSTS

To get the best deal, **book through a travel agent who will shop around.** Also **price local car-rental companies,** although the service and maintenance may not be as good as those of a major player. Remember to ask about required deposits, cancellation penalties, and drop-off charges if you're planning to pick up the car in one city and leave it in another. If you're traveling during a holiday period, also make sure that a confirmed reservation guarantees you a car.

Do **look into wholesalers,** companies that do not own fleets but rent in bulk from those that do and often offer better rates than traditional car-rental operations.

➤ LOCAL AGENCIES: **Alba Rent A Car** (☎ 305/444–3923). **Excellence Luxury Car Rental** (☎ 305/526–0000; 888/526–0055 in U.S. only). **Specialty Auto Rentals** (☎ 888/871–2770).

➤ MAJOR AGENCIES: **Alamo** (☎ 800/327–9633; 0181/759–6200 in the U.K.). **Enterprise** (☎ 800/736–8222 in town; 800/325–8007 out of town). **Thrifty** (☎ 305/871–5050 or 800/367–2277).

➤ WHOLESALERS: **Auto Europe** (☎ 207/842–2000 or 800/223–5555, FAX 800/235–6321, WEB www.autoeurope.com).

## INSURANCE

When driving a rented car you are generally responsible for any damage to or loss of the vehicle as well as for any property damage or personal injury that you may cause. Before you rent, see what coverage your personal auto-insurance policy and credit cards provide.

For about $15 to $20 per day, rental companies sell protection, known as a collision- or loss-damage waiver (CDW or LDW), which eliminates your liability for damage to the car.

In most states you don't need a CDW if you have personal auto insurance or other liability insurance. However, **make sure you have enough coverage to pay for the car.** If you do not have auto insurance or an umbrella policy that covers damage to third parties, purchasing liability insurance and a CDW or LDW is highly recommended.

## REQUIREMENTS AND RESTRICTIONS

In Florida you must be 21 to rent a car, and rates may be higher if you're under 25. You'll pay extra for child seats (about $3 a day), which are compulsory for children under five, and for additional drivers (about $2 per day). Non-U.S. residents need a reservation voucher (for prepaid reservations that were made in the traveler's home country), a passport, a driver's license, and a travel policy that covers each driver, when picking up a car.

## SURCHARGES

Before you pick up a car in one city and leave it in another, **ask about drop-off charges or one-way service fees,** which can be substantial. Note, too, that some rental agencies charge extra if you return the car before the time specified in your contract. **Check refueling fees upfront.** The price per gallon charged by the rental company is usually the same, if not lower, than local gas stations. The catch is you have to decide at time of rental and you're charged for a full tank, so you'll want to return the car as close to empty as possible. If you forego this option, don't change your mind later. The charge per gallon will be exorbitant and to avoid a hefty refueling fee, you'll have to fill the tank just before you turn in the car. Watch for gas stations near the rental outlet that overcharge.

## CAR TRAVEL

I–95 is the major expressway connecting South Florida with points north; State Road 836 is the major east–west expressway and connects to Florida's Turnpike, State Road 826, and I–95. Seven causeways link Miami and Miami Beach, with I–195 and I–395 offering the most convenient routes; the Rickenbacker Causeway extends to Key Biscayne from I–95 and U.S. 1. **Remember U.S. 1 (a.k.a. Dixie Highway)**—you'll hear it often in directions. It starts in Key West, hugs South Florida's coastline, and heads north straight through to Maine.

Greater Miami traffic is among the nation's worst, so definitely **avoid driving during the rush hours of 7–9 AM and 5–7 PM.**

Road construction is ubiquitous; **pay attention to the brightly lit, roadside Smart Signs that warn drivers of work zones and street closings.** During rainy weather, be especially cautious of flooding in South Beach and Key Biscayne. The Web site www.dot.state.fl.us lists roadwork updates for Florida's interstates, and www.ci.miami-beach.fl.us posts daily traffic advisories for Miami Beach.

Courtesy may not be the first priority of Miami drivers, who may suddenly change lanes or stop to drop off passengers where they shouldn't. **Watch out for short-tempered drivers** who may shout, gesticulate, honk, or even approach the car of an offending driver.

Even when your driving is beyond censure, you should **be especially careful in rental cars.** Despite the absence of identifying marks and the stepped-up presence of TOP (Tourist Oriented Police) patrols, cars piled with luggage or driven by hesitant drivers are prime targets for thieves. Keep car doors locked, and only ask questions at toll booths, gas stations, and other evidently safe locations. Don't stop if your car is bumped from behind, you see a disabled vehicle, or even if you get a flat tire. Drive to the nearest gas station or well-lighted locale and telephone the police from there. It's a good idea to **bring or rent a cellular phone,** as well.

### EMERGENCY SERVICES

If you're in a rental, your obvious choice is to call the rental company whose number should be with your rental papers in the glove compartment.

➤ CONTACTS: **AAA** (☎ 800/222–4357); **Aventura** (✉ 20801 Biscayne Blvd., Suite 101, ☎ 305/682–2100); **Kendall** (✉ 7074 S.W. 117th Ave., Snapper Creek Plaza, ☎ 305/270–6450); **South Miami** (✉ 6101 Sunset Dr., ☎ 305/661–6131).

### GASOLINE

Gas stations are usually open late or 24 hours and are self-serve; most accept credit or debit cards directly at the pump. Gasoline costs a few cents more per gallon here than in the rest of Florida (with the exception of the Keys).

### PARKING

Many parking garages fill up at peak times. This is particularly true in Miami Beach and Coconut Grove, where streetside parking is impossible and spaces in municipal lots cost a fortune. Thankfully, these neighborhoods are the most pedestrian-friendly in Greater Miami. On Miami Beach, valet parking is offered at most dining and entertainment venues (although it can cost as much as $20 on a busy weekend night). "Cabbing" it in South Beach is easy and inexpensive, but if you have to drive, call the **City of Miami Beach's Parking Hotline** (☎ 305/673–PARK) for garages convenient to where you're going. **Don't be tempted to park in a tow-away zone,** as the fees are high and you'll be surprised at how quickly the tow trucks arrive. If your car is towed, contact the municipality for details on how to retrieve your vehicle.

### ROAD CONDITIONS

During Florida's frequent summer lightning storms, power to street lights may temporarily go out; stop as you would at a four-way stop sign and proceed with caution. **Make sure your lights are on when it's raining** so other drivers can see you, and watch for flooding.

### RULES OF THE ROAD

Drive to the right and pass on the left. Keep change handy since toll roads are frequent and can range from 50¢ to as much as $1.50. Right turns are permitted at red lights (after a complete stop), unless otherwise indicated. At four-way stop signs, it's first-come, first-go; when in doubt, yield to the right. Speed limits are 55 mph on state highways, 30 mph within city limits and residential areas, and 55–70 mph on interstates and Florida's turnpike. Be alert for signs announcing exceptions and school zones (15 mph).

All front-seat passengers are required to wear seat belts, and children under five must be fastened securely in child safety seats or boosters; children under 12 are required to ride in the rear seat. Florida's Alcohol–Controlled Substance DUI Law is one of the toughest in the United States. A blood alcohol level of.08 or higher can have serious repercussions even for the first-time offender.

Cell phone use while driving is discouraged, although it's currently still legal.

## CHILDREN IN MIAMI

While Miami and Miami Beach's well-heeled reputation as a chic urban metropolis may be incongruous with traveling with children, fear not. Though somewhat weak in the attractions department, Greater Miami's ideal climate puts much of the attraction on the child-friendly outdoors. The tried-and-true beach experience is the most obvious choice; kids can't get enough of the water and Miami has more than 15 mi of beach. Expansive kid-friendly resorts with "water playgrounds," public pools, and lush, tropical parks give you even more options for tiring little ones. Miami also has a year-round calendar of special events and outdoor festivals, many of which are geared toward children or have special kid-friendly activities and areas.

Key to an enjoyable family vacation (underscore stress-free) is ensuring something for everyone—so do your homework before arriving. Call ahead and ask the visitors bureau to send you a copy of its "Fun & Sun Kids' Guide to Greater Miami and the Beaches." The best bet is ***South Florida Parenting Magazine*** (distributed free throughout the tri-county area) for ideas on what to see and do in any specific month; check for event roundups, as well as special offers at area restaurants.

*Fodor's Around Miami with Kids* (available in bookstores everywhere) can help you plan your days together.

**Don't forget sunscreen.** In winter, when it doesn't feel as warm, your kids (and you) might be burning and you won't even know it. Also, depending on where you're exploring, in summer you'll want to **bring along insect repellent and drinking water.** If you're renting a car, don't forget to **arrange for a car seat** when you reserve. For general advice about traveling with children, check out the family travel tips in the Family Travel section of www.fodors.com and consult *Fodor's FYI: Travel with Your Baby* (available in bookstores everywhere).

### BABY-SITTING

If you need a baby-sitter, check with your hotel concierge or front desk. Many hotels offer baby-sitting or can refer you to a reputable service. If you use the Yellow Pages, **be sure to double-check references.**

### DINING

Even though Miami's dining scene can be quite sophisticated, many places cater to young tastes. Weather permitting, **try to sit outside**; you'll enjoy a more leisurely meal since the kids will have more room to play and you won't worry (as much) about bothering other diners. Sidewalk cafés in Coconut Grove, South Miami, and South Beach are ideal for kid-style munchies; in season though there might be a wait for a table. If there's no children's menu, ask the wait staff if they split portions and if there's a charge. For additional local tips, *see* Dining With Kids *in* Dining.

### LODGING

If you're truly emphasizing a stress-free family vacation, then you don't want a sterile business hotel or a trendy hot spot. By nature, Miami's ocean resorts are usually family-friendly, although only a few offer organized children's programs. Short-term home or apartment rentals are an option and offer the benefit of added space and a kitchen (but then you have to cook). A plus is that family vacations are usually in summer, when good hotel deals abound in South Florida. Most hotels in Greater Miami allow children under a certain age to stay in their parents' room at no extra charge, but a few may charge for them as extra adults; be sure to **find out the cutoff age for children's discounts.** Some hotels include breakfast for kids under 12 gratis, and a few offer summer promotions that include a second room free. Make sure to ask about family packages. The resorts generally claim their children's programs are year-round, but double-check offerings for your vacation dates. Some hotels decrease program hours during slow periods or limit the number of participants. Also ask what charges there are, if any, and whether they accept children still in diapers. Kids' programs or not, make your stay more enjoyable by choosing accommodations with the right amenities. Rollaway beds and cribs, in-room microwaves, and refrigerators can make all the difference, but there may be added costs. If there's only a minibar in your room, note that it won't have much space to spare. If you have very young children, are the rooms childproofed? (Doubtful.) A few select hotels provide "kits" for this, but be prepared to bring your own.

➤ BEST CHOICES: **Doral Golf Resort and Spa's Camp Doral** (✉ 4400 N.W. 87th Ave., Doral, ☎ 305/592–2000), ages 5–12. **Fontainebleau Hilton Resort & Towers' Kid's Cove** (✉ 4441 Collins Ave., Miami Beach, ☎ 305/538–2000), ages 5–12. **Loews Miami Beach Hotel's SoBe Kid's Camp** (✉ 1601 Collins Ave., Miami Beach, ☎ 305/604–1601), ages 4–12. **Sonesta Beach Resort's Just Us Kids** (350 Ocean Dr., Key Biscayne, 33149, ☎ 305/361–2021 or 800/766–3782), ages 5–13.

### OUTDOOR FUN

Beaches are key to a Miami family vacation. Try the southern end of Haulover Park (the northern portion is home to a nude beach) or Bill Baggs Cape Florida State Recreation Area in Key Biscayne. In South Beach, families typically prefer Third Street Beach on Ocean Drive. Also in Key Biscayne, Crandon Park—rated among the top 10 beaches in the country by Dr. Beach (the Florida International University professor who issues a well-publicized yearly list)—has sand bars that at low tide extend out as much as 500 yards through the calm waters, perfect for little ones. Their Family Amusement Center has a historical carousel (open weekends 10 AM–5 PM, until 7 PM in summer), a tropical jungle hayride through Crandon Gardens on weekends, and a beachfront playground with marine play sculptures, a dolphin-shape spray fountain, and an old-fashioned outdoor roller rink. Oleta River State Recreation Area and Hammock Park have peaceful beaches, picnic shelters with shower facilities, and lush walking and bike trails. Fishing charters, kayak trips, wave runner excursions or a snorkeling adventure are other kid-friendly activities to consider.

Don't tell the kids, but South Florida's subtropical flora and fauna can be fun *and* educational. More adventurous families can overnight at Everglades National Park, south of Miami, the largest protected subtropical wilderness in the United States. There are campgrounds and lodging (you can even stay in a pontoon houseboat) at Flamingo Park, and the marina has bicycle, kayak, and canoe rentals. The biggest hits will probably be an airboat ride through the sawgrass and the alligator farm in the eastern portions of the Everglades. Or, for a day's fun, try Shark Valley at the park's north end—pack a lunch and grab a bicycle or take the tram tour. The nation's only underwater park, Biscayne National Park, has glass-bottom boats and organizes snorkeling on 25-ft-high coral reefs teeming with sea life. For more advice about these and other destinations, consult *Fodor's South Florida* (available in bookstores everywhere).

### SIGHTS AND ATTRACTIONS

Places that are especially appealing to children are indicated by a rubber-duckie icon (🐤) in the margin.

### TOP ATTRACTIONS

At the Miami Seaquarium the big draw now is W.A.D.E, the park's Water and Dolphin Exploration Program. The two-hour session offers one-on-one interaction with the dolphins, but you have to be at least 52" tall. It's expensive—$140 to touch, kiss, and swim with them, but the price does include park admission, towel, and snacks. Definitely call ahead to make reservations. The landmark Venetian Pool in Coral Gables is as much fun as it is historic. Aptly named, with secret caves and stone bridges, it has probably the most aesthetically pleasing wading pool you'll ever see (sorry, no children under three are allowed in the pool). Definitely at the top of Miami's attraction list for kids, Parrot Jungle & Gardens offers "free-flying" entertainment and lots of hands-on stuff—you can hand-feed the birds, let the parrots perch on your shoulders, and even stroke a tarantula! At the Miami MetroZoo, one of the largest cageless zoos in the country, younger kids can be steered to PAWS, the children's petting zoo and a great playground with age-appropriate areas. It's a pretty big place though and shading is at a premium so the little ones might get tired. Not to worry, hop on the monorail or try the tram tour.

## CONCIERGES

Concierges, found in many hotels, can help you with theater tickets, getting on a club's guest list, and dinner reservations: a good one with connections may be able to get you seats for a hot show or a table at the restaurant of the moment. You can also turn to your hotel's concierge for help with travel arrangements, sightseeing plans, services from aromatherapy to zipper repair, and emergencies. Always, **always tip** a concierge who has been of assistance.

## CONSUMER PROTECTION

Whenever shopping or buying travel services in Miami, **pay with a major credit card,** if possible, so you can cancel payment or get reimbursed if there's a problem. If you're doing business with a particular company for the first time, **contact your local Better Business Bureau and the attorney general's offices** in your state and (for U.S. businesses) the company's home state as well. Have any complaints been filed? Finally, if you're buying a package or tour, always **consider travel insurance** that includes default coverage.

➤ BBBs: **Council of Better Business Bureaus** (✉ 4200 Wilson Blvd., Suite 800, Arlington, VA 22203, ☎ 703/276–0100, FAX 703/525–8277, WEB www.bbb.org).

## CRUISE TRAVEL

The Dante B. Fascell Port of Miami, in downtown Miami near Bayside Marketplace and the MacArthur Causeway, justifiably bills itself as the cruise capital of the world. Home to 18 ships and the largest year-round cruise fleet in the world, the port accommodates more than 3 million passengers a year. It has 12 air-conditioned terminals, duty-free shopping, and limousine service. Taxicabs are at all terminals and Avis is at the port, although other rental companies offer shuttle service to off-site locations. Parking is $10 per day and short-term parking is a flat rate of $4. From here, 2-, 3-, 4-, 5- and 7-day cruises depart for the Bahamas, Belize, and Eastern and Western Caribbean, with longer sailings to the Far East, Europe, and South America.

To learn how to plan, choose, and book a cruise-ship voyage, check out Cruise How-to's on www.fodors.com and consult *Fodor's FYI: Plan & Enjoy Your Cruise* (available in bookstores everywhere).

➤ CRUISE LINES INFORMATION: **Carnival Cruise Lines** (☎ 800/327–9501). **Celebrity Cruises** (☎ 800/437–3111). **Norwegian Cruise Lines** (☎ 800/327–7030). **Port of Miami** (☎ 305/371–7678, WEB www.co.miami-dade.fl.us/portofmiami). **Royal Caribbean International** (☎ 800/255–4373).

➤ CRUISE TERMINAL INFORMATION: **Dante B. Fascell Port of Miami** (✉ 1015 North American Way, ☎ 305/371–7678).

## CUSTOMS AND DUTIES

### IN AUSTRALIA

Australian residents who are 18 or older may bring home $A400 worth of souvenirs and gifts (including jewelry), 250 cigarettes or 250 grams of tobacco, and 1,125 ml of alcohol (including wine, beer, and spirits). Residents under 18 may bring back $A200 worth of goods. Prohibited items include meat products. Seeds, plants, and fruits need to be declared upon arrival.

➤ INFORMATION: **Australian Customs Service** (Regional Director, ✉ Box 8, Sydney, NSW 2001, Australia, ☎ 02/9213–2000, FAX 02/9213–4000, WEB www.customs.gov.au).

### IN CANADA

Canadian residents who have been out of Canada for at least seven days may bring home C$500 worth of goods duty-free. If you've been away fewer than seven days but more than 48 hours, the duty-free allowance drops to C$200; if your trip lasts 24–48 hours, the allowance is C$50. You may not pool allowances with family members. Goods claimed under the C$500 exemption may follow you by mail; those claimed under the lesser exemptions must accompany you. Alcohol and tobacco products may be included in the seven-day and 48-hour exemptions but not in the 24-hour exemption. If you meet the age requirements of the province or territory through which you reenter Canada, you may bring in, duty-free, 1.14 liters (40 imperial ounces) of wine or liquor *or* 24 12-ounce cans or bottles of beer or ale. If you are 16 or older you may bring in, duty-free, 200 cigarettes and 50 cigars. Check ahead of time with Revenue Canada or the Department of Agriculture for policies regarding meat products, seeds, plants, and fruits.

You may send an unlimited number of gifts worth up to C$60 each duty-free to Canada. Label the package UNSOLICITED GIFT—VALUE UNDER $60. Alcohol and tobacco are excluded.

➤ INFORMATION: **Revenue Canada** (✉ 2265 St. Laurent Blvd. S, Ottawa, Ontario K1G 4K3, Canada, ☎ 613/993–0534; 800/461–9999 in Canada, FAX 613/991–4126, WEB www.ccra-adrc.gc.ca).

### IN NEW ZEALAND

Homeward-bound residents 17 or older may bring back $700 worth of souvenirs and gifts. Your duty-free allowance also includes 4.5 liters of wine or beer; one 1,125-ml bottle of spirits; and either 200 cigarettes, 250 grams of tobacco, 50 cigars, or a combination of the three up to 250 grams. Prohibited items include meat products, seeds, plants, and fruits.

➤ INFORMATION: **New Zealand Customs** (Custom House, ✉ 50 Anzac Ave., Box 29, Auckland, New Zealand, ☎ 09/300–5399, FAX 09/359–6730, WEB www.customs.govt.nz).

### IN THE U.K.

From countries outside the EU, including the United States, you may bring home, duty-free, 200 cigarettes or 50 cigars; 1 liter of spirits or 2 liters of fortified or sparkling wine or liqueurs; 2 liters of still table wine; 60 ml of perfume; 250 ml of toilet water; plus £136 worth of other goods, including gifts and souvenirs. If returning from outside the EU, prohibited items include meat products, seeds, plants, and fruits.

➤ INFORMATION: **HM Customs and Excise** (✉ Dorset House, Stamford St., Bromley, Kent BR1 1XX, U.K., ☎ 020/7202–4227, WEB www.hmce.gov.uk).

## DINING

Miami and Miami Beach's dining options are as diverse as its population. Foodies will find lots of notable chefs, gorgeously appointed restaurants, and plenty of Miami-inspired culinary flair. The restaurants we list are the cream of the crop in each price category. Properties indicated by ✕🏨 are lodging establishments whose restaurant warrants a special trip.

Some restaurants offer early bird specials to diners who order before 6 PM and, in off-season, discounts are ubiquitous—check local papers for coupons and special offerings.

A note of caution: raw oysters have been identified as a problem for people with chronic illnesses of the liver, stomach, or blood, and for people with immune disorders. Since 1993, all Florida restaurants serving raw oysters are required to post a notice in plain view of all patrons warning of the risks associated with consuming them. A good rule of thumb is to order raw oysters only during months with names containing the letter "R."

### RESERVATIONS AND DRESS

Reservations are always a good idea: we mention them only when they're essential or not accepted. Book as far ahead as you can, and reconfirm as soon as you arrive. We mention dress only when men are required to wear a jacket or a jacket and tie.

Even in warmer months, it's a good idea to bring a light sweater or jacket. The hotter it gets outdoors, the more air-conditioners are worked.

### WINE, BEER AND SPIRITS

The legal drinking age in Florida is 21; be prepared to show a photo ID if you're under 30. Some nightclubs where food is also served permit entrance to persons under 21. Each municipality has its own laws governing the sale of alcohol, but most prohibit sales before 1 PM on Sunday. It's illegal to walk with an open container of alcohol, and while driving, liquor must be unopened and in the trunk.

## DISABILITIES AND ACCESSIBILITY

At Miami International Airport, TDD services are readily accessible throughout the terminal and disabled parking is available in the Dolphin and Flamingo garages on the third level, close to the Moving Walkway. Most rest rooms can accommodate wheelchairs, but an already commenced $10 million rehab will ensure that all meet ADA requirements. Many of the larger rental car companies offer hand controls, but 24-hour notice or more may be required. Florida recognizes disabled parking permits from other states and Canada, but not those of other countries. You can get a 90-day permit for $15 from the **Miami-Dade County Tax Collector's** office; make sure to bring your disabled permit and passport. They don't take credit cards, but you can pay with traveler's checks.

On TriRail (☞ Metrorail and Commuter Trains), all trains and stations are accessible to persons with disabilities; Miami-Dade also offers lift-equipped buses on more than 50 routes, including one from the airport. Miami Beach has a tourism hot line with information on accessibility, sign language interpreters, rental cars, and area recreational activities for the disabled. Several parks have accessible tennis courts and water sports, and the beaches at 10th Street and Ocean Drive, and at 72nd Street and Collins Avenue have ramps and surf chairs. Miami Beach's boardwalk is accessible at South Pointe Park, 5th Street, and 46th Street.

➤ LOCAL RESOURCES: **ADA** (☎ 305/375–3566). **City of Miami Beach** (☎ 305/673–6427; 305/673–7575 TDD). **City of Miami Department of Parks and Recreation** (☎ 305/461–7201 or 305/860–3800). **Miami-Dade Parks & Recreation Leisure Access Services** (☎ Voice/TDD 305/755–7848). **Miami-Dade Tax Collector** (✉ 140 W. Flagler St., Miami, ☎ 305/375–5678). For information on public transportation, call the **Miami-Dade Transit Agency Special Transportation Service,** Monday–Friday, 8–5 (☎ 305/263–5400). **Randle Eastern Ambulance Service Inc.** (☎ 305/718–6400) operates at all hours. **Wheelchair Getaways** (☎ 561/748–8414 in Florida; 800/637–7577 in the U.S. and Canada) rents vans equipped with lifts.

**Deaf Services of Miami** (✉ 1320 S. Dixie Hwy., Ste. 760, Coral Gables 33146; ☎ 305/668–3323 TDD; 305/668–4407 voice) provides sign-language interpreter referrals. TDD service for the hearing-impaired is available when dialing 911 for fire, police, medical, and rescue emergencies. For **operator and directory assistance,** ☎ 800/688–4486 is TDD only. The operators at **Florida Relay Service** (☎ 800/955–8771 TDD; 800/955–8770 voice) can translate TDD messages into speech for nonusers, and vice-versa. No charges apply to local calls.

The **Miami Lighthouse for the Blind** (☎ 305/856–2288) serves as a clearinghouse for information to assist the visually impaired.

### LODGING

Despite the Americans with Disabilities Act, the definition of accessibility seems to differ from hotel to hotel. Some properties may be accessible by

ADA standards for people with mobility problems but not for people with hearing or vision impairments, for example.

If you have mobility problems, ask for the lowest floor on which accessible services are offered. If you have a hearing impairment, check whether the hotel has devices to alert you visually to the ring of the telephone, knock at the door, and a fire/emergency alarm. Some hotels provide these devices without charge. Discuss your needs with hotel personnel if this equipment isn't available, so that a staff member can personally alert you in the event of an emergency.

If you're bringing a guide dog, get authorization ahead of time and write down the name of the person you spoke with.

### RESERVATIONS

When discussing accessibility with an operator or reservations agent, **ask hard questions.** Are there any stairs, inside *or* out? Are there grab bars next to the toilet *and* in the shower/tub? How wide is the doorway to the room? To the bathroom? For the most extensive facilities meeting the latest legal specifications, **opt for newer accommodations.** If you reserve through a toll-free number, consider also calling the hotel's local number to confirm the information from the central reservations office. Get confirmation in writing when you can.

➤ COMPLAINTS: **Aviation Consumer Protection Division** (✉ U.S. Department of Transportation, Room 4107, C-75, Washington, DC 20590, ☎ 202/366–2220, WEB www.dot.gov/airconsumer) for airline-related problems. **Civil Rights Office** (✉ U.S. Department of Transportation, Departmental Office of Civil Rights, S-30, 400 7th St. SW, Room 10215, Washington, DC 20590, ☎ 202/366–4648, FAX 202/366–9371, WEB www.dot.gov/ost/docr/index.htm) for problems with surface transportation. **Disability Rights Section** (✉ U.S. Department of Justice, Civil Rights Division, Box 66738, Washington, DC 20035-6738, ☎ 202/514–0301 or 800/514–0301; 202/514–0383 TTY; 800/514–0383 TTY, FAX 202/307–1198, WEB www.usdoj.gov/crt/ada/adahom1.htm) for general complaints.

### TRAVEL AGENCIES

In the United States, the Americans with Disabilities Act requires that travel firms serve the needs of all travelers. Some agencies specialize in working with people with disabilities.

➤ TRAVELERS WITH MOBILITY PROBLEMS: **Access Adventures** (✉ 206 Chestnut Ridge Rd., Scottsville, NY 14624, ☎ 716/889–9096, dltravel@prodigy.net), run by a former physical-rehabilitation counselor. **Accessible Vans of America** (✉ 9 Spielman Rd., Fairfield, NJ 07004, ☎ 877/282–8267, FAX 973/808–9713, WEB www.accessiblevans.com). **CareVacations** (✉ 5-5110 50th Ave., Leduc, Alberta T9E 6V4, Canada, ☎ 780/986–6404 or 877/478–7827, FAX 780/986–8332, WEB www.carevacations.com), for group tours and cruise vacations. **Flying Wheels Travel** (✉ 143 W. Bridge St., Box 382, Owatonna, MN 55060, ☎ 507/451–5005 or 800/535–6790, FAX 507/451–1685, WEB www.flyingwheelstravel.com).

## DISCOUNTS AND DEALS

Be a smart shopper and **compare all your options** before making decisions. A plane ticket bought with a promotional coupon from travel clubs, coupon books, and direct-mail offers or on the Internet may not be cheaper than the least expensive fare from a discount ticket agency. And always keep in mind that what you get is just as important as what you save.

### DISCOUNT RESERVATIONS

To save money, **look into discount reservations services** with toll-free numbers, which use their buying power to get a better price on hotels, airline tickets, even car rentals. When booking a room, always **call the hotel's local toll-free number** (if one is available) rather than the central reservations number—you'll often get a better price. Always ask about special packages or corporate rates.

➤ AIRLINE TICKETS: ☎ **800/FLY–ASAP.**

➤ HOTEL ROOMS: **Accommodations Express** (☎ 800/444–7666, WEB www.accommodationsexpress.com). **Central Reservation Service (CRS)** (☎ 800/548–3311). **Hotel Reservations Network** (☎ 800/964–6835, WEB www.hoteldiscount.com). **Players Express Vacations** (☎ 800/458–6161, WEB www.

playersexpress.com). **Quikbook** (☎ 800/789–9887, WEB www.quikbook.com). **RMC Travel** (☎ 800/245–5738, WEB www.rmcwebtravel.com). **Steigenberger Reservation Service** (☎ 800/223–5652, WEB www.srs-worldhotels.com). **Travel Interlink** (☎ 800/888–5898, WEB www.travelinterlink.com). **Turbotrip.com** (☎ 800/473–7829, WEB www.turbotrip.com).

### PACKAGE DEALS

Don't confuse packages and guided tours. When you buy a package, you travel on your own, just as though you had planned the trip yourself. Fly/drive packages, which combine airfare and car rental, are often a good deal. In cities, ask the local visitors' bureau about hotel packages that include tickets to major museum exhibits or other special events.

## ECOTOURISM

Southern Florida encompasses two major nature preserves; naturalists the world over flock to Biscayne and Everglades national parks. When you visit these and other parks, follow the basic rule of environmental responsibility: take nothing but pictures, leave nothing but footprints. **Be careful around the fragile dunes and reefs and don't touch the underwater coral.** Don't pick the sea grass. Damage to the environment may also incur a stiff fine. For details about these parks, consult *Fodor's South Florida* (available in bookstores everywhere).

## EMERGENCIES

➤ DOCTORS AND DENTISTS: **Miami-Dade County Medical Association** (☎ 305/324–8717) is open weekdays 9–5 for medical referrals. **East Coast District Dental Society** (☎ 305/667–3647) is open weekdays 9–4:30 for dental referrals. After hours, stay on the line and a recording will direct you to a dentist. **Dental Referral Service** (☎ 800/577–7322) is open weekdays 8–8 for dental referrals. **Visitors Medical Hotline** (☎ 305/674–2273) is a 24-hour medical referral service provided by Mt. Sinai Medical Center and the visitors bureau.

➤ EMERGENCY SERVICES: Dial **911** for police, ambulance, or fire rescue. You can dial free from pay phones. For 24-hour **Poison Control,** call ☎ 800/282–3171.

➤ HOSPITALS: **Aventura Hospital** (✉ 20900 Biscayne Blvd., Aventura, ☎ 305/682–7000). **Baptist Hospital of Miami** (✉ 8900 N. Kendall Dr., Miami, ☎ 305/596–1960; 305/596–6556 emergency; 305/596–6557 physician referral). **Jackson Memorial Medical Center** (✉ 1611 N.W. 12th Ave., near Dolphin Expressway, Miami, ☎ 305/585–1111; 305/585–6901 emergency; 305/547–5757 physician referral). **Mercy Hospital** (✉ 3663 S. Miami Ave., Coconut Grove, ☎ 305/854–4400; 305/285–2171 emergency; 305/285–2929 physician referral). **Miami Children's Hospital** (✉ 3100 S.W. 62nd Ave., Miami, ☎ 305/666–6511, press 6 for emergencies). **Mt. Sinai Medical Center** (✉ 4300 Alton Rd., I–195 off Julia Tuttle Causeway, Miami Beach, ☎ 305/674–2121; 305/674–2200 emergency; 305/674–2273 physician referral). **Parkway Medical Center East** (✉ 160 N.W. 170th St., North Miami Beach, ☎ 305/651–1100; 888/836–3848 physician referral). **South Miami Hospital** (✉ 6200 S.W. 73rd St., South Miami, ☎ 305/661–4611; 305/662–8181 emergency; 305/596–6557 physician referral). **South Shore Hospital & Medical Center** (✉ 630 Alton Rd., Miami Beach, ☎ 305/672–2100 Ext. 3201 for emergencies).

➤ HOT LINES: **Abuse Registry** (☎ 800/962–2873; 800/453–5145 TTY). **Domestic Violence Hotline** (☎ 800/500–1119). **Drug Helpline** (☎ 800/662–4357). **Mental Health/Suicide Intervention** (☎ 305/358–4357). **Missing Children Information Clearing House** (☎ 888/356–4774). **Rape Treatment Center Hotline** (☎ 305/585–7273).

➤ 24-HOUR PHARMACIES: **Eckerd Drug** (✉ 9031 S.W. 107th Ave., Miami, ☎ 305/274–6776). **Walgreens** (✉ 4895 E. Palm Ave., Hialeah, ☎ 305/231–7454; ✉ 2750 W. 68th St., Hialeah, ☎ 305/828–0268; ✉ 12295 Biscayne Blvd., North Miami, ☎ 305/893–6860; ✉ 5731 Bird Rd., Miami, ☎ 305/666–0757; ✉ 1845 Alton Rd., South Beach, Miami Beach, ☎ 305/531–8868; ✉ 3007 Aventura Blvd., Aventura, ☎ 305/936–2483; ✉ 791 N.E. 167th St., North Miami Beach, ☎ 305/652–7332).

## GAY AND LESBIAN TRAVEL

Greater Miami in general and South Beach in particular are especially gay- and lesbian-friendly. Many of the shops post rainbow flags, and some hotels cater specifically to a gay clientele. Gay beaches include Ocean Drive at 12th Street in South Beach and Haulover Park's northernmost beach (enter at 159th Street and Collins Avenue). The largest concentration of gay nightspots is in the Art Deco District. South Beach tends to embrace everyone, though, and most clubs are decidedly gay-friendly. In March, the Dade Human Rights Foundation hosts the five-day Winter Party (www.winterparty.com) and the Colony Theater on Lincoln Road is home to the 10-day Gay & Lesbian Film Festival. By far the best-known gay event is Thanksgiving week's White Party (www.whitepartyweek.com) with more than 10,000 gay men and women gathering for county-wide festivities.

Pick up a copy of one of the many free publications distributed at clubs and retail establishments. For nightlife, good bets are the club rags *Miamigo, Hotspots,* and *TWN* (*The Weekly News*). TWN offers actual news, even running AP wire stories. Another good source is the free, weekly *New Times*. The *Miami Herald* runs a regular column, "Outlooks," detailing gay and lesbian life in South Florida. Also check out www.floridaoutlooks.com for links to a variety of community resources. The Miami Beach Visitor's and Convention Bureau and the South Beach Business Guild provide tourist information for gay and lesbian visitors.

For details about the gay and lesbian scene, consult *Fodor's Gay Guide to the USA* (available in bookstores everywhere).

➤ LOCAL INFORMATION: **South Beach Business Guild,** (✉ 1657 Drexel Ave., Miami Beach, ☎ 888/893–5595 or 305/534–3336).

➤ GAY- & LESBIAN-FRIENDLY TRAVEL AGENCIES: **Different Roads Travel** (✉ 8383 Wilshire Blvd., Suite 902, Beverly Hills, CA 90211, ☎ 323/651–5557 or 800/429–8747, FAX 323/651–3678, lgernert@tzell.com). **Kennedy Travel** (✉ 314 Jericho Turnpike, Floral Park, NY 11001, ☎ 516/352–4888 or 800/237–7433, FAX 516/354–8849, WEB www.kennedytravel.com). **Now Voyager** (✉ 4406 18th St., San Francisco, CA 94114, ☎ 415/626–1169 or 800/255–6951, FAX 415/626–8626, WEB www.nowvoyager.com). **Skylink Travel and Tour** (✉ 1006 Mendocino Ave., Santa Rosa, CA 95401, ☎ 707/546–9888 or 800/225–5759, FAX 707/546–9891, WEB www.skylinktravel.com), serving lesbian travelers.

## GUIDEBOOKS

Plan well and you won't be sorry. Guidebooks are excellent tools—and you can take them with you. You may want to check out pocket-size, color-photo-illustrated *Citypack Miami,* with a supersize city map, available at on-line retailers and bookstores everywhere.

## HEALTH

If you're unaccustomed to strong, subtropical sun, you run the risk of a severe sunburn or dehydration if you do not take adequate precautions. Try to hit the beach or the streets before 10 AM or after 3 PM. If you must be out at midday, **limit strenuous exercise, drink plenty of liquids, and wear a hat.** Even on overcast or cool days you are vulnerable to burning, so use a sunscreen with an SPF of at least 15, and have children wear waterproof SPF 30 or better.

Although in past years isolated incidents of mosquito-transferred encephalitis were reported in central and north Florida (and immediate precautions taken), mosquitoes and sand fleas (no-see-ums) aren't so much a health issue as a nuisance. In the wet, late spring and summer months, a good insect repellent is a priority. For kids, make sure to use a product that does not contain DEET, which can be toxic to some children.

### DIVERS' ALERT

**Do not fly within 24 hours of scuba diving.**

## HOLIDAYS

Major national holidays include New Year's Day (Jan. 1); Martin Luther King, Jr., Day (3rd Mon. in Jan.); President's Day (3rd Mon. in Feb.);

Memorial Day (last Mon. in May); Independence Day (July 4); Labor Day (1st Mon. in Sept.); Thanksgiving Day (4th Thurs. in Nov.); Christmas Eve and Christmas Day (Dec. 24 and 25); and New Year's Eve (Dec. 31).

## INSURANCE

The most useful travel-insurance plan is a comprehensive policy that includes coverage for trip cancellation and interruption, default, trip delay, and medical expenses (with a waiver for pre-existing conditions).

Without insurance you will lose all or most of your money if you cancel your trip, regardless of the reason. Default insurance covers you if your tour operator, airline, or cruise line goes out of business. Trip-delay covers expenses that arise because of bad weather or mechanical delays. Study the fine print when comparing policies.

Always **buy travel policies directly from the insurance company**; if you buy them from a cruise line, airline, or tour operator that goes out of business you probably will not be covered for the agency or operator's default, a major risk. Before making any purchase, **review your existing health and home-owner's policies** to find what they cover away from home.

➤ TRAVEL INSURERS: In the U.S.: **Access America** (✉ 6600 W. Broad St., Richmond, VA 23230, ☎ 800/284–8300, FAX 804/673–1491, WEB www.accessamerica.com). **Travel Guard International** (✉ 1145 Clark St., Stevens Point, WI 54481, ☎ 715/345–0505 or 800/826–1300, FAX 800/955–8785, WEB www.travelguard.com).

## FOR INTERNATIONAL TRAVELERS

For information on customs restrictions, *see* Customs and Duties.

### CAR TRAVEL

Gasoline costs varied from $1.13–$1.25 a gallon at press time. Stations are plentiful. Most stay open late (24 hours along large highways and in big cities), except in rural areas, where Sunday hours are limited and where you may drive long stretches without a refueling opportunity. Highways are well paved. Interstate highways—limited-access, multilane highways whose numbers are prefixed by "I–"—are the fastest routes. Interstates with three-digit numbers encircle urban areas, which may have other limited-access expressways, freeways, and parkways as well. Tolls may be levied on limited-access highways. So-called U.S. highways and state highways are not necessarily limited-access but may have several lanes.

Along larger highways, roadside stops with rest rooms, fast-food restaurants, and sundries stores are well spaced. State police and tow trucks patrol major highways and lend assistance. If your car breaks down on an interstate, pull onto the shoulder and wait for help, or have your passengers wait while you walk to an emergency phone. If you carry a cell phone, dial *55, noting your location on the small green roadside mileage markers.

Driving in the United States is on the right. Do **obey speed limits** posted along roads and highways. Watch for lower limits in small towns and on back roads. On weekdays between 6 and 10 AM and again between 4 and 7 PM **expect heavy traffic.** To encourage carpooling, some freeways have special lanes for so-called high-occupancy vehicles (HOV)—cars carrying more than one passenger.

Book stores, gas stations, convenience stores, and rest stops sell maps (about $3.50) and multiregion road atlases (about $10).

### CURRENCY

The dollar is the basic unit of U.S. currency. It has 100 cents. Coins include the copper-zinc penny (1¢); the silvery nickel (5¢), dime (10¢), quarter (25¢), and half-dollar (50¢); and the golden $1 coin, replacing a now-rare silver dollar. Bills are denominated $1, $5, $10, $20, $50, and $100, all green and identical in size; designs vary. The exchange rate at press time was US$1.44 per British pound, US$0.63 per Canadian dollar, US$0.51 per Australian dollar, and US$0.42 per New Zealand dollar.

### ELECTRICITY

The U.S. standard is AC, 110 volts/60 cycles. Plugs have two flat pins set parallel to each other.

### EMERGENCIES

For police, fire, or ambulance, **dial 911** (0 in rural areas).

### INSURANCE

Britons and Australians need extra medical coverage when traveling overseas.

➤ INSURANCE INFORMATION: In the U.K.: **Association of British Insurers** (✉ 51–55 Gresham St., London EC2V 7HQ, U.K., ☎ 020/7600–3333, FAX 020/7696–8999, WEB www.abi.org.uk). In Australia: **Insurance Council of Australia** (✉ Level 3, 56 Pitt St., Sydney NSW 2000, ☎ 03/9614–1077, FAX 03/9614–7924). In Canada: **RBC Insurance** (✉ 6880 Financial Dr., Mississauga, Ontario L5N 7Y5, Canada, ☎ 905/816–2400; 800/668–4342 in Canada, FAX 905/816–2498, WEB www.royalbank.com). In New Zealand: **Insurance Council of New Zealand** (✉ Box 474, Wellington, New Zealand, ☎ 04/472–5230, FAX 04/473–3011, WEB www.icnz.org.nz).

### PASSPORTS AND VISAS

When traveling internationally, **carry your passport** even if you don't need one (it's always the best form of ID) and **make two photocopies of the data page** (one for someone at home and another for you, carried separately from your passport). If you lose your passport, promptly call the nearest embassy or consulate and the local police.

Visitor visas are not necessary for Canadian citizens, or for citizens of Australia and the United Kingdom who are staying fewer than 90 days.

➤ AUSTRALIAN CITIZENS: **Australian Passport Office** (☎ 131–232). **U.S. Office of Australia Affairs** (✉ MLC Centre, 19-29 Martin Pl., 59th floor, Sydney NSW 2000, Australia).

➤ CANADIAN CITIZENS: **Passport Office** (☎ 819/994–3500; 800/567–6868 in Canada).

➤ NEW ZEALAND CITIZENS: **New Zealand Passport Office** (☎ 04/494–0700; 04/474–8100 for application procedures, WEB www.passports.govt.nz). **Embassy of the United States** (✉ 29 Fitzherbert Terr., Thorndon, Wellington, ☎ 04/462–6000 WEB usembassy.state.gov/wellington). **United States Consulate General** (✉ Citibank Center, 3rd floor, 23 Customs St. E, Auckland, ☎ 09/303–2724, WEB www.usembassy.state.gov/wellington).

➤ U.K. CITIZENS: **London Passport Office** (☎ 0870/521–0410) for application procedures and emergency passports. **U.S. Embassy Visa Information Line** (☎ 01891/200–290). **U.S. Embassy Visa Branch** (✉ 5 Upper Grosvenor Sq., London W1A 1AE, U.K.); send a self-addressed, stamped envelope. **U.S. Consulate General** (✉ Queen's House, Queen St., Belfast BTI 6EO, Northern Ireland).

### TELEPHONES

All U.S. telephone numbers consist of a three-digit area code and a seven-digit local number. Within most local calling areas, dial only the seven-digit number. Within the same area code, dial "1" first. To call between area-code regions, dial "1" then all 10 digits; the same goes for calls to numbers prefixed by "800," "888," and "877"—all toll-free. For calls to numbers preceded by "900" you must pay—usually dearly.

For Miami telephone information, *see* Telephones, *below.*

For international calls, dial "011" followed by the country code and the local number. For help, dial "0" and ask for an overseas operator. The country code is 61 for Australia, 64 for New Zealand, 44 for the United Kingdom. Calling Canada is the same as calling within the United States. Most local phone books list country codes and U.S. area codes. The country code for the United States is 1.

For operator assistance, dial "0". To obtain someone's phone number, call directory assistance, 555–1212 or occasionally 411 (free at public phones). To have the person you're calling foot the bill, phone collect; dial "0" instead of "1" before the 10-digit number.

At pay phones, instructions are usually posted. In Miami you insert coins in a slot (35¢ for local calls) and wait for a steady tone before dialing. When you call long-distance, the operator will tell you how much to insert; prepaid phone cards, widely available in various denominations, are easier. Call the number on the back, punch in the card's identification number when prompted, then dial your number.

## LANGUAGE

If you know Spanish you'll be well received in Greater Miami and better prepared to mix among both locals and international visitors. While the city's not officially considered bilingual, it may as well be.

## LIMOUSINES

Miami is a city of expensive cars and limos, so arranging for limousine service is not a problem. Expect at least $60 per hour with a three-hour minimum; airport service is about $60 and prior arrangements are necessary. Unfortunately, some companies are frequently in and out of business; if you rely on the Yellow Pages, look for a company that has a street address, not just a phone number. One of the oldest companies in town, Vintage Rolls-Royce Limousines, chauffeurs clients around in Rolls-Royces dating from the 1940s.

➤ LIMOUSINE SERVICES: **Carey South Florida Limousine** (☏ 305/893–9850 or 800/824–4820). **Sterling Limousine** (☏ 305/567–9200 or 888/239–9200). **Vintage Rolls-Royce Limousines** (☏ 305/662–5763 or 800/888–7657).

## LODGING

The lodgings we list are the cream of the crop in each price category. We always list the facilities that are available—but we don't specify whether they cost extra. When pricing accommodations, always ask what's included and what costs extra. Remember that ocean view balconies and proximity to the beach significantly increase rates. All hotels listed have private bath unless otherwise noted. Properties indicated by ✕🏨 are lodging establishments whose restaurant warrants a special trip.

Assume that hotels operate on the **European Plan** (EP, with no meals) unless we specify that they use the **Continental Plan** (CP, with a Continental breakfast), **Breakfast Plan** (BP, with a full breakfast), **Modified American Plan** (MAP, with breakfast and dinner), or the **Full American Plan** (FAP, with all meals).

### APARTMENT RENTALS

If you want a home base that's roomy enough for a family and comes with cooking facilities, **consider a furnished rental.** These can save you money, especially if you're traveling with a group. Home-exchange directories sometimes list rentals as well as exchanges.

In Miami and Miami Beach, condominium and apartment rentals run the gamut from the very affordable (usually off the beach) to the ultra luxe. A number of local real estate agencies handle short-term rentals; you can contact them through the chamber of commerce in the area you're visiting or through the visitors bureau (*see* Visitor Information).

➤ INTERNATIONAL AGENTS: **Hideaways International** (✉ 767 Islington St., Portsmouth, NH 03801, ☏ 603/430–4433 or 800/843–4433, FAX 603/430–4444, WEB www.hideaways.com; membership $129). **Hometours International** (✉ Box 11503, Knoxville, TN 37939, ☏ 865/690–8484 or 800/367–4668, WEB http://thor.he.net/~hometour). **Interhome** (✉ 1990 N.E. 163rd St., Suite 110, North Miami Beach, FL 33162, ☏ 305/940–2299 or 800/882–6864, FAX 305/940–2911, WEB www.interhome.com). **Vacation Home Rentals Worldwide** (✉ 235 Kensington Ave., Norwood, NJ 07648, ☏ 201/767–9393 or 800/633–3284, FAX 201/767–5510, WEB www.vhrww.com).

### B&BS

Greater Miami does not have many traditional bed and breakfasts, but there are a few standouts tucked away off the beaten path. Florida Bed & Breakfast Inns is an association of small and historic lodging properties throughout the state.

➤ RESERVATION SERVICES: **Florida Bed & Breakfast Inns** (✉ Box 6187, Palm Harbour, 34684, ☏ 800/524–1880, WEB www.florida-inns.com).

### HOME EXCHANGES

If you would like to exchange your home for someone else's, **join a home-exchange organization,** which will send you its updated listings of available exchanges for a year and will include your own listing in at least one of them. It's up to you to make specific arrangements.

➤ EXCHANGE CLUBS: **HomeLink International** (✉ Box 47747, Tampa, FL 33647, ☎ 813/975–9825 or 800/638–3841, FAX 813/910–8144, WEB www.homelink.org; $106 per year). **Intervac U.S.** (✉ Box 590504, San Francisco, CA 94159, ☎ 800/756–4663, FAX 415/435–7440, WEB www.intervacus.com; $50 yearly fee includes on-line access to listings, $99 per year pays for listing home in catalogue and on-line access).

### HOSTELS

No matter what your age, you can **save on lodging costs by staying at hostels.** In some 5,000 locations in more than 70 countries around the world, Hostelling International (HI), the umbrella group for a number of national youth-hostel associations, offers single-sex, dorm-style beds and, at many hostels, rooms for couples and family accommodations. Membership in any HI national hostel association, open to travelers of all ages, allows you to stay in HI-affiliated hostels at member rates; one-year membership is about $25 for adults (C$26.75 in Canada, £13 in the U.K., $30 in Australia, and $30 in New Zealand); hostels run about $10–$30 per night. Members have priority if the hostel is full; they're also eligible for discounts around the world, even on rail and bus travel in some countries.

➤ ORGANIZATIONS: **Hostelling International—American Youth Hostels** (✉ 733 15th St. NW, Suite 840, Washington, DC 20005, ☎ 202/783–6161, FAX 202/783–6171, WEB www.hiayh.org). **Hostelling International—Canada** (✉ 400–205 Catherine St., Ottawa, Ontario K2P 1C3, Canada, ☎ 613/237–7884, FAX 613/237–7868, WEB www.hostellingintl.ca). **Youth Hostel Association of England and Wales** (✉ Trevelyan House, 8 St. Stephen's Hill, St. Albans, Hertfordshire AL1 2DY, U.K., ☎ 0870/8708808, FAX 01727/844126, WEB www.yha.org.uk). **Australian Youth Hostel Association** (✉ 10 Mallett St., Camperdown, NSW 2050, Australia, ☎ 02/9565–1699, FAX 02/9565–1325, WEB www.yha.com.au). **Youth Hostels Association of New Zealand** (✉ Box 436, Christchurch, New Zealand, ☎ 03/379–9970, FAX 03/365–4476, WEB www.yha.org.nz).

### HOTELS

All hotels listed have private bath unless otherwise noted.

➤ TOLL-FREE NUMBERS: **Best Western** (☎ 800/528–1234, WEB www.bestwestern.com). **Choice** (☎ 800/221–2222, WEB www.hotelchoice.com). **Clarion** (☎ 800/252–7466, WEB www.hotelchoice.com). **Colony** (☎ 800/777–1700, WEB www.colony.com). **Comfort** (☎ 800/228–5150, WEB www.comfortinn.com). **Days Inn** (☎ 800/325–2525, WEB www.daysinn.com). **Doubletree and Red Lion Hotels** (☎ 800/222–8733, WEB www.doubletree.com). **Embassy Suites** (☎ 800/362–2779, WEB www.embassysuites.com). **Fairfield Inn** (☎ 800/228–2800, WEB www.marriott.com). **Hilton** (☎ 800/445–8667, WEB www.hilton.com). **Holiday Inn** (☎ 800/465–4329, WEB www.basshotels.com). **Howard Johnson** (☎ 800/654–4656, WEB www.hojo.com). **Hyatt Hotels & Resorts** (☎ 800/233–1234, WEB www.hyatt.com). **Inter-Continental** (☎ 800/327–0200, WEB www.interconti.com). **La Quinta** (☎ 800/531–5900, WEB www.laquinta.com). **Marriott** (☎ 800/228–9290, WEB www.marriott.com). **Omni** (☎ 800/843–6664, WEB www.omnihotels.com). **Quality Inn** (☎ 800/228–5151, WEB www.qualityinn.com). **Radisson** (☎ 800/333–3333, WEB www.radisson.com). **Ramada** (☎ 800/228–2828, WEB www.ramada.com). **Ritz-Carlton** (☎ 800/241–3333, WEB www.ritzcarlton.com). **Sheraton** (☎ 800/325–3535, WEB www.starwood.com). **Sleep Inn** (☎ 800/753–3746, WEB www.sleepinn.com). **Westin Hotels & Resorts** (☎ 800/228–3000, WEB www.westin.com). **Wyndham Hotels & Resorts** (☎ 800/822–4200, WEB www.wyndham.com).

### RVS AND CAMPING

There are more than 3,000 family camp sites in 45 Florida state parks. Under new state policy, campers without reservations at Florida state parks are assured that 10% of each park's sites will be available for walk-ins on a first-come, first-serve basis. Reservations in Florida state parks are made directly with the parks. For a free park guide, call ☎ 850/488–9872 or see www.dep.state.fl.us/parks.

➤ RV AND CAMPING INFORMATION: **Florida Association of RV Parks &**

**Campgrounds** (1340 Vickers Dr., Tallahassee, FL 32303–3041, ☎ 850/562–7151, WEB www.floridacamping.com).

## MAIL AND SHIPPING

For mail sent within the United States, you need at least a 37¢ stamp for first-class letters weighing up to 1 ounce (23¢ for each additional ounce) and 25¢ for domestic postcards. For overseas mail, you pay 60¢ for 1-ounce airmail letters to Canada and Mexico, 80¢ other countries; 50¢ for airmail postcards to Canada and Mexico, 70¢ elsewhere. For 70¢ you can buy an aerogram—a single sheet of lightweight blue paper that folds into its own envelope, stamped for overseas airmail.

The Miami General Mail Facility is open weekdays 7–7, and Saturday 8:30–2, although branch offices keep their own hours.

➤ POST OFFICES: **Miami General Mail Facility** (2200 N.W. 72nd Ave., Miami, FL 33152, ☎ 800/275–8777). **Miami Beach Post Office** (1300 Washington Ave., Miami Beach, FL 33139, ☎ 305/672–2447).

➤ FEDERAL EXPRESS: ☎ 800/463–3339.

➤ UPS: ☎ 800/742–5877.

### E-MAIL SERVICE

Cheaper than a phone call and quicker than post is e-mail. If you're sans laptop and modem, get a free e-mail account from any of the larger service providers or try www.hotmail.com. You can log on free at the local library, or try Kafka's Kafe in South Beach. A used bookstore, newsstand and cyber café, it's very Europeanlike. High-speed access for five minutes is $1, $9 for one hour, rates drop after 7 PM. If you're in one of the larger hotels, you can use their Business Center to send and receive e-mail.

➤ E-MAIL SERVICE: **Kafka's Cybernet Kafe** (✉ 1464 Washington Ave., Miami Beach, ☎ 305/673–9669, WEB www.kafkaskafe.citysearch.com).

## MEDIA

Greater Miami is a media hub, offering access to information from around the world and in many languages. For international and foreign language papers, check out one of the larger hotels or book store chains, or try the popular News Café in Coconut Grove or South Beach. The main Coral Gables branch of Books & Books, Inc. (✉ 265 Aragon Ave.) is a terrific independent bookstore that's worth a trip for magazines and books.

### NEWSPAPERS AND MAGAZINES

Greater Miami's major newspaper is the ***Miami Herald.*** Your best bet for weekend happenings is the free alternative weekly, ***New Times*** or ***Street,*** a free weekly with entertainment news, local art and film reviews, events, and nightlife. For Spanish-language news, turn to ***El Nuevo Herald.*** Regional editions of the ***Wall Street Journal*** and the ***New York Times*** can be found just about everywhere—including vending machines—and many of Europe and Latin America's major dailies and fashion glossies are available at newsstands.

### RADIO AND TELEVISION

Greater Miami is served by all the major cable networks. Major broadcast television stations include **WAMI** (Telefutur, Spanish–international), **WBFS** (UPN), **WBZL** (WB), **WFOR** (CBS), **WLTV** (Univision, Spanish–international), **WPBT** (PBS), **WPLG** (ABC), **WSCV** (Telemundo, Spanish–international), **WSVN** (Fox), and **WTVJ** (NBC).

Radio stations in Greater Miami include **WDNA/88.9** (jazz), **WEDR/99.1** (urban), **WHYI/100.7** (Top 40), **WIOD/610AM** (news), **WKIS/99.9** (country), **WLRN 91.3** (National Public Radio), **WQAM/560AM** (sports), **WZTA/94.9** (hard rock), and **WBGG/105.9** (classic rock). Near the airport, you can find basic tourist information, broadcast successively in English, French, German, Portuguese, and Spanish, on the low-wattage **WAEM/102.3.**

## METRORAIL AND COMMUTER TRAINS

Elevated Metrorail trains run from downtown Miami north to Hialeah and south along U.S. 1 to Dadeland. The system operates daily 5 AM–midnight. Trains run every six minutes during peak hours, every 15 minutes during weekday mid-hours, and every

30 minutes after 8 PM and on weekends. The fare is $1.25; 25¢ transfers to Metromover or Metrobus must be purchased at the station where you originally board the system. Parking at Metrorail stations costs $2.

Metromover runs on two loops around downtown Miami, linking major hotels, office buildings, and shopping areas. The system spans 4½ mi, including the 1½-mi Omni extension with six stations to the north, and the 1-mi Brickell extension with six stations to the south. Service runs daily, every 90 seconds during rush hour and every three minutes off-peak, 6 AM–midnight along the inner loop and 6 AM–10:30 PM on the Omni and Brickell extensions. The fare is 25¢; transfers to Metrorail are $1.

Tri-Rail, South Florida's commuter train system, offers daily service connecting Miami-Dade with Broward and Palm Beach counties via Metrorail (transfer at the TriRail–Metrorail Station at the Hialeah station, at 79th Street and East 11th Avenue). They also offer shuttle service to and from MIA from their airport station at 3797 N.W. 21st Street. Tri-Rail stops at 18 stations along a 71-mi route. Fares are established by zones, with prices ranging from $3.50 to $9.25 for a round-trip ticket.

➤ INFORMATION: **Metrorail** and **Metromover** (☎ 305/770–3131). **TriRail** (☎ 800/874–7245).

## MONEY MATTERS

Plastic is everywhere in Greater Miami and debit and credit cards are readily accepted. If not, there's sure to be an ATM nearby offering almost full-service bank services, including cash advances and money transfers. You can use a tried-and-true traveler's check at most restaurants, hotels, and stores as well, it's just not as convenient. Larger banks, especially in downtown Miami or South Beach, offer currency exchange.

Although Greater Miami is a relatively expensive destination, a smart shopper can find bargains in just about every category, from a $1 quick bite at a walk-up window in Little Havana to significantly lower room rates at hotels a few blocks off the beach. You can expect to spend an average of about $6 for breakfast, $12 for lunch, and $30 for dinner, while daily hotel rates average $136. Greens fees at public golf courses are $14–$20, but fees can approach $250 at the toniest private courses. Adult admission to area attractions typically costs $12–$14, but remember that the outdoors is a major attraction in itself, and many of Greater Miami's outdoor events and festivals are free.

Prices throughout this guide are given for adults. Substantially reduced fees are almost always available for children, students, and senior citizens. For information on taxes, *see* Taxes.

➤ CURRENCY EXCHANGE AND SERVICES: **Bank of America** (☎ 800/299–2265). **First Union** (☎ 800/275–3862). **Western Union** (☎ 800/325–6000).

### ATMS

ATMs may cost you as much as $2.50 per transaction, so **use your own bank's ATM** if possible. Be wary at night and go to a safe, well-lighted location (machines at Publix Groceries throughout Miami and Miami Beach are free and usually well-trafficked).

### CREDIT CARDS

Throughout this guide, the following abbreviations are used: **AE**, American Express; **D**, Discover; **DC**, Diners Club; **MC**, MasterCard; and **V**, Visa.

➤ REPORTING LOST CARDS: **American Express** (☎ 800/528–4800). **Diners Club** (☎ 800/234–6377). **Discover** (☎ 800/347–2683). **MasterCard** (☎ 800/826–2181). **Visa** (☎ 800/336–8472).

## MOTORCYCLE RENTAL

You'll notice that motorcycles, Vespas, and scooters are a popular mode of transportation. In Miami you can rent all of the above, including a Harley (at American Road Collection) or a Honda bike, with daily rentals starting at $109. Even with unlimited mileage, motorcycles still cost more than a car, but then that's not the point.

Expect to pay for insurance and a security deposit. Florida law doesn't require a helmet, but it's worth the additional charge. You must be 21 with a credit card, valid driver's license, and motorcycle endorsement.

Vespas and scooters are available at Deco Scooter Rentals from about $40 a day. Ask for hotel pick-up service.

➤ MOTORCYCLE RENTAL CONTACTS: **American Road Collection** (✉ 1416 18th St., Miami Beach, ☎ 305/673–8113). **Cruise America** (✉ 5801 N.W. 151st St., Miami, ☎ 800/327–7799 or 305/828–1198, www.cruiseamerica.com). **Deco Scooter Rentals** (✉ 215 6th St., Miami Beach, ☎ 305/538–0202).

## NATIONAL PARKS

Look into discount passes to save money on park entrance fees. The National Parks Pass ($50) gets you and your companions free admission to all parks for one year. (Camping and parking are extra.) A percentage of the proceeds from sales of the pass will fund National Parks projects. Both the Golden Age Passport ($10), for those 62 and older, and the Golden Access Passport (free), for travelers with disabilities, entitle holders to free entry to all national parks, plus 50% off fees for the use of many park facilities and services. You must show proof of age and of U.S. citizenship or permanent residency (such as a U.S. passport, driver's license, or birth certificate) and, if requesting Golden Access, proof of disability. The Golden Age and Golden Access passes are available at all national parks wherever entrance fees are charged. The National Parks Pass is available by mail or through the Internet.

➤ PASSES BY MAIL: **National Park Service** (✉ National Park Service–Department of Interior, 1849 C St. NW, Washington, DC 20240, ☎ 202/208–4747, WEB www.nps.gov). **National Parks Pass** (✉ 27540 Ave. Mentry, Valencia, CA 91355, ☎ 888/GO–PARKS, WEB www.nationalparks.org).

## PACKING

You can generally swim year-round in Greater Miami, so **pack a bathing suit.** If it's winter at home, don't fret. You can easily pick one up in the many South Beach shops. Although they're not cheap. **Bring a sun hat and sunscreen**; the sun can be fierce, even in winter when it might be chilly or overcast. Be prepared for sudden summer storms with a fold-up umbrella that fits easily into your luggage.

For the most part, daytime dress is casual—especially in flip-flop and sarong-wearing South Beach. In the evenings, although most restaurants won't require jacket or tie, there is opportunity to spiff up. Think trendy as opposed to dressy in South Beach—the term du jour is *casual chic*. For winter months, a sweater and a jacket are recommended; in the summer, air-conditioners are on overdrive so you might need a light sweater. Finally, comfortable walking shoes are a good idea for the many outdoor activities.

In your carry-on luggage, **pack an extra pair of eyeglasses or contact lenses and enough of any medication** you take to last the entire trip. You may also ask your doctor to write a spare prescription using the drug's generic name, since brand names may vary from country to country. In luggage to be checked, **never pack prescription drugs or valuables.** To avoid customs delays, carry medications in their original packaging. And don't forget to carry with you the addresses of offices that handle refunds of lost traveler's checks. Check *Fodor's How to Pack* (available in bookstores everywhere) for more tips.

### CHECKING LUGGAGE

You are limited to one carry-on bag and a personal item such as a purse or laptop computer. Don't pack scissors or pocket knives in your carry-ons; your manicure set should go in checked luggage. For the latest information on what's allowed in carry-ons, check the airport's Web site. Make sure that everything you carry aboard will fit under your seat or in the overhead bin, and get to the gate early. Note that if you have a seat at the back of the plane, you'll probably board first, while the overhead bins are still empty.

If you are flying internationally, note that baggage allowances may be determined not by piece but by weight—generally 88 pounds (40 kilograms) in first class, 66 pounds (30 kilograms) in business class, and 44 pounds (20 kilograms) in economy.

Airline liability for baggage is limited to $1,250 per person on flights within the United States. On international flights it amounts to $9.07 per pound or $20 per kilogram for checked baggage (roughly $640 per 70-pound bag) and $400 per passenger for unchecked baggage. You can buy additional coverage at check-in for about $10 per $1,000 of coverage, but it excludes a rather extensive list of items, shown on your airline ticket.

Before departure, **itemize your bags' contents** and their worth, and label the bags with your name, address, and phone number. (If you use your home address, cover it so potential thieves can't see it readily.) Inside each bag, **pack a copy of your itinerary.** At check-in, **make sure that each bag is correctly tagged** with the destination airport's three-letter code. If your bags arrive damaged or fail to arrive at all, file a written report with the airline before leaving the airport.

## REST ROOMS

Free public facilities are not widely available in Greater Miami, but most municipal buildings have free rest rooms that are open to the public during business hours. Along Miami Beach, rest rooms are free and open 'til 5; Miami-Dade County park facilities close at sundown. Rest rooms at gas, bus, and rail stations are an option, but may not be the cleanest choices. While not, strictly speaking, open to the public, rest rooms in lobbies of large hotels are often accessible; if there's an attendant, tip 25¢–50¢. Or order some refreshments from a restaurant and use theirs.

## SAFETY

Greater Miami is as safe for visitors as any American city its size, but it's always a good idea to exercise extra caution when you're on vacation. Unfamiliarity with a location combined with carrying more money than usual can increase your safety risks. Instead, **know where you're going,** and be especially wary when driving in strange neighborhoods and leaving the airport. With the exception of heavily trafficked areas in Miami Beach and Coconut Grove, it's also best not to walk alone at night. You can ask your concierge or front desk staff which areas to avoid. Don't assume that valuables are safe in your hotel room; **use in-room safes** or the hotel's safety deposit boxes. Carry your money like you do at home: in small amounts. And **don't carry a fanny pack**—it separates you from the locals. Try to use ATMs only during the day or in brightly lighted, well-traveled locals. If you're shopping, don't leave purchases in the car.

### BEACH SAFETY

Before swimming, **make sure there's no undertow.** Rip currents, caused when the tide rushes out through a narrow break in the water, can overpower even the strongest swimmer. If you do get caught in one, resist the urge to swim straight back to shore—you'll tire before you make it. Instead, stay calm. Swim parallel to the shore line until you are outside the current's pull, then work your way in to shore.

While at the beach, **steer clear of anything that looks like a blue bubble in the sand or water.** These are either jellyfish or Portuguese man-of-wars, and stings from their tentacles can cause a painful allergic reaction. Beaches with lifeguards usually post signs warning bathers. Don't forget lots of sunscreen and drinking water. Overexposure and dehydration are oft-treated medical emergencies in South Florida. While not too serious, they can quickly dampen vacation spirits.

## SENIOR-CITIZEN TRAVEL

Businesses in Miami and Miami Beach offer many discounts to seniors and AARP members. Restaurant discounts (Florida is famed for early bird specials) may be limited to certain menus, days, or hours, so call ahead to check. Nearly all hotels offer some sort of discount, as do many movie theaters and attractions. All Miami-Dade transit routes (via bus or rail) are discounted for seniors 65-plus.

To qualify for age-related discounts, **mention your senior-citizen status up front** when booking hotel reservations (not when checking out) and before you're seated in restaurants (not when paying the bill). When renting a car, ask about promotional car-rental discounts, which can be cheaper than senior-citizen rates.

➤ EDUCATIONAL PROGRAMS: **Elderhostel** (✉ 11 Ave. de Lafayette, Boston, MA 02111-1746, ☎ 877/426–8056, FAX

877/426–2166, WEB www.elderhostel.org). **Interhostel** (✉ University of New Hampshire, 6 Garrison Ave., Durham, NH 03824, ☎ 603/862–1147 or 800/733–9753, FAX 603/862–1113, WEB www.learn.unh.edu).

## SIGHTSEEING TOURS

### BICYCLE TOURS

A two-hour bike tour of the Art Deco District leaves from the **Miami Beach Bicycle Center** (✉ 601 5th St., Miami Beach, ☎ 305/674–0150) at 10:30 AM on the third Sunday of each month. This tour costs $20 with a rental bike and $10 with your own bike; make sure to call ahead as the schedule can be erratic.

### BOAT TOURS

***Island Queen, Island Lady, and Pink Lady*** (☎ 305/379–5119) are 150-passenger double-decker tour boats docked at Bayside Marketplace (✉ 401 Biscayne Blvd.). They offer daily 90-minute narrated tours of the Port of Miami and Millionaires' Row, at a cost of $14 per person, $7 under 12.

For something a little more private and luxe, ***RA Charters*** (☎ 305/854–7341 or 305/989–3959, www.racharters.com) sails out of the Dinner Key Marina in Coconut Grove. Full- and half-day charters include snorkeling and even sailing lessons, with extended trips to the Florida Keys and Bahamas. For a romantic night, have Captain Masoud pack some gourmet fare and sail sunset to moonlight while you enjoy Biscayne Bay's spectacular skyline view of Miami. Call for prices and details.

### HELICOPTER TOURS

For a bird's-eye view, try ***Biscayne Helicopters*** (☎ 305/252–3883). They're out of Tamiami Airport and $400 buys you a half hour for up to four passengers with flyovers of Miami International Airport, downtown Miami, South Beach, Key Biscayne, and the Biscayne Bay skyline.

### RICKSHAW TOURS

**Coconut Grove Rickshaw** operates two-person rickshaws along Main Highway in Coconut Grove's Village Center, nightly 8 PM–2 AM. You'll find them parked streetside throughout the neighborhood or in front of the major entertainment complexes. Prices start at $5 per person for a 10-minute ride through Coconut Grove or $10 per person for a 20-minute lovers' moonlight ride to Biscayne Bay.

### SPECIAL INTEREST TOURS

**Everglades Safari Park** (✉ 26700 S.W. 8th St., 9 mi west of Krome Ave., Miami, ☎ 305/226–6923) is actually an attraction featuring a jungle trail and an alligator show and farm, but the highlight is the airboat tour of the Everglades. Open daily, rain or shine (unless there's lightning), adults are $15, children 5–11 $5, and under 5 free. Leave an hour-plus for this one, more if you want to spend time on the jungle trail.

**Style Ventures** (✉ 1109 Ponce de León Blvd., ☎ 305/444–8428 or 888/255–4428) offers a variety of customized tours. Primarily a group operator with tour packages to other regions of Florida as well, private tours cost a little more ($29–$170 per person depending on number of participants and itinerary), but are well worth it. Choose from city, Everglades, deep-sea fishing, gallery, nightlife, and shopping tours, or plan your own with the professional staff. Accessible vehicles and trained guides are provided for travelers with special needs.

**Tropical Tours** (☎ 305/248–4181) provides an overview of southern Miami-Dade County's 80,000 acres of agriculture. Highlights include visits to an orchid nursery, tropical fruit grove, and U-Pick-Em field, which in winter offers plentiful bounty. Cost is $15 adult, $7.50 children under 15; tours are available on request and depart from the Robert is Here Fruit Stand (192nd Ave. and 344th St., Homestead).

### WALKING TOURS

The **Art Deco District Tour** (✉ 1001 Ocean Dr., Miami Beach, ☎ 305/531–3484), operated by the Miami Design Preservation League, is a 90-minute guided walking tour that departs from the league's welcome center at the Oceanfront Auditorium. It costs $10 (tax-deductible) and starts at 10:30 AM Saturday and 6:30 PM Thursday. Private group tours can be arranged with advance notice. You can go at your own pace with the league's self-guided $5 audio tour, which takes roughly an hour and a half and is available in English, Spanish, French, and German.

**Professor Paul George** (✉ 1345 S.W. 14th St., Miami, ☎ 305/858–6021), a history professor at Miami-Dade Community College and past president of the Florida Historical Society, leads a variety of walking and boat tours, as well as tours via Metrorail and Metromover. Pick from tours covering downtown, the Miami River, or neighborhoods such as Little Havana and Coconut Grove. George starts Saturdays at 10 and Sundays at 11 at various locations, depending on the tour; the tours generally last about 2½ hours. Call for each weekend's schedule and for additional tours by appointment. Tours start at $15 per person and prices vary by tour and group size.

## STUDENTS IN MIAMI

Although spring break does not assume the proportions in Miami and Miami Beach that it does elsewhere in Florida, Greater Miami is a popular destination for students, so discounts are ubiquitous. To qualify, make sure you mention your student status up front when booking hotel reservations—don't wait until checking out. Restaurants may restrict student discounts to certain menus, days, or hours. Miami-Dade public transportation offers student fares and some movie theaters, museums, and attractions also feature discounts. The biggest plus for students are discounts at area gyms, which can otherwise be expensive, and college nights at bars (try spots near area colleges and universities).

➤ IDs and Services: **STA Travel** (☎ 212/627–3111 or 800/781–4040, FAX 212/627–3387, WEB www.sta.com). **Travel Cuts** (✉ 187 College St., Toronto, Ontario M5T 1P7, Canada, ☎ 416/979–2406; 800/667–2887 in Canada, FAX 416/979–8167, WEB www.travelcuts.com).

## TAXES

### SALES TAX

Greater Miami's sales tax is currently 6.5%, but tourist taxes can raise the total to as much as 12.5% on accommodations and 8.5% on meals. It's all a bit complicated, since the tax may change depending on which municipality you're in and what you're buying. Ask about additional costs up front if they're not posted.

## TAXIS

Except in South Beach, it's difficult to hail a cab on the street; in most cases you'll need to call a cab company or have a hotel doorman hail one for you. Fares run $3 for the first mile and $2 every mile thereafter; flat-rate fares are also available from the airport to a variety of zones. Fares are set by the board of county commissioners, so if you have a question or complaint, call the **Metro-Dade Passenger Transportation Regulatory Service** (☎ 305/375–2460), informally known as the Hack Bureau. There's no additional charge for up to five passengers or for luggage. Many cabs now accept credit cards; inquire when you call or before you get in the car.

Recent taxi-regulating legislation, hospitality training, and increased competition should rein in most surly drivers. But Greater Miami still has cabbies who are rude and in some cases even dishonest, taking advantage of visitors who don't know the area, so **try to be familiar with your route and destination.**

➤ Taxi Companies: **Central Taxicab Service** (☎ 305/532–5555). **Diamond Cab Company** (☎ 305/545–5555). **Flamingo Taxi** (☎ 305/759–8100). **Metro Taxi** (☎ 305/888–8888). **Society Cab Company** (☎ 305/757–5523). **Super Yellow Cab Company** (☎ 305/888–7777). **Tropical Taxicab Company** (☎ 305/945–1025). **Yellow Cab Company** (☎ 305/633–0503).

## TELEPHONES

Area codes in Greater Miami are 305 and 786. All local calls must start with one of these area codes. In other words, local calls are 10-numbers long.

Calls from public telephone booths cost 35¢. Cell phone rental is available through some car rental agencies and many of the larger resort and convention hotels.

To reach an operator, dial 0. To reach directory assistance anywhere within the United States, dial 411.

### LONG-DISTANCE CALLS

The country code for the United States is 1. To place an international call from the United States, dial 011 before the country code and number you're calling.

For long distance or toll-free calls, always dial 1 before the area code. Toll-free calls begin with 800, 888, or 877; telephone numbers beginning with 900 are toll calls that could end up costing you several dollars per minute. Competitive long-distance carriers make calling within the United States relatively convenient and let you avoid hotel surcharges. By dialing an 800 number, you can get connected to the long-distance company of your choice. You may also want to consider long distance prepaid calling cards, sold in a variety of increments at most stores. Call the number on the back, punch in the card's identification number when prompted, then dial your number.

### LONG-DISTANCE SERVICES

AT&T, MCI, and Sprint access codes make calling long distance relatively convenient, but you may find the local access number blocked in many hotel rooms. First ask the hotel operator to connect you. If the hotel operator balks, ask for an international operator, or dial the international operator yourself. One way to improve your odds of getting connected to your long-distance carrier is to travel with more than one company's calling card (a hotel may block Sprint, for example, but not MCI). If all else fails, call from a pay phone.

➤ ACCESS CODES: **AT&T Direct** (☎ 800/435–0812). **MCI WorldPhone** (☎ 800/444–4141). **Sprint International Access** (☎ 800/877–4646).

## TIME

Miami is in the Eastern U.S. time zone and adopts Daylight Savings Time between April and October (clocks are set one hour ahead). For Miami time and temperature, call ☎ 305/324–8811.

## TIPPING

The customary tip for a doorman who calls for a taxi or a valet who brings your car around is $1. Bellhops are usually given $2 per bag in luxury hotels, $1 per bag elsewhere. Hotel maids should be tipped at least $2 per day of your stay. For concierge service, tips depend on the request: $3–$5 for basic dinner or tour reservations and perhaps $10 for above-and-beyond service, like getting you on the guest list of a popular club or having your laptop repaired. Taxi drivers should receive 15%–20% of the fare and skycaps $1 per bag.

If you're sitting at the bar, bartenders should get 50¢–$1 per drink. Maitre d's and wine stewards should be rewarded for special efforts.

Tip waiters 15%–20% of your bill before tax. **Check your bill before tipping** though, since many restaurants here do you the favor of adding the gratuity. Restaurants in Miami-Dade must now provide customers with written notice of their tipping policy and post an anti-discrimination statement in English, Spanish, and Creole—in other words, if they choose to charge an automatic 15%, they'd better post it.

## TOURS AND PACKAGES

Because everything is prearranged on a prepackaged tour or independent vacation, you spend less time planning—and often get it all at a good price.

For hundreds of out-of-the-ordinary tour options click on "Adventure Travel" at www.fodors.com.

### BOOKING WITH AN AGENT

Travel agents are excellent resources. But it's a good idea to collect brochures from several agencies as some agents' suggestions may be influenced by relationships with tour and package firms that reward them for volume sales. If you have a special interest, **find an agent with expertise in that area**; ASTA (☞ Travel Agencies) has a database of specialists worldwide.

Make sure your travel agent knows the accommodations and other services of the place they're recommending. Ask about the hotel's location, room size, beds, and whether it has a pool, room service, or programs for children, if you care about these. Has your agent been there in person or sent others whom you can contact?

Do some homework on your own, too: local tourism boards can provide information about lesser-known and small-niche operators, some of which may sell only direct.

### BUYER BEWARE

Each year consumers are stranded or lose their money when tour operators—even large ones with excellent reputations—go out of business. So **check out the operator.** Ask several travel agents about its reputation, and try to **book with a company that has a consumer-protection program.** (Look for information in the company's brochure.) In the United States, members of the National Tour Association and the United States Tour Operators Association are required to set aside funds to cover your payments and travel arrangements in the event that the company defaults. It's also a good idea to choose a company that participates in the American Society of Travel Agents' Tour Operator Program (TOP); ASTA will act as mediator in any disputes between you and your tour operator.

Remember that the more your package or tour includes the better you can predict the ultimate cost of your vacation. Make sure you know exactly what is covered, and **beware of hidden costs.** Are taxes, tips, and transfers included? Entertainment and excursions? These can add up.

➤ TOUR-OPERATOR RECOMMENDATIONS: **American Society of Travel Agents** (☞ Travel Agencies). **National Tour Association** (NTA; ✉ 546 E. Main St., Lexington, KY 40508, ☎ 859/226–4444 or 800/682–8886, WEB www.ntaonline.com). **United States Tour Operators Association** (USTOA; ✉ 342 Madison Ave., Suite 1522, New York, NY 10173, ☎ 212/599–6599 or 800/468–7862, FAX 212/599–6744, WEB www.ustoa.com).

## TRAIN TRAVEL TO AND FROM MIAMI

Amtrak provides service from 500 destinations to the Greater Miami area, including three trains daily from New York City. The trains make several stops along the way; north–south service stops in the major Florida cities of Jacksonville, Orlando, Tampa, West Palm Beach, and Fort Lauderdale. For extended trips, or if you want to visit other areas in Florida, come via Auto Train from Lorton, Virginia, just outside of Washington, D.C., to Sanford, Florida, just outside of Orlando. From there it's less than a four-hour drive to Miami. Note: you must be traveling with an automobile to purchase a ticket on the Auto Train.

### FARES AND SCHEDULES

The Auto Train runs daily with one departure at 4 PM (however, car boarding ends one hour earlier). Fares vary depending on class of service and time of year, but expect to pay between $269 and $346 for a basic sleeper seat and car passage each way.

➤ TRAIN INFORMATION: **Amtrak** (✉ 8303 N.W. 37th Ave., Miami, ☎ 800/872–7245).

## TRANSPORTATION AROUND MIAMI

Greater Miami's public transportation system leaves much to be desired. Waits at bus stops can be lengthy and locals complain that trains don't get you where you need to go—at least conveniently. The network consists of more than 600 Metrobuses on 70 routes, the 21-mi Metrorail elevated rapid-transit system, and the Metromover, an elevated light-rail system serving downtown Miami and vicinity. Free maps, schedules, information on special transportation services for the disabled, and a "First-Time Rider's Kit" are available from the Miami-Dade Transit Agency; reduced-fare tokens, sold 10 for $10, are available at all Metrorail stations (regular fare is $1.25; transfers are an additional 25¢. Miami Beach also has an inexpensive trolley system, Electrowave, that traverses the major shopping areas and key sites.

➤ TRANSIT INFORMATION: **Miami-Dade Transit Agency** (☎ 305/770–3131, weekdays 6 AM–10 PM and weekends 9 AM–5 PM or WEB www.co.miami-dade.fl.us/mdta).

## TRAVEL AGENCIES

A good travel agent puts your needs first. Look for an agency that has been in business at least five years, emphasizes customer service, and has someone on staff who specializes in your destination. In addition, **make sure the agency belongs to a professional trade organization.** The American Society of Travel Agents (ASTA), with 27,000 agents in some 170 countries, is the largest and most influential in the field. Operating under the motto "Integrity in Travel," it maintains and enforces a strict code of ethics and will step in to help mediate any agent-client disputes if necessary. ASTA also maintains a Web site that includes a directory of agents. (If a travel agency is also acting as your tour operator, *see* Buyer Beware *in* Tours and Packages.)

➤ LOCAL AGENT REFERRALS: **American Society of Travel Agents** (ASTA; ☎ 800/965–2782 24-hr hot line, FAX 703/739–7642, WEB www.astanet.com). **Association of British Travel Agents** (✉ 68-71 Newman St., London W1T 3AH, U.K., ☎ 020/7637–2444, FAX 020/7637–0713, WEB www.abtanet.com). **Association of Canadian Travel Agents** (✉ 130 Albert St., Suite 1705, Ottawa, Ontario K1P 5G4, Canada, ☎ 613/237–3657, FAX 613/237–7502, WEB www.acta.net). **Australian Federation of Travel Agents** (✉ Level 3, 309 Pitt St., Sydney NSW 2000, Australia, ☎ 02/9264–3299, FAX 02/9264–1085, WEB www.afta.com.au). **Travel Agents' Association of New Zealand** (✉ Box 1888, Wellington 10033, New Zealand, ☎ 04/499–0104, FAX 04/499–0827, WEB www.taanz.org.nz).

## TROLLEY TRAVEL

In Miami Beach, electric trolleys run every few minutes up and down Washington Avenue with turnabouts at Lincoln Road Mall and South Pointe Park. A newer route runs from 16th Street to 23rd Street on Collins Avenue, then along Washington Avenue to the convention center, the botanical gardens, and the Holocaust Memorial. Rides are 25¢ and trolleys operate Monday–Wednesday 8 AM–2 AM, Thursday–Saturday 8 AM–4 AM, and Sundays and holidays 10 AM–2 AM.

➤ INFORMATION: **Electrowave** (☎ 305/535–9160 or 305/843–9283).

## VISITOR INFORMATION

➤ TOURIST INFORMATION: **Florida Tourism Industry Marketing Corporation (FLA USA–Visit Florida)** (☎ 888/7FLA–USA automated).

➤ MIAMI METRO AREA CONVENTION AND VISITORS BUREAUS: **Greater Miami Convention & Visitors Bureau** (✉ 701 Brickell Ave., Suite 2700, Miami 33131, ☎ 305/539–3000 main number; 800/283–2707; 305/539–3063 visitor services in the U.S.; elsewhere, dial the country's toll-free AT&T access code followed by ☎ 800/240–4282; 0800–013–0011 in the U.K.; 800/881–011 in Australia; 800/225–5277 in Canada). **Sunny Isles Beach Resort Association Visitor Information Center** (✉ 17100 Collins Avenue, Suite 208, Sunny Isles Beach 33160, ☎ 305/947–5826). **Surfside Tourist Board** (✉ 9301 Collins Ave., Surfside 33154, ☎ 305/864–0722 or 800/327–4557, FAX 305/993–5128).

➤ MIAMI METRO AREA VISITOR CENTERS: **Bayside Marketplace** (✉ 401 Biscayne Blvd., Miami 33132, ☎ 305/539–8070). **Sears** (✉ 3655 S.W. 22nd St., Coral Gables, ☎ 305/460–3477; ✉ 1625 N.W. 107th Ave., Miami International Mall, Miami, ☎ 305/470–7863; ✉ 1625 W. 49th St., Westland Mall, Hialeah, ☎ 305/364–3827).

➤ MIAMI METRO AREA CHAMBERS OF COMMERCE: **Coconut Grove Chamber of Commerce** (✉ 2820 McFarlane Rd., Coconut Grove 33133, ☎ 305/444–7270, FAX 305/444–2498). **Coral Gables Chamber of Commerce** (✉ 50 Aragon Ave., Coral Gables 33134, ☎ 305/446–1657, FAX 305/446–9900). **Florida Gold Coast Chamber of Commerce** (✉ 1100 Kane Concourse, Suite 210, Bay Harbor Islands, 33154, ☎ 305/866–6020, FAX 305/866–0635) serves the beach communities of Bal Harbour, Bay Harbor Islands, Golden Beach, North Bay Village, Sunny Isles Beach, and Surfside. **Greater Homestead–Florida City Chamber of Commerce** (✉ 43 N. Krome Ave., Homestead 33030, ☎ 305/247–2332 or 888/FLCITY1). **Greater Miami Chamber of Commerce** (✉ 1601 Biscayne Blvd., Miami 33132, ☎ 305/350–7700, FAX 305/374–6902). **Greater North Miami Chamber of Commerce** (✉ 13100 W. Dixie Hwy., North Miami 33181, ☎ 305/891–7811, FAX 305/

893–8522). **Greater South Dade–South Miami–Kendall Chamber of Commerce** (✉ 6410 S.W. 80th St., South Miami 33143-4602, ☎ 305/661–1621, FAX 305/666–0508). **Key Biscayne Chamber of Commerce** (✉ Key Biscayne Bank Bldg., 87 W. McIntyre St., Key Biscayne 33149, ☎ 305/361–5207, FAX 305/361–9411). **Miami Beach Chamber of Commerce** (✉ 1920 Meridian Ave., Miami Beach 33139, ☎ 305/672–1270, FAX 305/538–4336).

## WEB SITES

Do check out the World Wide Web when planning your trip. You'll find everything from weather forecasts to virtual tours of famous cities. Be sure to **visit Fodors.com** (www.fodors.com), a complete travel-planning site. You can research prices, check out bargains, and book plane tickets, hotel rooms, rental cars, vacation packages, and more. In addition, you can post your pressing questions in the Travel Talk section and, in the site's Rants & Raves section, read comments about some of the restaurants and hotels in this book—and chime in yourself. Other planning tools include a currency converter and weather reports, and there are loads of links to travel resources.

For general visitor information, try the visitor bureau's www.tropicoolmiami.com. The *Miami Herald*'s entertainment section, at www.miami.com/herald, includes recent restaurant reviews and ratings, as well as links to other sites of interest to vacationers. There's a slew of local on-line guides, but good places to start are www.miami.com, www.miamicitysearch.com, and www.southbeach-usa.com.

## WHEN TO GO

Miami and Miami Beach are definitely year-round destinations, although most visitors come October through April, when snowbirds flee cold weather in the north. Hotels, restaurants, shops, and attractions are busy at this time of year, and special events and the performing arts take center stage—so be prepared for in-season rates and low availability. The summer months are still a good time for budget-minded visitors; many hotels lower their rates considerably, and even the nicer restaurants may offer discounts (check local newspapers). If you're traveling to other Florida destinations in addition to Greater Miami, you may also want to consider the fall and late spring shoulder seasons, when many rates are as good as in summer—and rates plummet in the Keys and Orlando.

### CLIMATE

Miamians brag that the reason they live in South Florida is for winter—dry, clear blue skies, temperatures in the 60s and low 70s, cotton-puff clouds, and humidity-free, good-hair days. Even better, there's very little difference between winter, late fall, and early spring. Good thing, since Greater Miami is often very hot and humid in the summer and air-conditioning is a must. Though Miami can be humid, its temperature rarely reaches the high 90s, even in the middle of summer. In fact, along the coast, ocean breezes make summer quite bearable, and afternoon thunderstorms disappear as quickly as they come. Hurricane season officially begins June 1 and ends on November 30. Severe storms can interrupt public services, including water and electricity. In the rare instance of hurricane-force winds, Miami-Dade County may order evacuation of storm-surge areas. Most hotels have emergency plans in place to assist tourists, although if availability is scarce at inland hotels, you may find yourself at an area shelter. If before you leave on vacation you're advised South Florida is under a hurricane watch, you might want to postpone your plans.

➤ FORECASTS: **Weather Channel Connection** (☎ 900/932–8437), 95¢ per minute from a Touch-Tone phone. **National Weather Forecast Service** (☎ 305/229–4522) offers local and marine conditions. **Miami-Dade Hurricane Hotline** (☎ 305/229–4470). You can also log on to www.weather.com; www.intellicast.com is best for tracking severe weather systems.

Following are average monthly minimum and maximum temperatures for **Greater Miami:**

| | | | | | | | | |
|---|---|---|---|---|---|---|---|---|
| Jan. | 75F | 24C | May | 85F | 29C | Sept. | 88F | 31C |
| | 59 | 15 | | 72 | 22 | | 76 | 24 |
| Feb. | 76F | 24C | June | 88F | 31C | Oct. | 85F | 29C |
| | 60 | 16 | | 75 | 24 | | 72 | 22 |
| Mar. | 79F | 26C | July | 89F | 32C | Nov. | 80F | 27C |
| | 64 | 18 | | 77 | 25 | | 67 | 19 |
| Apr. | 83F | 28C | Aug. | 89F | 32C | Dec. | 77F | 24C |
| | 68 | 20 | | 77 | 25 | | 62 | 16 |

### RAINFALL IN INCHES:

| | | | | | |
|---|---|---|---|---|---|
| Jan. | 2.01″ | May | 6.21″ | Sept. | 7.63″ |
| Feb. | 2.08″ | June | 9.33″ | Oct. | 5.64″ |
| Mar. | 2.39″ | July | 5.70″ | Nov. | 2.66″ |
| Apr. | 3.03″ | Aug. | 7.58″ | Dec. | 1.83″ |

### FESTIVALS AND SEASONAL EVENTS

➤ DECEMBER: The tennis careers of Seles, Agassi, and Evert were partly launched here, at the world's largest international youth sports-and-arts festival, **Junior Orange Bowl Festival** (☎ 305/662–1210), held throughout Miami-Dade County. It begins in October and lasts through January, but most of its more than 20 events take place in December. Since 1948 the festival has grown to include cultural activities, such as photography, chess, and creative writing, and such sports events as basketball, equestrian, golf, soccer, and tennis. Between Christmas and New Years, the youth-oriented **Junior Orange Bowl Parade** winds through downtown Coral Gables. The **Orange Bowl 5K** race kicks off the festivities accompanying January's football classic. A hilarious cast of characters spoofs each year's local and national newsmakers as it sashays through Coconut Grove during the **King Mango Strut** (☎ 305/445–1865), a raunchy send-up of the Orange Bowl Parade.

➤ JANUARY: Miami rings in each new year with the **FedEx Orange Bowl** (☎ 305/371–4600), preceded by the colorful **Orange Bowl Parade,** newly updated with modern floats. The second weekend in January, **Art Expo** (☎ 305/558–1758)—with live concerts and 100 juried artists booths—takes over Sunset Drive from U.S. 1 to 62nd Avenue. More than 500,000 people flood the streets of South Beach for **Art Deco Weekend** (☎ 305/672–2014), a celebration of the Miami that put Miami back on the map. Art deco antiques sales, history lectures, and performances by jazz, swing, and big band musicians make this perhaps the best time of year to see Miami. Usually held the third weekend of January, **Art Miami** (☎ 305/673–7311) fills the Miami Beach Convention Center with a massive art market that draws leading international collectors and exhibitors. Special exhibits showcase hot young talents from Latin America and the Caribbean. In the busy third weekend of January, the Lowe Art Museum presents **Beaux Arts Annual Festival of Art Weekend** (☎ 305/284–3535) on the University of Miami campus, a family-friendly event that includes the works of 250 juried exhibitors. The idea behind the **Coconut Grove Food and Music Festival** (☎ 305/444–7270) is simple: eat, drink, and be merry. The third weekend of the month, Coconut Grove's restaurateurs and chefs show their stuff alongside live music. More than 150 artists from around the world head to the island for the **Key Biscayne Art Festival** (☎ 305/361–0049) on a weekend at the end of January. This festival is held at the entrance to Cape Florida State Park, a gorgeous setting.

➤ FEBRUARY: The **Miami International Map Fair** (☎ 305/375–1492), held at the Historical Museum of Southern Florida the first weekend of February, brings together map dealers, collectors and enthusiasts from around the world for a weekend of browsing and buying. Each Presidents' Day weekend, the **Coconut Grove Arts Festival** (☎ 305/558–1758) brings hordes of people to the bohemian community to see, hear, and taste entries in the visual, performing, and culinary arts. Usually ranked among the top art festivals in the country, the three-day event is as much about fresh air, food, and fun as it is about serious art. For 10 days in late February and early March, an excellent selection of 26 to 30 international films is screened at the **FIU Miami Film Festival** (☎ 305/377–3456). More than 45,000 people, including many actors and directors, descend on the eye-popping Gusman Center for the Performing Arts and attend scores of galas and midnight parties on South Beach.

➤ MARCH: More than a million people attend the nine-day Latin blowout known as **Carnaval Miami** (☎ 305/644–8888), which turns Little Havana into Little Rio. The week includes beauty pageants, cooking competitions, and Noche de Carnaval, a downtown concert showcasing top international Latin performers. The nation's largest Hispanic celebration culminates in the 23-block-long one-day **Calle Ocho Festival,** with more dance, food, and top-notch entertainment. The **Miami International Orchid Show** (☎ 305/255–3656) brings more than half a million blooms and spectacular botanical exhibits to Coconut Grove in early March. The **Genuity Championship,** formerly known as the Doral-Ryder Open (☎ 305/477–4653), typically held the last week in February through the first week of March, attracts 144 of the world's top golfers to the famed "Blue Monster" at the Doral Golf Resort. For 11 days each spring, the **NASDAQ-100** (formerly the Ericsson Open; ☎ 305/442–3367) fills the Tennis Center at Crandon Park on Key Biscayne. The tournament is one of the world's largest in terms of attendance, and it has the cash clout to attract such international stars as Andre Agassi, Pete Sampras, Serena Williams, and Martina Hingis.

➤ APRIL: During the eight weeks of **Dade Heritage Days** (☎ 305/358–9572), from early March to mid-May, neighborhood associations organize tours, lectures, boat and trolley tours, nature walks, and canoe trips throughout the county. In mid-April the weeklong **South Beach Film Festival** (☎ 305/532–1233), highlighting independent films, arrives at the Colony Theater.

➤ MAY: **Dade Heritage Days** continue through mid-May. The **South Beach Dive & Seafood Fest** (☎ 305/672–1270), during the first weekend of the month, includes aquatic activities such as a sandcastle-building contest, an underwater film festival, and offshore diving.

➤ JUNE: Things slow down in Miami during the warmer months, but there's no better time for the **Miami–Bahamas Goombay Festival** (☎ 305/372–9966). The street party in the heart of Coconut Grove highlights the culture and contributions of Miami's early Bahamian settlers, with junkanoo parades, appearances by the Royal Bahamas Police Band, a golf tournament, and plenty of Bahamian food. With around 600,000 participants, the three-day festival claims to be the largest black heritage festival in the U.S. During the two-week **Florida Dance Festival** (☎ 305/674–3350) at the end of the month, dance companies from all over the United States perform here. Catch local talent at the City Theatre company's very popular **Summer Shorts Festival** (☎ 305/365–5400, WEB www.citytheatre.com)—short plays, that is—held at the University of Miami in Coral Gables.

➤ JULY: **America's Birthday Bash** (☎ 305/358–7550), in Bayfront Park, is an old-fashioned July 4th extravaganza, with lots of rides, music, food, fireworks, and a petting zoo. Key Biscayne's **4th of July Parade & Fireworks Display** (☎ 305/365–8901) is one of South Florida's longest and largest fireworks shows. The parade passes by the Village Green; a spot here or on the beach will give you a prime view of the action. The **International Mango Festival** (☎ 305/667–1651), held the second weekend of July at Fairchild Tropical Garden, extols the king of tropical fruits with smoothies and other taste treats, plus mango medics, and a celeb-studded mango auction.

➤ SEPTEMBER: As summer draws to a close, the University of Miami School of Music hosts the six-week **Festival Miami** (☎ 305/284–4940) from mid-September through the end of October. From jazz to flamenco and traditional Cuban music to chamber music recitals and symphony concerts, the festival brings together guest artists and award-winning student performers. Depending on the show, admission is free or runs up to $35—not bad when a musician like Wynton Marsalis shows up.

➤ OCTOBER: The **Hispanic Heritage Festival** (☎ 305/541–5023), one of the oldest Hispanic cultural festivals in the United States, takes place throughout the month. A food fair kicks off the festivities; other highlights are Discovery of America Day (on Columbus Day weekend), a beauty pageant, and the Festival of the Americas, a huge street party.

➤ NOVEMBER: The first weekend of the month, the juried **South Miami Art Festival** (☎ 305/661–1621) brings more than 150 artists and craftspeople to Sunset Drive along the downtown business district. For the 11 days leading up to Thanksgiving, literary lions and book lovers gather for **Miami Book Fair International** (☎ 305/237–3258), an international author's congress and book exhibition. Top authors give nightly readings, plug their books, mingle with their peers and readers, and host lectures. A weekend street fair with more than 300 book exhibitors (including rare-book sellers) makes this one of Miami's most civilized and entertaining events. It's held downtown at the Wolfson Campus of Miami-Dade Community College.

# 1 DESTINATION: MIAMI AND MIAMI BEACH

No Place Quite Like It

What's Where

Pleasures and Pastimes

Fodor's Choice

Great Itineraries

# NO PLACE QUITE LIKE IT

**SUN AND SAND, SALSA AND STYLE,** Miami is distinctly different from any other city in America—or any city in Latin America, for that matter. This is no sleepy little beach outpost, no drowsy southern town. How could anyone nod off knowing a hurricane might blast through or swallow-size mosquitoes could attack at any moment? Seriously: how could anyone nap knowing there's so much excellent shopping, dining, and people-watching to be done?

Both logically and geologically, the city of Miami shouldn't even be here. Way back when, it was not much more than a swamp between the Everglades and the Atlantic Ocean. The first inhabitants were the Tequesta, who called this area home long before Spain's gold-hungry treasure ships sailed along the Gulf Stream a few miles offshore. They were followed by the Seminole, who learned how to prosper in the local ecosystem. Eventually the Seminole skedaddled, less likely because of the floods and hurricanes than because of Andrew Jackson. Today's residents don't have to worry about Old Hickory, and modern technology seems to be keeping the mosquitoes at bay, so why not head south for a little fun in the sun?

The end of the 20th century brought big changes to Miami. In the early 1980s, Miami Beach was an oceanside geriatric ward. Today's South Beach residents have a hip that doesn't break. The average age of locals dropped from the mid-sixties in 1980 to a youthful early forties today. Toned young men outnumber svelte young women two to one, and hormones are as plentiful as cell phones. At night, the revitalized Lincoln Road Mall gets into full swing as crowds descend on its restaurants, cafés, galleries, and theaters—but the Road also suffers from the vacancies that come with rapidly rising rents. Those who have seen how high rents can crush a dream are heading to the northern beaches and to the southern reaches of South Beach, whose derelict buildings, once a flashback to the pre-renaissance days of the 1980s, are being refitted as affordable apartments and boutique hotels. This is where the Miami Beach revival is taking place.

In Miami (as opposed to Miami Beach), boom times started in the 1970s for a small group of Latin American drug dealers. These "Cocaine Cowboys," as they were known, made and spent millions in Miami, investing in real estate and launching major construction projects. Their day ended in the 1980s, but by then economic development had its own—legal—momentum. Today, 150-plus U.S. and multinational companies have their Latin American headquarters here. Greater Miami is home to more than 40 foreign bank agencies, 11 Edge Act banks, 23 foreign trade offices, 31 binational chambers of commerce, and 53 foreign consulates.

As North America's gateway to the Southern Hemisphere and Latin America, Miami has become a multicultural metropolis that works and plays with vigor and that invites the world to celebrate its diversity. Miami is largely Cuban, as a result of two major waves of immigration, one in the early 1960s, then another in the 1980s. No matter where you spin your radio dial, virtually every announcer punctuates his harangue with an emphatic "COOBAH!" Look around and you'll see Spanish on billboards, hear it in elevators, and pick it up on the streets. *Newsweek* called Miami "America's Casablanca," and the comparison may be apt. Many Cuban Americans straddle the Cuba–America divide, maintaining ties with their families back home and creating a culturally rich life in Miami. Some, perhaps with less affluence or resources, are less successful: in 1999 both the United States and Cuba followed the plight of young Elian Gonzalez, whose citizenship was hotly debated when his mother perished at sea in an illegal attempt to emigrate.

In addition to the Cuban population, there are also residents from Brazil, China, Colombia, El Salvador, Germany, Greece, Haiti, Iran, Israel, Italy, Jamaica, Lebanon, Malaysia, Nicaragua, Panama, Puerto Rico, Russia, Sweden, and Venezuela—all speaking in their own tongue and carrying on their own traditions. Miami seems to know it will remain a montage of nationalities, and it celebrates the cultural diversity at festivals, world-music performances, and a wealth of exotic restaurants.

Miami has always attracted its fair share of hucksters, scammers, and fly-by-nighters and celebs, too. From the carpetbaggers to Al Capone, from the Colombian druglords of the '80s to the Russian mafia in the '90s, this city opens its arms to anyone with flash and cash. Miami bid farewell to Madonna and Sylvester Stallone, who swept into town for a few years, and extended an uneasy greeting to O. J. Simpson and his children. High profile hometown heroes Gloria and Emilio Estefan lead the list of Latin artists who spend much of their time here, along with Jon Secada, Julio Iglesias, Albita, and Andy Garcia. Thanks to a booming film industry and Miami's appeal to fashion magazines, year-round movie and photo shoots attract squadrons of beautiful people, filling up chic restaurants and VIP lounges of SoBe clubs.

Although you might not think it to look around, Miami's restaurant scene isn't mere glam without culinary gusto. The city is teeming with celebrity chefs, and most have an inventive flair derived from flavors found in kitchens around the globe. Miami's New World Cuisine was formed about a decade ago, when a group of master chefs dubbed the Mango Gang created a new genre that makes splendid use of fresh native fruits and vegetables and local seafood, spiced up with Caribbean and Latin influences. Tropical treats such as mango, starfruit, avocado, papaya, cilantro, yucca, guava, and plantains are used lavishly, and stone crabs, conch, grouper, and Florida lobster make frequent mouthwatering appearances, sometimes along more contemporary or Continental items. Do try the obvious: Cuban medianoche sandwiches, Brazilian barbecue, Nicaraguan grilled steaks, Jamaican jerk chicken. Then seek out Peruvian ceviche, Haitian *griots* (seasoned, fried cubes of pork), and some of the innovative Pan-Asian combinations that are born not of fad, but bona fide cultural fusion. With an emphasis on its cultural heritage, many old neighborhoods are being rediscovered and revivified through special monthly events, such as Little Havana's Cultural Fridays, Homestead's Friday Fests, and Coral Gables's Gallery Nights. Other up-and-coming areas are emerging—lively Brickell Village in the financial district, the trendy Miami Design District, and the residential Morningside and Belle Meade Districts north of Downtown, where gracious homes are being restored and antiques shops are replacing blighted storefronts along Biscayne Boulevard. Equally impressive are efforts to shed, for once and for all, Miami's image as a cultural backwater. The long-delayed Performing Arts Center, with a concert hall, ballet and opera house, and black box theater, has finally secured funding and is expected to revitalize the Omni area, just north of Downtown. In Miami Beach, the Collins Park Cultural Center will eventually be returned to a park with an ocean view—as it incorporates the renovated Bass Museum and the new Miami City Ballet.

You can easily have the kind of fun here that will drain your wallet. But look for less flashy ways to explore Miami, too. Skip the chichi restaurant and go for an ethnic eatery. Tour Lincoln Road Mall, downtown Coral Gables, or Coconut Grove on foot. Or take South Beach's colorful Electrowave shuttle, Florida's first electric transportation system, which really works for getting around traffic-clogged SoBe. Winter *is* the best time to visit, but if money is an issue, come in the off-season—after Easter and before October. You'll find plenty to do, and room rates can come down considerably. Summer brings many European and Latin American vacationers who find Miami congenial despite the heat, humidity, and intense afternoon thunderstorms. Like millions of others, they've discovered the many natural and unnatural pleasures to be had year-round in America's southernmost metropolis.

So whaddya waitin' for? Grab your lotion and head to the ocean.

— Gary McKechnie;
revised by Gretchen Schmidt

# WHAT'S WHERE

Miami is a lot like New York City, except that here cops swab zinc oxide on their noses. Its neighborhoods are also as distinct as the Big Apple's five boroughs.

### Coconut Grove

Not just a commercial outpost of manufactured charm, the quirky Grove really does have a history of its own. Under the guidance of Ralph Munroe, Coconut Grove established a yacht club, library, post office, churches, and a school for the New England intellectuals, Bahamian blacks, and Key Westers who settled in the neighborhood. Although today's artists and writers keep a lower profile than their predecessors, there's still a creative energy here generated by the mingling of carefree young people and the older, wealthier residents who like being considered slightly off center.

### Coral Gables

In the 1920s, George Merrick envisioned an American Venice, and then he built it. Canals, stunning homes, the majestic Biltmore Hotel, and the most beautiful municipal swimming pool in America are all right here. Sadly, Merrick's work was halted by the 1926 hurricane and ensuing depression. Still, what he built set the stage for a bustling shopping district (Miracle Mile) and the University of Miami. Fine restaurants, a thriving arts scene, and a well-behaved nightlife are turning the Gables into a delightful destination.

### Downtown Miami

After winter freezes obliterated much of Florida's orange crop in 1894–95, Miami landowner Julia Tuttle mailed some fresh orange blossoms to railroad developer Henry Flagler to prove that sunny Miami was worth a stop on his line. Flagler built the railroad, and in its wake came hotels, businesses, and people looking for winter warmth. Although downtown has gone through some hard times, it's definitely rebounded with the arrival of the AmericanAirlines basketball arena, shopping mall, and major financial institutions. Downtown is now remarkably vital, with lots of small shops and restaurants, particularly in Brickell Village, independent merchants, the gorgeous Gusman Theatre, and the Miami-Dade Cultural Center.

### Key Biscayne and Virginia Key

Perhaps the best-preserved section of Miami, this pair of islands south of Miami Beach is part residential, part recreational, and primarily natural. At the public beaches, windsurfers dart about the waves and picnickers park beneath Australian pines to enjoy the bay. Two large and beautiful parks, Bill Baggs Cape Florida State Recreation Park and Crandon Park, have beaches, walking and skating trails, and golf courses. Crandon Park also has courts aplenty at the Tennis Center, home of the NASDAQ-100 Open (formerly the Ericsson Open).

### Little Havana

In the 1960s the aging neighborhood west of downtown first became a magnet for refugees fleeing Castro's Cuba. Today, Little Havana, home to Spanish-speaking refugees from Cuba and Central America, seems every bit as Cuban—and in some places as destitute—as the original. It's intriguing to visit cigar shops where the product is hand-rolled by a Cuban-trained master and to glimpse a separate world whose residents seem entirely self-sufficient.

### Miami Beach North of 23rd Street

Miami Beach encompasses 17 islands east of Miami, stretching from South Beach (on the south) to North Beach, and west to exclusive private islands such as Palm, Star, and Hibiscus. The central and northern beaches have an identity all their own, separate from the trendy frenzy of South Beach. Mid-beach you'll find the huge, throwback resort hotels like the Fontainebleau, and farther north you'll hit Bal Harbour. Although it occupies only a third of a square mile, Bal Harbour glitters with businesses like the Bal Harbour Shops and the Sheraton Bal Harbour. So get those credit cards ready, folks.

### North Miami and North Miami Beach

The northernmost reaches of oceanside Miami still resemble the Florida of the 1950s and '60s, complete with tacky souvenir shops and motels. But they're rapidly being bulldozed to make way for huge condos. An influx of Asian, Russian, and other immigrants has added spice to the mix. The neighborhood is also home to some peaceful nature preserves. The City of Aventura to the north has a popular mall and the terrific contemporary Allen Susser eatery, Chef Allen's. The manicured neighborhood Bal Harbour, known for its chichi shops, borders Miami Beach to the south.

### South Beach

South Beach, the shiniest jewel in the Miami Beach strand, is where you'll find sun worshipers, tourists, conventioneers, hippies, club hoppers, fashionistas, and super models. Look a little closer and you'll also find residential neighborhoods, city parks, and a surprisingly enjoyable "walking town" hidden in the middle of the city. Its epicenter is the Art Deco District, called by some "America's Riviera." Fronted on the east by Ocean Drive and on the west by Alton Road, the heart of the district runs from 5th to 17th avenues. Cafés, shops, nightclubs, the fabled art deco hotels, and the glorious beach make the area pulse with possibility.

### South Miami

South Miami is only a few miles away from downtown, but it's worlds away in attitude. Tree-lined Sunset Drive threads its way through this suburb of fine old homes and an old-fashioned commercial district. Equally picturesque attractions such as Parrot Jungle (now moving to Watson Island), and good local restaurants, like Two Chefs, have long drawn tourists, and the arrival of the Shops at Sunset Place, a huge shopping and entertainment complex, hasn't diminished its small-town friendliness.

## PLEASURES AND PASTIMES

### Beaches

Greater Miami has numerous free beaches to fit every oceanfront mood. A sandy, 300-ft-wide beach with several distinct sections extends for 10 mi from the foot of Miami Beach north to Haulover Beach Park. Amazingly, it's all man-made. Seriously eroded during the mid-1970s, the beach was restored between 1977 and 1981, and restoration remains an ongoing project for environmental engineers, who spiff up the sands every few years. Between 23rd and 44th streets, the city of Miami Beach built boardwalks and protective walkways atop a dune landscaped with sea oats, sea grapes, and other native plants whose roots keep the sand from blowing away. Key Biscayne adds more great strands to Miami's collection. Even if the Art Deco District didn't exist, the area's beaches would be enough to satisfy tourists.

### Boating

It's not uncommon for traffic to jam at boat ramps, especially on weekend mornings, but the waters are worth the wait. If you have the opportunity to sail, do so. Blue skies, calm seas, and a view of the city skyline make for a pleasurable outing—especially at twilight, when the fabled "moon over Miami" casts a soft glow on the water. Key Biscayne's calm waves and strong breezes are perfect for sailing and windsurfing, and though Dinner Key and the Coconut Grove waterfront remain the center of sailing in Greater Miami, sailboat moorings and rental firms are located all along the bay.

### Dining

Whether you've got a couple of bucks in your wallet or a couple hundred, you can sample from such an array of dishes here that it's only fair to call Miami's culinary reaches global. Dishes native to Spain, Cuba, and Nicaragua as well as China, India, Thailand, Vietnam, and other Asian cultures create a veritable United Nations of dining experiences. The Miami-born New World Cuisine also blends culinary influences from throughout the Americas. Tropical combinations of fresh, natural ingredients—especially seafood—and classic Caribbean island flavors have yielded an American cuisine that is sometimes called Floribbean. Try the work of über-popular chefs or strike out on your own—you may come across your best Miami meal at a little ethnic eatery.

### Nightlife

Fast, hot, and as transient as the crowds who pass through their doors, Miami's nightspots are as sizzling as their New York and L.A. counterparts. Clubbing is a 24-hour-a-day art form here. The densest concentration of clubs is on South Beach along Washington Avenue, Lincoln Road Mall, and Ocean Drive. Other nightlife centers on Little Havana and Coconut Grove, and on the fringes of downtown Miami. Miami's nightspots offer jazz, reggae, salsa, various forms of rock, disco, and Top 40 sounds, most played at a body-thumping, ear-throbbing volume. Some clubs refuse entrance to anyone under 21, others to those under 25, so if that is a concern, call ahead. If you prefer to hear what people are saying, try the many lobby bars at South Beach's art deco hotels. Throughout Greater Miami, bars and cocktail lounges in larger, newer hotels operate nightly discos with live weekend entertainment. Many hotels extend their bars into open-air courtyards, where patrons dine and dance under the stars throughout the year.

### Shopping

Miami is a serious shopping city. Chichi shopping districts like Lincoln Road and come-spend-here enclaves like Coral Gables and Bal Harbor are rather astonishing sociological spheres, drawing locals day and night. Here, the question easily comes to mind, Does anyone work during the day? If your cold-weather hometown makes finding a bathing suit impossible, fret not. You'll find one here with ease.

### Spectator Sports

Greater Miami has franchises in basketball, football, and baseball. Fans still turn out en masse for the Dolphins, and—in the best fair-weather-fan tradition—show up for basketball's Heat and Sol and the 1997 World Series champion Marlins. Miami also hosts top-rated events in boat racing, auto racing, jai alai, golf, and tennis. Each winter, the FedEx Orange Bowl Football Classic highlights college football.

## FODOR'S CHOICE

### Dining

**Aria.** Choose a view—a spot near the exhibition kitchen or outside overlooking the landscaped gardens or beaches—then your artistic meal, made from mouth-watering ingredients like beef cheeks and truffles. Both at this Key Biscayne spot in the Ritz-Carlton are irresistible. *$$$$*

**Blue Door at the Delano.** Claude Troisgros of the famous French culinary family and executive-chef Elizabeth Barlow oversee the kitchen in this hippest of South Beach hotels. Tropical and Asian flavors guest star on their soundly French menu. *$$$$*

**Chef Allen's.** Beyond a huge picture window in Aventura, chef Allen Susser creates a different menu nightly. Try rock-shrimp hash with roasted corn, followed by the double-chocolate soufflé. *$$$$*

**Norman's.** Considered by many to be Miami's best, this Coral Gables restaurant perfects the New World cuisine for which South Florida is famous. *$$$$*

**Pacific Time.** The joyous bustle at this South Beach favorite attests to the beauty of chef-owner Jonathan Eismann's food, which simmers with magical American and Asian influences. *$$$–$$$$*

**Azul.** Hotel restaurants sure are better than they used to be. Chef Michelle Bernstein's exotically rendered French–Caribbean cuisine does wonders for redeeming the genre and service is crisp and somehow comforting, with house pashminas for the sleeveless and reading glasses for the forgetful. *$$–$$$*

**Pascal's on Ponce.** Unlike the capricious Miami that lives for the moment, Pascal Oudin's stream-lined French cuisine disdains trends and discounts flash. Instead substantive delicacies are matched with proper service and just the right wine. And, ooh la la, les desserts. *$$–$$$*

### Fun in the Sun

**Bill Baggs Cape Florida State Recreation Area.** Great beaches, sunsets, boardwalks, fishing piers, picnic shelters, and bike paths are all the reason you need to drive to Key Biscayne's southern tip. Plus, there's a lighthouse that's the oldest structure in South Florida.

**Crandon Marina.** The deep-sea fishing off Miami has always been great, and Crandon Marina has an international reputation for its knowledgeable captains and good catches.

**Doral Golf Resort and Spa.** The five excellent 18-hole courses here are par 70–72; there's also a driving range and a learning center. Play the famed Blue Monster, where the pros battle at the annual Genuity Championship.

**Haulover Beach Park.** Good old-fashioned fun is to be had at this fully equipped Sunny Isles beach, which is popular with families. Barbecue grills, volleyball courts, bike trails, a concession stand, and showers make a day here more than just a day at the beach.

**Venetian Pool.** Sculpted from a rock quarry in 1923 and fed by artesian wells, this fantastical municipal Coral Gables pool has secret caves, stone bridges, and a delightful wading pool. Spend an afternoon cooling off where Johnny Weissmuller and Esther Williams once swam.

## Lodging

**Biltmore Hotel.** A Coral Gables classic, this 1926 palace offers large guest rooms with a Moorish air. The Biltmore chefs are constantly sharpening their skills, and a spa, tennis courts, and scenic golf course allow you to work off the fruits of their labor. *$$$$*

**Casa Grande.** A little piece of Bali on Ocean Drive, this first-rate palace of teak and mahogany combines South Beach–cool with a warm, inviting atmosphere. Large baths and full kitchens make the rooms seem more like apartments than the average hotel unit, and are a welcome retreat from the hectic scene outside. *$$$$*

**Delano.** Ian Schrager's Miami masterpiece is still the see-and-be-seen capital of South Beach style. The trendsetting (and smallish) stark-white rooms are really just a way station between trips to the pool and the hip bar, which is set off from the lobby by a huge, billowing curtain. If you go, bring your haute couture. *$$$$*

**Sonesta Beach Resort Key Biscayne.** Quiet Key Biscayne is home to one of Greater Miami's nicer resorts, notable for its family-friendly approach to hospitality. In addition to familiar oceanfront resort activities like tennis courts and parasailing, it offers extensive programs for kids ages 3–17. *$$$$*

**Turnberry Isle Resort & Club.** This may be Miami Beach's grandest resort, its varied accommodations scattered across 300 superbly landscaped acres. Moor your yacht at the marina or play a round on one of the two Robert Trent Jones, Sr., golf courses. *$$$$*

**Fontainebleau Hilton Resort and Towers.** Singers, movie stars, and every president since Eisenhower have made the pilgrimage to this original mecca of Miami cool. A grande dame reinventing itself for the 21st century, the Fontainebleau is outsize and often outlandish, but never boring. Soak up soothing sensations at the beachfront spa, and bring the family: the Cookie's World water playland is a kid magnet. *$$$–$$$$*

**Kent.** A light-hearted redesign of this midmarket Island Outpost hotel has pushed it to the top tier of South Beach bargains. There are toys in the lobby, beanbags in the corridors, and funky chrome fixtures throughout; add in reasonably spacious rooms (for South Beach) and a location a block from the beach, and you have a winner. *$$*

## Sights to See

**Art Deco District.** All the fuss about South Beach started with the neighborhood's concentration of whimsical, evocative art deco architecture. Restoration of many structures has earned the area, which includes some 800 significant buildings, a place on the National Register of Historic Places. Stop by the Art Deco District Welcome Center to hire a guide or to rent a taped tour.

**Bal Harbour Shops.** This is the swankiest shopping to be had in Florida outside of Palm Beach, with an open-air collection of 100 shops, boutiques, and department stores from Prada to Pratesi.

**Española Way.** Lined with Mediterranean Revival buildings, this pretty South Beach street has drawn bohemians since the 1920s. It's a great spot for strolling and shopping any time, but it really comes to life each Sunday afternoon. The street closes to traffic and vendors set up stalls to sell everything from handmade jewelry to discount CDs, all to the strains of live music and the scents of Latin cooking.

**Fairchild Tropical Garden.** In the southern reaches of Coral Gables, the largest tropical botanical garden in the continental United States showcases orchids, bellflowers, coral trees, bougainvillea, rare palms, and flowering trees. Windows to the Tropics houses rare tropical plants, and a 2-acre exhibit displays tropical rain-forest plants from around the world.

**Miami-Dade Cultural Center.** Come downtown for a taste of what Miami's coming to. This complex contains the Miami Art Museum, site of major touring exhibitions; the Historical Museum of Southern

Florida, which celebrates Miami's multicultural heritage and history; and the Miami-Dade Public Library, which offers rotating art exhibits.

**Vizcaya Museum and Gardens.** Built by industrialist James Deering in 1914–1916, this neoclassical Coconut Grove residence is surrounded by 10 acres of formal gardens with fountains. It's filled with paintings, sculpture, antique furniture, and other fine and decorative arts in Renaissance, baroque, rococo, and neoclassical style.

# GREAT ITINERARIES

## If You Have 1 Day

To recuperate from your journey to paradise, grab a towel and your suntan lotion, and head for the sand in South Beach to catch some rays. Afterward, take a guided or self-guided tour of the Art Deco District to see what all the fuss is about. Keep track of where you've been so you can later revisit the places that piqued your interest. Chances are one place will be the Lincoln Road Mall, where shops and sidewalk cafés spread for several blocks along a pedestrian mall. Take time to hit Collins Avenue between 6th and 8th streets for some traditional shopping. Have a quiet dinner at one of the grand hotels of Collins Avenue (the Delano or the National), and complete the night with a drink or two at the sidewalk cafés of happening Ocean Drive.

## If You Have 3 Days

Follow the first day's itinerary and on Day Two reward yourself for being smart enough to take a vacation. Swing through Little Havana for a taste of Miami's Cuban culture (and to snag a stogie). At the Venetian Pool in Coral Gables, lay out a towel, swab on the sunscreen, and ponder that the lushly landscaped waterfalls were formed out of a rockpit. If you prefer to do something, head to the Gables's incredible Fairchild Tropical Garden. Or you might want to check out the interactive Parrot Jungle Gardens, especially if you have children in tow. After a dip or a look at the flora, try one of the area's fine restaurants for lunch. In the afternoon, take in some window-shopping along Miracle Mile and then hop in the car to get lost in the Coral Gable neighborhoods, working your way over to the grand Biltmore Hotel. That evening, cruise over to Coconut Grove. At night, the village is jumping from CocoWalk along Main Highway to the Taurus. Movie theaters, rowdy bars, smoky dives, and the traditional tourist fare of chain restaurants are at your service. The festive atmosphere should drain the last ounce of energy from your body and prepare you for a good night's sleep.

On Day Three, sleep in and then pamper yourself with a trip to the beaches of Key Biscayne. Just before the William T. Powell bridge, pull off to take windsurfing lessons or just park and enjoy the tranquillity of this laid-back slice of Miami. Key Biscayne is one very large beach, and you can keep driving to reach Bill Baggs Cape Florida State Recreation Area, where you'll find more beaches and tackle stores; pick up gear for pier fishing. A fleet of deep-sea charters is moored at Crandon Marina for more adventurous sport fishing. Keep in mind the half-day charters don't come cheap, but if this is a once-in-a-lifetime trip, anchors aweigh! Whether you lounge on the shore or sail on the sea, that evening you can return to your favorite nightspot in South Beach, Coconut Grove, or Coral Gables.

## If You Have 5 Days

Follow the suggested three-day itinerary, and on Day Four use the morning to visit South Miami's Italian Renaissance–style villa, Vizcaya Museum and Gardens. Afterward, head to burgeoning Brickell Village for lunch; it's a relaxed area with shops and restaurants between the Miami River and downtown. If you're here on the right evening, take in a performance at the ornate Gusman Theatre. Even if the theater's dark, the bayfront should still be going strong. Join the throng over at Bayside Marketplace, or the nightspots at the dazzling high-tech AmericanAirlines Arena. Another option is to board a gambling cruise and live the high life at sea.

On your final day, head north on Collins Avenue to explore monolithic tourist hotels such as the Fontainebleau Hilton and Eden Roc. Each has more restaurants, pools, and activities than many American towns. From here, you're more than halfway to Bal Harbour, whose shops—Chanel, Tiffany & Co., Armani, Dolce & Gabbana—are simply among the finest in the world. That evening, return to South Beach for dinner and a walk up Washington Avenue, down Collins and back up Ocean Drive to return to your favorite deco hotels. Since you plan to call in sick when you get back home, pick a nightclub and party into the morning.

# 2 EXPLORING MIAMI AND MIAMI BEACH

Miami and Miami Beach may be the most exotic cities Americans can visit without a passport. On a typical evening in South Beach, you'll witness the energy and passion of Rio, Monte Carlo, Havana, and Hemingway's Paris. Other neighborhoods, such as Coral Gables and Little Havana, show off architecture and cultural events derived from their distinct historical legacies. Born as a tourist spot in the 1920s, raised as a southern metropolis in the 1960s, Greater Miami has become one of the country's sexiest, though still evolving, destinations.

Revised by Gretchen Schmidt and updated by Kathy Foster

**THINK OF MIAMI AS A TEENAGER:** a young beauty with growing pains, cocky yet confused, quick to embrace the latest fads, exasperating yet lovable. It may help you understand how best to tackle this imperfect paradise.

As cities go, Miami and Miami Beach really are young. Just a little more than 100 years ago, Miami was mosquito-infested swampland, with an Indian trading post on the Miami River. Then hotel builder Henry Flagler brought his railroad to the outpost known as Fort Dallas. Other visionaries—Carl Fisher, Julia Tuttle, William Brickell, and John Sewell, among others—set out to tame the unruly wilderness. Hotels were erected, bridges were built, the port was dredged, electricity arrived. The narrow strip of mangrove coast was transformed into Miami Beach. And the tourists started to come.

Greater Miami is many destinations in one. At its best, it offers an unparalleled multicultural experience: melodic Latin and Caribbean tongues, international cuisines and cultural events, and an unmistakable joie de vivre—all against a frankly beautiful beach backdrop. In Little Havana, the air is tantalizing with the perfume of strong Cuban coffee. In Coconut Grove, Caribbean steel drums ring out during the Goombay Street Festival. Anytime in colorful Miami Beach, restless crowds form outside nightclubs waiting for entry to the hottest new club.

Many visitors don't know that Miami and Miami Beach are really separate cities. Miami, on the mainland, is South Florida's commercial hub. Miami Beach, on 17 islands in Biscayne Bay, is sometimes considered America's Riviera, luring refugees from winter with its warm sunshine; sandy beaches; graceful, shady palms; and tireless nightlife. The natives know well that there's more to Greater Miami than the bustle of South Beach and its Art Deco District. In addition to well-known places such as Coconut Grove and Bayside, the less reported-upon spots, like the Museum of Contemporary Art, in North Miami, the burgeoning Design District in Miami, and the mangrove swamps of Matheson Hammock Park, in Coral Gables, are great insider destinations.

Don't mistake the great Miami outdoors for the beach. Hang up your beach towel long enough to check out Fairchild Tropical Garden, a serene oasis of lush palms, flowering vines, and tranquil overlooks. Take a canoe ride on the Oleta River, and you'll be surrounded by unspoiled tropical hammocks and mangrove forests. On Key Biscayne grassy dunes and fertile wetlands seem a world away from the urban hubbub. Whatever you do, savor the moment. Miami may grow up one of these days, and when it does, it won't be quite the same.

## Orientation

Miami-Dade County sprawls over 2,000 square mi along the southeastern tip of Florida. Unless you don't intend to leave your hotel or your immediate neighborhood, you'll need a car to see the sights. Public transportation exists, but it does not easily reach many places you'll want to visit. Rent a convertible if you can—there's nothing quite like putting on some shades and feeling the wind in your hair as you drive across one of the causeways that links Miami to Miami Beach and Key Biscayne.

Downtown has become the lively hub of the mainland city, now more accessible thanks to the Metromover rail extension. Park at one of the outlying Metrorail stations and take the train in, connecting to the Metromover if need be. In South Beach you absolutely don't need a car. Park it and use the inexpensive Electrowave shuttle—or your feet—to get around. In Coconut Grove metered street parking is hard to come by; try parking at CocoWalk, Streets of Mayfair, or the garage at Mary Street and Oak Avenue and stroll the neighborhood.

Finding your way around Greater Miami is easy if you know how the street numbering system works. Miami is laid out on a grid with four quadrants—northeast, northwest, southeast, and southwest—centered at Miami Avenue and Flagler Street. Miami Avenue separates east from west, and Flagler Street separates north from south. Avenues and courts run north–south; streets, terraces, and ways run east–west. Roads run diagonally, northwest–southeast. In Miami Beach the numbering on north–south thoroughfares gives you a pretty accurate idea of the nearest cross street: 500 Ocean Drive is at 5th Street, 7100 Collins Avenue is at 71st Street, 17800 Ocean Boulevard is at 178th Street, and so forth. So far, so good.

Confusion arises because Coral Gables, Hialeah, and Miami Beach do not generally follow the same system. Even some longtime Coral Gables residents don't know the names of their streets. And along the curve of Biscayne Bay, the symmetrical grid shifts diagonally. It's best to buy a detailed map, stick to the major roads, and ask directions early and often. However, make sure you're in a safe neighborhood or public place when you seek guidance; cabbies and cops are good resources.

# NORTH MIAMI AND NORTH MIAMI BEACH

If you want to catch a glimpse of what Florida looked like to visitors in the 1950s and 1960s, drive north along the stretch of A1A from the Sunny Isles Causeway at Northwest 163rd Street. But hurry. The most precious resource of northeast Miami-Dade County—its land—is being tapped by developers, and the tacky souvenir malls and beachfront motels of old are quickly being supplanted by luxury condos. A bevy of colorful neighborhood restaurants reveals this area's diverse ethnic makeup. North Miami Beach is home to dozens of Asian eateries, and tiny restaurants in North Miami serve up savory East Indian and Jamaican specialties such as oxtail, curried goat, and jerk chicken. This buzz of activity, however, is offset by a number of remarkably unspoiled nature enclaves.

*Numbers in the text correspond to numbers in the margin and on the Miami Beach and North map.*

## A Good Tour

Start your tour at the south end of **Haulover Beach Park** ①. From here you'll have one of the area's few unimpeded beachfront views. Head north on A1A into Sunny Isles Beach, where uncrowded beaches attract groups of Latin American and European visitors. As you cruise through Sunny Isles, keep an eye out for classic tourist landmarks, such as the Newport Fishing Pier, at 170th Street, where you can rent fishing gear, buy bait, and cast in, plus mom-and-pop souvenir stores and swimwear shops. Catch a fleeting glimpse of the corny '50s architectural details, such as the Sphinxes at the Suez Oceanfront Resort at 18215 Collins Avenue, and the nomads and camel statues at the Sahara Beach Club Ocean Condos, 18335 Collins Avenue—these will soon disappear as these motels are torn down to make way for luxury condos. As you continue north, you'll enter the tiny, wealthy town of **Golden Beach** ②. At County Line Road at the end of Golden Beach, turn around and head south until you reach the William Lehman Causeway. Following the causeway west, you'll pass the sleek condos of Aventura. Once you've had an eyeful of Aventura's upscale diversions—consisting primarily of shopping (Aventura Mall is one of South Florida's largest) and spas—head south on Biscayne Boulevard. To the west you'll see **Greynolds Park** ③, spreading out south of Route 856. A little farther on you'll pass the **Ancient Spanish Monastery** ④. Stop here to see an example of Romanesque architecture from 12th-century Spain. Continue south to the Sunny Isles Causeway at 163rd Street. On the east side of the boulevard, toward the water, is the **Oleta River State Recreation Area** ⑤. Here you can spy endangered West Indian manatees and waterbirds in the lagoon surrounding a mangrove island. The last stop on your tour can be the **Museum of Contemporary Art (MoCA)** ⑥, a dramatic warehouselike space that houses a cutting-edge collection.

TIMING
A driving tour of the area requires about 45 minutes. Add to this any time you plan to spend in parks, shops, at the MoCA, or at the beach.

## Sights to See

❹ **Ancient Spanish Monastery.** Tucked away in a peaceful hammock only a few blocks from a busy commercial district, this medieval structure is one of the oldest buildings in the western hemisphere. Originally constructed in Segovia, Spain, in the 1100s, the monastery was occupied by Cistercian monks for nearly 700 years before it was converted into a granary and stable. In 1925 William Randolph Hearst purchased the cloisters and outbuildings and had them dismantled, planning to reconstruct them on his San Simeon, California, estate. Twenty-six years and some financial troubles later, the 11,000 crates holding the stones were sold at auction, and the buildings were reassembled here. An opportunity to admire the Romanesque architecture is the main reason to come here. ✉ *16711 W. Dixie Hwy., at N.E. 167th St., North Miami Beach, Miami Beach,* ☎ *305/945–1461,* WEB *www.spanishmonastery.com.* 🎫 *$5.* ⏲ *Mon.–Sat. 9–5, Sun. 1:30–5.*

**Arch Creek Park and Museum.** Site of a unique natural stone bridge used by ancient Native American tribes, this park has 8 acres of tropical hardwood hammock, a museum–nature center, a wildlife sanctuary, and naturalist-guided tours. ✉ *1855 N.E. 135 St., North Miami,* ☎ *305/944–6111,* WEB *www.co.miami-dade.fl.us/parks/mpattra5.htm.* 🎫 *Free.* ⏲ *Daily dawn–dusk.*

❷ **Golden Beach.** You won't actually be able to visit the sand in this 2-mi-long enclave of private oceanfront homes—the beaches are for residents only. But as you drive through town, you'll appreciate the beautifully landscaped properties, a welcome sight after miles of high-rise condos. ✉ *A1A between N.E. 195th St. and County Line Rd., Sunny Isles, Miami Beach.*

❸ **Greynolds Park.** Tranquil Greynolds Park has bike and nature trails and a place where you can rent paddleboats. A rookery provides roosting and nesting areas for wading birds. In the mangrove wetland, you may spot cattle egrets, anhingas, white ibis, green herons, or double-crested cormorants. There are also guided bird walks and owl prowls. ✉ *17530 W. Dixie Hwy., north of 163rd St., North Miami Beach, Miami Beach,* ☎ *305/945–3425,* WEB *www.co.miami-dade.fl.us/parks.* 🎫 *Weekdays free, parking weekends $4.* ⏲ *Daily dawn–dusk.*

NEED A BREAK? Since 1954 **Wolfie Cohen's Rascal House** (✉ 17190 Collins Ave., at 172nd St., Sunny Isles, Miami Beach, ☎ 305/947–4581) has been one of Florida's best delis. They open early and close as late as 2 AM on

Miami Beach and North
AVENTURA
GOLDEN BEACH
SUNNY ISLES
NORTH MIAMI BEACH
NORTH MIAMI
BAL HARBOUR
SURFSIDE
MIAMI SHORES
MIAMI BEACH
SOUTH BEACH
Miami Gdns. Dr.
N. Miami Beach Blvd.
N.E. 6th Ave.
Biscayne Blvd.
Arch Creek Park
N.E. 135th St.
Broad Causeway
Gratigny Rd.
Collins Ave.
North Shore Open Space Park
N.E. 103rd St.
N.E. 95th St.
North Beach
Isle of Normandy
N.W. 79th St.
JFK Causeway
N. Miami Ave.
N.E. 2nd Ave.
N.W. 54th St.
Julia Tuttle Causeway
Biscayne Bay
ATLANTIC OCEAN
N.W. 20th St.
Venetian Causeway
Parrot Jungle & Gardens
MacArthur Causeway
95
441
856
826
1
909
915
195
395
A1A
N
0
3 miles
3 km

weekends. Grab a booth or order takeout for the beach. And don't miss their breakfasts. As soon as you sit down, you're greeted with baskets of breads, rolls, and danishes—and you can load them in a doggie bag when you leave.

★ ❶ **Haulover Beach Park.** Haulover, far from the action of South Beach, preserves the Miami of 35 years ago. You can fire up the barbecue grills, get in on a pickup volleyball game, rent kayaks, or bike on one of the trails. There are also showers and a concession stand. Sand on the eroded beach hasn't been replaced, and the narrow strand is perfect for beachgoers who don't relish a trek across hot sand to get to the water. Kite flying is popular here, and there are kite shops to get you started. An underground path leads to the Haulover Park Marina, home to the largest charter–drift fishing fleet in South Florida. A clearly marked clothing-optional section at the north end of the beach draws 5,000–7,000 birthday-suited beachgoers on any given Sunday. ✉ *10800 Collins Ave., north of Bal Harbour, Miami Beach,* ☎ *305/947–3525,* WEB *www.co.miami-dade.fl.us/parks/mpbeach1.htm.* *$4 per vehicle.* ⏲ *Daily dawn–dusk.*

❻ **Museum of Contemporary Art (MoCA).** Inaugurated in 1996 in a Charles Gwathmey–designed facility, this museum seeks to keep abreast of the latest trends in all artistic media. The permanent collection numbers more than 350 works, and exhibitions place an emphasis on promising new artists. ✉ *770 N.E. 125th St., between N.E. 7th Ct. and 8th Ave., North Miami,* ☎ *305/893–6211,* WEB *www.mocanomi.org.* *$5.* ⏲ *Tues.–Sat. 11–5, Sun. noon–5.*

★ ❺ **Oleta River State Recreation Area.** The largest urban park in Florida, Oleta has nearly 1,000 acres of lush greenery that provide a welcome respite from urban clutter. In this tranquil wilderness are bald eagles, dolphins, ospreys, and manatees, who stay the winter. Outdoor adventurers can fish, bike, or rent canoes or kayaks. The 30-ft hill is a virtual mountain in flat Florida, and mountain bikers will find 10 miles of trails for beginners and intermediates, a dual slalom course, and various bridges. ✉ *3400 N.E. 163rd St., between Biscayne Blvd. and Collins Ave., North Miami Beach, Miami Beach,* ☎ *305/919–1846,* WEB *www.dep.state.fl.us/parks/district5/oletariver.* *$4 per vehicle, $1 per person on bike or on foot.* ⏲ *Daily 8–dusk.*

# MIAMI BEACH NORTH OF 23RD STREET

The Miami Beach of picture postcards—glamorous sprawling hotels and showgirls with feathered headdresses—doesn't only survive here, it thrives. Multimillion-dollar renovations in recent years to such landmark 1950s hotels as the Fontainebleau and Eden Roc have revived their glitzy splendor, not subdued it. And amid the high-rise hotels and condominium communities that characterize the area are some delightfully uncrowded beaches.

*Numbers in the text correspond to numbers in the margin and on the Miami Beach and North map.*

## A Good Tour

Take Arthur Godfrey Road (41st Street) east to Collins Avenue and head north. Immediately in front of you, you'll see Robert Haas's huge trompe l'oeil mural on the side of the **Fontainebleau Hilton Resort and Towers** ⑦. As you round the corner, the front of the massive curved building will come into view, followed by the **Eden Roc Renaissance Resort and Spa** ⑧ and **Wyndham Miami Beach Resort** ⑨, all of which recapture the glamour of the 1950s and '60s.

As you continue driving north on Collins, the condo canyon begins, high-rise after nondescript high-rise. If you're looking for some low-key self-indulgence, stop at the Castle Beach Club, at 54th Street, for a soak in the **Russian and Turkish Baths** ⑩. At 74th Street check out the mosaic wall and band shell, used by the community for dances and skating. To the east is North Beach, a section of waterfront preferred by families and those who like things quiet; metered parking is plentiful, and there's a pleasant old shopping street to meander along. Continuing north, you'll come upon the family-friendly North Shore Open Space Park, a pristine strip of sand dunes and sea grapes, with a boardwalk. Between 88th and 96th streets you'll pass through the peaceful French Canadian enclave of Surfside, with its quiet beaches, family-operated motels, and time-warp hotels. Then it's on to ritzy **Bal Harbour** ⑪, home to world-class shops and elegant condos.

TIMING

Allow about 30 minutes for this drive, plus additional time to relax on the beach, explore hotels, or shop at Bal Harbour.

## Sights to See

★ ⓫ **Bal Harbour.** Best known for its elegant shopping mall, this manicured village is the smallest and one of the wealthiest municipalities in Miami-Dade County. Bal Harbour, a planned community, was incorporated in 1946 after having served as a United States Air Force training facility during World War II. The barracks are long gone, and today along the date palm–lined stretch of Collins Avenue are luxury condos, the Sheraton Bal Harbour Beach Resort, and the restored Sea View and Beach House hotels. At the posh Bal Harbour Shops, white-helmeted guards stand at the door. ✉ *Collins Ave. between 96th and 103rd Sts., Bal Harbour, Miami Beach,* WEB *www.balharbourshops.com.*

❽ **Eden Roc Renaissance Resort and Spa.** Renovations have returned this immense Morris Lapidus creation to the flamboyant splendor of its heyday—note the dramatic sunken lobby and golden fleur-de-lis motifs throughout the majestic lobby. The Eden Roc drew top entertainers in the 1960s—Frank Sinatra, Dean Martin, and Sammy Davis, Jr., all took the stage here. Today the hotel is well known for its sybaritic attraction, the Spa of Eden, and its popular beachside bar. ✉ *4525 Collins Ave., between 45th and 46th Sts., Miami Beach,* ☎ *305/531–0000,* WEB *www.edenrocresort.com.*

❼ **Fontainebleau Hilton Resort and Towers.** Whether or not garish opulence is your cup of tea, this Morris Lapidus–built 1950s extravaganza is worth a look. As you enter the vast lobby, you can easily imagine a parade of guests in evening wear gliding down the grand staircase, illuminated by the awe-inspiring chandeliers and reflected in the many mirrored columns. Outside, amid tropical foliage, the lagoon pool and waterfall, complete with a bar hidden inside, cover a half acre. Latin-accented floor shows with scantily clad performers and a 10-piece orchestra live on at the Club Tropigala. ✉ *4441 Collins Ave., between 44th and 45th Sts., Miami Beach,* ☎ *305/538–2000,* WEB *www.fontainebleau.hilton.com.*

OFF THE BEATEN PATH

**PARROT JUNGLE GARDENS –** South Florida's original tourist attraction—it opened in 1936—closed in October 2002 with plans to move to an island of its own between Miami and Miami Beach in early 2003. In South Miami, the park was home to more than 1,100 exotic birds, a few orangutans, and a rare albino alligator, plus amazing orchids and flowering plants. All this and more, like a new Japanese garden and a squadron of Caribbean flamingos, are expected at the new location. An increase in admission and hours of operation are expected, so call ahead. ✉ *Watson Island (off I–395 MacArthur Causeway) east of downtown Miami), Miami,* ☎ *305/666–7834,* WEB *www.parrotjungle.com.* 🎫 *$15.95.* ⏲ *Daily 9:30–6, last admission 4:30; café daily 8–5.*

OFF THE BEATEN PATH

**PELICAN HARBOR SEABIRD RESCUE STATION** – Walk among pelicans and other seabirds who are being nursed back to health after encounters with fish hooks, commercial nets, and other man-made dangers. ✉ *1275 N.E. 79th St. Causeway (JFK Causeway), north side causeway in Pelican Harbor Marina, North Bay Village, Miami,* ☎ *305/751–9840,* WEB *www.pelicanharbor.bizland.com.* 🎫 *Free.* ⏲ *Daily dawn–dusk.*

10 **Russian and Turkish Baths.** Pamper yourself without all the trappings of a designer spa. These baths, at the Castle Beach Club, include a salt-water whirlpool, tiled Russian sauna, redwood Finnish sauna, and a Turkish *hamam*—a wet eucalyptus steam room. Towels are provided, and you can sweat all day for one price, or buy extra services such as an oak leaf *platza* (massage), mud rubs, salt scrubs, or regular massages. ✉ *5445 Collins Ave., at 54th St., Miami Beach,* ☎ *305/867–8313.* 🎫 *$21 per day.* ⏲ *Daily noon–midnight.*

NEED A BREAK?

A hotel filled with 1950s cars? But of course. At **Dezerland Hotel** (✉ 8701 Collins Ave., at 87th St., Surfside, Miami Beach, ☎ 305/865–6661), vintage Caddies and T-Birds decorate the lobby. In the buffet-style restaurant you can dine in booths fashioned from the backseats of vintage cars. As gimmicks go, this one will make you smile.

9 **Wyndham Miami Beach Resort.** The Wyndham, another monument to Miami Beach's past, was once the famed Doral. Renovators made it a point to keep intact the legendary Starlight Room, a rooftop nightspot with a ceiling of thousands of twinkling lights, although now it's used just for private functions. ✉ *4833 Collins Ave., Miami Beach,* ☎ *305/532–3600.*

# SOUTH BEACH

The hub of South Beach (no self-respecting local calls it SoBe) is the 1-square-mi Art Deco District, fronted on the east by Ocean Drive and on the west by Alton Road. In recent years the story of South Beach has become a big part of the story of Miami. Back in the early 1980s, the neighborhood's vintage hotels were badly run down, catering mostly to retirees on fixed incomes. Some were abandoned, and some served as crack houses. The Morris Lapidus–designed Lincoln Road pedestrian mall, known as the 5th Avenue of the South during its heyday in the 1950s, languished. The entire area had a decidedly depressed feel. But a group of visionaries led by the late Barbara Baer Capitman, a spirited New York transplant, saw this group of buildings as architecturally significant and worth protecting from mindless urban renewal. Even then, the buildings of South Beach composed a peerless collection of art deco architecture dating from the 1920s to the 1950s.

Capitman was well into her sixties when she stepped in front of bulldozers ready to tear down the Senator, an art deco hotel. The Senator fell, but thanks to preservationists, 40 others were saved. As the movement picked up, investors started restoring the interiors and repainting the exteriors of classic South Beach buildings. The area is now distinguished as the nation's first 20th-century district to be listed on the National Register of Historic Places, with 800 significant buildings making the roll.

As the restoration proceeded, South Beach's vibrant pastel palette (a sign of artistic liberty—originally, the deco hotels were primarily white) was made famous by the classic 1980s television show *Miami Vice*. Talented chefs and restaurateurs saw the potential of the increasingly attractive, hotel-intensive neighborhood. A $16 million face-lift revived Lincoln Road Mall. Fashion photographers, music video producers, and movie directors took note of the emerging location and began shooting here. Ocean Drive emerged as an emblem of hip style. As South Beach gained exposure, celebrities such as singer Gloria Estefan, the late designer Gianni Versace, and recording mogul Chris Blackwell bought a piece of the action.

Life along Ocean Drive unfolds 24 hours a day. Beautiful people pose in hotel lounges and sidewalk cafés, tanned cyclists zoom past palm trees, and visitors flock to see the action. If Ocean Drive is the heartbeat of South Beach, then Lincoln Road has become its soul. Its quirky blend of cultural venues, artists' galleries, boutiques, restaurants, and cafés has recently fallen victim to high rents, and a new movie and retail complex at the Alton Road end of the mall has not been universally well received. But Lincoln Road still has character. Café crowds spill onto the sidewalks, weekend markets draw all kinds of visitors and their dogs, and, thanks to a few late-night lounges, the scene is just as present and alive at night.

You'll notice right away that several things are plentiful in South Beach. Besides the plethora of surgically enhanced bodies and cell phones, there are a lot of cars for a small area, and plenty of attentive meter maids. On-street parking is scarce, tickets are given freely when meters expire, and towing charges are high. Check your meter to see when you must pay to park; times vary by district. No quarters? Try the municipal lot west of the Convention Center; the 17th Street Garage between Pennsylvania and Meridian; the 16th Street Garage between Collins and Washington; or the 7th Street Garage at Washington and Collins. Better yet, take advantage of the Electrowave shuttle—it only costs a quarter and runs until the wee hours of the morning.

*Numbers in the text correspond to numbers in the margin and on the South Beach map.*

## A Good Walk

Start this walk early (8 AM) if you want to watch the awakening city without distraction—at this hour you're also likely to see a fashion photo shoot in progress, since photographers like early morning light. On the other hand, a walk later in the day puts you in the thick of South Beach's action. That action has made the stretch of Ocean Drive from 1st to 23rd streets—primarily the 10-block stretch from 5th to 15th streets—the most talked-about beachfront in America. A bevy of art deco jewels hugs the drive, while across the street lies palm-fringed **Lummus Park** ①, whose south end is a good starting point for a walk. Cross to the west side of Ocean Drive, where there are many sidewalk cafés; find one that's open and have some breakfast. Then walk north, taking note of the Park Central Hotel (No. 640), built in 1937 by deco architect Henry Hohauser. If you're in the vicinity of 10th Street between 11 AM and 6 PM, recross Ocean Drive to the beach side and visit the **Art Deco District Welcome Center** ②, in the 1950s-era Oceanfront Auditorium. Rent a tape or hire a guide for an Art Deco District tour.

Look back across Ocean Drive and take a peek at the wonderful flying-saucer architecture of the Clevelander, at No. 1020. On the next block you'll see the late Gianni Versace's Spanish Mediterranean **Casa Casuarina** ③, formerly known as the Amsterdam Palace. Graceful

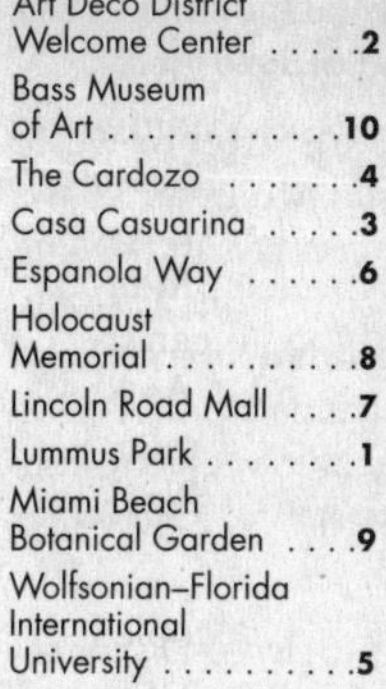

Art Deco District Welcome Center . . . . .2
Bass Museum of Art . . . . . . . . . . . .10
The Cardozo . . . . . . .4
Casa Casuarina . . . . .3
Espanola Way . . . . . .6
Holocaust Memorial . . . . . . . . . .8
Lincoln Road Mall . . . .7
Lummus Park . . . . . . . .1
Miami Beach Botanical Garden . . . .9
Wolfsonian–Florida International University . . . . . . . . . .5


## South Beach

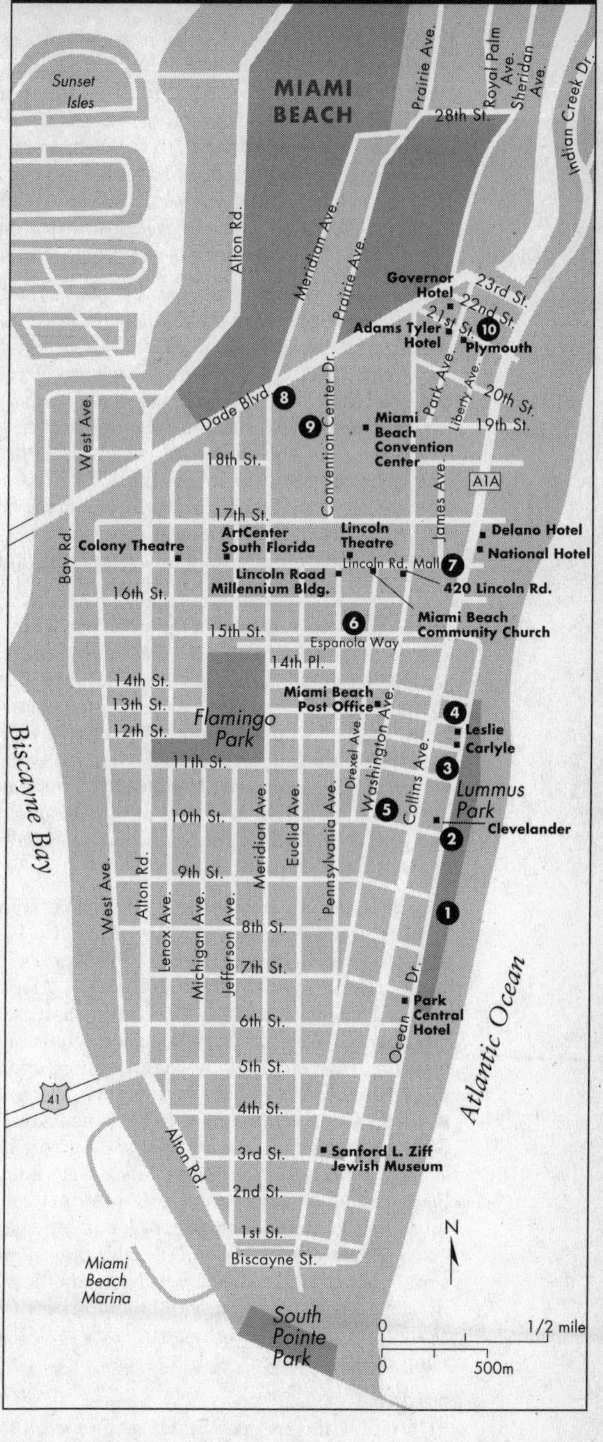

fluted columns stand guard at the Leslie (No. 1244) and the empty 1941 Carlyle; to their north is the much-photographed **Cardozo** ④.

Walk two blocks west (away from the ocean) on 13th Street to Washington Avenue, and step inside the 1937 Depression Moderne Miami Beach Post Office, designed by Howard Cheney, to see the rotunda and the Works Project Administration–era mural. Turn left on Washington and walk 2½ blocks south to the **Wolfsonian–Florida International University** ⑤, where design and art used as propaganda from 1885 to 1945 is the focus. Along the way, you'll notice the mix of chic restaurants, club-kid and alternative shops, delicatessens, and nightclubs that have spiced up a once derelict neighborhood.

Return north on Washington past 14th Street, and turn left on **Espanola Way** ⑥, a narrow street of Mediterranean Revival buildings, eclectic shops, and a weekend market. Continue west to Meridian Avenue and turn right. Three blocks north of Espanola Way is the redesigned **Lincoln Road Mall** ⑦, part of must-see South Beach. Look beyond the lively parade of pedestrians and you'll see such architectural gems as the massive 1940s keystone building at 420 Lincoln Road, with a 1945 Leo Birchanky mural in the lobby; the 1921 Mission-style Miami Beach Community Church at Drexel Avenue; and the fabulous Cadillac dealership sign discovered underneath the facade of the Lincoln Road Millennium Building on the south side of the mall, at Pennsylvania Avenue.

The next main street north of Lincoln Road is 17th Street, and to the east is the Miami Beach Convention Center, where Muhammad Ali (then known as Cassius Clay) defeated Sonny Liston for the world heavyweight boxing championship in 1964. It was also the site of the highly charged 1968 Republican National Convention and both the Republican and Democratic National Conventions in 1972. Walk behind the massive building to the corner of Meridian Avenue and 19th Street to see the chilling **Holocaust Memorial** ⑧, a monumental record honoring the 6 million Jewish victims of the Nazi Holocaust. Just east is the compact **Miami Beach Botanical Garden** ⑨, home to a Japanese garden and other tropical displays.

As you head along Park Avenue, take note of some off-the-beaten-path architectural jewels: the Adams Tyler Hotel at 2030 Park, with rooftop ornamentation—inspired by the 1939 World's Fair—pointing toward space; the Streamline Plymouth at 336 21st Street, its distinctive sculpted facade concealing an elevator shaft; and the 1939 Governor Hotel at 435 21st Street, rich in such details as a shiny stainless-steel marquee, glass etched with wildlife figures, and a terrazzo floor. Continue east through Collins Park and its enormous baobab trees to the **Bass Museum of Art** ⑩, a stark 1930 Streamline building that once housed Miami Beach's first library, then walk across the street and peek inside the windows of the Miami City Ballet's home, where dancers may be practicing their arabesques. Return to Ocean Drive in time to pull up a chair at an outdoor café, order an espresso, and settle down for some people-watching, South Beach's most popular pastime. Or grab some late rays at the beach, which has unofficial gay, mixed, and family zones. You can go back to Lummus Park to play volleyball or to skate, or head north to the boardwalk for a stroll (skating and bicycling are not allowed).

#### TIMING

To see only the art deco buildings on Ocean Drive, allow one hour. Depending on your interests, schedule at least five hours for the whole tour and include a drink or meal at a café and browsing time in the shops on Ocean Drive, along Espanola Way, and at Lincoln Road Mall.

Start your walking tour as early in the day as possible. In winter the street becomes increasingly crowded as the day wears on, and in summer afternoon heat and humidity can be unbearable, wilting even the hardiest soul. Finishing by midafternoon also enables you to hit the beach and cool your heels in the warm sand.

## Sights to See

❷ **Art Deco District Welcome Center.** Run by the Miami Design Preservation League, the center provides information about the buildings in the District. A gift shop sells 1930s–1950s art deco memorabilia, posters, and books on Miami's history. Several tours—covering Lincoln Road, Espanola Way, North Beach, the entire Art Deco District, and more—start here. You can rent audiotapes for a self-guided tour, join the regular Saturday-morning or Thursday-evening walking tours, or take a bicycle tour—all of the options provide detailed histories of the art deco hotels. Don't miss their special boat tours during Art Deco Weekend in early January. A second location (✉ 520 Lincoln Rd., ☎ 305/672–2014), behind the Miami Beach Community Church, has art deco merchandise and furniture. ✉ *1001 Ocean Dr., at Barbara Capitman Way (10th St.), South Beach,* ☎ *305/531–3484.* 💰 *Tours $10–$15.* ⏲ *Sun.–Thurs. 10–10, Fri.–Sat. 10 AM–midnight.*

❿ **Bass Museum of Art.** The newly expanded Bass in historic Collins Park is part of the new Miami Beach Cultural Park, which includes the Miami City Ballet's Arquitectonica-designed facility and the Miami Beach Regional Library. The original building, constructed of keystone, has unique Maya-inspired carvings. The new expansion designed by Japanese architect Arata Isozaki houses another wing, a café, and an outdoor sculpture garden. Special exhibitions join a diverse collection of European art. Works on permanent display include *The Holy Family,* a painting by Peter Paul Rubens; *The Tournament,* one of several 16th-century Flemish tapestries; and works by Albrecht Dürer and Henri de Toulouse-Lautrec. Special exhibits often cost a little extra. ✉ *2121 Park Ave., at 21st St., South Beach,* ☎ *305/673–7530,* WEB *www.bassmuseum.org.* 💰 *$6.* ⏲ *Tues.–Sat. 10–5, except 2nd and 4th Thurs. of each month 1–9, Sun. 1–5.*

NEED A BREAK? If your feet are giving out, head to the **Delano Hotel** (✉ 1685 Collins Ave., at 17th St., South Beach, ☎ 305/672–2000) for a drink. This surrealistic place lives up to its hype, with a soaring lobby-bar-restaurant area that epitomizes South Beach style. Or, for a more historically accurate ambiance, have a martini in the 1930s Press Room bar in the lobby of the **National Hotel** (✉ 1677 Collins Ave., south of 17th St., South Beach, ☎ 305/532–2311), then take a peek at the pool.

❹ **The Cardozo.** This 1939 Hohauser-designed Streamline Moderne classic, owned by Gloria Estefan, was one of the first art deco hotels to be revived, and it is now one of the most photographed hotels on the beach. It's beautifully restored inside and out, with wrought-iron furniture and hardwood floors. Look for the eyebrows over the windows. ✉ *1300 Ocean Dr., at 13th St., South Beach.*

❸ **Casa Casuarina.** In the early 1980s, before South Beach turned fabulous, the late Italian designer Gianni Versace purchased this Spanish Mediterranean–style residence built before the arrival of art deco. Today the ornate three-story palazzo includes a guest house and a copper-dome rooftop observatory and pool. In July 1997 Versace was tragically shot and killed in front of his home. The spot where he fell has turned into a morbid tourist attraction where hundreds of people have their picture taken every day. ✉ *1114 Ocean Dr., at 11th St., South Beach.*

NEED A BREAK? Take a respite from the crowds and the heat at the **Front Porch Café** (✉ 1418 Ocean Dr., between 14th and 15th Sts., South Beach, Miami Beach, ☎ 305/531–8300), where you can have a salad or a sandwich. If you're hungry but don't have time to stop, pick up a bite at **Le Sandwicherie** (✉ 229 14th St., between Collins and Washington Aves., South Beach, ☎ 305/532–8934).

★ 6 **Espanola Way.** There's a decidedly Bohemian feel to this street lined with Mediterranean Revival buildings constructed in 1925. Al Capone's gambling syndicate ran its operations upstairs at what is now the Clay Hotel, a youth hostel. At a nightclub located here in the 1930s, future bandleader Desi Arnaz strapped on a conga drum and started beating out a rumba rhythm. Visit this quaint avenue on a Sunday afternoon, when merchants and craftspeople set up shop to sell everything from handcrafted bongo drums to fresh flowers. Between Washington and Drexel avenues, the road has been narrowed to a single lane, and Miami Beach's trademark pink sidewalks have been widened to accommodate sidewalk cafés and shops selling imaginative clothing, jewelry, and art. ✉ *Espanola Way, between 14th and 15th Sts. from Washington to Jefferson Aves., South Beach.*

8 **Holocaust Memorial.** A bronze sculpture depicts refugees clinging to a giant bronze arm that reaches out of the ground and 42 ft into the air. Enter the surrounding courtyard to see a memorial wall and hear the music that seems to give voice to the 6 million Jews who died at the hands of the Nazis. It's easy to understand why Kenneth Triester's dramatic memorial is in Miami Beach: the city's community of Holocaust survivors was once the second largest in the country. ✉ *1933–1945 Meridian Ave., at Miami-Dade Blvd., South Beach,* ☎ *305/538–1663,* WEB *www.holocaustmmb.org.* *Donations welcome.* *Daily 9–9.*

★ 7 **Lincoln Road Mall.** A playful 1990s redesign spruced up this open-air pedestrian mall, adding a grove of 20 towering date palms, five linear pools, and colorful broken-tile mosaics to the futuristic 1950s vision of Fontainebleau designer Morris Lapidus. Many of the shops are owner-operated boutiques with a delightful variety of clothing, furnishings, garden supplies, and decorative design. Even remnants of tired old Lincoln Road—beauty supply and discount electronic stores on the Collins end of the strip—somehow fit nicely into the mix. The new Lincoln Road is fun, lively, and friendly for people old, young, gay, and straight—and their dogs. Folks skate, scoot, bike, or jog here. The best times to hit the road are during Sunday morning farmers markets and on weekend evenings, when cafés bustle, art galleries open shows, street performers make the sidewalk their stage, and stores stay open late. To the west, toward Biscayne Bay, the street is lined with chic food markets, cafés, and boutiques. At Euclid Avenue, there's a monument to Lapidus, who in his 90s watched the renaissance of his whimsical creation. ✉ *Lincoln Rd. between Collins Ave. and Alton Rd., South Beach.*

In the **Lincoln Theatre** (✉ 541–545 Lincoln Rd., at Pennsylvania Ave., South Beach), a classical four-story art deco gem with friezes, the New World Symphony, a national advanced-training orchestra led by Michael Tilson Thomas, rehearses and performs. Concerts are often broadcast via loudspeakers, to the delight of visitors. On Lincoln Road's western stretch is the **ArtCenter–South Florida** (✉ 924 Lincoln Rd., between Jefferson and Michigan Aves., South Beach, ☎ 305/674–8278), home to one of the first arts groups to help resurrect the area. A black-and-white art deco movie house with a Mediterranean barrel-tile roof is now the **Colony Theater** (✉ 1040 Lincoln Rd., at Lenox Ave., South Beach), where live theater and experimental films are presented.

NEED A BREAK? Lincoln Road is a great place to cool down with an icy treat while touring South Beach. Try the homemade ice cream and sorbets—including Indian mango, key lime, and litchi—from the **Frieze Ice Cream Factory** (✉ 1626 Michigan Ave., South Beach, ☎ 305/538–2028). Or try an authentic Italian gelato at the sleek glass-and-stainless-steel **Gelateria Parmalat** (✉ 670 Lincoln Rd., between Euclid and Pennsylvania Aves., South Beach, ☎ 786/276–9475). Or on Sunday visit one of the many juice vendors, who will whip up made-to-order smoothies from mangos, oranges, and other fresh local fruits.

❶ **Lummus Park.** Its goofy, colorful lifeguard stands are fitting symbols for this popular beach. Once part of a turn-of-the-20th-century plantation owned by brothers John and James Lummus, this palm-shaded oasis on the beach side of Ocean Drive attracts families to its children's play area. Senior citizens predominate early in the day; then younger folk take over with volleyball, in-line skating along the wide and winding sidewalk, and a lot of posing. In the center of it all, a natural venue has emerged for outdoor concerts that have included big-name performers such as Luciano Pavarotti, Cab Calloway, and Lionel Hampton. ✉ *East of Ocean Dr. between 5th and 15th Sts., South Beach.*

❾ **Miami Beach Botanical Garden.** Much like the rest of Miami, the Botanical Garden is a work in progress, as the community works to restore the 40-year-old site, which was neglected for decades. Already this 5-acre patch of tropical foliage, sandwiched between the huge Miami Beach Convention Center and the Holocaust Memorial, is a tranquil oasis just blocks from frenetic South Beach, and a venue for cultural events. There's a Japanese Garden and gift shop. ✉ *2000 Convention Center Dr., South Beach,* ☎ *305/673–7256.*

OFF THE BEATEN PATH **PALM, STAR, AND HIBISCUS ISLANDS** – Off the MacArthur Causeway, these private islands offer luxurious shelter to affluent residents and low-key celebrities. One of their most notorious residents, Al Capone, lived on Palm Island in the 1920s; local-girl-made-good Gloria Estefan lives here now. You can drive through and ogle the houses.

**SOFI** – The up-and-comingest part of South Beach lies *S*outh of *Fi*fth Street. In addition to more art deco architecture and a slew of nightclubs, you'll find the **Sanford L. Ziff Jewish Museum of Florida: Home of MOSAIC** here, housed in a former synagogue built in 1936. The building is listed on the U.S. National Register of Historic Places and has art deco chandeliers and 80 impressive stained-glass windows. A permanent exhibit, *MOSAIC: Jewish Life in Florida,* depicts more than 235 years of the Florida Jewish experience. The museum also hosts changing exhibits and events and has a museum store. ✉ *301 Washington Ave., at 3rd St., South Beach,* ☎ *305/672–5044,* WEB *www.jewishmuseum.com.* *$5.* *Tues.–Sun. 10–5.*

At the southern tip of Miami Beach is **South Pointe Park,** a great place to enjoy the ocean. From the 50-yard Sunshine Pier, which adjoins the 1-mi-long jetty at the mouth of Government Cut, you can fish or just relax while watching huge ships pass. Facilities include two observation towers, rest rooms, and volleyball courts. No bait or tackle is available in the park. ✉ *1 Washington Ave., at Biscayne St., South Beach.*

★ ❺ **Wolfsonian–Florida International University.** An elegantly renovated 1927 storage facility is now both a research center and home to the 70,000-plus item collection of modern design and "propaganda arts" amassed by Miami native Mitchell ("Micky") Wolfson Jr., a world traveler and connoisseur. Broad themes of the 19th and 20th centuries—nationalism, political persuasion, industrialization—are addressed in permanent and traveling shows. Included in the museum's eclectic holdings, which represent art deco, art moderne, art nouveau, Arts and Crafts, and other aesthetic movements, are 8,000 matchbooks collected by Egypt's King Farouk. ✉ *1001 Washington Ave., at 10th St., South Beach,* ☎ *305/531–1001,* WEB *www.wolfsonian.fiu.edu.* *$5.* ⏲ *Mon.–Tues. and Fri.–Sat. 11–6, Thurs. 11–9, Sun. noon–5.*

# DOWNTOWN MIAMI

Downtown Miami dazzles from a distance. Its complex skyline of stark marble monoliths, gaudily illuminated glass towers, a futuristic arena, and sleek steel structures suggests a thoroughly modern metropolis. Rapid transit trains zoom across a neon-hue bridge arcing high over the Miami River before disappearing into a cluster of high-rises. Enormous white cruise ships hover in the background at the Port of Miami, and jets steadily descend on their approach to Miami International Airport. The city looks equipped for the 21st century.

Yet zoom in on Flagler Street, downtown's epicenter, and it resembles nothing so much as an international marketplace. Music blares from storefront radios, food vendors tout their wares, garish shops lure passersby with discounted sneakers and cameras and electronics, while throngs of people, speaking everything but English, go about their business.

By day downtown Miami's streets are clogged with Latin American shoppers loading up on bargains. Yet downtown Miami is not always high on the list of places to visit. Because of traffic congestion and expensive parking, locals tend to avoid the area (except in November, when the Miami Book Fair International draws an astonishing half-million attendees). Other than catching a Miami Heat game at the new downtown arena, or bringing out-of-towners to the touristy Bayside Marketplace, residents don't much venture downtown.

And that's a pity, because it's an area that deserves exploring. There are architectural landmarks, such as the Gusman Center and the sturdy Flagler Palm Cottage. Bayfront Park is a beautiful patch of green and a great place to contemplate the bay, where sea breezes seem to soften the city's hard edges and bathe the surroundings in a dreamy mist. And the neighborhood is home to the Historical Museum of Southern Florida, the Miami Art Museum, and other sophisticated attractions.

Thanks to the Metromover, which runs inner and outer loops through downtown, plus north and south extensions, this is an excellent tour to take by rail. Attractions are conveniently located within about two blocks of the nearest station. If you're coming from north or east of downtown, leave your car near a Metromover stop and take the Omni Loop downtown. If you're coming from south or west of downtown, park your car at a Metrorail station and take a leg of the 21-mi elevated commuter system downtown.

*Numbers in the text correspond to numbers in the margin and on the Downtown Miami map.*

## A Good Tour

Make your way to the Metrorail/Metromover Government Center Station and board the Brickell Avenue Loop. Ride onto that line's southern spur and get off at the Financial District stop. From the station turn left heading toward **Brickell Avenue** ①, where sleek high-rises, international banks, and a handful of restaurants have replaced the mansions of yesteryear. Cross Brickell at Southeast 8th Street to look at the First Presbyterian Church, a 1949 keystone structure with a dis-

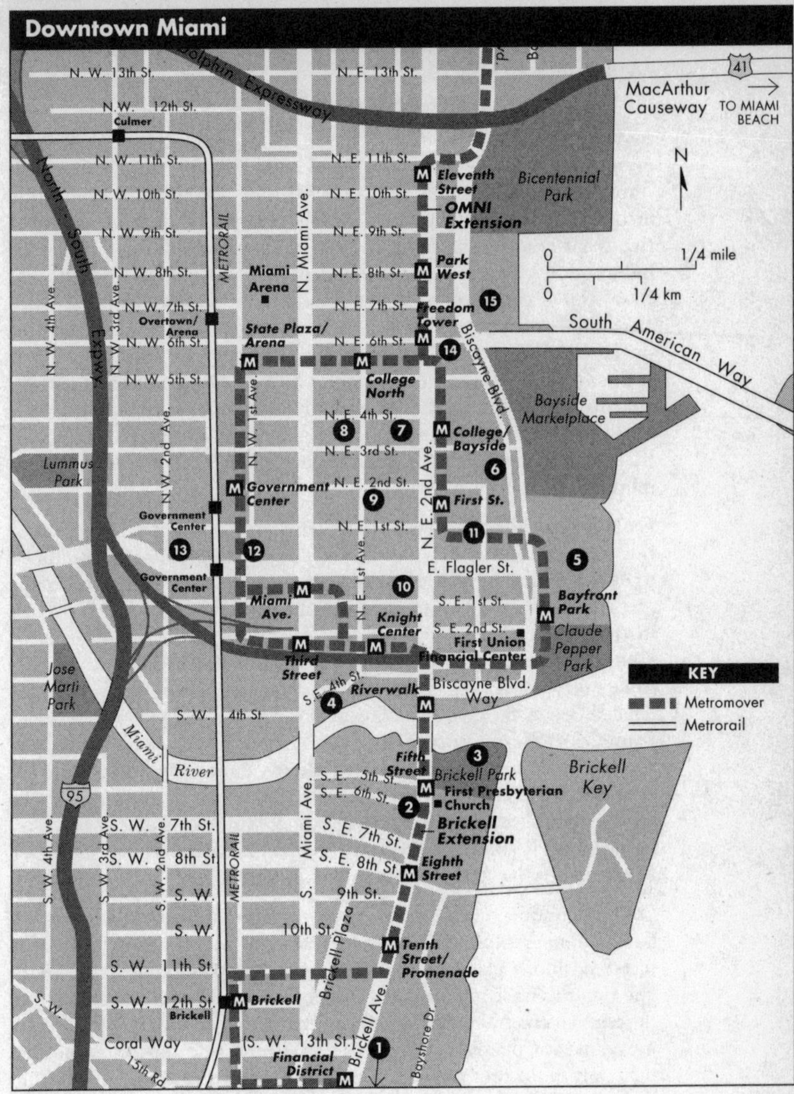


AmericanAirlines Arena . . . . . . . . . . 15
Brickell Avenue . . . . 1
Brickell Village . . . . . 2
Dade County Courthouse . . . . . . . 12
Flagler Palm Cottage . . . . . . . . . 4
Freedom Tower . . . 14
Galeria International Mall . . . . . . . . . . . 11
Gusman Center for the Performing Arts . . . 10
Historic Gesu Church . . . . . . . . . . 9
Miami Circle . . . . . . 3
Miami-Dade Community College . . . . . . . . . . 7
Miami-Dade Cultural Center . . . . 13
Mildred and Claude Pepper Bayfront Park . . . . . . 5
Plaza Bolivar . . . . . . 6
U.S. Courthouse . . . . 8

tinctive verdigris roof. As you head north on Brickell toward downtown, you'll arrive at **Brickell Village** ②. This burgeoning neighborhood of low-rise condos and shops near Fifth Street Station has some rather popular restaurants, particularly for the evening.

As you head across the Miami River via the Brickell Avenue Bridge, notice the bridge's bronze plaques of native wildlife and its dramatic statue of a Tequesta Indian, one of Miami's original inhabitants, his arrow poised toward the sun. From the bridge check out the parcel of riverfront land on the right, the site of the **Miami Circle** ③. A multimillion-dollar development was halted here when archaeologists discovered a circular stone formation and other ancient artifacts. After crossing the bridge, go left to the Hyatt Regency Miami, adjacent to the James L. Knight Convention Center. Walk down Southeast 4th Street to an old yellow-frame house, **Flagler Palm Cottage** ④, a 19th-century anachronism in this modern neighborhood. From the adjoining Bijan's Fort Dallas Restaurant and Raw Bar, you can look out over the Miami River, a hub of Native American commerce hundreds of years ago (and, more recently, drug running).

From here you can reboard the Metromover at Riverwalk Station to ride past the following sights, or you can remain on foot to head back to Brickell (which becomes Southeast 2nd Avenue) and walk up to Southeast 2nd Street. You'll instantly notice the proliferation of Brazilian flags in the storefronts. This lively part of downtown draws crowds of South American shoppers. Turn right at Southeast 2nd Street and continue for two blocks, passing the monumental 55-story First Union Financial Center, the tallest building in Florida; royal palms grace its 1-acre Palm Court plaza. Proceed until you reach Biscayne Boulevard at the southwest corner of **Mildred and Claude Pepper Bayfront Park** ⑤. Across the street is the Hotel Inter-Continental Miami, a 34-story marble monolith with *The Spindle,* a huge sculpture by Henry Moore, in the lobby. Rising up in the corner of the park is the white *Challenger* Memorial to the space shuttle that exploded in 1986.

On foot continue north on Biscayne, past **Plaza Bolivar** ⑥, a tribute by Cuban immigrants to their adopted country. You'll reach the JFK Torch of Friendship, a plaza adorned with plaques representing all the South and Central American countries except Cuba, and Bayside Marketplace, the popular entertainment, dining, and retail complex. Get off the Metromover at the College/Bayside Station to visit Bayside and to continue the next part of the tour on foot. From Bayside cross Biscayne and walk up Northeast 3rd Street to Northeast 2nd Avenue, where you'll come upon **Miami-Dade Community College** ⑦, home of two worthy art galleries. One block farther west stands the **U.S. Courthouse** ⑧, notable for the epic Depression-era mural inside that depicts Floridian progress.

Turn south on Northeast 1st Avenue and walk one block to Northeast 2nd Street. On the corner stands the 1922 **Historic Gesu Church** ⑨, one of South Florida's oldest. Return to Northeast 2nd Avenue; then turn right. Before you is the architectural clutter that characterizes downtown Miami: a cacophony of gaudy outlet shops, homely storefronts, and the occasional gem of a building. One of those is the 1938 Art Moderne Alfred I. DuPont Building, between Northeast 1st Street and Flagler, notable for its distinctive facade and ornate marble floors; another, the 1927 Italian Renaissance Ingraham Building at 25 Southeast Second Avenue, has hand-painted ceilings in the lobby. Across the street at 174 East Flagler, the landmark **Gusman Center for the Performing Arts** ⑩ is a stunning movie palace that now serves as a concert hall. If you feel like doing some shopping in a Latin American setting, **Galeria International Mall** ⑪ is right next door.

Continue west on Flagler Street, downtown Miami's commercial spine. As you pass through a cluster of busy electronics, sporting goods, and shoe stores, you'll be in one of the first areas of Miami to be carved out of the pine woods and palmetto scrub when Henry Flagler's railroad arrived in 1896. You'll see the 1936 Streamline Moderne building housing Burdines department store. (On the back of the building is a huge mural of whales painted by the artist Wyland. It's visible from the outer loop of the Metromover route.) Continue up Flagler for one block until the **Dade County Courthouse** ⑫ comes into view; it still bears its old name even though the county is now called Miami-Dade. If you're here between October and March, look for the flock of urban vultures (literally) that circle above the ziggurat roof. Crossing Southwest 1st Avenue, you'll arrive at the **Miami-Dade Cultural Center** ⑬, home of the Miami Art Museum, the Historical Museum of Southern Florida, and the Miami-Dade Public Library.

From the adjacent Metrorail–Metromover Government Center Station, you can reboard the Metromover and get a bird's-eye view of the downtown area. As you pass the State Plaza–Arena Station, look two blocks north to see the pink Miami Arena, a venue for concerts and community events. If you are riding the Omni Loop, you'll get a close-up look at the **Freedom Tower** ⑭, as the track curves onto its northern spur. To see the tower and the new Cuban-American museum, once a processing center for Cuban refugees, up close, walk north from Edcom Station to Northeast 6th Street, then two blocks east to Biscayne. The Omni spur continues north over the MacArthur Causeway past the Miami Herald Building, past the site of the Performing Arts Center scheduled to open in fall 2004, and on to Omni International Mall, a hotel and shopping center. Stay on the train for the return trip and a beautiful view of the **AmericanAirlines Arena** ⑮, the architecturally progressive venue that replaced the Miami Arena as home of the Miami Heat.

TIMING

To walk and ride to the various points of interest, allow three hours. If you want to spend additional time eating and shopping at Bayside, allow at least five hours. To include museum visits, allow seven hours.

## Sights to See

15 **AmericanAirlines Arena.** This 20,000-seat arena, built by the noted Miami-based firm Arquitectonica, hosts the NBA Miami Heat and WNBA Miami Sol, concerts, and other events. Part of the bayfront renewal, the sleek, futuristic arena has shops and restaurants, including Gloria and Emilio Estefan's pineapple-topped Bongos Cuban Café. The arena will link to Bayside Marketplace via a pedestrian bridge. ✉ *Biscayne Blvd. between N.E. 8th and 9th Sts., Downtown,* ☎ *305/577–4328.*

OFF THE BEATEN PATH

**AMERICAN POLICE HALL OF FAME AND MUSEUM –** With a cop car mounted Spiderman-style on its facade, this museum exhibits more than 11,000 law enforcement–related items, including weapons, a jail cell, and an electric chair. A guillotine, gas chamber, and a replica of a "tramp chair," an iron chair used to hold prisoners in the Old West, are also on display, and a 400-ton marble memorial lists the names of American police officers killed in the line of duty since 1960. ✉ *3801 Biscayne Blvd., at 38th St., Buena Vista,* ☎ *305/573–0070.* *$12.* *Daily 10–5:30.*

1 **Brickell Avenue.** A canyon rimmed by tall buildings, Brickell (rhymes with fickle) has the densest concentration of international banking offices in the United States. From the end of the Metromover line you

can look south to where several architecturally interesting condominiums rise between Brickell Avenue and Biscayne Bay. Arquitectonica designed three of these buildings: the **Palace** (⊠ 1541 Brickell Ave.), the **Imperial** (⊠ 1627 Brickell Ave.), and the **Atlantis** (⊠ 2025 Brickell Ave.). Israeli artist Yacov Agam painted the rainbow exterior of **Villa Regina** (⊠ 1581 Brickell Ave.). ⊠ *Brickell Ave. between 15th Rd. and Biscayne Blvd. Way.*

2 **Brickell Village.** You can spend a delightful evening outdoors in Brickell Village, a neighborhood rarely discovered by visitors. Get your bearings now among the shops and condos and return at sunset for drinks at the **Big Fish** (⊠ 55 S.W. Miami Avenue Rd., at S.E. 5th St. Brickell Village, ☎ 305/373–1770), a riverfront restaurant decorated with metal fish scales that's hard to find but worth the effort. From here you can see downtown's dazzling skyline, the neon art that adorns the span of the Metrorail bridge, and the nonstop activity along the Miami River. One of Brickell Village's hottest nightspots—for drinks or dinner—is **Hardaway's Firehouse Four** (⊠ 1000 S. Miami Ave., at 10th St., Brickell Village, ☎ 305/371–3473), a restored 1923 building with shiny brass fire poles that invoke the building's past incarnation. You can get homemade gelato or tiramisu at **Perricone's Marketplace and Café** (⊠ 15 S.E. 10th St., Brickell Village, ☎ 305/374–9449). The venerable blues and rock bar (est. 1912) **Tobacco Road** (⊠ 626 S. Miami Ave., Brickell Village, ☎ 305/374–1198) is a great stop for live music. And there's no hurry to leave, they close at 5 AM. Just north at the Miami River is the **Brickell Avenue Bridge.** More of an outdoor art piece than a mere bridge, it's decorated with a bronze sculpture of a Tequesta Indian, a collage of native wildlife, and a series of smaller bronze plaques of area fauna on both sides of the bridge, works of Manuel Carbonell (1995). ⊠ *Brickell Ave. between S.E. 5th St. and Biscayne Blvd. Way, Downtown.*

12 **Dade County Courthouse.** Built in 1928, this was once the tallest building south of Washington, D.C. It may not be as romantic as California's San Juan Capistrano, where swallows return every year, but turkey vultures roost here each winter—just look overhead, and you'll see them soaring in graceful circles over downtown. ⊠ *73 W. Flagler St., at N. Miami Ave., Downtown,* ☎ *305/349–7000.*

4 **Flagler Palm Cottage.** Now somewhat wedged between huge modern structures, this modest but cheerful-looking 1897 house, built of local pine, was once scheduled for demolition but was moved from its previous downtown location to this site for preservation. It's the only building of its type and age in downtown Miami. Though not open to visitors, its exterior is an interesting example of late-19th-century Miami architecture. ⊠ *66 S.E. 4th Ave., between S. Miami Ave. and S.E. 1st St., Downtown.*

14 **Freedom Tower.** In the 1960s this imposing Spanish baroque structure was the Cuban Refugee Center, processing more than 500,000 Cubans who entered the United States after fleeing Fidel Castro's regime. Built in 1925 for the *Miami Daily News,* it was inspired by the Giralda, an 800-year-old bell tower in Seville, Spain. Preservationists were pleased to see the tower's exterior restored in 1988, and a Cuban-American museum in 2002. ⊠ *600 Biscayne Blvd., at N.E. 7th St., Downtown.*

11 **Galeria International Mall.** If you have any doubt that you're in a bustling international city, step inside this indoor mall. Packed with visitors from South America, Europe, and beyond, the food court brims with authentic ethnic fast food: grilled meats from Brazil, *masala dosa* (Southern Indian rice and split-pea pancakes filled with spicy pota-

toes), *empanadas*, and fruit shakes from Cuba, and subs from the United States. ✉ *243 E. Flagler St., between N.E. 1st and 2nd Sts., Downtown,* ☎ *305/371–4536.*

★ 10 **Gusman Center for the Performing Arts.** Rudy Vallee, Martha Raye, Elvis Presley, and Jackie Gleason all performed in this former movie palace, now restored as a concert hall with a fabulous marquee. Resembling a Moorish courtyard inside, with twinkling "stars" in the "sky," it hosts the annual Miami Film Festival and other cultural events. ✉ *174 E. Flagler St., at N.E. 2nd Ave., Downtown,* ☎ *305/372–0925.*

9 **Historic Gesu Church.** The oldest Miami church to remain on its original site, this 1922 building was designed in the Venetian style, with Spanish influences. Salient architectural features are the three-story portico, stained-glass windows by Franz Mayer, and a rose window. There are 25 masses weekly in both English and Spanish. ✉ *118 N.E. 2nd St., at N.E. 1st Ave., Downtown,* ☎ *305/379–1424.* ⏲ *Daily 8–5.*

OFF THE BEATEN PATH

**LITTLE HAITI** – Once known as Lemon City, for the fragrant fruit grown here by early settlers, Little Haiti is now a colorful Caribbean community, with brightly painted buildings, Creole-language signs, and attractive storefront murals. This is not a wealthy community but one in which refugees from the western hemisphere's poorest country seek their share of the American dream. By day Little Haiti is a reasonably safe neighborhood to explore, but there is little here at night.

The heart of Little Hàiti is on North Miami Avenue, from 54th to 59th streets. The **Caribbean Marketplace** (✉ 5927 N.E. 2nd Ave., Little Haiti), patterned after the Iron Market in Port-au-Prince, is now shuttered. Throughout Little Haiti, tiny *botanicas* (a spiritual kind of drug store) sell candles and potions, a reminder that voodoo is a real and living faith in the neighborhood. But there are also countless storefront *églises* (Christian churches). Several small, inexpensive restaurants serve specialties such as pigeon peas and rice, oxtail, and goat stew. Among these, **Gourmet Creole** (✉ 8427 N.E. 2nd Ave., Little Haiti, ☎ 305/759–8802) cooks up inexpensive Haitian food that's popular with locals.

3 **Miami Circle.** When a construction project got under way here in 1998, workers uncovered a 38-ft-diameter stone formation and other mysterious relics. After heated pleas from archaeologists, preservationists, and Native Americans, the county decided to acquire the land and preserve the site. The area is covered and protected while plans for preservation are worked out. ✉ *East of the Brickell Ave. bridge at Miami River, Downtown,* WEB *www.nps.gov/bisc/miamicircle.htm.*

7 **Miami-Dade Community College.** The campus houses two galleries: the third-floor **Centre Gallery** mounts photography, painting, and sculpture exhibitions, and the fifth-floor **Frances Wolfson Art Gallery** presents smaller photo exhibits. ✉ *300 N.E. 2nd Ave., between N.E. 3rd and 4th Sts., Downtown,* ☎ *305/237–3278.* 🎫 *Free.* ⏲ *Mon.–Wed., Fri. 10–4, Thurs., 12–6.*

★ 13 **Miami-Dade Cultural Center.** Containing three cultural resources, this fortresslike 3-acre complex is a focal point of downtown. The **Miami Art Museum** (☎ 305/375–3000, WEB www.miamiartmuseum.org) presents major touring exhibitions of work by international artists, focusing on art since 1945. Open Tuesday–Friday 10–5 and weekends noon–5, the museum charges $5 admission; for $1 more your ticket also includes admission to the Historic Museum. At the **Historical Museum of Southern Florida** (☎ 305/375–1492, WEB www.historical-museum.org), you'll be treated to pure South Floridiana, with exhibits celebrating

Close-Up

## THE MIAMI CIRCLE: UNCOVERING A CITY'S ANCIENT HISTORY

PRESENT-DAY MIAMIANS have always been aware of the Native American roots planted here long before the arrival of Spanish explorers—after all, the city's name is believed to be the word for "sweet water" in an indeterminate Native American tongue. But there is little visible evidence of the activities of its first people, the Tequesta. It wasn't until 1998, with the discovery of a unique archaeological finding—a mysterious 38-ft ring of stone, dubbed the Miami Circle—that the community decided its prehistoric past just might be worth preserving.

At a routine dig at the mouth of the Miami River, the site of a new condo project, archaeologists discovered a series of basins cut into limestone bedrock in a perfect circular pattern when viewed from above. The circle contained postholes, a carving that resembled an eye, and other artifacts, including charcoal samples carbon-dated to AD 100. The circle's east–west alignment suggested it may have been an astronomical tool to signal the summer and winter solstice or a Tequesta temple or council house.

State and county government have now acquired the site, and are planning how best to preserve this fascinating relic for future generations, who may discover the Miami Circle's yet-unknown purpose.

Miami's multicultural heritage and history, including an old Miami streetcar, cigar labels, and a railroad exhibit, plus a display on prehistoric Miami. Admission is $5–$6—this includes admission to the Miami Art Museum—and hours are Monday–Wednesday and Friday–Saturday 10–5, Thursday 10–9, and Sunday noon–5. The **Miami-Dade Public Library** (☎ 305/375–2665)—open June–September, Monday–Wednesday and Friday–Saturday 9–6, Thursday 9–9; October–May, Monday–Wednesday and Friday–Saturday 9–6, Thursday 9–9, Sunday 1–5—contains nearly 4 million holdings and a Florida Department that includes rare books, documents, and photographs recording Miami history. It also has art exhibits in the auditorium and in the second-floor lobby. ✉ *101 W. Flagler St., between N.W. 1st and 2nd Aves., Downtown,* ☎ *305/375–2665.*

OFF THE BEATEN PATH

**MIAMI INTERNATIONAL ARTS AND DESIGN DISTRICT** – Just north of downtown Miami, the Design District consists of 1 square mi of furniture showrooms, eclectic accessories boutiques, art studios, and interior design firms that are open to the public. Some design showrooms, like **Holly Hunt** (✉ 3833 N.E. 2nd Ave., Design District), combine furniture with art and photography exhibits, thereby merging the discrete worlds of decor and visual art. Murals on either side of the Buick Building mark the entrance to the neighborhood, which also has its own arts-oriented high school. Grab a bite to eat at the lush **Piccadilly Garden Restaurant and Lounge** (✉ 35 N.E. 40th St., Design District, ☎ 305/573–8221). ✉ *N.E. 2nd Ave. between 39th and 42nd Sts., Design District.* ⏲ *Weekdays 10–5; some stores by appointment.*

5 **Mildred and Claude Pepper Bayfront Park.** An oasis among the skyscrapers, this park extends east from busy, palm-lined Biscayne Boulevard to the bay. A landfill in the 1920s, it became the site of a World War II memorial in 1943, which was revised in 1980 to include the names of later war victims. Japanese sculptor Isamu Noguchi redesigned the park in 1989 to include two amphitheaters, a memorial to the *Challenger* space shuttle astronauts, and a fountain honoring the late Florida congressman Claude Pepper and his wife. At the park's north end, the Friendship Torch, dedicated in 1964, honors John F. Kennedy and includes plaques representing Peru, Bolivia, Venezuela, Ecuador, Colombia, and Panama—and an empty space where Cuba should be.

6 **Plaza Bolivar.** Flags of South and Central American countries fly, and there's a statue of Ponce de León and a plaque inscribed with A CUBAN SALUTE TO THE BICENTENNIAL. The plaque was presented by—according to the inscription—THE CUBANS WHO LEFT BEHIND FAMILY, FRIENDS AND ALL OUR POSSESSIONS IN SEARCH OF FREEDOM AND OPPORTUNITY. AND ONLY IN AMERICA, THE LAND OF ENDLESS OPPORTUNITY, HAVE WE FOUND THE RIGHTS THAT WE LOST IN OUR HOMELAND. ✉ *Biscayne Blvd. between 2nd and 3rd Sts., Downtown.*

OFF THE BEATEN PATH

**RUBELL FAMILY COLLECTION** – A must-see for contemporary-art lovers, the private collection of Mera and Don Rubell includes work by artists from the 1970s to the present, including Jeff Koons, Cindy Sherman, Damien Hirst, Keith Haring, and Ansel M. Keifer. It's housed in a 40,000-square-ft former Drug Enforcement Agency confiscation center. Exhibitions are rotated, and there are public programs November–May. ✉ *95 N.W. 29th St., between N. Miami Ave. and N.W. 1st Ave., near Design District, Downtown,* ☎ *305/573–6090.* 🎫 *Free.* ⏲ *Thurs.–Sat. 11–4 or by appointment.*

8 **U.S. Courthouse.** Built of keystone in 1931, the Neoclassical Revival courthouse originally housed Miami's main post office as well (the post office moved out in the 1980s). In what was once the second-floor central courtroom is *Law Guides Florida Progress,* a huge Depression-era mural by Denman Fink. Surrounding the central figure of a robed judge are several images that define the Florida of the 1930s: fish vendors, palm trees, beaches, and a Pan Am airplane winging off to Latin America. No cameras or tape recorders are allowed in the building. ✉ *300 N.E. 1st Ave., between N.E. 3rd and 4th Sts., Downtown,* ☎ *305/523–5075.* ⏲ *Building weekdays 8:30–5.*

# LITTLE HAVANA

First settled en masse by Cuban exiles 40 years ago, following that country's Communist revolution, Little Havana holds a potent brew of Latin cultures from throughout the Americas. This is a predominantly working-class area of recently arrived immigrants and elderly residents on fixed incomes, for as each exile generation prospers, it moves west. But the neighborhood is still the core of Miami's Hispanic community and a magnet for Anglos looking to immerse themselves in Latin culture. Little Havana, especially East Little Havana, brims with immigrant optimism, and new arrivals are welcomed every day. Spanish is the language that predominates, but don't be surprised if the cadence is less Cuban and more Salvadoran or Nicaraguan.

Abutting the Miami River and downtown Miami to the east (and Northwest 7th Street and Coral Way, to the north and south, respectively), Little Havana treats its western boundary on Southwest 27th Avenue as its point of entry. The main commercial zone is bounded by

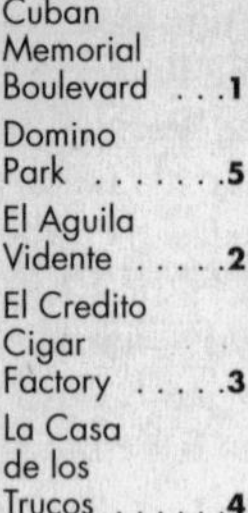


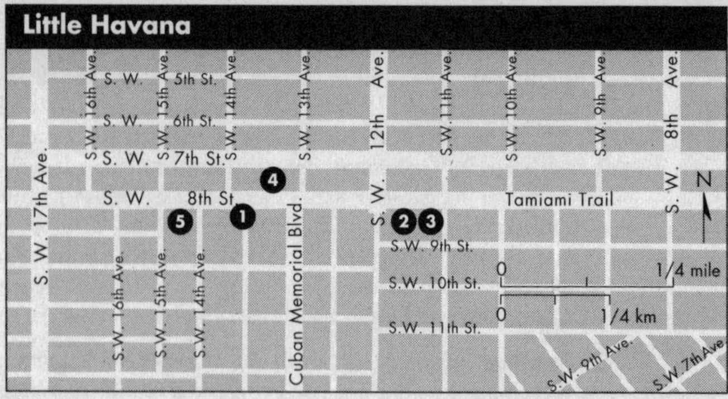


Northwest 1st Street, Southwest 9th Street, Ronald Reagan Avenue (Southwest 12th Avenue), and Teddy Roosevelt Boulevard (Southwest 17th Avenue). Calle Ocho, or Southwest 8th Street, is the axis of the neighborhood.

Little Havana sprawls over a number of old Miami neighborhoods first settled in the early 20th century, following Miami's incorporation in 1896. Suburbs sprang up west of the Miami River and south of Flagler Street's commerce. Riverside—as Little Havana was then known—quickly became home to well-heeled southern families, who were followed in the 1930s by Miami-Dade County's growing Jewish population. A predominantly Jewish community throughout the '40s and '50s, Little Havana was then home to jazz clubs that marqueed Nat King Cole and Count Basie and was also home to kosher butcher shops that eventually gave way to Cuban meat markets. Present-day residents live in streets lined with a mix of humble little houses, well-preserved coral-rock bungalows vernacular to the turn of the last century, and time-worn tenements.

The area began to redefine itself in the '50s, when Cubans opposed to Fulgencio Batista's dictatorship began trickling in, but it was Fidel Castro's takeover of Cuba in 1959 and the later Freedom Flights of the '60s and early '70s that indelibly altered the local landscape. Members of Cuba's middle class fled their homeland, bringing very little with them except an entrepreneurial spirit. They quickly filled the fading neighborhood's relatively cheap housing, as family and friends joined them. Soon, boarded-up stores reopened with the familiar merchant names of prerevolutionary Cuba, restaurants were dishing up Latin comfort food, and a bustling economy emerged.

In 1980 more change came to Little Havana when upward of 125,000 Cuban refugees flooded into South Florida during the exodus from the Port of Mariel. Many were poor and uneducated, and more than 10,000 came directly from Cuba's prisons and mental institutions. A run-down way station for Latin Americans headed toward bigger and better things, the area is Miami's version of Ellis Island, a jumping-off point for each new wave of immigrants. Indeed, Little Havana is now a misnomer. The influx of Cubans has been somewhat limited by U.S. immigration policy, but the *balseros* (rafters) still trickle in illegally. Now, most of the new arrivals are Central and South American refugees fleeing difficult economies and oppressive governments. As the political epicenter for the Latin American community, whatever the country, Little Havana's main drags—Flagler Street and Calle Ocho—are often sites of protests, demonstrations, and flag-waving, horn-honking, traffic-stopping marches. They frequently make international headlines, as in the recent case of Elián González, the Cuban youngster who arrived in South Florida via an inner tube, his mother perishing on the way.

In the neighborhood, corner bodegas seem derived from another place and time, and their regulars gather to share neighborhood gossip and political opinions. Elaborate, costly statues of saints stand in tiny, overgrown yards in front of dingy houses. Street vendors sell plastic bags filled with ripe tomatoes, peeled oranges, fat limes. Cuban cafeterias share the street with Nicaraguan bakeries and Central American taquerías.

Some of the restaurants host traditional flamenco performances and Sevillaña *tablaos* (dances performed on a wood-plank stage, using castanets), and some clubs feature recently arrived Cuban acts. Intimate neighborhood theaters host top-notch productions ranging from Spanish classics to contemporary satire. Throughout the year a variety of festivals commemorate Miami's Hispanic heritage, and residents from no fewer than five countries celebrate their homeland's independence days in Little Havana. If you're in Miami in March—and don't mind huge crowds—plan on attending the granddaddy of them all, the Calle Ocho Street Party. The 23-block extravaganza is part of Carnaval Miami and features top Latin entertainment. On the last Friday of every month, Little Havana takes its culture to the streets between 7 and 10 PM on Eighth Street at 15th Avenue for Cultural Fridays. Art expositions, music, and avant-garde street performances bring a young, hip crowd to the neighborhood.

*Numbers in the text correspond to numbers in the margin and on the Little Havana map.*

## A Good Walk

An ideal place to discover the area's flavor, both literally and figuratively, is along Calle Ocho (Southwest 8th Street), at the eastern end of Tamiami Trail between Southwest 12th and 27th avenues. You'll need to drive in, but definitely park, since the only way to really experience the neighborhood is on foot; metered spots are readily available, and it's not too hard to find a free spot on a side street. Throughout your walk make sure to stop in the sundry retail establishments; perhaps buy a breezy guayabera shirt—always in vogue in white cotton. It's hard to miss the record stores, whose speakers flood the street with the sounds of salsa and *danzones* (danceable Cuban music). Browse through neighborhood bookstores for Spanish titles from Gabriel García Marquez to Zoe Valdes, and others—you may even find some editions in English.

Start at Southwest 13th Avenue and Southwest 8th Street, at **Cuban Memorial Boulevard** ①. Memorials to Cuban patriots line the boulevard, and the plaza is the scene of frequent political rallies. On Mother's Day older women adorn a statue of the Virgin Mary with floral wreaths and join in song to honor her. Believers claim a miracle occurs here each midafternoon, when a beam of sunlight shoots through the foliage overhead directly onto the Christ child in the Virgin's arms. Religious faith of a different sort is evident near the kapok tree that towers over the boulevard: you may see an offering left by a Santero (practitioner of Santería) hoping to win the blessings of a saint.

On Calle Ocho to the east of the boulevard is **El Aguila Vidente** (The Seeing Eagle) ②, one of many neighborhood *botánicas* that cater to Santeros. The shop welcomes the respectfully curious. A particularly worthwhile stop is next door at the **El Credito Cigar Factory** ③. At this family-owned business, one of about a half-dozen cigar factories in the neighborhood, employees deftly hand-roll more than a million stogies each year. If you enjoy cigars, you'll be more than impressed by the ones they sell here.

On Calle Ocho, between Southwest 13th and 17th avenues, you'll find the Walkway of the Stars. The Latin version of its Hollywood namesake, the strip of sidewalk embedded with stars honors many of the world's top Hispanic celebrities, among them salsa queen Celia Cruz, crooner Julio Iglesias, and superstar Gloria Estefan. The newly renovated Tower Theater is a center for cultural activities and headquarters of the Hispanic Film Festival, held each spring. Stop in at **La Casa de los Trucos** ④, a magic store where the owners sometimes demonstrate their skills. Farther west on Calle Ocho is **Domino Park** ⑤, at 15th Avenue. The game tables are always two deep with guayabera-clad men—it wasn't until the last decade that the park's male domino aficionados even allowed women into their domain. The colorful backdrop, a mural of world leaders, was painted by schoolchildren in honor of the Summit of the Americas held in Miami in 1994. A display outside the park's doors has photos of the City of Miami dating to the early 1900s.

TIMING

If a quick multicultural experience is your goal, set aside an hour or two to do this tour on foot. For real ethnic immersion, allow more time; eating is a must, as well as a peek at the area's residential streets lined with distinctive homes. Especially illuminating are Little Havana walking and bike tours led by Dr. Paul George (1345 S.W. 14th St., Miami, ☎ 305/858–6021), a history professor at Miami-Dade Community College and past president of the Florida Historical Society.

## Sights to See

❶ **Cuban Memorial Boulevard.** Two blocks in the heart of Little Havana are filled with monuments to Cuba's freedom fighters. Among the memorials are the *Eternal Torch of the Brigade 2506,* commemorating those who were killed in the failed Bay of Pigs invasion of 1961, a bust of 19th-century hero Antonio Maceo, and a bas-relief map of Cuba depicting each of its *municipios.* There's also a bronze statue in honor of Tony Izquierdo, who participated in the Bay of Pigs invasion, served in Nicaragua's Somozan forces, and interestingly enough was also on the CIA payroll. ✉ *S.W. 8th St. at S.W. 13th Ave., Little Havana.*

❺ **Domino Park.** Officially named Máximo Gomez Park, it's really known as a gathering place for Miami's domino players. Anti-Castro politics are as fierce as the clacking of domino tiles and as thick as the cigar smoke among the Cuban men who spend hours at the tables. Unwelcome in the past, women have started to make inroads into this macho setting. Although some of the male regulars seem less than friendly, others seem happy to compete with any good player with a few dollars to stake. ✉ *S.W. 8th St. at S.W. 15th Ave., Little Havana.* ⏲ *Daily 9–6.*

❷ **El Aguila Vidente (The Seeing Eagle).** This store offers one-stop shopping for practitioners of Santería, an Afro-Cuban religion that incorporates some tenets of Catholicism. Santeros worship patron saints, both evil and good, by making offerings; the saints are said to bestow love, money, and even revenge. Some Santeros are uncomfortable with too many questions, so practice tact. ✉ *1122 S.W. 8th St., between 11th and 12th Aves., Little Havana,* ☎ *305/854–4086.* ⏲ *Mon.–Sat. 11–7.*

❸ **El Credito Cigar Factory.** Many of the workers at this family business dating back three generations learned their trade in prerevolutionary Cuba. Today the tobacco leaf they use comes primarily from the Dominican Republic and Mexico and the wrappers from Connecticut, making theirs a truly multinational product. A walk-in humidor has more than 40 brands, favored by customers such as Arnold Schwarzenegger, Bill Clinton, Robert De Niro, and Bill Cosby. ✉ *1106 S.W. 8th St., near S.W. 11th Ave., Little Havana,* ☎ *305/858–4162.* ⏲ *Weekdays 8–6, Sat. 8–4.*

OFF THE BEATEN PATH

**ELIAN GONZALEZ'S HOUSE** – This humble two-bedroom home was where 6-year-old Gonzalez stayed for nearly six months after surviving a raft journey from Cuba that killed his mother. From this same house, he was removed by federal agents in a predawn raid that ultimately united him with his father, who took him home to Cuba. The Miami relatives have since moved, but bought the property to turn it into a shrine and museum. ✉ *2319 N.W. 2nd St., at N.W 23rd Ave., Little Havana.* *Free.* ⏲ *Sun. 10–6.*

❹ **La Casa de los Trucos.** This popular magic store first opened in Cuba in the 1930s. Its exiled owners reopened it here in the '70s, and when they're in, they perform magic acts for customers. ✉ *1343 S.W. 8th St., Little Havana,* ☎ *305/858–5029.* ⏲ *Mon.–Sat. 10–6.*

NEED A BREAK?

Sorry, there's no Starbucks in Little Havana—the locals probably wouldn't touch the stuff, anyway—but everywhere are walk-up windows peddling the quick energy of thimble-size *café cubano* for as little as 35¢. The locals call it *un cafecito* (literally, a small coffee), but be warned that it's high-octane and is sure to keep you going through this tour. In the mood for something refreshing? Try **Las Pinareños** *frutería* (✉ 1334 S.W. 8 St., Little Havana) for fresh cold coconut juice served in a whole coconut, mango juice, or other *jugos* (juices).

# COCONUT GROVE

Eclectic and intriguing, Miami's Coconut Grove has from the beginning stayed true to its nature—and to its natural surroundings. First inhabited in 1834, the oldest settlement in South Florida was formally established in 1873, a full two decades before Miami arrived on the scene. By then the village was already home to a multicultural collection of new residents; Bahamian blacks, white Key Westers (called "Conchs"), and New England intellectuals lured to the balmy sliver of a village on pristine Biscayne Bay. The community they built attracted artists, writers, and scientists, who established winter homes here. By the end of World War I more people listed in *Who's Who* had addresses in Coconut Grove than in any other place in the United States. It might be considered the tropical equivalent of New York's Greenwich Village.

Just as it was 80 years ago, Coconut Grove is still a haven for writers and artists. Confined within a relatively small area, the Miami neighborhood has never quite outgrown its image as a small village, even though it covers 3 square mi. And the Grove has changed over the decades. In the 1960s it went through a hippie period, the 1970s brought out a laid-back funkiness, and it withstood an invasion of new-wave teenyboppers in the 1980s. Things seem to have balanced out, and today the tone is upscale, urban, and fun.

During the day it's business as usual in Coconut Grove, much like in any other Miami neighborhood. But in the evening, especially on weekends, it seems as if someone flips a switch and the streets come alive. Locals and tourists jam into small boutiques, sidewalk cafés, and stores lodged in two massive retail-entertainment complexes. For blocks in every direction, students, honeymooning couples, families,

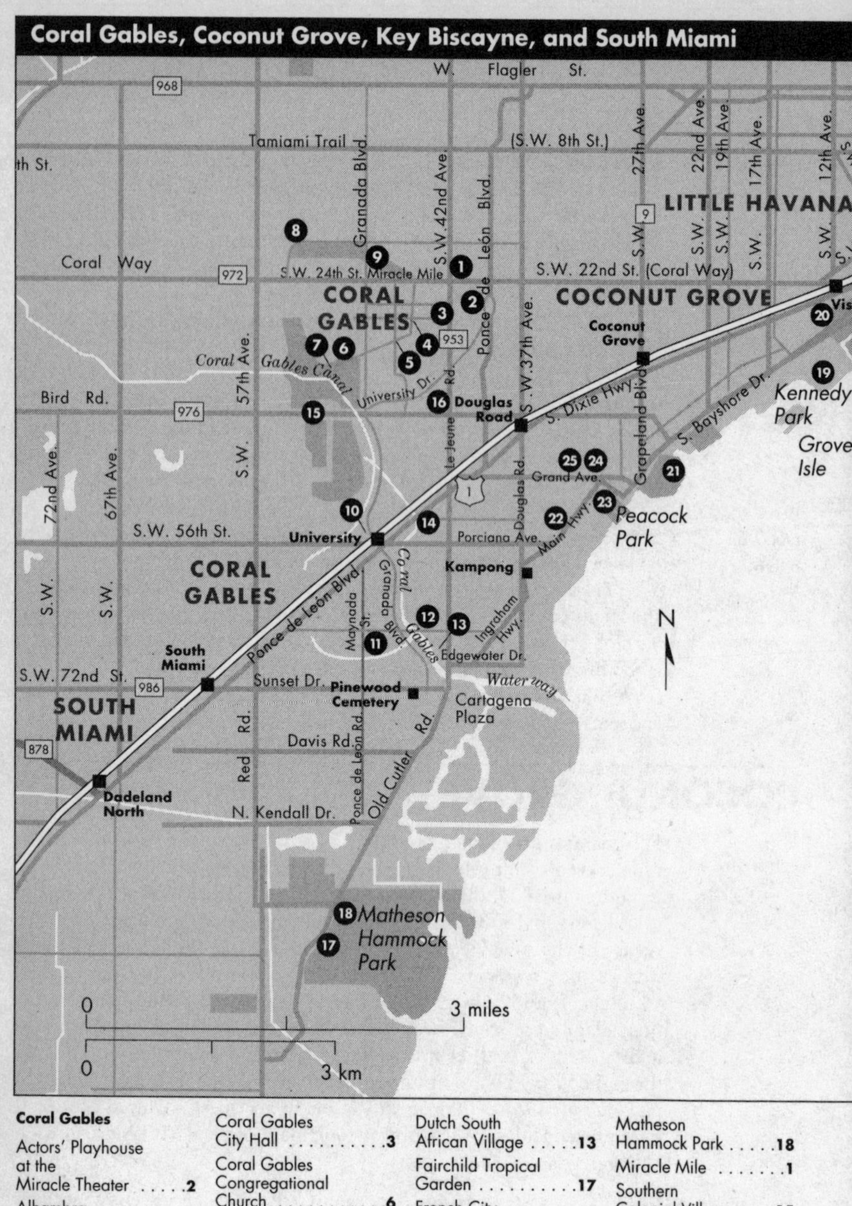


**Coral Gables**

- Actors' Playhouse at the Miracle Theater . . . . . 2
- Alhambra Water Tower . . . . . . . 8
- Biltmore Hotel . . . . . . 7
- Chinese Village . . . . 14
- Coral Gables City Hall . . . . . . . . . . 3
- Coral Gables Congregational Church . . . . . . . . . . . 6
- Coral Gables Merrick House and Gardens . . . . . . . 9
- De Soto Plaza and Fountain . . . . . . . 5
- Dutch South African Village . . . . . 13
- Fairchild Tropical Garden . . . . . . . . . . 17
- French City Village . . . . . . . . . . 11
- French Country Village . . . . . . . . . . 12
- French Normandy Village . . . . . . . . . . 16
- Matheson Hammock Park . . . . . 18
- Miracle Mile . . . . . . . 1
- Southern Colonial Village . . . . 15
- University of Miami . . . . . . . . . . . 10
- Venetian Pool . . . . . . . 4

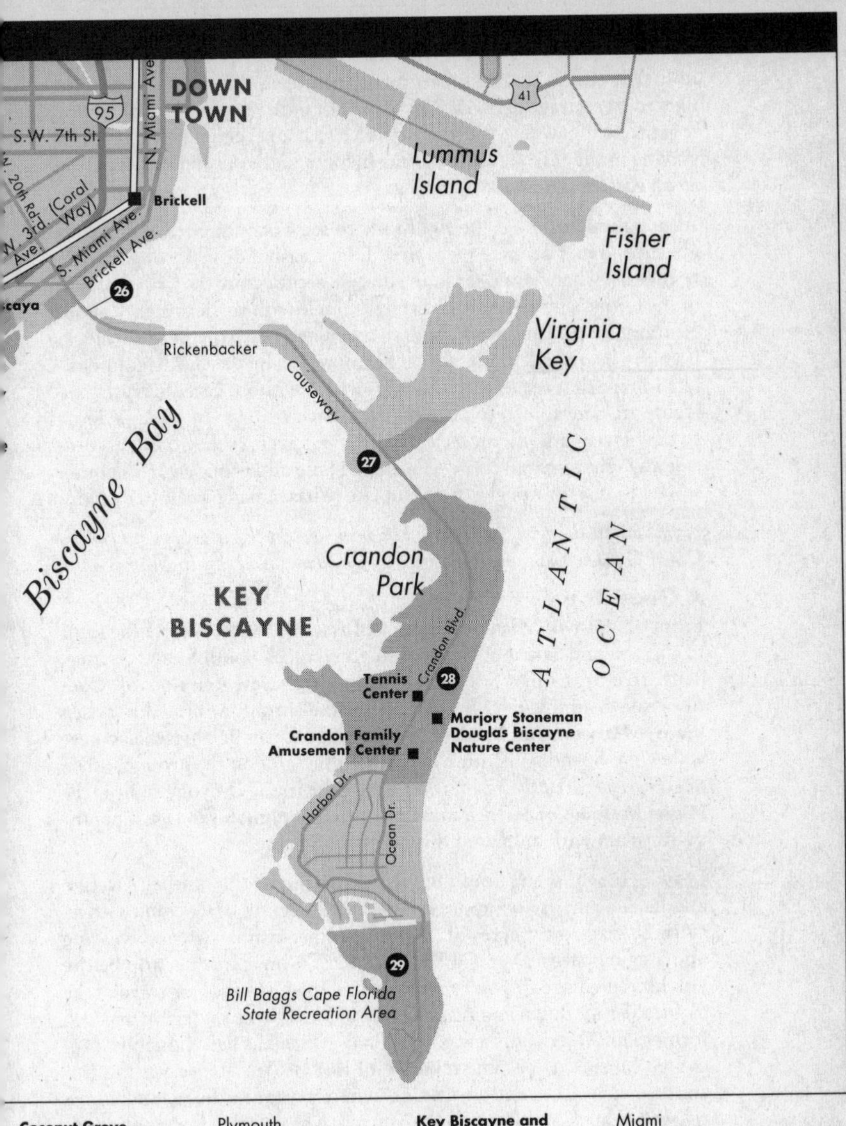


**Coconut Grove**

Barnacle State Historic Site . . . . . . . **23**

CocoWalk . . . . . . . . **24**

Miami City Hall . . . . **21**

Miami Museum of Science and Space Transit Planetarium . . . **20**

Plymouth Congregational Church . . . . . . . . . . **22**

Streets of Mayfair . . . . . . . . . . **25**

Vizcaya Museum and Gardens . . . . . . . . . **19**

**Key Biscayne and Virginia Key**

Bill Baggs Cape Florida State Recreation Area . . . . . . . . . . . . **29**

Crandon Park . . . . . **28**

Miami Seaquarium . . . . . . . **27**

Old Rickenbacker Causeway Bridge . . . **26**

and prosperous retirees flow in and out of a mix of galleries, restaurants, bars, bookstores, comedy clubs, and theaters. With this weekly influx of traffic, parking can pose a problem. There's a new well-lighted city garage at 3315 Rice Street, or look for police to direct you to parking lots where you'll pay $5–$10 for an evening's slot. If you're staying in the Grove, leave the car behind, and your night will get off to an easier start.

Although nighttime is the right time to see Coconut Grove, don't neglect the area's daytime pleasures. Take a casual drive through neighborhoods, where you'll see in the diverse architecture the varied origins of the Grove's pioneers. Posh estates mingle with rustic cottages, modest frame homes, and stark modern dwellings, often on the same block. If you're into horticulture, you'll be impressed by the Garden of Eden–like foliage that seems to grow everywhere without care. In truth, residents are determined to keep up the Grove's village-in-a-jungle look, so they lavish attention on exotic plantings even as they battle to protect any remaining native vegetation. These and other efforts demonstrate just how thoroughly Coconut Grove has remained true to its roots.

*Numbers in the text correspond to numbers in the margin and on the Coral Gables, Coconut Grove, Key Biscayne, and South Miami map.*

## A Good Tour

From downtown Miami take Brickell Avenue south. Follow the signs to Vizcaya and Coconut Grove, and you'll reach South Miami Avenue. This street turns into South Bayshore Drive a few miles down. Continue south and watch on your left for the entrance to the don't-miss **Vizcaya Museum and Gardens** ⑲, an estate with an Italian Renaissance–style villa. Spend some time in the building and on the grounds; then head less than 100 yards farther down the road. On your right is the **Miami Museum of Science and Space Transit Planetarium** ⑳, a hands-on museum with animated displays for all ages.

Leaving the museum, South Bayshore switches from four lanes to two and back again as you approach the village center of Coconut Grove. With 28 waterfront acres of Australian pine, lush lawns, and walking and jogging paths, David T. Kennedy Park is one pleasant stop before you hit the village. If you're interested in the history of air travel, take a quick detour down Pan American Boulevard to see the 1930s art deco former Pan American Airways terminal, which has been horribly "renovated" inside to become **Miami City Hall** ㉑. You'll also see the Coconut Grove Convention Center, where antiques, boat, and home shows are held, and Dinner Key Marina, where seabirds soar and sailboats ride at anchor. As South Bayshore curves to the right, you'll see placid Peacock Park in front of you, a bayfront oasis with boardwalks, and across the street on your right, a 1921 oolitic limestone building called The Housekeepers Club, listed on the National Register of Historic Places.

South Bayshore heads directly into McFarlane Road, which takes a sharp right into the center of the action. Forsake the earthly for a moment and turn left on Main Highway, driving less than a half mile to Devon Road and the coral-rock **Plymouth Congregational Church** ㉒.

Return to Main Highway and to the historic village of Coconut Grove. As you reenter the village center, note on your left the Coconut Grove Playhouse. On your right, beyond the benches and shelter, is the entrance to the **Barnacle State Historic Site** ㉓, a residence built by Commodore Ralph Munroe in 1891. The house and grounds offer a glimpse into Miami's early Anglo years. After getting your fill of history, relax and spend the evening mingling with Coconut Grove's artists and intellectuals. Shop along Grand Avenue and Mary Street, and be sure to check out **CocoWalk** ㉔ and the **Streets of Mayfair** ㉕, two collections of stores and restaurants.

TIMING

Plan on devoting from six to eight hours to enjoy Vizcaya, other bayfront sights, and the village's shops, restaurants, and nightlife.

## Sights to See

㉓ **Barnacle State Historic Site.** A pristine bayfront manse sandwiched between cramped luxury developments, Barnacle is Miami's oldest house still standing on its original foundation. To get here, you'll hike along an old buggy trail through a tropical hardwood hammock and landscaped lawn leading to Biscayne Bay. Built in 1891 by Florida's first snowbird—New Yorker Commodore Ralph Munroe—the large home, built of timber Munroe salvaged from wrecked ships, has many original furnishings, a broad sloping roof, and deeply recessed verandas that channel sea breezes into the house. If your timing is right, you may catch one of the monthly Moonlight Concerts, and the old fashioned picnic on the Fourth of July is popular. ✉ *3485 Main Hwy., Coconut Grove,* ☎ *305/448–9445,* WEB *www.barnacle.cjb.net.* 💵 *$1, concerts $5.* ⏲ *Fri.–Mon. 9–4; tours 10, 11:30, 1, and 2:30, but call ahead; group tours (10 or more) Tues.–Thurs. by reservation; concerts on evenings near the full moon, 6–9, call ahead for exact dates.*

㉔ **CocoWalk.** This indoor-outdoor mall has three floors of nearly 40 name-brand (Victoria's Secret, Gap, Banana Republic, etc.) and independent shops that stay open almost as late as its popular restaurants and clubs. Kiosks with beads, incense, herbs, and other small items are scattered around the ground level; street entertainers hold court on weekends; and the movie theaters and nightspots are upstairs. If you're ready for an evening of touristy people-watching, this is the place. ✉ *3015 Grand Ave., Coconut Grove,* ☎ *305/444–0777,* WEB *www.cocowalk.com.* ⏲ *Sun.–Thurs. 11 AM–10 PM, Fri.–Sat. 11 AM–midnight.*

**The Kampong.** With nearly 10 acres of exquisite, flamboyant flowering trees and fruits, this former home and garden of horticulturist Dr. David Fairchild is a one of five gardens administered by the Hawaii-based National Tropical Botanical Garden. ✉ *4013 Douglas Rd., Coconut Grove,* ☎ *305/442–7169,* WEB *www.ntbg.org/kampong.html.* 💵 *$10.* ⏲ *Tours by appointment, second Sat. Sept.–Apr.*

㉑ **Miami City Hall.** Built in 1934 as the terminal for the Pan American Airways seaplane base at Dinner Key, the building retains its nautical-style art deco trim. Sadly, the interior is generic government, but a 1938 Pan Am menu on display (with filet mignon, *petit pois au beurre,* and Jenny Lind pudding) lets you know Miami officials appreciate whence they came. ✉ *3500 Pan American Dr., Coconut Grove,* ☎ *305/250–5400.* ⏲ *Weekdays 8–5.*

OFF THE BEATEN PATH

**MIAMI METRO ZOO–** Don't miss a visit to this top-notch zoo, 14 mi south of Miami, which is the only subtropical zoo in the continental U.S. Its 290 acres are home to about 800 animals that roam on islands surrounded by moats. Take the monorail for a cool overview, then walk around to take a closer look at such attractions as the Tiger Temple, where white tigers roam; the African Plains exhibit, where giraffes, ostriches, and zebras graze in a simulated natural habitat; and the refreshing Asian River Life exhibit, with real komodo dragons. There's also a petting zoo for children (with a new meerkat exhibit) and interactive opportunities, like at Dr. Wilde's World. Kids can also touch Florida animals such as alligators and opossums at the Ecology Theater. An educational and entertaining Wildlife Show is offered three times daily. In addition to standard fare, the snack bar offers local favorites such as Cuban sandwiches, arepas, and Cuban coffee—and cold beer. ✉ *12400 Coral Reef Dr. (S.W. 152nd St.), Richmond Heights, Miami,* ☎ *305/251–0400.* 🎟 *$8, 45-min tram tour $2.* ⏲ *Daily 9:30–5:30, last admission at 4.* WEB *www.magni.com/MetroZoo/*

---

20 **Miami Museum of Science and Space Transit Planetarium.** This museum is chock-full of hands-on sound, gravity, and electricity displays for children and adults alike. A wildlife center houses native Florida snakes, turtles, tortoises, and birds of prey. Outstanding traveling exhibits appear throughout the year, and virtual reality, life-science demonstrations, and Internet technology are on hand every day. Its recent association with the Smithsonian Institution means top-notch exhibitions and, within the next few years, the creation of the waterfront Science Center of the Americas, which will feature the latest technology; interactive exhibits on topics such as dinosaurs, ecosystems, and the ancient Americas; large-screen theaters; and research and education facilities. Stick around after dark on Friday and Saturday nights for the laser-light rock-and-roll shows presented in the planetarium. ✉ *3280 S. Miami Ave., Coconut Grove,* ☎ *305/854–4247 museum; 305/854–2222 planetarium information,* WEB *www.miamisci.org.* 🎟 *Museum exhibits, planetarium shows, and wildlife center $6–10; laser show $6.* ⏲ *Daily 10–6, closed Thanksgiving and Christmas.*

---

NEED A BREAK? Coconut Grove is packed with places to eat, from humble to grand. One congenial waterfront choice is **Monty's Stone Crab–Seafood House** (✉ 2550 S. Bayshore Dr., Coconut Grove, ☎ 305/441–2100), for fresh seafood or delectable stone crab claws.

---

22 **Plymouth Congregational Church.** Opened in 1917, this coral-rock church is built in the Mission style. The front door, made of hand-carved walnut and oak with wrought-iron fittings, came from an early 17th-century monastery in the Pyrénées. Also on the 11-acre grounds are the first schoolhouse in Miami-Dade County (one room), which was moved to this property, and the site of the original Coconut Grove waterworks and electric works. ✉ *3400 Devon Rd., Coconut Grove,* ☎ *305/444–6521.* ⏲ *Weekdays 9–4:30, Sun. service 10 AM.*

25 **Streets of Mayfair.** Home to the *other* News Café, the Limited, Borders, and other shops and restaurants, this mall is best known for its entertainment venues: a comedy club; and the Iguana Cantina, a nightclub. On Saturday, there's a farmers market with fresh produce, flowers, baked goods, and handicrafts. ✉ *2911 Grand Ave., Coconut Grove,* ☎ *305/448–1700,* WEB *www.streetsofmayfair.com.* ⏲ *Sun.–Thurs. 11–10, Fri.–Sat. 11–11.*

★ 19 **Vizcaya Museum and Gardens.** Of the 10,000 people living in Miami between 1912 and 1916, about 1,000 of them were gainfully employed by Chicago industrialist James Deering to build this Italian Renaissance–style winter residence. Once comprising 180 acres, the grounds now occupy a 30-acre tract that includes a native hammock and more than 10 acres of formal gardens, with fountains overlooking Biscayne Bay. The house, open to the public, contains 70 rooms, 34 of which are filled with paintings, sculpture, antique furniture, and other fine and decorative arts. The pieces date from the 15th through the 19th centuries and represent the Renaissance, Baroque, Rococo, and Neoclassical movements. So unusual and impressive is Vizcaya that visitors have included many major heads of state. Guided tours are available. Moonlight tours, in particular, offer a unique look at the gardens;

call for reservations. ✉ *3251 S. Miami Ave., Coconut Grove,* ☎ *305/250–9133,* WEB *www.vizcayamuseum.com.* 🎫 *$10.* ⏲ *House and ticket booth daily 9:30–4:30, garden daily 9:30–5:30.*

# CORAL GABLES

You can easily spot Coral Gables from the window of a Miami-bound jetliner—just look for the massive orange tower of the Biltmore Hotel rising from a lush green carpet of trees, concealing the city's gracious homes. The canopy is as much a part of this planned city as its distinctive architecture, all attributed to the vision of George E. Merrick nearly 100 years ago.

The story of this city began in 1911, when Merrick inherited 1,600 acres of citrus and avocado groves from his father. Through judicious investment he nearly doubled the tract to 3,000 acres by 1921. Merrick dreamed of building an American Venice here, complete with canals and homes. Working from this vision, he began designing a city based on centuries-old prototypes from Mediterranean countries. Merrick embraced the Garden City theory of urban planning that was so popular in the 1920s and planned lush landscaping, magnificent neighborhood entrances, and broad boulevards named for Spanish explorers, cities, and provinces. Relying on the advice of his uncle, artist Denman Fink, Merrick hired architects trained abroad to create neighborhoods, or villages, with a single architectural or historical style, such as Florida pioneer, Chinese, French, Dutch South African, and Italian.

Unfortunately for Merrick, the devastating no-name hurricane of 1926, followed by the Great Depression, prevented him from fulfilling many of his plans. He died at 54, an employee of the post office. His city languished until after World War II, but then it grew rapidly. Today, Coral Gables has a population of about 42,000. In its bustling downtown, more than 140 multinational companies maintain headquarters or regional offices, and the University of Miami campus in the southern part of the Gables brings a youthful vibrancy to the area—the median age of residents here is 36. A southern branch of the city extends down the shore of Biscayne Bay through neighborhoods threaded with canals. The gorgeous Fairchild Tropical Garden and beachfront Matheson Hammock Park dominate this part of the Gables.

Like much of Greater Miami, Coral Gables has realized the aesthetic and economic importance of historic preservation and has passed a Mediterranean design ordinance that rewards businesses for maintaining their buildings' original architectural style. Even the street signs are preserved for their historical value. These ground-level markers are hard to see in daylight, impossible to see at night, but such inconveniences can be tolerated, and not only to honor the memory of Merrick. The community of broad boulevards and Spanish-Mediterranean architecture is entirely justified in calling itself the City Beautiful.

*Numbers in the text correspond to numbers in the margin and on the Coral Gables, Coconut Grove, Key Biscayne, and South Miami map.*

### A Good Tour

Heading south from downtown Miami on Brickell Avenue, turn right onto Coral Way, a historic roadway characterized by an arch of banyan trees, until you reach the grand entrance onto **Miracle Mile** ①. Actually only a half mile long, this stretch of Coral Way, from Douglas Road (Southwest 37th Avenue) to Le Jeune Road (Southwest 42nd Avenue), is the heart of downtown Coral Gables. Park your car and take time to explore it on foot. Cafeterias stand cheek by jowl with top-notch bistros, and independent bookstores share customers with major book chains. There's a heavy concentration of bridal shops here, as well as ever-changing owner-operated boutiques that are a welcome change from typical mall fare.

Back on wheels, head west on Coral Way past the plentiful shops, and you'll pass the 1930s **Actors' Playhouse at the Miracle Theater** ② on your left. Cross Le Jeune Road and bear right to continue on Coral Way, catching an eyeful of the ornate 1928 Spanish Renaissance **Coral Gables City Hall** ③ and the adjacent Merrick Park. Turn left at Toledo Street and continue for four blocks until you reach the gates surrounding the Merrick-designed **Venetian Pool** ④, which Esther Williams made famous. There's parking on your right, and immediately ahead is the **De Soto Plaza and Fountain** ⑤, also Merrick-designed.

Head to 12 o'clock (the opposite side) of the roundabout surrounding the fountain and stay on De Soto for a magnificent vista of the Merrick-designed Biltmore Hotel. Before you reach the hotel, you'll see the **Coral Gables Congregational Church** ⑥, on your right, one of the first churches built in this planned community. At the **Biltmore Hotel** ⑦ there's parking to the right; enjoy the grounds and public areas. After you've visited the hotel, double back to the De Soto Fountain, this time circling the roundabout to 9 o'clock and entering Granada Boulevard. Several blocks away you'll arrive at the Granada Golf Course—the oldest operating course in Florida—where you'll turn left onto North Greenway Drive. As you cruise along the street, notice the stands of banyan trees that separate the fairways. At the end of the golf course the road makes a horseshoe bend, but continue west and cross Alhambra Circle to loop around the restored **Alhambra Water Tower** ⑧, a city landmark dating from 1924. By the way—it's Merrick-designed.

Return to Alhambra and follow it south to the next light, at Coral Way, where you can turn left and ogle the beautifully maintained Spanish-style homes from the 1920s. Although there is only a small sign to announce it, at the corner of Coral Way and Toledo streets is the **Coral Gables Merrick House and Gardens** ⑨, Merrick's boyhood home. After a stop there, take a right back onto Coral, turn left on Granada, and follow its winding way south past Bird Road; you'll eventually reach Ponce de León Boulevard. Turn right and follow the boulevard until you reach the entrance to the main campus of the **University of Miami** ⑩. Turn right at the first stoplight (Stanford Drive) to enter the campus, and park in the lot on your right, which is designated for visitors to the Lowe Art Museum, where you can view fine art.

Now take a drive through Merrick's internationally themed Gables neighborhoods, which he called villages. He planned these residential areas, some of which are very small, to contrast with the Mediterranean look of the rest of the city. From Lowe Art Museum, cross Ponce De León and follow Maynada Street south to Hardee Road. Turn left on Hardee; between Leonardo and Cellini streets is **French City Village** ⑪. Continuing east on Hardee, you'll pass **French Country Village** ⑫ between San Vincente and Maggiore streets. When you reach Le Jeune, turn right and drive seven blocks south to Riviera Drive to see **Dutch South African Village** ⑬. Turn around and drive north on Le Jeune, crossing Poinciana Avenue and proceeding three more blocks to Castania Avenue, on your left. Two blocks in, at the corner of Riviera, is **Chinese Village** ⑭. Return once again to Le Jeune, take a left, cross Dixie Highway, and turn left on Blue Road. Blue wends its way west through Riviera Country Club to Santa Maria Street, where you'll turn right. As you head north through the golf course toward Bird you'll encounter **Southern Colonial Village** ⑮, also known as Florida Pioneer Village.

When you reach Bird, take a right and proceed back to Le Jeune. Turn left on Le Jeune and drive four blocks north to Viscaya Avenue. If you turn right here, you'll shortly reach **French Normandy Village** ⑯.

Returning to Le Jeune, you can head north, back to Miracle Mile, or south, to scenic Old Cutler Road. Old Cutler Road curves down through the uplands of southern Florida's coastal ridge toward the 83-acre **Fairchild Tropical Garden** ⑰. After admiring the tropical flora, backtrack a quarter mile north on Old Cutler Road to the entrance of the lovely **Matheson Hammock Park** ⑱ and its beach.

TIMING

To see all the sights described here, you'll need two full days. Strolling Miracle Mile should take a bit more than an hour unless you plan to shop (don't forget the side streets); in that case, allow four hours. Save time—perhaps an hour or two—for a refreshing dip at the Venetian Pool, and plan to spend at least an hour getting acquainted with the Biltmore, longer if you'd like to order a drink and linger poolside or enjoy the elaborate Sunday brunch. Allow an hour to visit the Lowe Art Museum and another hour for the drive through the villages. You'll need a minimum of two hours to do Fairchild Tropical Garden justice, and if you want to spend time at the beach, Matheson Hammock Park will require at least another two hours.

## Sights to See

❷ **Actors' Playhouse at the Miracle Theater.** The 1940s-era movie house was renovated in the late 1990s and now stages theatrical productions. The majority of performances here are good family fare, with theater pros presenting shows like *Man of La Mancha, Pajama Game,* and *West Side Story.* There are productions of musical theater for younger audiences in the 300-seat Children's Balcony Theatre. ✉ *280 Miracle Mile, near Salzedo, Coral Gables,* ☎ *305/444–9293,* WEB *www.actorsplayhouse.org.*

❽ **Alhambra Water Tower.** Finished in 1924, this city landmark (which used to store water) has a decorative Moorish-style exterior. After more than 50 years of disuse and neglect, the lighthouselike tower was completely restored in 1993, with a copper-rib dome and playful multicolor frescoes. It remains empty and unused. ✉ *Alhambra Circle, Greenway Ct., and Ferdinand St., Coral Gables.*

★ ❼ **Biltmore Hotel.** Bouncing back stunningly from dark days as an army hospital, this hotel has become the jewel of Coral Gables—a dazzling architectural gem with a colorful past. First opened in 1926, it was a hotspot for the rich and glamorous of the Jazz Age until it was converted to an Army–Air Force regional hospital in 1942. The Veterans Administration continued to operate the hospital after World War II, until 1968. Then the Biltmore lay vacant for nearly 20 years before it underwent extensive renovations and reopened as a luxury hotel in 1987. Its 16-story tower, like the Freedom Tower in downtown Miami, is a replica of Seville's Giralda Tower. The magnificent pool, the largest hotel pool in the continental United States, is steeped in history—Johnny Weissmuller of Tarzan fame was a lifeguard there, and in the 1930s grand aquatic galas featuring alligator wrestling, synchronized swimming, and bathing beauties drew thousands. More recently, it was President Clinton's preferred place to stay and golf. To the west is the Biltmore Country Club, a richly ornamented Beaux Arts–style structure with a superb colonnade and courtyard; it was reincorporated into the hotel in 1989. On Sunday free tours are offered at 1:30, 2:30, and 3:30. ✉ *1200 Anastasia Ave., near De Soto Blvd., Coral Gables,* ☎ *305/445–1926,* WEB *www.biltmorehotel.com.*

14 **Chinese Village.** These eight homes, intended to resemble a traditional Chinese residential compound, are easily the most exotic of Merrick's creations, since his Persian and Tangiers villages never got past the drawing board. Their designer, Henry Killam Murphy, was an expert in Chinese architecture; he also designed several universities in China. Among the borrowed architectural elements that set these homes apart are the latticework on balconies, the blue-tile eaves and roofs, and the window grills. Notice the bamboolike ornamentation on the concrete-and-stucco wall that defines the block. ⊠ *5100 blocks of Riviera Dr. and Maggiore St. between Sansovino and Castania Aves., Coral Gables.*

3 **Coral Gables City Hall.** This 1928 building has a three-tier tower topped with a clock and a 500-pound bell. A mural by Denman Fink (George Merrick's uncle and artistic adviser during the planning of Coral Gables) inside the dome ceiling on the second floor depicts the four seasons. Although not as well known as Maxfield Parrish, Fink clearly shares his contemporary's utopian vision. Far more attractive (at least on the outside) than many modern city halls, this municipal building also displays paintings, photos, and advertisements touting 1920s Coral Gables. The Junior Orange Bowl parade starts here in late December every year, and a farmers market runs on Saturday 8 AM–1 PM, mid-January through the end of March. ⊠ *405 Biltmore Way, at Hernando Ave., Coral Gables,* ☎ *305/446–6800.* ⏲ *Weekdays 8–5.*

6 **Coral Gables Congregational Church.** With George Merrick as a charter member (he donated the land on which it stands), this parish was organized in 1923. Rumor has it Merrick built this small church, the first in the Gables, in honor of his father, a Congregational minister. The original interiors are still in magnificent condition, and a popular jazz series is held here. ⊠ *3010 De Soto Blvd., at Anastasia Ave., Coral Gables,* ☎ *305/448–7421.* ⏲ *Weekdays 8:30–7, Sun. services at 9:15 AM and 10:45 AM.*

9 **Coral Gables Merrick House and Gardens.** In 1976 the city of Coral Gables acquired George Merrick's boyhood home. Restored to its 1920s appearance, it contains Merrick family furnishings and artwork. The breezy veranda and oolitic limestone construction—also called coral rock—are architectural details you'll see repeated on many of the grand homes along Coral Way. ⊠ *907 Coral Way, at Toledo St., Coral Gables,* ☎ *305/460–5361.* 🎟 *House $5, grounds free.* ⏲ *House Wed. and Sun. 1–4; grounds daily 8–dusk. Also by appointment.*

5 **De Soto Plaza and Fountain.** Water flows from the mouths of four faces sculpted on a classical column that stands on a pedestal in this Denman Fink–designed fountain from the early 1920s. The closed eyes of the face looking west symbolize the day's end. ⊠ *Intersection of Granada Blvd. and Sevilla Ave., Coral Gables.*

13 **Dutch South African Village.** Marion Syms Wyeth designed these five homes to recall Dutch South Africa; they're distinguished by their white-stucco walls, round windows, and ornamented facades. ⊠ *Le Jeune Rd. at Maya Ave., Coral Gables.*

OFF THE BEATEN PATH

**EVERGLADES ALLIGATOR FARM –** Here's your chance to see gators, gators, gators—2,500 or so—and other wildlife, of course. Alligator wrestling, reptile shows, and other animal exhibits are here. You can also take airboat rides (they're not allowed inside Everglades National Park) and see blue herons, snowy egrets, and perhaps a rare roseate spoonbill. It's a little over 30 mi south of Miami, just south of the former pioneer town of Homestead. ⊠ *40351 S.W. 192 Ave., Florida City,* ☎ *305/247–2628,* WEB *www.everglades.com.* 🎟 *$14.50 includes airboat tour.* ⏲ *Daily 9–6.*

★ 17 **Fairchild Tropical Garden.** With 83 acres of lakes, sunken gardens, a 560-ft vine pergola, orchids, bellflowers, coral trees, bougainvillea, rare palms, and flowering trees, Fairchild is the largest tropical botanical garden in the continental United States. The tram tour highlights the best of Southern Florida's flora; then set off exploring on your own. The newest addition is the 2-acre rain forest exhibit, with tropical rain forest plants from around the world amid a waterfall and stream. The conservatory, Windows to the Tropics, houses rare tropical plants, including the Titan Arum (*Amorphophallus titanum*), a fast-growing variety that attracted thousands of visitors when it bloomed in 1998. (It was only the sixth documented bloom in this country in the 20th century.) The Keys Coastal Habitat provides food and shelter to resident and migrant birds. Check out the Montgomery Botanical Center, a research facility devoted to palms and cycads. Spicing up Fairchild's calendar are plant sales, moonlight strolls, symphony concerts, and genuinely special events year-round, such as the Ramble in November and the International Mango Festival the second weekend in July. The excellent bookstore–gift shop carries books on gardening and horticulture, and the Garden Café serves sandwiches and, seasonally, smoothies made from the garden's own crop of tropical fruits. ✉ *10901 Old Cutler Rd., Coral Gables,* ☎ *305/667–1651,* WEB *www.fairchildgarden.org.* *$8.* *Daily 9:30–4:30.*

11 **French City Village.** The homes on the north side of this stretch of Hardee Road reflect the inspiration of formal 17th- and 18th-century French Empire design, and the walls surrounding the cluster feature pavilionlike entryways. ✉ *1000 block of Hardee Rd. between Leonardo and Cellini Sts., Coral Gables.*

12 **French Country Village.** These 18 homes were designed by Frank Forster, Edgar Albright, and Philip Goodwin. The houses represent a range of styles predominant in 18th-century rural France. Among them you'll spot a châteaulike residence with a slate roof and cylindrical turret. ✉ *500 block of Hardee Rd. between San Vincente and Maggiore Sts., Coral Gables*

OFF THE BEATEN PATH

**PINEWOOD CEMETERY** – Once the preserve of the Tequesta Indians 3,000–4,000 years ago, this hidden wooded site in the midst of affluent suburbia was recently restored. Gravestones bear the names of pioneer families and much of the native flora has been identified, making this a pleasant place to wander around. ✉ *Sunset Dr. and Erwin Rd., Coral Gables.*

16 **French Normandy Village.** When designing these 11 homes, architects John and Coulton Skinner used half-timbering and shingled gable roofs to evoke 15th- and 16th-century provincial France. In the 1930s this village was a men's dormitory for the University of Miami. ✉ *Le Jeune Rd. at Viscaya Ave., Coral Gables.*

NEED A BREAK?

For a burger and a beer, stop by **JohnMartin's** (✉ 253 Miracle Mile, at Ponce de León Blvd., Coral Gables, ☎ 305/445–3777) Irish pub. The popular spot also offers updated Irish dishes.

18 **Matheson Hammock Park.** In the 1930s the Civilian Conservation Corps developed this 100-acre tract of upland and mangrove swamp on land donated by a local pioneer, Commodore J. W. Matheson. The park, one of Miami-Dade County's oldest and most scenic, has a bathing beach where the tide flushes a saltwater "atoll" pool through four gates. The marina has 243 slips, 71 dry-storage spaces, a bait-and-tackle shop, and a top-rated seafood restaurant built into a historic coral

rock building. ✉ *9610 Old Cutler Rd., Coral Gables,* ☎ *305/665–5475,* WEB *www.co.miami-dade.fl.us/parks/mpbeach1.htm#.* 🎫 *Parking for beach and marina $4 per car, $10 per RV; limited free upland parking.* ⏲ *Daily 6–dusk; pool winter, daily 8:30–5; summer, weekends 8:30–6.*

★ ❶ **Miracle Mile.** Even with competition from some impressive malls, this half-mile stretch of retail stores continues to thrive because of its intriguing mixture of unique boutiques, bridal shops, art galleries, charming restaurants, and upscale nightlife venues. ✉ *Coral Way between S.W. 37th Ave. and S.W. 42nd Ave., Coral Gables.*

OFF THE BEATEN PATH

**SOUTH MIAMI** – Just southwest of the University of Miami is a picturesque city called South Miami, not to be confused with the even more southerly region known as South Miami-Dade. Stately old homes and towering trees line Sunset Drive—a one-horse-drawn carriage road 'til the early 1900s—and now a city-designated Historic and Scenic Road to and through the town. (Sunset Drive is the western extension of Coral Gables's Sunset Road.) The town's distinctive commercial district of friendly shops and restaurants now includes a huge retail and entertainment complex, the Shops of Sunset Place. The mall's offerings—among which are Steven Spielberg's GameWorks, a Virgin Megastore, Nike-Town, and an IMAX theater—are especially popular with teenagers but have added to the traffic woes of the community.

⓯ **Southern Colonial Village.** Also known as Florida Pioneer Village (the name used by architects John and Coulton Skinner), this collection of five homes adapts Greek Revival and Colonial Revival styles. ✉ *Santa Maria St. at Mendavia Ave., Coral Gables.*

❿ **University of Miami.** With almost 14,000 full-time, part-time, and noncredit students, UM—the largest private research university in the Southeast—enters a new era under new president Donna Shalala, the former Health and Human Services Secretary under the Clinton administration. Walk around campus and visit the **Lowe Art Museum,** which hosts traveling exhibitions and has a permanent collection of 8,000 works that include Renaissance, Baroque, American, Latin American, and Native American arts and crafts. In 1999 the museum merged with the Cuban Museum of the Americas, bringing a rich collection of art and artifacts to the campus. Rain or shine, the **John C. Gifford Arboretum,** on the northwest corner of the campus at San Amaro and Robbia streets, is a perfect place to stroll through the palms and flowering trees. UM is also the site of the popular Beaux Arts Festival the third weekend in January. ✉ *1301 Stanford Dr., near Ponce de León Blvd., Coral Gables,* ☎ *305/284–3535 or 305/284–3536,* WEB *www.miami.edu.* 🎫 *$5.* ⏲ *Tues.–Wed. and Fri.–Sat. 10–5, Thurs. noon–7, Sun. noon–5.*

★ ❹ **Venetian Pool.** Sculpted from a rock quarry in 1923 and fed by artesian wells, this 825,000-gallon municipal pool remains quite popular due to its themed architecture—a fantasized version of a waterfront Italian village—created by Denman Fink. The pool has earned a place on the National Register of Historic Places and showcases a nice collection of vintage photos depicting 1920s beauty pageants and swank soirées held long ago. Paul Whiteman played here, Johnny Weissmuller and Esther Williams swam here, and you should, too (but no kids under 3). A snack bar, lockers, and showers make this must-see user-friendly as well. ✉ *2701 De Soto Blvd., at Toledo St., Coral Gables,* ☎ *305/460–5356,* WEB *www.venetianpool.com.* 🎫 *Apr.–Oct., $8; Nov.–Mar. $5, free parking across De Soto Blvd.* ⏲ *June–Aug.,* *weekdays 11–7:30, weekends 10–4:30; Sept.–Oct. and Apr.–May, Tues.–Fri. 11–5:30, weekends 10–4:30; Nov.–Mar., Tues.–Fri. 10–4:30, weekends 10–4:30.*

# KEY BISCAYNE AND VIRGINIA KEY

Once upon a time, these barrier islands were an outpost for fishermen and sailors, pirates and salvagers, soldiers and settlers. The 95-ft Cape Florida Lighthouse stood tall during Seminole Indian battles and hurricanes. Coconut plantations covered two-thirds of Key Biscayne, and there were plans as far back as the 1800s to develop the picturesque island as a resort for the wealthy.

Fortunately, the state and county governments set much of the land aside for parks, and both keys are now home to top-ranked beaches and golf, tennis, softball, and picnicking facilities. The long and winding bike paths that run through the islands are favorites for in-line skaters and cyclists. Incorporated in 1991, the village of Key Biscayne is a hospitable community of about 9,000 that enjoys hosting friendly community events such as a popular Fourth of July parade; Virginia Key remains undeveloped at the moment, making these two playground islands especially family-friendly.

*Numbers in the text correspond to numbers in the margin and on the Coral Gables, Coconut Grove, Key Biscayne, and South Miami map.*

## A Good Tour

Day or night, there are few drives prettier than the one to Key Biscayne and Virginia Key. And if you're in a convertible on a balmy day—well, this kind of drive is what South Florida living is all about. You can also make this tour on in-line skates or bicycle.

From I–95 take the Key Biscayne exit to the Rickenbacker Causeway (a $1 toll covers your round-trip). If you plan to skate or bike, just park anywhere along the causeway after the toll booth and take off. The beaches on either side of the causeway are popular for water sports, with sailboards, sailboats, and Jet Skis available for rental. Officially known as the William Powell Bridge, the causeway bridge rises 75 ft, providing a spectacular if fleeting view of the cruise ships at the Port of Miami, to the north. You can also see the high-rises looming at the tip of South Beach to the northeast, the bright blue Atlantic straight ahead, and sailboat-dotted Biscayne Bay to the south. South of Powell Bridge you'll see anglers fishing off the **Old Rickenbacker Causeway Bridge** ㉖ among the hungry seabirds.

After the causeway turns southeast on Virginia Key, you'll see the gold geodesic dome of the **Miami Seaquarium** ㉗, a longtime sightseeing attraction, and the University of Miami Rosenstiel School of Marine and Atmospheric Science. Visit the undersea world of South Florida and beyond; then cross the Bear Cut Bridge (popular for fishing) onto lush Key Biscayne. Past the marina on your right, winding Crandon Boulevard takes you to **Crandon Park** ㉘, whose Tennis Center is the site of the NASDAQ-100 Open (formerly the Ericsson Open) each March. The park is also home to one of South Florida's best-loved beaches.

As you approach the village of Key Biscayne, take note of the iguana-crossing signs warning motorists of the many green reptiles that scamper about the area. Follow Crandon through Key Biscayne's downtown, where shops and a village green mainly serve local residents. As you drive through town, you'll see luxurious beachfront condos and smaller buildings on your left and single-family houses on your right. Peek down some of the side streets—especially those along waterways—and you can spot spectacular bay-front mansions. Crandon turns into Grapetree Drive as you enter **Bill Baggs Cape Florida State Recreation Area** ㉙, a 460-acre park with great beaches, two excellent cafés, picnic areas, and, at its southern tip, the brick Cape Florida Lighthouse and light keeper's cottage.

After you've taken the sun, or perhaps a bicycle ride, in the park, backtrack on Crandon to the causeway. On your way to the mainland, there's a panoramic view of downtown Miami as you cross the bridge.

TIMING

Set aside the better part of a day for this tour, saving a few late-afternoon hours for Crandon Park and the Cape Florida Lighthouse.

## Sights to See

★ ㉙ **Bill Baggs Cape Florida State Recreation Area.** Thanks to great beaches, sunsets, and a lighthouse, this park at Key Biscayne's southern tip is worth the drive. It has boardwalks, 18 picnic shelters, and two cafés that serve light lunches. A stroll or ride along walking and bicycle paths provides wonderful views of Miami's dramatic skyline. From the southern end of the park, you can see a handful of houses rising over the bay on wooden stilts, the remnants of Stiltsville, built in the 1940s and now dying a natural death. Bill Baggs has bicycle and skate rentals, a playground, fishing piers, kayak rentals, and, on request, guided tours of the cultural complex and the **Cape Florida Lighthouse,** South Florida's oldest structure. The lighthouse was erected in 1845 to replace an earlier one destroyed in an 1836 Seminole attack, in which the keeper's helper was killed. Recent plantings around the lighthouse and keeper's cottage recall the island's past. The restored cottage and cookhouse offer free tours at 10 AM and 1 PM Thurs.–Mon. Be there a half hour beforehand. ✉ *1200 S. Crandon Blvd., Key Biscayne,* ☎ *305/361–5811 or 305/361–8779,* WEB *www.dep.state.fl.us/parks/district_5/BillBaggs/index.htm.* *$4 per vehicle with up to 8 people; $1 per person on bicycle, bus, motorcycle, or foot.* ⏲ *Daily 8 AM–dusk.*

㉘ **Crandon Park.** This laid-back park in northern Key Biscayne is popular with families, and many educated beach enthusiasts rate the 3½-mi beach here among the top 10 beaches in North America. The sand is soft, there are no riptides, there's a great view of the Atlantic, and parking is both inexpensive and plentiful. Because it's a weekend favorite of locals, you'll get a good taste of multicultural Miami flavor: salsa and hip-hop, jerk chicken and barbecue ribs. The **Crandon Family Amusement Center** (☎ 305/361–0099) at Crandon Park was once the site of a zoo. Now it has a restored carousel (it's $1 for 3 rides), splash pool, outdoor roller rink, and playground. There are even swans, waterfowl, and hundreds of huge iguanas running loose. A jungle hayride, available from 10 AM to 1 PM on Saturdays, includes a narrated tour where you can hear the tales of Tequesta Indians and pirates that once inhabited this lush barrier island. At the north end of the beach is the free **Marjory Stoneman Douglas Biscayne Nature Center** (☎ 305/642–9600). Here you can explore seagrass beds on a tour with a naturalist; see red, black, and white mangroves; and hike along the beach and hammock in the Bear Cut Preserve. Nature center hours vary, so call ahead. ✉ *4000 Crandon Blvd., Key Biscayne,* ☎ *305/361–5421,* *Free. Parking $4 per vehicle,* WEB *www.co.miami-dade.fl.us/parks/crandon.htm.* ⏲ *Daily 8–dusk.*

㉗ **Miami Seaquarium.** This classic visitor attraction stages shows with sea lions, dolphins, and Lolita the killer whale. A new exhibit, Crocodile Flats, has 26 Nile crocodiles. You can visit a shark pool, a tropical reef aquarium, and West Indian manatees. Discovery Bay, an endangered mangrove habitat, is home to indigenous Florida fish and rays, alligators, herons, egrets, and ibis. You can tour the park and watch the ongoing presentations, or (for an additional fee) take part in the newest program, Dolphin Encounter, to learn about and swim with the popular mammals. The Seaquarium is awaiting approval for a major expansion; in the meantime, the only sure thing that's being added is a halfway house and hospital for the huge, gentle manatees who too often fall victim to boat propellers. ✉ *4400 Rickenbacker Causeway, Virginia Key,* ☎ *305/361–5705.* *$24.45, parking $4.* ⏲ *Daily 9:30–6, last admission 4:30.*

NEED A BREAK? For some really gritty local flavor and color, seek out **Jimbo's** (✉ off Rickenbacker Causeway at Arthur Lamb Jr. Rd., Virginia Key, ☎ 305/361–7026), a hard-to-find but impossible-to-miss hangout on Virginia Key. To get here, turn on Arthur Lamb Jr. Road just south of the MAST (Maritime and Science Technology) Academy. Tell the toll booth attendant you're headed to Jimbo's, and you'll save the $3 charge assessed to beachgoers. Follow the road past the sewer plant until you see a cluster of ramshackle buildings. This is the place. Have a cold beer and wander around the joint. Domestic wildlife—roosters, chickens, and dogs—shares space with herons and pelicans, and you might spot a manatee in the lagoon. The atmospheric shacks, sometimes occupied by rowdy live bands, have been used for countless TV, movie, video, and still-photo shoots. The lagoon in back was a location for the television series *Flipper.* Relax, watch the crusty characters playing boccie, and you'll feel delightfully removed from civilization.

26 **Old Rickenbacker Causeway Bridge.** Here you can watch boat traffic pass through the channel, pelicans and other seabirds soar and dive, and dolphins cavort in the bay. Park at its entrance, about a mile from the tollgate, and walk past anglers tending their lines to the gap where the center draw span across the Intracoastal Waterway was removed. On the right, on cool, clear winter evenings, the water sparkles with dots of light from hundreds of shrimp boats. ✉ *Rickenbacker Causeway south of Powell Bridge, east of Coconut Grove.*

NEED A BREAK? If you're none too eager to return to the mainland, stop at the **Rusty Pelican** (✉ 3201 Rickenbacker Causeway, Virginia Key, ☎ 305/361–3818), one of the few eateries in the area. Kick back, ignore the so-so seafood menu, order a cold beer or a frozen margarita, and admire the splendid view of the Miami skyline.

# 3 DINING

During the past decade Miami-Dade County has achieved a radical culinary turnaround: ten years ago you couldn't get a decent meal; now it's hard not to get one. But locals and visitors alike aren't satisfied with "good enough." In fact, inventive, inspired chefs, experimenting with all manner of international influences, have raised the bar so high that eateries unable to make the jump from mediocre to superior simply go out of business. Those that do spark interest in this competitive scene are handsomely rewarded—the typical Miami diner is as loyal as your shadow.

Revised by Jen Karetnick

**THE DINING SCENE IN MIAMI AND MIAMI BEACH** is much like the cities themselves: a quirky mix of exotic adventure and upscale glamour. You can sample dishes from all over the globe and pay just a few dollars, or you can have the meal of a lifetime and spend accordingly. Indeed, deep-pocketed diners can easily empty their wallets here. In the process you can enjoy the work of the celebrity chefs who have pioneered New World cuisine, a loose fusion of Latin American, Asian, and Caribbean flavors, using fresh, local ingredients.

The most famous, and best, of Miami's high-end restaurants is Norman's, run by Norman Van Aken, who has moved into the big leagues with a truly dazzling New World menu. Van Aken's competition includes Allen Susser, at Chef Allen's, a stylish Aventura place where international influences combine the finest of contemporary cuisine. At Nemo, a trendy near-oceanside spot, chef-proprietor Michael Schwartz puts a global spin on a seafood-oriented menu. As locally renowned as Van Aken is nationally, Jonathan Eismann maintains his Lincoln Road eatery, Pacific Time, a pan-Asian take on New World cuisine. And in South Miami, Two Chefs, run by Jan Jorgensen and Soren Bredahl, provides fine dining to the suburbs.

Miami's Latin-American influence is a fact of dining life that no food-loving resident would want to change. You can sample Brazilian *rodizio* (barbecue) at Porcao downtown; taste Nicaraguan at Guayacan, in Little Havana, or at Los Ranchos, in multiple locations throughout Miami; dip into Colombian at Patacón's several outlets; or peruse Puerto Rican at the Puerto Rico Restaurant, in Miami. It's almost impossible not to experience Cuban cuisine with the hundreds of cafés and bodegas that abound here; head to the glamorous but inexpensive Versailles, on Calle Ocho, home of South Florida's strongest shot of Cuban coffee.

Miami's most unusual import, though, comes from Vietnam: amid the bodegas of Little Havana, Hy-Vong, a frustratingly slow but deliciously rewarding hole-in-the-wall, serves up chicken in pastry with watercress sauce and dolphin sautéed with mangos and green peppercorns. In the Gables, Miss Saigon Bistro delivers authentic Vietnamese fare in more sophisticated surroundings, complemented by live orchids.

Dining out is an essential part of Miami nightlife, and many restaurants don't even expect customers until late in the evening. Others cater to neighborhood folk and close just when places like South Beach start to heat up. No matter which type of restaurant you choose, you should double-check its status before you set out for the evening.

## Prices

The price of eating in Miami continues to rise. Typical entrée prices in the upper-echelon restaurants hover near the $30 mark, and even in more casual spots a $20 dish is typical. At lunch you can have a representative meal at a given restaurant, sometimes at half the cost of dinner. Another strategy is to order two or three appetizers and skip the entrée. Starters are usually more creative, and by ordering a selection, you get a good idea of the chef's oeuvre. Dollar for dollar, the best values are still to be found in the city's ethnic restaurants. Sometimes you may have to sacrifice atmosphere, but the savings and the experience are usually worth it.

| CATEGORY | COST* |
|---|---|
| $$$$ | over $30 |
| $$$ | $20–$30 |
| $$ | $10–$20 |
| $ | under $10 |

**per person, for a main course at dinner*

### Tipping

When you get your check, you'll be reminded once again of Miami's international flavor: for the convenience of the city's many European and Latin American visitors, who are accustomed to the practice, a 15%–18% gratuity is included on most restaurant tabs. You can reduce or supplement that amount depending on your opinion of the service.

### Dress

Jackets and ties are rarely required, even at the fancier restaurants. In their place a dress category called "casual chic" has emerged. It loosely translates to "black and expensive" (whether a T-shirt or a little dress). Shorts are appropriate in many places at lunchtime and at casual spots for dinner. Don't be embarrassed to call ahead and ask what to wear.

### Reservations

It's a fact of Miami life that a lot of people want to eat at the best restaurants, so at many of the hot spots you'll need a reservation to avoid a long wait—we only mention when they're essential or not accepted. Try to reserve a few days in advance, and if you change your mind or your plans, cancel your reservation—it's only courteous. Tables can be hard to come by if you want to dine between 8 and 10, and some places don't really get rolling until even later.

## North Miami-Dade, North Miami Beach, North Miami

### American

**$–$$$** ✕ **Magnum.** From the outside, this hidden speakeasy looks almost deserted. Enter through the back alley, though, and you're in a world of jazz, martinis, hamburgers, and crab cakes. A popular gay hangout on weeknights, Magnum caters to an upscale local crowd on weekends, and owners Jeffrey Landsman and Kurt Schmidt, who also run ever-popular Jeffrey's on South Beach, make sure no one feels neglected. ✉ *709 NE 79th St., Shorecrest, North Miami-Dade,* ☎ *305/757–3368. AE, MC, V. No lunch.*

**$–$$$** ✕ **Soyka.** This eponymously named eatery is the fourth in restaurateur Mark Soyka's (News and Van Dyke cafés) empire. Slightly more upscale than the others, it serves marinated skirt steak, calves' liver with caramelized onions, and sesame-seared salmon for dinner. Most proponents appreciate the day menu more, with omelets, burgers, salads, pizza, and sandwiches. Love the food or merely tolerate it, no one can deny this urban eatery is a great space, with lots of chrome and cement, good martinis, and comforting desserts. ✉ *5556 Biscayne Blvd., Morningside, North Miami-Dade,* ☎ *305/759–3117. AE, D, DC, MC, V.*

### Chinese

**$–$$** ✕ **Macau Chinese Bakery.** Peer into the cases stocked with homemade Chinese baked goods and grab something to go. Or if your agenda includes more than a bag of almond cookies or home-baked pork buns—that is, a full-blown multicourse feast—option one of the dozen tables inside. Highly personalized service guides you through a menu that ranges from the predictable Americanized favorites to outrageously Chinese dishes. Chicken with sweet corn, and watercress with pork are pleasantly mild soups perfect for a winter cold snap; shrimp

Close-Up

# DINING WITH KIDS: A GUIDE

MIAMI'S LEGACY OF ELDERLY residents and more recent history of nightlife aficionados has left folks with children in a peculiar place. The remaining retired citizens resent noise or intrusions of any kind in their habitual places of culinary worship, and even the funkier restaurants simply don't want—or know what to do with—real kids as opposed to club kids. Hardly any restaurants have children's menus, let alone high chairs. What's a family to do?

1. Look for tile floors. Consider any restaurant that has a tile floor fair game, simply because it's easy to sweep up debris and wipe up spills. Eateries like David's Cafe II (✉ 1654 Meridian Ave., Miami Beach, ☏ 305/672–8707), a modern art deco dining room serving Cuban fare, may not look as if it's up to toddlers throwing handfuls of black beans. But the management is quick to assure you that any mess the babies make, the staff will clean. The superb food here is worth a little parental embarrassment.

2. Go Latin. This may be a generalization, but most Latinos, whether Cuban, South American, or Central American, love children. Especially kids who like to eat. And even if the child is picky or cranky, the Latin culture demands that children be with their parents rather than be left at home. It's not unusual to see fairly young children sharing late-night black beans and suckling pig with their folks, even in the trendier spots such as Lario's on the Beach (✉ 820 Ocean Dr., Miami Beach, ☏ 305/532–9577).

3. Ask about high chairs. If a restaurant has just one representative high chair, go. But reserve it for your offspring in advance. Even better are those eateries in the suburbs like K. C. Kagney & Co. (✉ 11230 S.W. 137th Ave., Kendall, ☏ 305/386–1555), a wacky diner with a fun menu and cute decor. Not only do you get a choice between high chairs and booster seats, the staff isn't at all mystified by little people.

4. Eat outside. You may prefer your child to have her temper tantrums in the open air. On the flip side, if you frequent outdoor cafés like those on Lincoln Road, a walking mall, or Ocean Drive, both on South Beach, it's guaranteed there will be plenty of distractions during those rants—in the forms of human foot traffic, pedigreed canines, and the occasional parrot or iguana.

5. Peer groups tell the story. If a restaurant has already seated someone else's child, it's safe to assume that management considers a child an appropriate member of a dining party. And don't go by the old adage that two's company, three's a crowd. Rather, the more the merrier. In other words, children can keep each other company. At best, if another child is misbehaving, you can revel in your own wee one's table manners. At worst, you can apply peer pressure: "Look how nicely that child is behaving, eating, sitting still."

6. Tip big. 'Nuff said.

—Jen Karetnick

Andiamo . . . . . . . . . 23
Andre's Restaurant . . . 10
Arnie & Richie's . . . . 25
Artichoke's . . . . . . . . 8
Atlantic . . . . . . . . . . 15
Biscayne Wine Merchants . . . . . . . . 12
Cafe Del Mar . . . . . . 17
Café Prima Pasta . . . . 21
Chef Allen's . . . . . . . . 2
Crystal Café . . . . . . . 27
5061 Eaterie and Deli . . . . . . . . . . . . 24
The Forge . . . . . . . . . 26
Hanna's Gourmet Diner . . . . . 11
Kebab Indian Restaurant . . . . . . . . . 6
Kyung Ju . . . . . . . . . . 5
La Paloma . . . . . . . . . 16
Las Delicias del Mar Peruano . . . . . . . . . . 30
Macau Chinese Bakery . . . . . . . . . . . . 7
Magnum . . . . . . . . . . 18
Oasis Café . . . . . . . . 28
Oggi Café . . . . . . . . 19
Paquito's . . . . . . . . . . 9
Paramount Grill . . . . . . 1
Patacón . . . 3, 20, 29, 31
Shula's Steak House . . . . . . . . . . . . 4
Soyka . . . . . . . . . . . 22
Sushi Republic . . . . . . 14
Tani Guchi's Place . . . 13

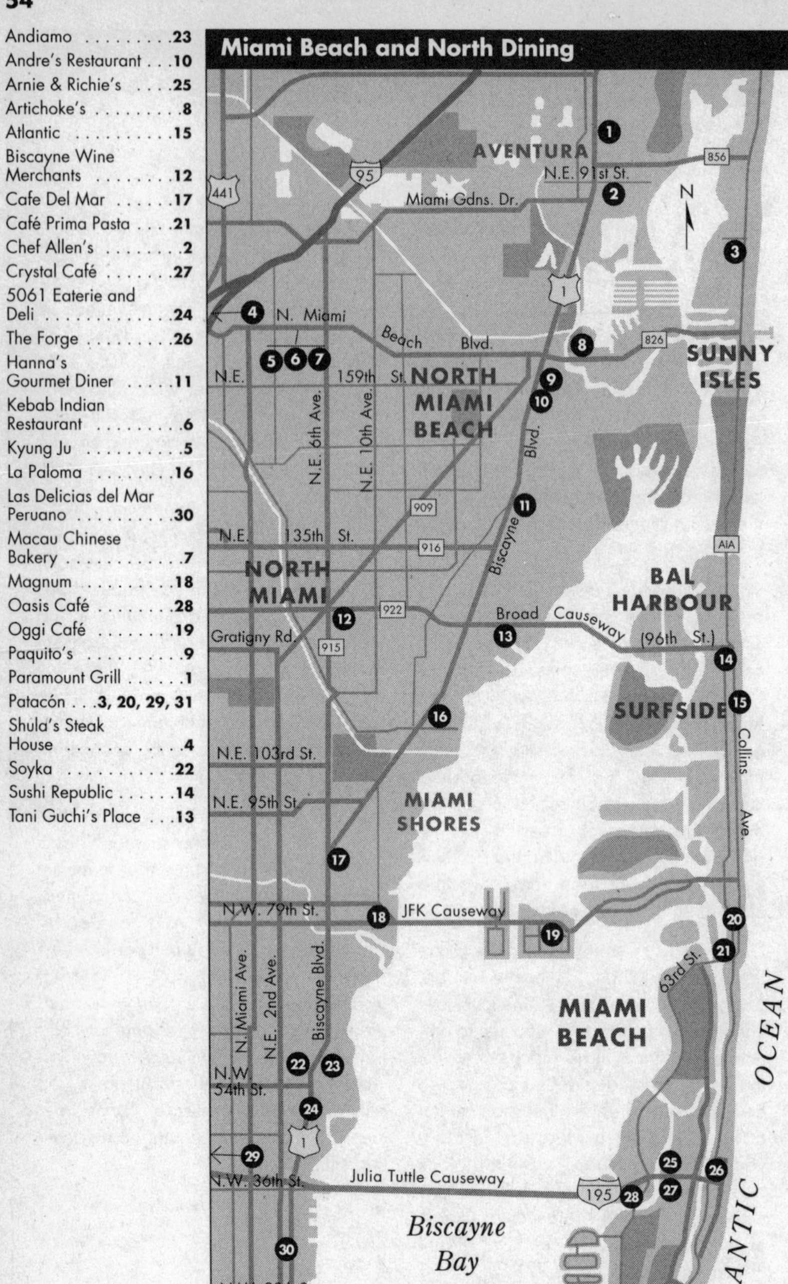

with salty pepper flavor is stimulating any time of year. ✉ *520 N.E. 167th St., Little Asia, North Miami Beach,* ☎ *305/947–5594. MC, V.*

## Colombian

$–$$ ✕ **Patacón.** If you haven't familiarized yourself with Colombian cuisine, let this minimally decorated minichain initiate you. And a delicious intro it can be, too—crisp *empanaditas,* stuffed with ground meat and potato, are elevated by green chili sauce. Don't fill up, though. Main-dish soups, especially the *sancocho,* a stew including hen, tripe, oxtail, and corn on the cob—basically, whatever the cook has on hand—comfort the hungry soul. And so does the signature dish, *patacón pisao,* a huge, flattened fried plantain on which you can spread such condiments as shrimp, chicken, shredded meat, beans, and guacamole. ✉ *18230 Collins Ave., Sunny Isles, North Miami Beach,* ☎ *305/931–3001;* ✉ *7902 N.W. 36th St., Miami,* ☎ *305/591–8866;* ✉ *13720 N. Kendall Dr., Kendall,* ☎ *305/382–3717. AE, DC, MC, V.*

## Contemporary

$$$–$$$$ ★ ✕ **Chef Allen's.** At the 25-ft-wide picture window, you can watch Allen Susser, a member of the original, self-designated Mango Gang, create contemporary American masterpieces from a global menu that changes nightly. After a salad of baby greens and warm wild mushrooms or a rock-shrimp hash with roasted corn, consider swordfish with conch-citrus couscous, macadamia nuts, and lemon or grilled lamb chops with eggplant timbale and a three-nut salsa. It's hard to resist the dessert soufflé; order it when you order your appetizer to eliminate a mouthwatering wait at the end of your meal. ✉ *19088 N.E. 29th Ave., Aventura,* ☎ *305/935–2900. AE, DC, MC, V.*

$$–$$$ ✕ **Cafe Del Mar.** Natives of Nice, and Miami Shores residents since 1992, proprietors Patricia and Jacques Ardisson opened this much-needed neighborhood eatery and fish market in summer 2001. The mostly seafood menu has everything from ceviche to bouillabaisse to sushi. You can bet on freshness with nightly dinner specials like paella or stone crabs. An excellent Sunday brunch buffet is value-oriented, as is a small but well-chosen wine list. Can't make it in? No worries—Cafe Del Mar ships stone crabs Fed Ex. ✉ *8699 Biscayne Blvd., North Miami-Dade,* ☎ *305/759–1100. AE, MC, V.*

$$–$$$ ✕ **5061 Eaterie and Deli.** Also a deli, market, and bookshop that sponsors readings and performances, 5061 is a 41-wines-by-the-glass addition to a fast-expanding neighborhood run by Parisian proprietor Xavier Lesmarie (who also owns Les Deux Fontaines and Hotel Ocean). The extensive menu has hearty specialty salads and crusty quiches, roasted (free-range) chicken and steamed fish and more elaborate preparations like roasted and grilled vegetables mille-feuille or beef tenderloin with horseradish-herb butter. And yes, "Eaterie" is spelled that way deliberately, to invoke the French spelling of shops like boulangerie and patisserie. ✉ *5061 Biscayne Blvd., Morningside,* ☎ *305/756–5051. AE, DC, MC, V.*

$$–$$$ ✕ **Hanna's Gourmet Diner.** Meals are served in a long, silvery structure riveted across the street from the Florida East Coast Railway tracks, although this amusingly eclectic, mainly French-influenced diner won't remind you a bit of the fare on Amtrak. Hannah's is the place to head when you have a hankering for sautéed calves liver—or grilled snapper, rack of lamb, rare tuna, a big, juicy New York strip, or chicken *chasseur* (wine and mushroom sauce). Helpful hint: the fruit tart, one of Miami's best desserts, is in heavy demand on busy nights, so order your slice when you choose your main course. ✉ *13951 Biscayne Blvd., North Miami Beach,* ☎ *305/947–2255. AE, MC, V.*

$-$$$ ✕ **Paramount Grill.** Don't quibble about it being located on the second story of a shopping mall. It's a handsomely appointed, bistro-style place that begs the question—why put up with a food court? Creative innovations may include pizza topped with smoked salmon and citrus cream cheese; rock shrimp cakes with lemon aioli; Caribe-crusted skirt steak; or key lime chicken with yuca fries—at about half the dough you'd spend elsewhere. Sit under the flickering gaslights, lean against a red-brick column, and raise a toast to mall eateries. ✉ *Aventura Mall, 19501 Biscayne Blvd., Aventura,* ☎ *305/466–1466. AE, MC, V.*

$-$$ ★ ✕ **Artichoke's.** This quirky spot on North Miami Beach's main drag is a dual tribute to art and artichoke—but not, you should note, to red meat. Set off the road in a strip mall, the health-oriented, veggie-focused restaurant can be easily overlooked by travelers but is usually packed with locals. In this setting the artichoke flourishes as it does nowhere else: get it broiled whole with a zesty dipping sauce, flicked into salads, tossed with pasta, and more. The spa-cuisine seafood dishes can be sort of bland, but the pastas—especially the vegetarian ones—excel. ✉ *3055 N.E. 163rd St., North Miami Beach,* ☎ *305/945–7576. AE, D, MC, V.*

$-$$ ★ ✕ **Biscayne Wine Merchants.** True to its name, this casually elegant establishment lines its walls with wine racks; untrue to its moniker, it's no longer in its original spot on Biscayne Boulevard. That's only relevant if you get lost, though. The specials change often—not the location—but look for Brie in phyllo with kumquat jalapeño glaze, Portobello mushrooms in red wine sauce, steak with bordelaise sauce, classic bouillabaisse, and cassoulet with lamb shank, sausage, and duck. As for the wine, you're sure to quaff a good vintage—and at a more reasonable price than you're probably accustomed. ✉ *738 N.E. 125th St., North Miami,* ☎ *305/899–1997. AE, D, MC, V.*

## Continental

$$-$$$ ✕ **La Paloma.** Contemporary diners could find this Swiss Continental restaurant somewhat old-fashioned, but it's really a total sensory experience: fine food, impeccable service, and the ambience of an art museum with Baccarat crystal, Limoges china, Meissen porcelain, and Sèvres clocks to hold grandmas and collectors alike in thrall. The multilingual staff serves freshly prepared local fish and shellfish, Wiener schnitzel, veal chops with morel sauce, and herb-encrusted lamb chops with a quiet flamboyance appropriate to its Old Europe setting. ✉ *10999 Biscayne Blvd., North Miami,* ☎ *305/891–0505. AE, MC, V. No lunch weekends.*

## Indian

$-$$ ★ ✕ **Kebab Indian Restaurant.** Private, curtain-shrouded booths in this small, rather creaky, and certainly aromatic place set the mood for romantic interludes or serious business dealings—and some delicious Indian food. Get your meat fix with the mixed tandoori grill, featuring beef, lamb, and chicken. Shrimp vindaloo is thick, savory, and spicy; ask for it hot, and ye shall receive, as there's no downplaying to sissified American palates here. Cool yourself off with fragrant nan bread, *raita* (yogurt-cucumber dip), or a homemade sweet *lassi* (yogurt drink). ✉ *514 N.E. 167th St., Little Asia, North Miami Beach,* ☎ *305/940–6309. AE, DC, MC, V.*

## Italian

$$-$$$ ✕ **Andre's Restaurant.** In a glamorous dining room appointed with French advertisements and white-linen covered tables, chef-proprietor Andre Filosa showcases his northern Italian and French-influenced cuisine. He coddles seafood—check out "Andre's Fever," a buttery sauté of sea scallops and jumbo shrimp over angel hair—and stocks enough

fresh fish daily to tempt a dolphin. Nightly specials include his famed osso buco, which sells out so rapidly the servers will tell you right away and without inquiry how many orders are left. Interestingly, Andre's also caters to folks with early bird agendas and dietary concerns, offering lighter, less calorie-laden dishes. ✉ *16145 Biscayne Blvd., North Miami Beach,* ☎ *305/919–9962. AE, MC, V.*

$–$$ ✕ **Andiamo.** Miami's not renowned for its pizza—until now, that is. The addition of Andiamo, a storefront pizzeria connected to a car wash, has residents raving about brick ovens and high-quality gourmet toppings like roasted eggplant, broccoli rabe, kalamata olives, and truffle oil. Order one of the specialty pizzas—like the divine Genovese, with potatoes, pancetta, caramelized onions, rosemary, and Gorgonzola cheese—or make up your own. Paninis and salads are pretty much the only alternatives here, but when the main item is so absorbing, nobody really minds. ✉ *5600 Biscayne Blvd., Morningside, North Miami,* ☎ *305/762–5751. AE, D, MC, V.*

## Japanese

$–$$ ✕ **Tani Guchi's Place.** Kosher sushi—try saying that three times fast. Or abandon the linguistic effort, pick up a pair of chopsticks, and put your mouth to work in more useful ways. Granted, *glatt* kosher means no bagel rolls (with salmon and cream cheese)—dairy is a no-no—and shellfish is off limits, too. But you can still indulge in salmon teriyaki and lightly fried vegetable tempura, in addition to more innovative house specials made with tofu, and you won't walk away hungry. Banana tempura with Tofutti, an ice cream substitute, for dessert may even make you feel blessed. ✉ *2224 N.E. 123rd St., North Miami,* ☎ *305/892–6744. AE, D, DC, MC, V. No dinner Fri., no lunch weekends.*

## Korean

$–$$$ ✕ **Kyung Ju.** Serving the spiciest of Asian cuisines—Korean—this unstylish but wonderfully tasty spot has terrfic tofu in a searing sauce of sesame, soy, ginger, and dried chilies; spicy seasoned beef and vegetable soup with ginger and garlic; and seasoned, boiled black codfish casserole. Mongolian barbecue is a grill-your-own house specialty and everyone gets a free festival of vegetable garnishes: kimchi (pickled cabbage), spinach with sesame seeds, mustard greens, and pickled bean sprouts. The atmosphere is limited to a TV, but the food is excitement enough. ✉ *400 N.E. 163rd St., Little Asia, North Miami Beach,* ☎ *305/947–3838. AE, DC, MC, V.*

## Mexican

$$ ✕ **Paquito's.** A Mexican place to please both the gourmand and the glutton, Paquito's enlivens an otherwise massive, impersonal strip-mall hacienda with bright, colorful decor and ultrafriendly staff. All the standards—enchiladas, burritos, tortilla chips—are masterfully prepared. More ambitious cuisine includes tortilla soup with cheese *and* sour cream; a zesty mole *verde* with chicken, pork, or beef; turkey meatballs in *chipotle* (chile) sauce; or dolphin (mahimahi) with tomato, capers, and green olives. *Sopaipillas* (fried bits of dough with cinnamon and brown sugar) provide a sweet finish. ✉ *16265 Biscayne Blvd., North Miami Beach,* ☎ *305/947–5027. AE, DC, MC, V.*

## Steak

$$$–$$$$ ✕ **Shula's Steak House.** Prime rib, fish, and steaks displayed on a cart along with live, 3-pound lobsters are almost an afterthought to the *objets de sport* in this shrine for the NFL-obsessed. Dine in a manly wood-lined setting with a fireplace, surrounded by memorabilia of retired coach Don Shula's perfect 1972 season with the Miami Dolphins. Polish off the 48-ounce porterhouse steak and achieve a sort of immortality—your name on a plaque and an autographed picture of Shula to take

home. Also for fans, there's shula's steak 2 (lowercase borrowed from espn2™), a sports-celebrity hangout in the resort's hotel section, as well as a branch at the Alexander Hotel in Miami Beach. ✉ *7601 N.W. 154th St., Miami Lakes,* ☎ *305/820–8102;* ✉ *5225 Collins Ave., Miami Beach,* ☎ *305/341–6565. AE, DC, MC, V.*

## Miami Beach North of 23rd Street

### American

$$–$$$ ✕ **Atlantic.** Cookbook guru Sheila Lukins runs the kitchen in the Ralph Lauren–designed Nantucket-style Beach House hotel. The menu emphasizes her no-nonsense American classics—think rack of lamb with roasted new potatoes and green beans—along with executive chef Jason Miller's seafood-accentuating list. Sip a martini at the Seahorse Bar—where an aquarium houses the namesake—then dine outside to experience the far-from-Florida atmosphere. ✉ *Beach House Bal Harbour, 9449 Collins Ave., Bal Harbour,* ☎ *305/695–7930. AE, MC, V.*

### Contemporary

$$–$$$ ✕ **Crystal Café.** As cozy as Grandma's dining room, this New Continental restaurant takes the classics and lightens 'em up. Beef Stroganoff and chicken *paprikash* are two such updated stars; osso buco literally falls off the bone. More contemporary items include chicken Kiev, stuffed with goat cheese and topped with a tricolor salad, and pan-seared duck breast with raspberry sauce. Multiple Golden Spoon award–winning Macedonian chef-proprietor Klime Kovaceski takes pride in serving more food than you can possibly manage, including home-baked rhubarb pie. ✉ *726 41st St., Miami Beach,* ☎ *305/673–8266. AE, D, DC, MC, V. Closed Mon. No lunch.*

### Continental

$$$–$$$$ ✕ **The Forge.** Often compared to a museum, each intimate dining salon in this landmark eatery has its own historical artifacts, including a chandelier that hung in James Madison's White House. The wine cellar contains 380,000 bottles—including more than 500 dating from 1822 (and costing as much as $35,000). In addition to steak, specialties include Norwegian salmon with spinach vinaigrette and free-range Wisconsin duck roasted with black currants. For dessert try the blacksmith pie. This place is a hot party spot on Wednesday night, and the adjoining club, Café Nostalgia, is very popular with the "I remember Cuba" crowd. ✉ *432 Arthur Godfrey Rd., Miami Beach,* ☎ *305/538–8533. Reservations essential. AE, DC, MC, V. No lunch.*

### Delicatessens

$–$$ ✕ **Arnie and Richie's.** Take a deep whiff when you walk in, and you'll know what you're in for: onion rolls, smoked whitefish salad, half-sour pickles, herring in sour cream sauce, chopped liver, corned beef, pastrami. Deli doesn't get more delicious than in this family-run operation. Casual to the extreme, most customers are regulars and seat themselves at tables that have baskets of plastic knives and forks; if you request a menu, it's a clear sign you're a newcomer. Service can be brusque, but it sure is quick. ✉ *525 41st St., Miami Beach,* ☎ *305/531–7691. AE, MC, V.*

### Italian

$–$$$ ★ ✕ **Café Prima Pasta.** One of Miami's many signatures is this exemplary Argentine-Italian spot, which rules the emerging North Beach neighborhood. Service can be erratic, but you forget it all on delivery of fresh-made bread with a bowl of spiced olive oil. Tender carpaccio and plentiful antipasti are a delight to share, but the real treat here is the hand-rolled pasta, which can range from crab-stuffed ravioli to sim-

Close-Up

# A FLASH IN THE PAN?

**ONE OF MIAMI'S VIRTUES** is also one of its greatest vices: the inability to remain static. While constant progress makes for an exciting day-by-day life for residents, this quick-change artist of a town can be frustrating for visitors who never know if a recommended restaurant will still be in place. Indeed, many notable restaurants that are still in the planning stages or have just opened obviously haven't stood the test of tourist season, but they're worth mentioning and even exploring, that is if the local telephone directory can find the number for you.

For instance, the famed Japanese chef-proprietor Nobu Matsuhisa has finally debuted a branch of his New York Nobu restaurant on Miami Beach. However, the Shore Club resort that it's located in (✉ 1901 Collins Ave., ☎ 305/695–3232) has been struggling financially, and rumors about the hotel's permanence—and therefore Nobu's and sister restaurant Sirena's existence—abound.

Another recently launched South Beach eatery called 6 Degrees (✉ 685 Washington Ave., ☎ 305/538–2212) shows plenty of potential. Madonna's brother Christopher Ciccone designed it; longtime Beach residents own it; and chef Jason Strom's strengths lie in his ability to combine global ingredients. Salza Grill (✉ 524 Ocean Dr., ☎ 305/535–0090), in the erstwhile Ricky Martin Casa Salsa space, is trying to make Nuevo Latino food a more profitable venture this go-round.

A couple of restaurants are new to Lincoln Road. The Cafeteria, an offshoot of the Chelsea Cafeteria in New York, is under a $2.5 million renovation. It will be on the vintage site of Miami's first Cadillac dealership, and will have a roof garden and 24-hour service. Bobby Rifkin, who owns the popular Touch on Lincoln Road, has just added an avant-garde steak house to his budding empire. Called KISS (✉ 301 Lincoln Rd., ☎ 305/695–4445), it's currently the topic of discussion, thanks to the dancers who entertain the beef-eaters here.

Elsewhere, in Coral Gables, AMMO (✉ 1915 Ponce de León Blvd., ☎ 305/444–3357) promises terrific pastas like homemade tortelli stuffed with loin of lamb mousse in a truffle-duck reduction. Just down the street, the former proprietor of Casa Rolandi, a long-running Gables favorite that went out of business some years ago has returned with his namesake Fabio Rolandi (✉ 2626 Ponce de León Blvd., ☎ 305/448–2626), a creative Northern Italian trattoria and designer pizzeria.

Whether any of these restaurants will fulfill the promise of the advance press or last the season remains to be seen. But as always in Miami, the capricious culinary scene is, at the very least, an adventure.

— Jen Karetnick

ple fettuccine with seafood. If overexposed tiramisu hasn't made an enemy of you yet, try this legendary one in order to add espresso notes to your unavoidable garlic breath. ✉ *414 71st St., North Beach, Miami Beach,* ☎ *305/867–0106. MC, V.*

$–$$$ ✕ **Oggi Café.** It opened simply as a storefront pasta factory and local patrons hungry for Italian started to wander in. That's all it took to quickly became a vital staple in the North Bay Village community—and since the place has been expanded twice. Along with handmade pastas, grilled beef, poultry, and fresh fish dishes also rate raves. Breads, desserts, and salad dressings are all made on the premises, too, but don't worry if you can't get a seat—Oggi still supplies many of the finer area restaurants with its products, so chances are you'll run across them somewhere else. ✉ *1740 79th St. Causeway, North Bay Village,* ☎ *305/866–1238. Reservations essential. AE, D, MC, V. No lunch weekends.*

### Japanese

$–$$ ✕ **Sushi Republic.** A long and narrow storefront with sponge-painted walls, this eatery prides itself on welcoming customers, so don't be surprised when the sushi chefs say, "Hi!" when you walk in. Nor should you expect anything but the freshest sashimi, which is elegantly presented and perfectly succulent. As far as cooked fare goes, the Republic is more like a democracy—everything is even and consistent. *Shumai,* soft shrimp dumplings with *ponzu* (soy, rice vinegar, sake, seaweed, and dried bonito flakes) dipping sauce; whole fried soft-shell crab; and salmon teriyaki are particularly noteworthy. ✉ *9583 Harding Ave., Surfside, Miami Beach,* ☎ *305/867–8036. AE, D, DC, MC, V. Closed Mon. No lunch Sun.*

### Mediterranean

$–$$ ✕ **Oasis Café.** The emphasis in Mediterranean cuisine is on health, and Oasis, a coolly tiled spot with breezy decor, makes sure you don't keel over at the tables—the chefs here stuff grape leaves, not arteries. In other words, natural-food enthusiasts feel right at home, with delicacies such as eggplant salads, hummus, grilled sesame tofu, and sautéed garlic spinach for starters, and for entrées, pan-seared turkey chop, roasted vegetable lasagna, grilled fresh fish on focaccia, or penne with turkey, tomato, saffron, and pine nuts. The homemade rum cake is a superb way to drink dessert. ✉ *976 41st St., Miami Beach,* ☎ *305/674–7676. AE, D, DC, MC, V.*

## South Beach

### American

$$–$$$ ✕ **Joe Allen.** Crave a good martini along with a terrific burger? Locals head to this hidden hangout in an exploding neighborhood of condos, town houses, and stores. The eclectic crowd includes kids and grandparents, and the menu has everything from pizzas to calves' liver to steaks. Start with an innovative salad, such as arugula with pear, prosciutto, and a Gorgonzola dressing, or roast beef salad on greens with Parmesan. Desserts are home style as well, including banana cream pie and ice cream and cookie sandwiches. ✉ *1787 Purdy Ave., South Beach,* ☎ *305/531–7007. MC, V.*

### American/Casual

$–$$ ★ ✕ **Big Pink.** The decor in this innovative diner may remind you of a roller-skating rink—everything is pink Lucite, stainless steel, and campy (think sports lockers as decorative touches). And the menu is a virtual book, complete with table of contents. But the food is solidly all-American, with dozens of tasty sandwiches, pizzas, turkey or beef burgers, and side dishes, each and every one composed with a gourmet flair. Customers comprise club kids and real kids, who alternate, de-

Astor Place . . . . . . . 25
Balan's . . . . . . . . . . 4
Bambú . . . . . . . . . . . 9
Big Pink . . . . . . . . . 34
Blue Door at the Delano . . . . . . . . . . 13
Café Efesus . . . . . . . 20
Charlie's Roast Beef . . . . . . . . . 3
China Grill . . . . . . . . 31
Dab Haus . . . . . . . . 26
11th Street Diner . . . 19
Escopazzo . . . . . . . . 18
Gaucho Room . . . . . 14
Joe Allen . . . . . . . . . 2
Joe's Stone Crab Restaurant . . . . . . . . 35
Maiko Japanese Restaurant and Sushi Bar . . . . . . . . . 21
Nemo . . . . . . . . . . . 33
News Café . . . . . . . . 28
Osteria del Teatro . . . 16
Pacific Time . . . . . . . . 6
Red Square . . . . . . . 32
Rumi . . . . . . . . . . . . 12
Samba Room . . . . . . 15
Spiga . . . . . . . . . . . 22
Sport Café . . . . . . . . 29
Sushi Hana . . . . . . . 23
SushiSamba Dromo . . . . . . . . . . . 10
SUVA . . . . . . . . . . . 8
Tambo . . . . . . . . . . . 1
Tantra . . . . . . . . . . 17
Touch . . . . . . . . . . . 5
Tuscan Steak . . . . . . 30
1220 at the Tides . . . 23
Van Dyke Café . . . . . . 7
Wish . . . . . . . . . . . . 27
Yuca . . . . . . . . . . . . 11

## South Beach Dining

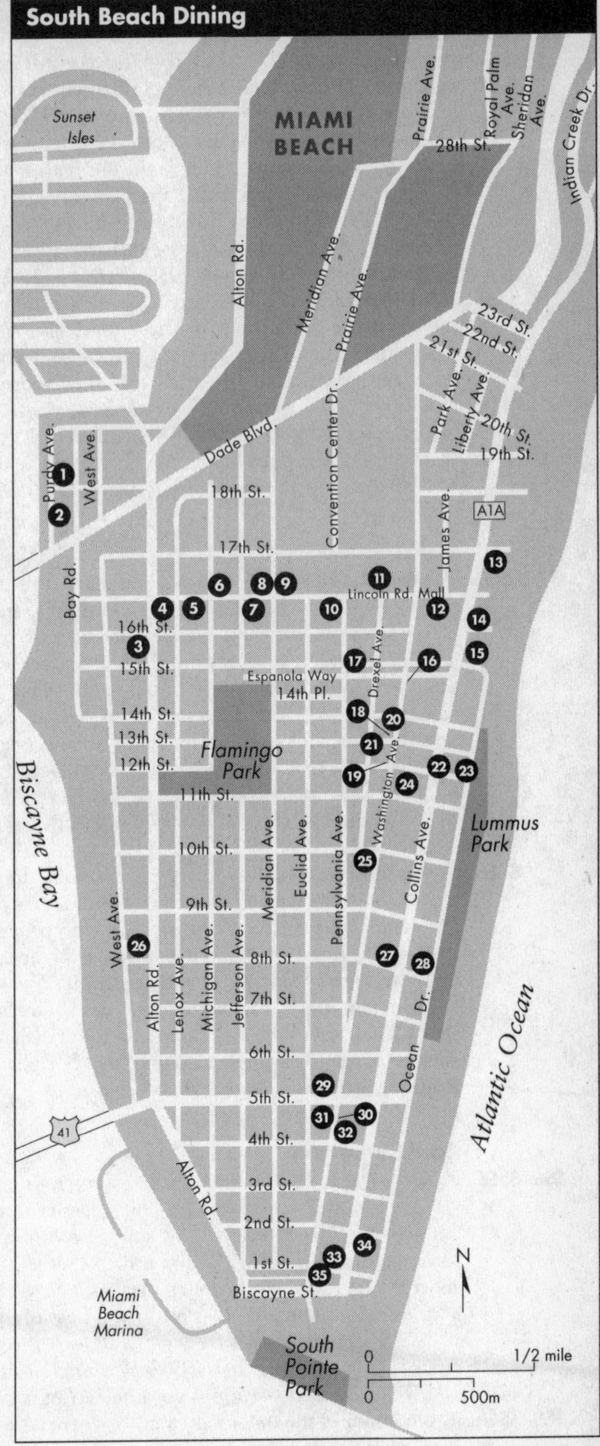

pending on the time of day—Big Pink makes a great spot for brunch—but both like to color with the complimentary crayons. ✉ *157 Collins Ave., South Beach,* ☎ *305/532–4700. AE, MC, V.*

$–$$ ✕ **Charlie's Roast Beef.** Yes, it's fast food. And okay, it's a chain, albeit one from Colombia (this is the only U.S. location). But these plump roast beef sandwiches enchant everyone who takes a bite, from gourmets to gourmands. Sample the one with smoked barbecue sauce, or the roast beef on a bagel special with sautéed mushrooms and onions. The truly hungry can indulge in a full rack of ribs and an order of deep-fried onion rings, thick-cut, batter dipped, and juicy. ✉ *1570 Alton Rd., South Beach,* ☎ *305/531–9555. MC, V.*

$–$$ ✕ **11th Street Diner.** Since serving its first plate of meat loaf in 1992, this diner has become a low-price, unpretentious hangout for locals. The best time to visit is weekend mornings, when the stragglers from the night before and early birds with their morning papers converge for conversation. At this busy, bustling eatery in a 1948 deco-style dining car, you can grab a corner booth and order a cherry cola, a blue plate special, or a milkshake and pretend you've traveled back in time. ✉ *1055 Washington Ave., South Beach,* ☎ *305/534–6373. AE, DC, MC, V.*

## Cafés

$–$$$ ★ ✕ **News Café.** An Ocean Drive landmark, this 24-hour café attracts a crowd with snacks, light meals, and drinks, and the people parade on the sidewalk out front. Most prefer sitting outside, where they can feel the salt breeze and gawk at the human scenery. Offering a little of this and a little of that—bagels, pâtés, chocolate fondue, sandwiches, and a terrific wine list—this joint has something for everyone. Although service can be indifferent to the point of laissez-faire, the café remains a scene. Note that a second location in Coconut Grove closes at 11 PM. ✉ *800 Ocean Dr., South Beach,* ☎ *305/538–6397;* ✉ *2901 Florida Ave., Coconut Grove,* ☎ *305/774–6397. Reservations not accepted. AE, DC, MC, V.*

$–$$ ✕ **Van Dyke Café.** Just as its parent, News Café, draws the fashion crowd, this offshoot attracts the artsy crowd. Indeed this place seems even livelier than its Ocean Drive counterpart, with pedestrians passing by on the Lincoln Road Mall and live jazz playing upstairs every evening—or, more to the point, every early morning. The kitchen serves dishes from mammoth omelets with home fries to soups and grilled dolphin sandwiches to basil-grilled lamb and pasta dishes, though it's best to stick to basics. There's an enticing list of drinks like Bellinis and Kir Royales. ✉ *846 Lincoln Rd., South Beach,* ☎ *305/534–3600. AE, DC, MC, V.*

## Contemporary

$$$–$$$$ ★ ✕ **Astor Place.** The Hotel Astor has a reputation for exceptional service, so it's only natural that its chic and airy restaurant, as light and ambient as a greenhouse, follow suit. The setting is complemented by smoked-tomato soup with mini grilled cheese (Brie) sandwiches; the short stack of wild mushroom pancakes; and the "duck, duck, goose" entrée that presents the two birds in a host of different ways on the plate. The menu changes frequently, so look for more signature, delicious humor. ✉ *Hotel Astor, 956 Washington Ave., South Beach,* ☎ *305/672–7217. Reservations essential. AE, DC, MC, V.*

$$$–$$$$ ★ ✕ **Blue Door at the Delano.** In a hotel where style reigns supreme, this high-profile restaurant provides both glamour and tantalizing cuisine. Acclaimed consulting chef Claude Troisgros and executive chef Elizabeth Barlow combine the flavors of classic French cuisine with South American influences to create dishes such as the Big Ravioli, filled with crab-and-scallop mousseline, and osso buco in Thai curry sauce with

caramelized pineapple and bananas. Equally pleasing is dining with the crème de la crème of Miami (and New York, and Paris) society. Don't worry if you don't recognize some apparent bigwig next to you—eavesdrop on their cell phone conversation, and you'll no doubt be filled in pronto. ✉ *1685 Collins Ave., South Beach,* ☏ *305/674–6400. Reservations essential. AE, D, DC, MC, V.*

$$$–$$$$ ✕ **Rumi.** Rumi is what happens when club kids and party organizers like Alan Roth and Sean Saladino grow up: they open a sophisticated dinner lounge named for a mystical poet. Co-chefs J. D. Harris and Scott Fredel contribute to the seductive, heavy-lidded atmosphere with such culinary delectations as Florida pompano with truffled Peruvian potatoes or Sonoma duck breast with orange crepes. After 11 or so, the two-story storefront turns into a club, complete with velvet rope and mandatory champagne purchases if you intend on sitting at a table. ✉ *330 Lincoln Rd., South Beach,* ☏ *305/672–4353. Reservations essential. AE, MC, V. No lunch.*

$$$–$$$$ ★ ✕ **Tantra.** South Beach's reigning palace of sensuality appeals even to the world-weary. Upon entrance, you tread softly upon a grassy sod floor in the entryway and lounge, smell burning incense, hear Middle Eastern music spun by a DJ, and can even swing in a rope hammock. Food is serious business here, courtesy of chef Willis Loughhead. The Tantra "love apple" appetizer—a Homestead (local) tomato spiked with Laura Chenel goat cheese; lobster, scallops, and golden chanterelle cobbler; and sea-salted foie gras perched on a peppered plantain cake are representative of the cuisine. Smoke a house-provided hookah stuffed with flavored Turkish tobacco for an even more decadent touch. ✉ *1445 Pennsylvania Ave., South Beach,* ☏ *305/672–4765. Reservations essential. AE, DC, MC, V. No lunch weekends.*

$$$–$$$$ ✕ **Touch.** Touch stands among the more mundane Lincoln Road eateries like a radiant diva. Executive chef Sean Brasel wraps his dishes in a haze of acceptable sins—Sonoma quail stuffed with wild rice, foie gras, and black plums with plum-vanilla glacé is just one example of his brand of decadence. The red curry–crusted ahi or the veal chop marinated Tahitian style also entices. Atmospheric elements mimic the kitchen's creativity, with tufted silk on the walls, lambskin cushions, and palm trees growing out of the corners of the bar. The hip crowd that dallies here makes it impossible to get past the velvet ropes without a reservation. ✉ *910 Lincoln Rd., South Beach,* ☏ *305/532–8003. Reservations essential. AE, MC, V. No lunch.*

$$$–$$$$ ✕ **1220 at the Tides.** It's undeniably beautiful, done almost entirely in white—linens, candles, and original terrazzo floor—and seems out of place on increasingly tacky Ocean Drive. Designed by executive chef Roger Ruch, the progressive American fare is innovative without being overwhelming. Dishes such as the Island Princess, a conch tempura appetizer, and the citrus-glazed sea bass with plantain mash and banana catsup entrée acknowledge tropical influences; while more classic dishes such as the wood-roasted tenderloin of beef with truffle-honey demi-glace prove why this eatery is considered the last bastion of civilization on the Drive. ✉ *The Tides hotel, 1220 Ocean Dr., South Beach,* ☏ *305/604–5130. AE, D, MC, V.*

$$–$$$$ ★ ✕ **Nemo.** In a neighborhood that has emerged as a South Beach hot spot, Michael Schwartz's Nemo was a SoFi (South of Fifth Street) pioneer. The open-air atmosphere, bright colors, copper fixtures, and tree-shaded courtyard lend casual comfort; but its location is not why Nemo receives the raves it does. The menu, which blends Caribbean, Asian, Mediterranean, and Middle Eastern influences, promises an explosion of cultures in each bite. And it delivers. Popular appetizers include garlic-cured salmon rolls with Tabiko caviar and wasabi mayo, and crispy prawns with spicy salsa *cruda*. Main courses might include

wok-charred salmon or grilled Indian-spice pork chop. Hedy Goldsmith's funky pastries are exquisitely sinful. ✉ *100 Collins Ave., South Beach,* ☎ *305/532–4550. AE, MC, V.*

$$–$$$$ ✕ **Wish.** If what you wish for is stupendous cuisine served in a designer-deco environment, consider your wish granted. Fashion designer Todd Oldham, a part-time resident of South Beach, redesigned the former Tiffany Hotel, the art deco beauty that houses this fresh, youthful restaurant. His whimsical, colorful design (you'll marvel at the creative use of something like 50 hanging light fixtures) provides an apt setting for chef E. Michael Redit's French-Brazilian cuisine. His sensibility results in dishes like seared scallops over *brandade* (a puree of salt cod, garlic, and cream) and brandied onions or rare tuna with charred watermelon and avocado Hollandaise, which make as much of a statement as the room. ✉ *The Hotel, 801 Collins Ave., South Beach,* ☎ *305/674–9474. AE, D, DC, MC, V.*

## Eclectic

$–$$ ✕ **Balan's.** The British are coming, all right—to Lincoln Road, with this medium-price, stylish spot. But aside from its breakfast and desserts, this outpost of an English chain scarcely bears the stamp of its mother country. Instead, a fusion menu of Mediterranean, Middle Eastern, and Thai elements delights the fashionable crowd here. Try deep-fried goat cheese and mushrooms in a beer-and-caraway bread crust, Moroccan chicken with spicy *harissa* (red pepper) sauce, sea bass over oven-roasted Italian tomatoes and sautéed potato slices, or sirloin steak with balsamic glaze and black lentils. The place is especially busy at breakfast, when it serves the traditional English platter of undeniably tasty cholesterol. ✉ *1022 Lincoln Rd., South Beach,* ☎ *305/534–9191. AE, D, MC, V.*

## German

$–$$ ✕ **Dab Haus.** Picture the inside of a U-boat, and you've got the idea: black-painted walls, scarred-wood furniture, a haze of cigarette smoke that never dissipates, and art that can only be described as weird. But the food is the star at this German pub, which is almost totally removed from the hubbub of South Beach. All the German favorites are here, including a wonderfully spicy goulash, sauerbraten, schnitzels, homemade spaetzle, and sausages such as bratwurst and currywurst. Big draft beers—the servers recommend the thirst-quenching, cloudy *hefe weizen*—wash it all down, even the Nutella (chocolate and hazelnut spread) crepes that are just too darn hard to resist. ✉ *852 Alton Rd., South Beach,* ☎ *305/534–9557. AE, D, DC, MC, V.*

## Italian

$$–$$$$ ★ ✕ **Tuscan Steak.** Dark wood, mirrors, and green upholstery define this masculine, chic, expensive place, where big platters of meats and fish are served family style, but as if your family were a royal one. Part of the restaurant empire run by China Grill Management, Tuscan can be busy as a subway stop, and still the staff will be gracious and giving. The chefs take their cues from the Tuscan countryside, where pasta is rich with truffles and main plates are simply but deliciously grilled. Sip a deep red Barolo with any of the house specialties: three-mushroom risotto with white truffle oil, gnocchi with Gorgonzola cream, Florentine T-bone with roasted garlic puree, whole yellowtail snapper with braised garlic, or filet mignon with a Gorgonzola crust in a red wine sauce. ✉ *431 Washington Ave., South Beach,* ☎ *305/534–2233. AE, DC, MC, V.*

$$–$$$ ✕ **Escopazzo.** A romantic storefront takes you away, like Calgon, from the din of bustling Washington Avenue. The northern Italian menu offers some of the area's best—and most expensive—Italian food. But innovative treatments of standard ingredients make it worth the out-

lay of cash. Sea bass gets "scales" of crusty potato, goat cheese and arugula are mixed into a risotto, and various soufflés feature vegetables and mixed seafood. Service can be slow as a speedboat in a manatee zone; pass the time by taking a tour of the 1,000-bottle wine cellar. ✉ *1311 Washington Ave., South Beach,* ☎ *305/674–9450. AE, DC, MC, V. No lunch.*

$$–$$$ ★ ✕ **Osteria del Teatro.** Thanks to word of mouth, this northern Italian restaurant is constantly full. Orchids grace the tables in the intimate gray-on-gray room with a low, laced-canvas ceiling, deco lamps, and the most refined clink and clatter along Washington Avenue. Regulars know not to order off the printed menu, however. A tremendous variety of daily specials offers the best options here. A representative appetizer is poached asparagus served over polenta triangles with a Gorgonzola sauce. Stuffed pastas, including spinach crepes overflowing with ricotta, can seem heavy but taste light; fish dishes yield a rosemary-marinated tuna or salmon in a pink peppercorn–citrus sauce. ✉ *1443 Washington Ave., South Beach,* ☎ *305/538–7850. Reservations essential. AE, DC, MC, V. Closed Sun. No lunch.*

$–$$ ✕ **Spiga.** When you need a break from Miami's abundant exotic fare, savor the modestly priced Italian standards served with flair in this small, pretty place. Homemade is the hallmark here, where pastas and breads are fresh daily. Carpaccio *di salmone* (thinly sliced salmon with mixed greens) is a typical appetizer, and the *zuppa di pesce* (fish stew) is unparalleled. Entrées include ravioli *di vitello ai funghi shiitaki,* homemade ravioli stuffed with veal and sautéed with shiitake mushrooms. The cozy restaurant has become a neighborhood favorite, where customers sometimes bring in CDs for personalized enjoyment. ✉ *1228 Collins Ave., South Beach,* ☎ *305/534–0079. AE, D, DC, MC, V.*

$–$$ ✕ **Sport Café.** When World Cup season comes around, there's no question this place is run by true Italians, and you can't get a seat or hear anything much but go-o-o-o-o-o-o-o-al. The supercasual bistro is dominated by a giant TV inside and has many tables outside that afford a cityscape view. Pastas here are wonderfully good and even more wonderfully inexpensive. Lighter appetites appreciate the spry salad of white beans, tuna, and red onion; the light vegetable-puree soups; and bubbling thin-crust pizza. A good power-lunch spot, Sport has two sister restaurants, both called Rosinella, one on Lincoln Road and the other downtown. ✉ *538 Washington Ave., South Beach,* ☎ *305/674–9700. MC, V.*

## Japanese

$$$–$$$$ ✕ **SushiSamba Dromo.** With the eclectic pairing of Japanese cuisine with Brazilian, this sibling to the New York City SushiSamba is perhaps the most eagerly awaited sushi restaurant next to Nobu. The results are fabulous if a bit mystifying: seared yellowfin tuna marinated in sugarcane juice; chicken teriyaki with Peruvian potato puree; shrimp and Latino vegetable tempura; and caramel rice pudding served in green tea leaf cups. Immediately swamped with customers, SushiSamba has a vibe that hurts the ears but warms the trendy heart. ✉ *600 Lincoln Rd., South Beach,* ☎ *305/673–5337. Reservations essential. AE, MC, V.*

$$$–$$$$ ✕ **Tambo.** Cross ceviche with sushi and you've got "Nikkei" cuisine, a blend of Japanese and Peruvian flavors that originally wowed Venezuela before arriving in Miami. Proprietor Alejandro Sucre named this cozy but elegant spot after the small inns in Peru, and it does have that exclusive, out-of-the-way feel. So take respite with items like carpaccio of diver scallops with tomato ceviche; snapper with wasabi-whipped potatoes; and a host of sushi, sashimi, ceviche toradito (thin-sliced marinated fish) concoctions. ✉ *1801 Purdy Ave., South Beach,* ☎ *305/535–2414. AE, D, DC, MC, V. Closed Sun. No lunch.*

$-$$$ ✕ **Sushi Hana.** You could describe the decor in this long-standing sushi house as Zen versus South Beach—soothing waterfalls and fountains vie with giant TV screens blasting music videos. Then again, dichotomy makes the world go around. For more unusual pairings, look to the extensive list of rolls, which include the French roll (shrimp, snow crab, avocado, cucumber, cream cheese, and roe), a combo that tastes like sushi in a crepe. Take advantage of the sashimi by ordering *chirashi,* a mixed assortment of raw fish on rice, or request a beautifully built ark that, like Noah's, houses just about two of everything. ✉ *1131 Washington Ave., South Beach,* ☎ *305/604–0300. AE, DC, MC, V. No lunch.*

$-$$ ✕ **Maiko Japanese Restaurant and Sushi Bar.** Ever-popular, ever-ready . . . it's not a battery, just a dependable place to order sushi standards, plus an amorous-sounding creation called the kissing roll—crab, avocado, and cucumber coated with the tiny flying fish eggs. Models hang around for the steamed dumplings with *ponzu* sauce, while club kids line their bellies with flavorful teriyaki, sautéed eel, and soba noodle soups before drinking the night away. They also get a good jump on the evening with the sake, which Maiko presents in warm abundance. ✉ *1255 Washington Ave., South Beach,* ☎ *305/531–6369. AE, DC, MC, V.*

## Latin

$$$-$$$$ ★ ✕ **Yuca.** Yuca, the potatolike staple of Cuban kitchens, also stands for the kind of *Y*oung *U*rban *C*uban-*A*merican clientele the top-flight, indoor-outdoor eatery courts. The Nuevo Latino food rises to high standards: traditional corn tamales filled with conch and a spicy jalapeño-and-creole-cheese pesto; the namesake yuca stuffed with Mamacita's *picadillo* (spiced ground meat) and dressed in wild mushrooms on a bed of sautéed spinach; and plantain-coated dolphin with a tamarind tartar sauce. Desserts include classic Cuban rice pudding in an almond basket and coconut pudding in its shell. ✉ *501 Lincoln Rd., South Beach,* ☎ *305/532–9822. AE, DC, MC, V.*

$$-$$$ ✕ **Samba Room.** A 25-ft canvas titled "Cuba 1957" by Rolando Diaz contributes to the pre-Castro Havana feel of the Samba Room. Executive chef Philip Butler's Latin fusion fare incorporates culinary elements from Peru to Puerto Rico, but is often Cuban-influenced: *ropa vieja* (shredded beef) served like a Sloppy Joe on a Cuban bun; beef tenderloin garnished with sugarcane; plantain chips with black bean–tomato salsa. Lounge lizards are especially happy with the outdoor sofas and deep, comfy club chairs that encourage dawdling. ✉ *1501 Collins Ave., South Beach,* ☎ *305/672–6223. AE, D, DC, MC, V.*

## Pan-Asian

$$$-$$$$ ✕ **Bambú.** Cameron Diaz may be an in-name owner only, but do anticipate glam surroundings and customers who are (or think they are) equal to her status. Bambú's muted khaki colors, woven raffia drapes, bars formed from river rocks and coconut wood, and spectacular 14-ft granite waterfall provide some Zen for the world-weary—props to Astor Place hotelier and restaurateur Karim Masri and his partner, Hubert Baudoin. But the real beauty here lies in executive chef Rob Boone's fare: tuna hand rolls with avocado, cilantro, and pickled eggplant; soy-lacquered cod with tempura chrysanthemum leaves; and Kobe beef with tiny Asian vegetables and lotus root. ✉ *1661 Meridian Ave., South Beach,* ☎ *305/531–4800. Reservations essential. AE, MC, V. No lunch.*

$$$-$$$$ ✕ **China Grill.** This crowded, noisy ever-vaunted celebrity haunt turns out not Chinese food but rather "world cuisine," and in large portions meant for sharing. Crispy duck with scallion pancakes and caramelized black-vinegar sauce is a nice surprise, as is pork and beans with green apple and balsamic *mojo* (a garlicky Cuban marinade). Mechanical ser-

vice delivers the acceptable broccoli rabe dumpling starter, the wild mushroom pasta entrée, or the flash-fried crispy spinach that shatters like a good martini glass thrown into a fireplace. Unless you're frequent diners Boris Becker or George Clooney, don't expect your drinks to arrive before your food. ✉ *404 Washington Ave., South Beach,* ☎ *305/534–2211. Reservations essential. AE, DC, MC, V. No lunch Sat.*

$$$–$$$$ ★ ✕ **Pacific Time.** Packed nearly every night, chef-proprietor Jonathan Eismann's superb eatery has a high blue ceiling, banquettes, plank floors, and an open kitchen. The brilliant American-Asian cuisine includes such entrées as cedar-roasted salmon, rosemary-roasted chicken, and dry-aged Colorado beef grilled with shiitake mushrooms. The cuttlefish appetizer and the Florida pompano entrée are masterpieces. Desserts include a fresh pear-pecan spring roll. (FYI: Eismann recently opened a sibling restaurant called Thom in New York's SoHo district.) ✉ *915 Lincoln Rd., South Beach,* ☎ *305/534–5979. Reservations essential. AE, DC, MC, V.*

$$–$$$ ✕ **SUVA.** Named for the capital of Fiji, and run by China Grill Management, the restaurant reflects a South Seas theme, with a unique sandbox bar, Pandana bush fronds, masks, gauze curtains, and bamboo wall sconces lighting the way. It's just as easy to be as enthusiastic about the tuna tartare served in a giant clam shell or the Fijian fisherman stew spilling out of a coconut. Family-size portions (à la China Grill) encourage sharing the Bora Bora banana split with homemade guanabana (a tart, yellow-green fruit, also called soursop) ice cream for dessert—but do keep the mango-spiked champagne cocktail all to yourself. ✉ *801 Lincoln Rd., South Beach,* ☎ *305/925–0051. AE, MC, V. No lunch.*

## Russian

$$–$$$$ ✕ **Red Square.** The management of China Grill have proven that Americans will happily dine at a Soviet-theme restaurant, even one that features a statue of Lenin in the foyer. No wonder, when you can sip one of 100 vodkas at a bar made of ice. Barbara Scott's wide-ranging menu is eclectic yet only barely Russian. The fusion dishes, such as Siberian nachos and fried wontons topped with smoked salmon and crème fraîche vie with spicy Georgian fried chicken or turkey–shiitake mushroom meat loaf for your attention—which, let's face it, may be limited in this see-and-be-seen atmosphere. ✉ *411 Washington Ave., South Beach,* ☎ *305/672–0200. Reservations essential. AE, MC, V.*

## Seafood

$$–$$$$ ✕ **Joe's Stone Crab Restaurant.** Because it's somewhat of a Miami phenomenon, Joe's stubbornly operates by its own rules and does not take reservations even though it attracts phenomenal crowds. Go prepared to wait up to an hour just to register your name for a table, and resign yourself to waiting up to another *three* hours before you finally sit down to eat. The centerpiece of the ample à la carte menu is, of course, stone crab, with a piquant mustard sauce. Popular side orders include creamed garlic spinach, french-fried onions, fried green tomatoes, and hash browns. Desserts range from a justifiably famous key lime pie to apple pie with a crumb-pecan topping. If you can't stand loitering hungrily while self-important patrons try to grease the maître d's palm, come for lunch or go next door for Joe's takeout. ✉ *11 Washington Ave., South Beach,* ☎ *305/673–0365; 305/673–4611 for takeout; 800/780–2722 for overnight shipping. Reservations not accepted. AE, D, DC, MC, V. Closed May–Oct. 15. No lunch Sun.–Mon.*

## Steak

$$$–$$$$ ✕ **Gaucho Room.** You'll never bite down on a more succulent steak anywhere than in this Argentine-cowboy-themed room. But don't you

dare call this a steak house. The chef cut his culinary teeth on fusion cuisine, and he takes the Latin beat and puts the metronome on vivace. The results are seen in pulled duck empanada with smoked chili sauce or Chilean sea bass with *boniato*-ginger puree. Which is not to say that you shouldn't order the supple *churrasco,* a whole skirt steak that is marinated, grilled, and then sliced table-side. And service may be the finest and most solicitous in South Beach—a compliment indeed. ✉ *Loews hotel, 1601 Collins Ave., South Beach,* ☎ *305/604–5290. Reservations essential. AE, D, DC, MC, V. Closed Mon. No lunch.*

### Turkish

$$ ✕ **Café Efesus.** Turkish cooking in a whimsical setting satisfies the predominantly Turkish clientele who hang out in this South Beach hideaway drinking beer and telling stories for hours. Their presence heralds the authenticity you'll find on the inexpensive, varied menu. Cold yogurt soup is a refreshing opener. Grape leaves, hummus, and phyllo stuffed with feta are good starters, as are various treatments of chickpeas. The chicken is tasty with garlic and tomato, or you can have a gyro sandwich filled with meat sliced right from a vertical spit. ✉ *1339 Washington Ave., South Beach,* ☎ *305/674–0078. AE, DC, MC, V.*

## Downtown Miami

### American/Casual

$–$$ ✕ **Hardaway's Firehouse Four.** Thanks to billboard-owner NBA star Tim Hardaway, this restored 1930s firehouse has a new lease on life. Influenced by every region from Asia to Latin America to the Caribbean, fare such as tenderloin tips sprinkled with lime and garlic or boniato-leek soup can be iffy on busy nights. It's best to stick with innovative sandwiches, such as the tuna burger with soba-noodle salad or the Euro-Cuban sandwich, a conglomeration of roast pork, ham, Swiss cheese, and red onion layered on focaccia. Better yet, skip the eats and head for the drinks—Firehouse Four's Friday happy hour is legendary, with normally sedate businessfolk thronging the streets like college students on spring break. ✉ *1000 S. Miami Ave., Brickell Village,* ☎ *305/371–3473. AE, D, DC, MC, V.*

$–$$ ✕ **Tobacco Road.** If you like your food the way you like your blues—gritty, honest, and unassuming—then this octogenarian joint will earn your respect. A musician wailing the blues also cooks jambalaya onstage, although entertainment varies. And no one's weeping about the food. The Road-burger is a popular choice, as are the chili worthy of a fire hose and appetizers such as nachos and chicken wings. Don't let the rough-edged exterior deter you from finer dining. On Tuesday during the season, Tobacco Road offers a Maine lobster special, and fine single-malt Scotches are stocked behind the bar. ✉ *626 S. Miami Ave., Downtown,* ☎ *305/374–1198. AE, D, DC, MC, V.*

### Chinese

$$ ✕ **Tony Chan's Water Club.** On the outstanding menu of more than 200 appetizers and entrées are minced quail tossed with bamboo shoots and mushrooms wrapped in lettuce leaves. Indulge in a seafood spectacular of shrimp, conch, scallops, fish cakes, and crabmeat tossed with broccoli in a bird's nest, or go for pork chops sprinkled with green pepper in a black bean–garlic sauce. A lighter favorite is steamed sea bass with ginger and garlic. Don't let the delicate flavors fool you—this restaurant is not just for the nosher but for the power-hungry power luncher who also wants a bay view. ✉ *Doubletree Grand Hotel, 1717 N. Bayshore Dr., Downtown,* ☎ *305/374–8888. AE, D, DC, MC, V. No lunch weekends.*

| | |
|---|---|
| Azul | 6 |
| Capital Grille | 8 |
| Fishbone Grille | 13 |
| Garcia's | 15 |
| Hardaway's Firehouse Four | 11 |
| Indigo | 5 |
| Japengo | 4 |
| Las Delicias del Mar Peruano | 1 |
| Los Ranchos | 3 |
| Morton's | 9 |
| Perricone's Marketplace and Café | 12 |
| Porcao | 7 |
| Rosinella's | 12 |
| Tobacco Road | 3 |
| Tony Chan's Water Club | 2 |

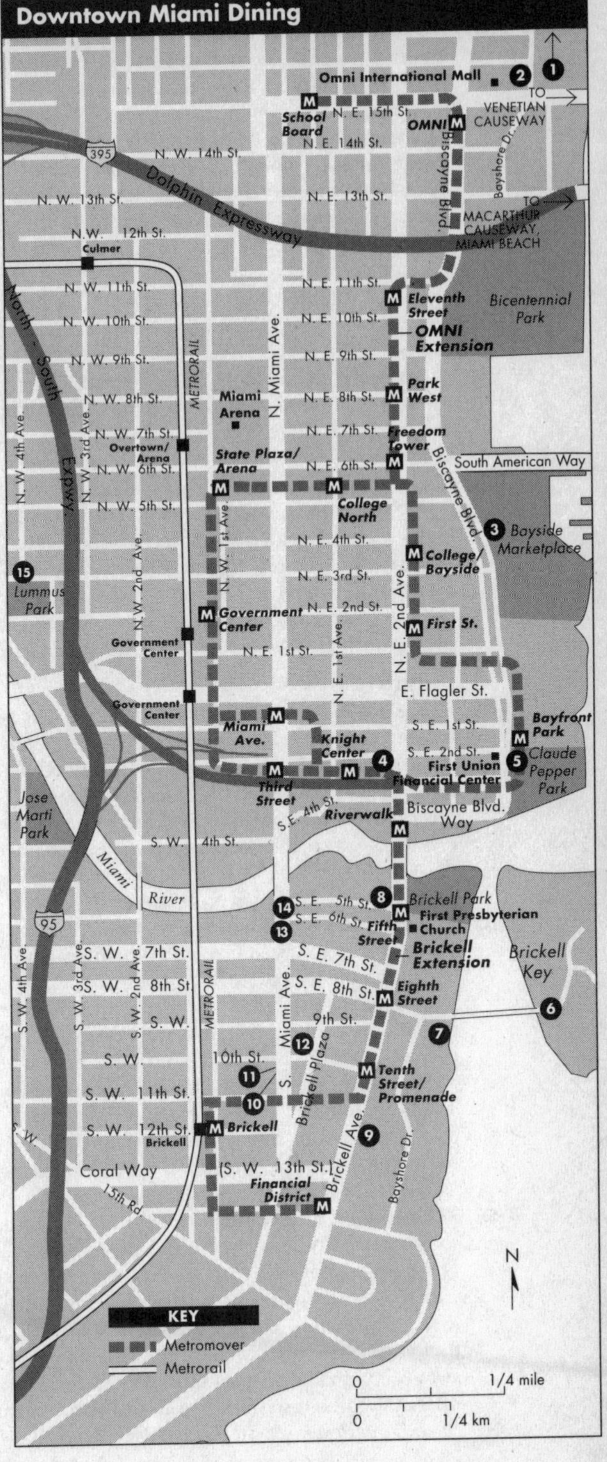

## Contemporary

$$–$$$$ ★ ✕ **Azul.** Azul has sumptuously conquered the devil in the details. In addition to chef Michelle Bernstein's exotically rendered French–Caribbean cuisine, the thoughtful touches in service graciously anticipate your broader dining needs. Does your sleeveless blouse mean your shoulders are too cold to properly appreciate the poached eggs with lobster-knuckle hollandaise? Ask for one of the house pashminas, available in a variety of fashionable colors. Forgot your reading glasses and can't decipher the hanger steak with foie gras sauce? Request a pair from the host. Want to see how the other half lives? Descend the interior staircase to Cafe Sambal, the all-day casual restaurant downstairs. ✉ *Mandarin Oriental Hotel, 500 Brickell Key Dr., Brickell Key,* ☏ *305/913–8288. Reservations essential. AE, MC, V. Closed Sun. No lunch Sat.*

$$–$$$ ✕ **Indigo.** When the Hotel Inter-Continental decided to redo its restaurants, it didn't fool around. Now the entire lobby is one big open-wall eatery, where you can watch vacationers get ready to depart for the cruise ships—unless you're one of them—and sup on the globally influenced cuisine. The menu's a trifle too cutesy for serious gourmets, with categories like "salappzs and ladles" and "dare 2 share." Stone crab *croquetas* are a notable starter, and Moroccan *tagine* (stew) can be shared as an entrée. A great wine list and moderately priced brunches, lunch buffets, and happy-hour spreads suit the suits who work in nearby downtown. ✉ *Hotel Inter-Continental, 100 Chopin Plaza, Downtown,* ☏ *305/854–9550. AE, D, DC, MC, V.*

## Italian

$–$$ ★ ✕ **Basilico Ristorante.** The neighborhood just north of Miami International Airport has few interesting dining options, but this one is worth investigating. Run by an Argentine family, Basilico has a quiet dining room insulated from all the takeoffs and landings. Delicate, delightful food at a low price includes seafood with linguine, ravioli stuffed with lobster, a lusty dish of veal nestled in mashed potatoes, and homemade desserts. ✉ *5879 N.W. 36th St., Virginia Gardens,* ☏ *305/871–3585. AE, DC, MC, V. Closed Sun. No lunch Sat.*

$–$$ ✕ **Perricone's Marketplace and Café.** Brickell Avenue south of the Miami River is burgeoning with Italian restaurants. This is the biggest and most popular among them, housed in a 120-year-old Vermont barn. The recipes were handed down from grandmother to mother to daughter, and the cooking is simple and good. Buy your wine from the on-premises deli and bring it to your table for a small corking fee. Enjoy a glass with homemade minestrone; a generous antipasto; linguine with a sauté of jumbo shrimp, fresh asparagus, and chopped tomatoes; or gnocchi with four cheeses. The homemade tiramisu and fruit tart are top-notch. ✉ *15 S.E. 10th St., Brickell Village,* ☏ *305/374–9449. AE, MC, V. Closed Sun. No lunch Sat.*

$–$$ ✕ **Rosinella's.** Owner Tonino Doino and his mother, Rosinella, run this stylish pasta house with true Italian touches. A luscious appetizer of veal with creamy sauce of pureed tuna precedes beautiful grilled fish with greens and pastas with zesty sauces (especially the red-pepper-infused *arrabbiata*). Pureed vegetable soups are good and light, and thin-crust pizzas are delicious. If Rosinella has made gnocchi that day, ask for it with Gorgonzola sauce. A sister restaurant on Lincoln Road offers the same tasty fare in a busier atmosphere. ✉ *1040 S. Miami Ave., Downtown,* ☏ *305/372–5756. AE, DC, MC, V.*

## Latin

$–$$$ ✕ **Los Ranchos.** Sustaining the tradition of Managua's original Los Ranchos, this steak-house chain serves Argentine-style beef—lean, grass-fed tenderloin with *chimichurri* (a thick sauce of olive oil, vinegar, cayenne, and herbs). The Nicaraguan sauces include a tomato-based marinara and a fiery *cebollitas encurtidas* (with jalapeño and pickled onion). Specialties include spicy chorizo and *cuajada con maduro* (skim cheese with fried bananas). Don't look for veggies or brewed decaf—that's just not the Latin way—but there is live entertainment. ✉ *Bayside Marketplace, 401 Biscayne Blvd., Downtown,* ☎ *305/375–8188 or 305/375–0666;* ✉ *125 S.W. 107th Ave., Sweetwater,* ☎ *305/221–9367;* ✉ *2728 Ponce de León Blvd., Coral Gables,* ☎ *305/446–0050;* ✉ *The Falls, 8888 S.W. 136th St., Suite 303, Kendall, South Miami,* ☎ *305/238–6867. AE, DC, MC, V.*

## Pan-Asian

**$$$** ✕ **Japengo.** Hotel restaurants sure aren't the disappointments they used to be. This one, named for Marco Polo's handle for Japan, has an outstanding photographic mural of Hong Kong and a stunning quantity of hand-carved Lalique glass—not to mention top-rate sushi (if a rather traditional assortment). Pan-Asian dishes, including warm charsu duck on mixed baby greens with vegetable root chips and fresh plums, take Hawaii, China, Thailand, and even South America into account. Too exotic for your typical business traveler tastes? Don't worry—the place also supplies a grilled hamburger on focaccia. ✉ *Hyatt Regency, 400 S.E. 2nd Ave., Downtown,* ☎ *305/679–3055. AE, MC, V.*

## Peruvian

**$–$$** ★ ✕ **Las Delicias del Mar Peruano.** If ever there were a mom-and-pop place, this is it. Especially if Mom and Pop are Peruvian. This salute to the coastal cuisine of western Peru snaps with wonderfully fresh food and surprising flavors. Start with *papa a la huancaina,* a traditional boiled-potato appetizer whose creamy white cheese sauce is enlivened with chilies. Move from land to sea with shrimp creole, a creamy revelation with a pink sauce that's a silky delight, or try *cau cau de los mariscos,* a seafood stew that startles with its combination of mint and potato. The vast menu has plenty of landlubber eats, too. ✉ *2937 Biscayne Blvd., Edgewater,* ☎ *305/571–1888. AE, MC, V.*

## Seafood

**$$–$$$** ★ ✕ **Garcia's.** Pull up your rowboat for outdoor waterfront dining at this tiny seafood joint on the Miami River. The menu is simple and limited, but the fish sure is fresh. Grilled dolphin—on a sandwich or with various Cuban-style side dishes—is juicy and well-seasoned. Grouper chowder, the classic Cuban fish soup, excels here, and fried calamari benefits from a peppy cocktail sauce. The conch fritters are truly packed with conch, or you can enjoy fish, shrimp, and chicken on kabobs, the primary entrée option. There's also a fish market inside. ✉ *398 N.W. North River Dr., Downtown,* ☎ *305/375–0765. MC, V.*

**$–$$** ✕ **Fishbone Grill.** The artsy humor of this place is evident in the campy decor, but the fish here is sincerely artful. Start with cakelike jalapeño cornbread served alongside a small salad with homemade tomato-basil dressing. Then order your fish from the blackboard and have it grilled, blackened, sautéed, baked, or Française- or Asian-style. Pizzas are available, too, as is a mean cioppino, the San Francisco–style fish stew in a tomato base. Fishbone serves beer and wine only and has a reasonably priced, varied selection. Watch for winemakers' dinners, when superb vintages are paired with the chef's whims. ✉ *650 S. Miami Ave., Downtown,* ☎ *305/530–1915. AE, MC, V. No dinner Sun.*

## Steak

**$$$–$$$$** ✕ **Morton's.** Morton's has the atmosphere of a private club, complete with dark mahogany paneling, spacious leather booths, subdued lighting, and crisp white tablecloths. Not bad for a chain. The open kitchen shows you how a real steak restaurant prepares double filet mignon,

New York strip sirloin, and broiled Block Island swordfish steak. The unfussiest item here is also the best bargain—an umpteen-ounce sirloin burger, with a side of hash browns and only available at lunch. ✉ *1200 Brickell Ave., Downtown,* ☎ *305/400–9990;* ✉ *17355 Biscayne Blvd., North Miami Beach,* ☎ *305/945–3131. AE, MC, V.*

$$$ ★ ✕ **Capital Grille.** Downtown's most elegant restaurant is a palace of protein. That is, the menu is traditional and oriented to beef, and the dining room handsome and filled mostly with men on a power lunch. Porterhouse, steak au poivre, various sirloins, and fillets, many of which hang in a locker in the center of the dining room to age, head the list. All is à la carte, even the baked potato. The cheesecake is tops. Still, service can be so relentlessly formal it's ridiculous—the waiters will walk miles to ensure that women get their menus first. ✉ *444 Brickell Ave., Downtown,* ☎ *305/374–4500. AE, D, DC, MC, V.*

$$$ ✕ **Porcao.** How now, Porcao—what's not to love? Not only does this Brazilian churrascaria serve outstanding *rodizio,* grilled meats sliced off skewers right at the table, a creative and enormous salad bar is included in the fixed $34 price. Pair pickled quail eggs with marinated chicken hearts, or veer toward the less exotic with thin-sliced prosciutto and bacon-wrapped chicken thighs. Satisfy the inner carnivore with lamb, filet mignon, and sirloin and the obvious sweet tooth with à la carte desserts such as flan in caramel sauce. Just don't weigh yourself afterward. ✉ *801 S. Bayshore Dr., Downtown,* ☎ *305/373–2777. AE, DC, MC, V.*

## Little Havana and Vicinity

### Cuban

$–$$$ ✕ **Casa Larios.** Yes, South Florida has 1,000 Cuban restaurants, but this one stands out for its consistently excellent food. The chicken soup is golden yellow, pearly, salty—the perfect elixir. Look for specials like roast pork loin, roasted lamb, *caldo gallego* (white-bean soup with ham and greens), and the Argentine-inspired *churrasco,* a boneless strip steak with *chimichurri* (a sauce of oil, vinegar, and herbs). The restaurant spawned Larios on the Beach, on Ocean Drive, where Gloria Estefan and husband Emilio Estefan are partners, and who, if you're lucky, can sometimes be glimpsed. ✉ *7705 W. Flagler St., near Mall of the Americas,* ☎ *305/266–5494. AE, MC, V.*

$–$$ ✕ **Versailles.** Cubans meet to dine on Calle Ocho in what is quite possibly the most ornate budget restaurant you'll ever see, all mirrors and candelabras. And the royal treatment is not limited to decor in this veritable institution. The food is terrific, especially such classics as ropa vieja, *arroz con pollo* (chicken and rice), *palomilla* (thin, boneless) steak, *sopa de platanos* (plantain soup), ham shank, and roast pork. To complete the experience, have the town's strongest Cuban coffee and terrific flan or sweet *tres leches* (literally, "three milks," a creamy Latin dessert) to finish. ✉ *3555 S.W. 8th St. between S.W. 35th and S.W. 36th Aves., Little Havana,* ☎ *305/444–0240. AE, D, DC, MC, V.*

### Italian

$–$$ ✕ **Tutto Pasta.** Some of the best Italian in town for the money comes out of this kitchen. Entrées rarely top $10, but they always please, especially homemade pastas with red sauces. Start with delicious bruschetta, mozzarella with pignoli, prosciutto and sun-dried tomatoes, or a homemade soup. Spaghetti with marinara, the cheapest entrée, might well be the best because the sauce is that good. Pleasant service matches the casual atmosphere. Fettuccine with chicken, mushrooms, and sun-dried tomatoes; homemade ravioli with spinach and ricotta; and a stew of snapper, seafood, and tomato sauce excel, as do house-baked desserts. ✉ *1751 S.W. 3rd Ave. at S.W. 18 Rd., Miami,* ☎ *305/857–0709. MC, V.*

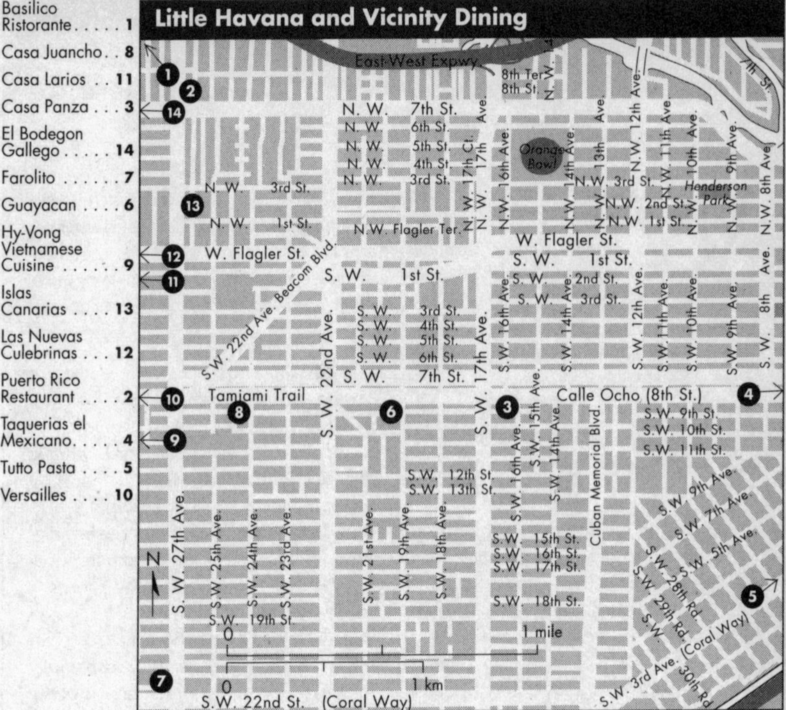


## Latin

$–$$ ✕ **Guayacan.** Offering counter service and a comfortable if simple dining room, this family-run place serves all the traditional Nicaraguan foods to a lot of traditional Nicaraguans: the signature grilled churrasco steak; a sticky sweet tres leches; and rich, mellow Victoria beer. A simple half-chicken or a boneless strip steak served with three lusty, spicy sauces: pico de gallo, chimichurri, and a basic hot sauce, sparks the palate. All come with *gallo pinto* (red beans with rice and plenty of seasoning) and a good smattering of local politics, culture, and around-town happenings. ✉ *1933 S.W. 8th St., Little Havana,* ☏ *305/649–2015. AE, MC, V.*

★

$–$$ ✕ **Puerto Rico Restaurant.** Puerto Rican mementos set the scene for the wonderfully authentic food here. The weekend buffet is the best bet, with various salads, soups, and meats served hot and fresh, all you can eat. Off the menu, try *asapao de pollo,* a tasty chicken soup with rice; *alcapurria,* mashed green banana stuffed with ground beef and fried; *sancocho,* hen stew with plantain, white potato, carrot, chicken, and cilantro; and *mofongo* (the national dish of Puerto Rico), plantain mashed and fried and mixed with various meats. There's live music some nights and always a friendly staff. ✉ *711 N.W. 27th Ave., Little Havana,* ☏ *305/642–6269. No credit cards.*

$ ✕ **Islas Canarias.** Since 1976 this has been a gathering place for Cuban poets, pop-music stars, and media personalities. Murals depict a Canary Islands street scene (owner Santiago Garcia's grandfather came from Tenerife). The low-priced menu, which includes breakfast, carries such Canary Islands dishes as baked lamb, ham hocks with boiled potatoes, and *tortilla española* (Spanish omelet with onions and chorizo), as well as Cuban standards like *palomilla* steak and fried kingfish. Don't miss the three superb varieties of homemade chips—potato, *malanga* (a tropical tuber), and plantain. ✉ *285 N.W. 27th Ave., Little Havana,* ☏ *305/649–0440. D, MC, V.*

Close-Up

# FLORIDA FOODS

WHEN THE LOCAL CHEFS claim they cook with indigenous items "right out of the backyard," they're telling the truth. South Florida's fortunate enough to have two growing seasons annually, and plenty of warm, soothing ocean for tropically oriented fish and shellfish. In other words, Florida supplies fresh ingredients year-round, and it's not just about oranges and grapefruits anymore.

Take mangos, for instance. Lush and lovable, mangos show up on restaurant menus in salsas, coulis, smoothies, and of course, desserts. They have to—hundreds of varieties grow here, yielding thousands of pounds of fruit, and anyone with a mango tree knows they ripen almost faster than you can eat 'em.

The same goes for avocados, which are big and bright green and have a firm, fleshy texture. And size does count. Florida avocados, also called by the fanciful name "alligator pears," have about half the fat and twice the girth of California avocados. They make excellent guacamole, but they're even better sliced simply over field greens along with some hearts of palm, another South Florida specialty.

Key limes have gotten more play in recent years than Dan Marino, taking over the orange's infamy. Though key limes—small, jaundiced-looking citrus fruit with as many seeds as Jim Carrey has teeth—can be bitter, cooks prize them for their acidic qualities and particularly enjoy using them in tart custard pastries called key lime pies.

The key lime pucker usually comes at the end of a meal, while fish native to Florida waters receive prime-time attention. The snapper family—including red, yellowtail, and hog varieties—is a mainstay on local menus. Although dolphin, also known as mahimahi, is a longtime favorite, grouper has almost replaced it in popularity, since its mild but fleshy fillets adhere well to almost any recipe. The coastal waters off the Florida shoreline also yield some flavorful shrimp: look especially for Key West pinks, which are as pretty as a sunrise.

Stone crabs—a delicacy native to the region—ensure a predinner smile. You can enjoy these simply steamed claws, which are only in season from October to May, for several reasons: they're succulent and mild, with tender flesh; they're usually dressed with a creamy mustard dip; and while the crab sacrifices a claw, it isn't killed. In fact, stone crab anglers take one claw from the crab and throw it back into the water, where a new claw will generate over time. Now that's a good growing season.

— Jen Karetnick

### Mexican

$ ✕ **Taquerias el Mexicano.** Locals swear by the ultracheap, superspicy cooking at this restaurant and Mexican grocery. Browse for your favorite dried chilies and contemplate a large menu loaded with typical favorites and a few surprises. The world's best hangover remedy might be *posole* (a rich stew with hominy and beef broth). Thick pork chops are bathed in a spicy green tomatillo sauce, and chicken fajitas bear no resemblance to the mall chain version: they're spicy, juicy, and delightful. Swab everything with any of three homemade sauces, but be warned: the one designated "hot" will taste like a midday August sun. ✉ *521 S.W. 8th St., Little Havana,* ☎ *305/858–1160;* ✉ *1961 S.W. 8th St., Little Havana,* ☎ *305/649–9150;* ✉ *6974 Collins Ave., North Beach, Miami Beach,* ☎ *305/864–5220. AE, MC, V.*

### Peruvian

$–$$ ★ ✕ **Farolito.** The menu at this small but tasteful storefront can be summed up easily: seafood, beef, pasta, and potato, the big four of Peru. Primary education begins with potatoes prepared in the traditional style, with creamy white cheese sauce, black olives, and egg. Continue on to middle school with a bracing ceviche, then attend high school with a thin boneless steak served with thick spaghetti and pesto. Hearty cilantro-laden beef stew is for the college-level appetite, and a surprising shredded chicken in a creamy sauce of minced walnut, garlic, egg, and milk is clearly graduate work. ✉ *2885 Coral Way, Little Havana,* ☎ *305/446–4122. AE, D, DC, MC, V.*

### Spanish

$$–$$$$ ✕ **Casa Juancho.** This meeting place for the movers and shakers of the Cuban *exilio* community is also a haven for lovers of fine Spanish regional cuisine. Strolling balladeers serenade you among brown brick, rough-hewn dark timbers, and walls adorned with hanging smoked meats and colorful Talavera platters. Try the hake prepared in a fish stock with garlic, onions, and Spanish white wine or the *carabineros a la plancha* (jumbo red shrimp with head and shell on, split and grilled). For dessert *crema Catalana* is a rich pastry custard with a delectable crust of burnt caramel. The house features the largest list of reserved Spanish wines in the States. ✉ *2436 S.W. 8th St., Little Havana,* ☎ *305/642–2452. AE, D, DC, MC, V.*

$$ ✕ **Casa Panza.** The sign on the door aptly describes the philosophy of this restaurant—HASTA QUE EL CUERPO AGUANTE (until the body gives). Here you'll have no problem getting your fill of authentic Spanish cuisine, such as fat tortillas, fish sautéed with tomato and garlic, and sautéed octopus, and of traditional tapas, such as rich *manchego* cheese, chorizo, and garlic-sautéed shrimp. Try a Spanish wine from the expansive cellar, and after your meal enjoy a hand-rolled stogie in the cigar room. ✉ *1620 S.W. 8th St., Little Havana,* ☎ *305/643–5343. AE, MC, V.*

$ ✕ **El Bodegon Gallego.** Ridiculously cheap and relentlessly craving inducing, this shabby little Spanish-only storefront serves tasty tapas and hefty main courses. Although the menu may escape those who only speak English, sign language will get you an absurdly large order of chickpeas sautéed with chorizo or a lusty seafood soup or yellow rice with chicken and shrimp. Consider the wrought iron on the windows not as an indication of how bad the neighborhood is, but how good the creamy desserts flavored with alcohol are—most customers will willingly put themselves behind bars just for a single spoonful. ✉ *3174 N.W. 7th Ave., at N.W. 32nd St., Downtown,* ☎ *305/649–0801. No credit cards.*

### Vietnamese

$$ ★ ✕ **Hy-Vong Vietnamese Cuisine.** Spring springs forth in spring rolls of ground pork, cellophane noodles, and black mushrooms wrapped in

## Coconut Grove, South Miami and Coral Gables Dining

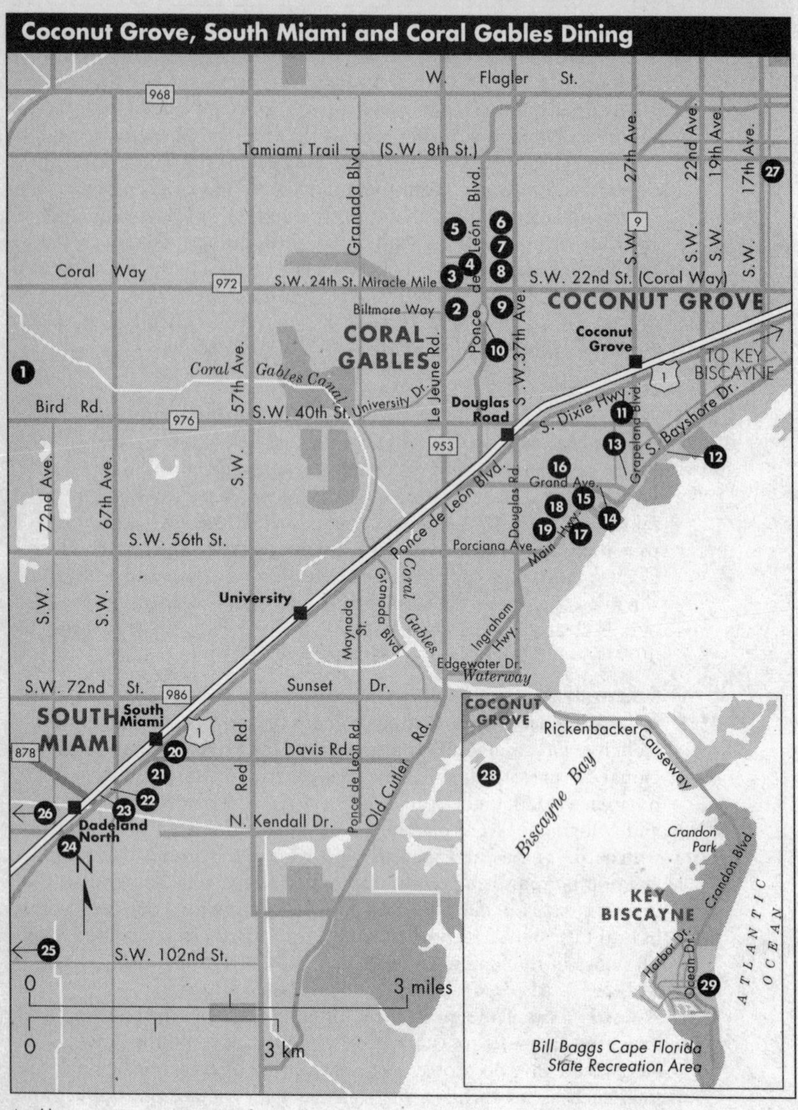


Anokha . . . . . . . . . 18
Aria . . . . . . . . . . . 29
Baleen . . . . . . . . . 28
Bice . . . . . . . . . . . 12
Cafè Tu Tu Tango . . 15
Caffè Abbracci . . . . 3
Captain's Tavern . . 24
Chrysanthemum . . . 13
Daily Bread Marketplace . . . . . 27
Don Quixote . . . . . 19
Empeek Cheke . . . . 25
Giacosa . . . . . . . . . 4
Il Tulipano . . . . . . 11
La Dorada . . . . . . . . 6
Lan . . . . . . . . . . . . 22
Le Bouchon du Grove . . . . . . . . . . 17
Le Festival . . . . . . . . 5
Mayfair Grill and Orchids Champagne and Wine Bar . . . . 14
Miss Saigon Bistro . . . . . . . . . . . 7
Norman's . . . . . . . . 9
Otranique on the Mile . . . . . . . . . . . 2
Pascal's on Ponce . . . . . . . . . . 10
Punjab Palace . . . . 26
Restaurant St. Michel . . . . . . . . 8
Sandbar Grill . . . . . 16
Shorty's Bar-B-Q . . . 23
Siam Lotus Room . . . . . . . . . . 21
Tropical Chinese Restaurant . . . . . . . . 1
Two Chefs . . . . . . . 20

homemade rice paper. Folks'll mill about on the sidewalk for hours—come before 7 PM to avoid a wait—to sample the whole fish panfried with *nuoc man,* a garlic-lime fish sauce, not to mention the thinly sliced pork barbecued with sesame seeds, almonds, and peanuts. Beer-savvy proprietor Kathy Manning serves a half-dozen top brews (Double Grimbergen, Moretti, and Spaten, among them) to further inoculate the experience from the ordinary. Well, as ordinary as a Vietnamese restaurant on Calle Ocho can be. ✉ *3458 S.W. 8th St., Little Havana,* ☎ *305/446–3674. AE, D, MC, V. Closed Mon. No lunch.*

## Coconut Grove and Key Biscayne

### Chinese

$–$$ ✕ **Chrysanthemum.** Forget all you know about Chinese food. You can't possibly appreciate how delicate and exotic a stir-fry can be unless you eat it here. Flash-fried crispy spinach, tossed with peppered chicken, is a revelation, and the high point of a dinner here is the Peking duck: moist, dark meat and skin wrapped in a pancake with scallions and plum sauce, the breast meat carved table-side, and the remnants stir-fried with bean sprouts. Don't bother with the run-of-the-Chinese-mill desserts; instead, stroll tourist-friendly Coconut Grove for alternatives. ✉ *Streets of Mayfair, 2911 Grand Ave., Coconut Grove,* ☎ *305/443–6789. AE, DC, MC, V.*

### Contemporary

$$$$ ★ ✕ **Aria.** Choose your view: the 126-seat dining room near the exhibition kitchen? Or the alfresco area with views of landscaped gardens or breeze-brushed beaches? Then select your food, which may be even more difficult, given chef Jeff Vigila's artistry—items range from asparagus cappuccino with crab frittata and nutmeg foam to braised veal cheeks with langoustines, lentil ragout, and summer truffles. Aria is fortunate to have master sommelier Marita Leonard, whose palate is impeccable and whose wine list is impossible to resist. ✉ *Ritz-Carlton, Key Biscayne, 455 Grand Bay Dr., Key Biscayne,* ☎ *305/365–4500. Reservations essential. AE, D, DC, MC, V.*

$$$–$$$$ ✕ **Mayfair Grill and Orchids Champagne and Wine Bar.** It can seem Old World, thanks to its muffled atmosphere and carpeted elegance, but the cooking is more innovative than the decor would suggest: Thai crab cakes with *panko* crumbs and a sesame-chili glaze; Colorado buffalo loin carpaccio splashed with white truffle oil; roulade of free-range chicken stuffed with spinach and goat cheese; and rack of lamb barbecued with notes of apple and ancho chile. If it all sounds a bit too filling, head instead for the outdoor courtyard at Orchids, the only champagne bar in town, where bubbly personalities can feel free to be themselves. ✉ *Mayfair House, 3000 Florida Ave., Coconut Grove,* ☎ *305/441–0000. AE, D, DC, MC, V. No lunch.*

$$–$$$$ ✕ **Baleen.** Culinary director Robbin Haas earned his New World stripes at a variety of South Beach restaurants. Some of his signature dishes, like tangy Caesar salad or salmon tartare with Thai spices and citron caviar, have carried over from eatery to eatery, but others are reinvented: hummus-parsley-crusted salmon with tahini butter, for instance, or Roquefort-crusted filet mignon with red wine sauce. Main plates are à la carte, with steak house–type side dishes padding the bill. The Sunday brunch is stellar. ✉ *Grove Isle Resort, 4 Grove Isle Dr., Grove Isle Coconut Grove,* ☎ *305/858–8300. Reservations essential. AE, D, DC, MC, V.*

### French

$$–$$$ ✕ **Le Bouchon du Grove.** Waiters tend to lean on chairs while taking orders and managers and owners freely mix with the clientele making

Le Bouchon perhaps the last remaining vestige of the Grove's bohemian days. The result is one big happy family, all enjoying traditional French pâtés, gratins, quiches, cassoulets, and steak frites. The supercharged atmosphere inside is equally matched by the throngs that tour the Grove outside the French doors. ✉ *3430 Main Hwy., Coconut Grove,* ☎ *305/448–6060. AE, MC, V.*

## Indian

$$–$$$ ✕ **Anokha.** "There is no doubt that all Indians love food," the menu says at Anokha, and there's also no doubt that all Miamians love *this* Indian food: shrimp cooked in pungent mustard sauce, fish soothed with an almond-cream curry, chicken wrapped in spinach and cilantro. The wait between starters—such as the Anokha roll, a combo of chicken and coriander enclosed in an egg-battered roti, and main courses such as the Kashmiri *rogan josh*, lamb in red curry sauce—can seem as long as a cab ride in Manhattan during rush hour. Don't fret—there's only one cook in the kitchen, and she's worth the delay. ✉ *3195 Commodore Plaza, Coconut Grove,* ☎ *786/552–1030. AE, MC, V. Closed Mon.*

## Italian

$$–$$$$ ✕ **Bice.** This Milan-based worldwide chain, run by the Ruggeri family, took over the dining room in the sumptuous Wyndham Grand Bay Hotel and, despite doubts hurled by the skeptics, actually improved upon it. A multihue wood floor and a huge mural backdrop are drop-dead decor highlights. Even more interesting is the Italian menu, with choices such as pumpkin ravioli in sage sauce, followed by Nebraska-raised filet mignon. ✉ *Wyndham Grand Bay Hotel, 2669 S. Bayshore Dr., Coconut Grove,* ☎ *305/860–0960. AE, DC, MC, V.*

$$–$$$$ ★ ✕ **Il Tulipano.** When an veteran establishment moves, folks get nervous, but Il Tulipano is still deemed worthy by its many proponents. Tuck into *funghi* (mushrooms) sautéed with baby artichokes; a salad with chopped plum tomatoes, mozzarella, radicchio, and Portobellos; and mussels in white wine sauce. Lamb chops are ruby red and succulent; the snapper broiled in bread crumbs is delicate and zesty. It's all topped off with traditional desserts—and excruciatingly polite service. ✉ *2833 Bird Ave., Coconut Grove,* ☎ *305/529–1115. MC, V.*

## Latin

$$$$ ✕ **Don Quixote.** This elaborate, multiroom, multistory Spanish restaurant takes up a good city block, practically. The menu is proportionately grand: you need about as much time to read it as you do the eatery's namesake novel. Chances are you'll put down the menu halfway through, if only because you were tempted by too many tapas, including brandy-flamed Spanish sausage or marinated octopus on a bed of potatoes. If you can make it to main courses, veal chops braised with Port and sautéed sea bass with asparagus and a hard-boiled egg are among the blue ribbons. ✉ *3148 Commodore Plaza, Coconut Grove,* ☎ *305/443–2774. AE, D, MC, V.*

$ ✕ **Café Tu Tu Tango.** An artistic concept follows from the Rococo-modern arcades, where local artists set up their easels, through to the menu, which allows you to pick appetizers as if you were selecting paints from a palette of chips, dips, breads, and spreads. House specials include frittatas, crab cakes, *picadillo* empanadas (pastries stuffed with spicy ground beef and served with cilantro sour cream), and chicken and shrimp orzo paella, all to be enjoyed with some of the best sangria in the city. ✉ *CocoWalk, 3015 Grand Ave., Coconut Grove,* ☎ *305/529–2222. AE, MC, V.*

### Mexican

$ ✕ **Sandbar Grill.** The name doesn't invoke the Baja Peninsula quite the way it should, given the fish tacos, shrimp burritos, and huevos rancheros on the menu. No matter. After imbibing one of the ten signature "hurricane" drinks, you won't care what the place is called, or even the fact that it's about as far from a sandbar as a real hurricane is from landfall in, say, January. ✉ *3064 Grand Ave., Coconut Grove,* ☎ *305/444–5270. AE, MC, V.*

### Middle Eastern

$ ✕ **Daily Bread Marketplace.** Go pan–Middle Eastern with falafel, gyro pita pockets—some of the most tempting in the county, Arabic meat pies, and Greek spinach pies. Desserts are uniformly sticky with honey, drenched with butter, and encrusted with nuts—not a bad way finish a meal, whether you eat in at the self-service market tables or take out. A new South Beach location adds ethnic allure to the South of Fifth neighborhood. ✉ *2400 S.W. 27th St., Coconut Grove,* ☎ *305/856–5893. AE, D, MC, V.*

## Coral Gables

### Caribbean

$$–$$$ ✕ **Ortanique on the Mile.** Named after an exotic citrus fruit, this restaurant screams "island"—or, more accurately, island resort—from the breezy interior decorated like a Jamaican terraced garden to the exquisite pan-Caribbean cuisine. Proprietor Delius Shirley and chef-proprietor Cindy Hutson offer such favorites as pumpkin soup; fried calamari salad; whole yellowtail snapper; and jerk pork loin. Dessert doesn't get better than drunken banana fritters, unless you accompany them with a press pot of Blue Mountain coffee, direct from Jamaica and practically vibrating with caffeine. ✉ *278 Miracle Mile, Coral Gables,* ☎ *305/446–7710. AE, DC, MC, V. No lunch weekends.*

### Contemporary

$$$–$$$$ ★ ✕ **Norman's.** Chef Norman Van Aken has created an international buzz by perfecting the art of New World cuisine—an imaginative combination rooted in Latin, North American, Caribbean, and Asian influences. Bold tastes are delivered in every dish, from a simple black-and-white-bean soup with sour cream, chorizo, and tortillas to a rum-and-pepper-painted grouper on a mango-*habañero* sauce. The emphasis here is on service, and the ultragracious staff never seems harried, even when all seats are filled (usually every minute between opening and closing). ✉ *21 Almeria Ave., Coral Gables,* ☎ *305/446–6767. Reservations essential. AE, DC, MC, V. Closed Sun. No lunch.*

$$–$$$$ ✕ **Restaurant St. Michel.** Chef Stuart Bornstein's lace-curtained café with sidewalk tables would be at home across from a railroad station in Avignon or Bordeaux. The setting is utterly French, the little hotel it's in evokes the Mediterranean, and the cuisine is global. Lighter dishes include moist couscous chicken and pasta primavera. Among the heartier entrées are a plum-, soy-, and lemon-glazed fillet of salmon; sesame-coated loin of tuna; and local yellowtail snapper. ✉ *Hotel Place St. Michel, 162 Alcazar Ave., Coral Gables,* ☎ *305/444–1666. AE, DC, MC, V.*

### French

$$$$ ✕ **La Palme D'Or.** You may not be able to "d'afford the d'Or," but if you've got the bucks, this upscale French restaurant has the goods. Chef Philippe Ruiz pairs wild turbot with baby leeks and caviar, conjoins caramelized cod with Spanish sausage chips, and cranks out a superior Colorado lamb with garam masala jus. Talk about universal ap-

peal. French fare has never been more inviting, especially when Michelin-starred chefs visit for the first week of every month. As long as you don't feel shut out by the check, that is. ✉ *Biltmore Hotel, 1200 Anastasia Ave., Coral Gables,* ☎ *305/445–1926. Reservations essential. AE, MC, V. No lunch.*

$$–$$$ ★ ✕ **Le Festival.** The canopied entrance to this classical French restaurant hints at the elegance within, a Parisian *moderne* room featuring etched-glass filigree and burgundy-, mahogany-, and rose-tinted details. A second room, for smokers, is more gilded. Main courses include fillet of grouper in bouillabaisse sauce; stuffed quail with a grape and red-wine sauce; chateaubriand for two; and milk-fed veal sautéed with mushrooms, grapes, and brandy cream sauce. For dessert, choose among various pastries, mousses, and soufflés—or another bottle from the 100-plus selection wine list. ✉ *2120 Salzedo St., Coral Gables,* ☎ *305/442–8545. Reservations essential. AE, D, DC, MC, V. Closed Sun. No lunch Sat.*

$$–$$$ ★ ✕ **Pascal's on Ponce.** He's not a native son, but he might as well be. Chef-proprietor of Pascal's, Pascal Oudin, has been cooking here since the 1980s, when he opened Dominique's in the Alexander Hotel. His stream-lined French cuisine disdains trends and discounts flash. Instead, you're supplied with substantive delicacies such as sautéed sea bass wrapped in a crispy potato crust with braised leeks, veal rib eye au jus, and tenderloin of beef sautéed with snails and wild mushrooms. Service is proper, textures are perfect, and wines ideally complementary. The only dilemma is deciding between Oudin's own tarte tatin or a cheese course for dessert. ✉ *2611 Ponce de León Blvd., Coral Gables,* ☎ *305/444–2024. Reservations essential. AE, D, DC, MC, V. No lunch weekends.*

## Italian

$$$ ✕ **La Palma.** Romantics read on: Italian restaurant La Palma is perhaps Miami's most love-inducing atmosphere. We're talking garden courtyards, white linens, candles, piano bar, impressionist art, even lounge singers—the sentimental works. Fortunately the food doesn't inspire weeping but rather laughing with joy, especially the osso buco and lobster risotto. While there's not much on the menu in the way of innovation, the warm, formal service and inviting decor make this a noteworthy recluse à deux. ✉ *116 Alhambra Circle, Coral Gables,* ☎ *305/445–8777. Reservations essential. AE, D, MC, V.*

$$–$$$ ✕ **Caffè Abbracci.** Long-running and much-beloved, this Italian restaurant is more like a club than an eatery. Patrons tend to fare better when they're recognized, so go with a local or pretend you've been there before. Confidently order some cold and hot antipasti—including various carpaccios, porcini mushrooms, calamari, grilled goat cheese, shrimps, mussels—and a few festive entrées. Most pasta is made fresh, so consider sampling two or three, maybe with pesto sauce, Gorgonzola, and fresh tomatoes. ✉ *318 Aragon Ave., Coral Gables,* ☎ *305/441–0700. Reservations essential. AE, DC, MC, V. No lunch weekends.*

$$–$$$ ★ ✕ **Giacosa.** From the moment your server places your napkin in your lap to the moment he discreetly presents your check, you'll feel more than well tended to. While you contemplate your choices, a tower of airy pita bread with a carafe of olive oil appears on your table. Consider the *tricolore* sala, which imparts the bitter kiss of arugula; pastas, veal, and fresh seafood are all prepared for peak taste. Whenever you request it, Parmesan is freshly grated to the plate. ✉ *394 Giralda Ave., Coral Gables,* ☎ *305/445–5858. AE, DC, MC, V. No lunch weekends.*

## Spanish

$$$–$$$$ ✕ **La Dorada.** Named after the royal sea bream, the restaurant brings in fresh fish daily from the Bay of Biscay, rather than Biscayne Bay, setting the standard for fine Spanish cuisine in the city. Preparations are both classic and excellent: scallops sautéed with grapes, monkfish

stuffed with shrimp, whole fish baked in rock salt. Not a lot of English is spoken here, thanks to an all-Spanish staff, so service can be a little off. But they do make an effort to please, catering to those whims that get across language barriers. ✉ *177 Giralda Ave., Coral Gables,* ☎ *305/446–2002. AE, MC, V.*

**$–$$** ✕ **Las Nuevas Culebrinas.** A Spanish *tapacería* (house of little plates) is a place to live each meal as if it were your last, though you may wait for it as long as some inmates do for an appeal. Tapas are not small at all; some are entrée size, such as a succulent mix of garbanzos with ham, sausage, red peppers, and oil, or the Spanish tortilla, a giant Frisbee-shape omelet. Indulge in a tender fillet of crocodile, fresh fish, grilled pork, or the kicker, goat in Coca-Cola sauce. For dessert there's a bit of drama—*crema Catalana,* caramelized right at your table with a blowtorch. This is a good time to remind your kids not to touch. ✉ *4700 W. Flagler St., at N.W. 47th Ave., Coral Gables,* ☎ *305/445–2337. AE, MC, V.*

### Vietnamese

**$–$$** ✕ **Miss Saigon Bistro.** The musical was the inspiration for this family-run restaurant, and yes, the soundtrack plays ad nauseam. But overall the effect is quaint rather than campy, and the dining room, decorated with orchids, is serene. The first act commences with delicate spring rolls, pork-stuffed crepes, or steamed mussels. Take intermission with tangy green papaya salad, then return to the second act for chicken with lemongrass or caramelized pork. Close down the show with grilled salmon with mango, then toast curtain calls with a bottle from the reasonably priced wine list. ✉ *146 Giralda Ave., Coral Gables,* ☎ *305/446–8006. AE, DC, MC, V. No lunch weekends.*

## South Miami, Kendall, South Miami-Dade

### Barbecue

**$–$$** ✕ **Shorty's Bar-B-Q.** Since 1951, when Shorty Allen opened his barbecue restaurant in a log cabin, it's been a local institution with two locations. Meals are served family style at long picnic tables, and cowboy hats hang on the walls along with animal horns, saddles, and mounted heads of boar and caribou. Longtime fans come for the barbecued pork ribs, chicken, and pork steak, all slow-cooked over hickory logs and drenched in Shorty's own warm, spicy sauce. If you've got room, try side orders of tangy baked beans, corn on the cob, and coleslaw. ✉ *9200 S. Dixie Hwy., South Miami,* ☎ *305/670–7732;* ✉ *11575 S.W. 40th St., Westchester, Miami,* ☎ *305/227–3196. D, MC, V.*

### Chinese

**$–$$$** ✕ **Tropical Chinese Restaurant.** This big, lacquer-free room feels as open and busy as a railway station and the extensive menu is filled with tofu combinations, poultry, beef, pork, and tender seafood. You'll find unfamiliar items on the menu, too—early spring leaves of snow pea pods, for example, which are sublimely tender and flavorful. An exuberant dim sum lunch—brunch on the weekends—allows you to choose an assortment of small dishes from wheeled carts. In the open kitchen, 10 chefs prepare everything as if for dignitaries. ✉ *7991 S.W. 40th St. (Bird Rd.), west of S.W. 79th Ave., Westchester, Miami,* ☎ *305/262–7576 or 305/262–1552. AE, DC, MC, V.*

### Contemporary

**$$–$$$$** ✕ **Two Chefs.** Meet the two chefs—Jan Jorgensen and Soren Bredahl—both Danes, who've been cooking together for decades. Their restaurant, decorated like a Williams-Sonoma catalog, has an ever-changing menu, but scan for seared foie gras with gnocchi, an unusually textured combination that features reduced boysenberries. The chefs pride themselves on the unexpected and think nothing of pairing goat meat with lobster or composing an escargot potpie. ✉ *8287 S. Dixie Hwy., South Miami,* ☎ *305/663–2100. AE, D, DC, MC, V. Closed Sun.*

## Indian

**$–$$** ✕ **Punjab Palace.** The food here, adjusted to American palates, is a less-spicy-than-usual take on Indian. Chicken soup is plenty flavorful, though, and lentil soup is also terrific, strongly flavored with cilantro and ginger. The salads are fresh, enlivened by a yogurt, lemon, and cilantro dressing. Convince the staff you can handle a little heat in your food, and you'll find the tandoori chicken is downright peppy. Fried pastry balls in sugar and honey sure are an improvement over Dunkin' Donuts. ✉ *11780 N. Kendall Dr., Kendall,* ☎ *305/274–1300. AE, DC, MC, V.*

## Native American

**$$–$$$$** ✕ **Empeek Cheke.** Members of the Miccosukee Indian tribe spared no expense when they created this luxe steak house, on the second floor of the new art deco casino–hotel complex. "Everglades cuisine" figures highly here—check out alligator tail Provençal or panfried frogs' legs for a starter. Then move on to venison tenderloin, buffalo sirloin, or baked Florida grouper with lobster-shrimp sauce. Do read prices carefully—even less exotic meats such as filet mignon can cost you, and the casino downstairs is limited to video slot machines, poker, and bingo, so don't expect a huge windfall to pay for your eats. ✉ *Miccosukee Casino and Resort, 500 S.W. 177th Ave., Redlands,* ☎ *305/925–2559. AE, D, DC, MC, V. No lunch.*

## Pan-Asian

**$–$$$** ✕ **Lan.** Aside from rolls and summer-fresh sashimi, Lan, on the ground floor of an inaccessible megamall, supplies the connoisseur of all cuisines Asian with satays, pot stickers, braised ribs, and sake-steamed clams. The sushi bar's more interesting items include a "Tahi bomb"—lemongrass-chili-infused shrimp and calamari rolled in rice and sesame. Vegetarians get a nod, too, with "green plates," a grilled mushroom sampler or spinach seared with garlic and chilies. Innovative desserts include spring rolls or wontons stuffed with fruit and chocolate. ✉ *Dadeland Station, 8332 S. Dixie Hwy., South Miami,* ☎ *305/661–8141. AE, MC, V.*

## Seafood

**$$–$$$$** ✕ **Captain's Tavern.** The paneled walls may be hokey, but the interesting menu fortified with Caribbean and South American influences can take your mind off the surroundings. Beyond good versions of the typical fare—conch chowder and conch fritters—you'll find Portuguese fish stew, fish with various tropical fruits, a delightful black bean soup, and oysters in cream sauce with fresh rosemary, not to mention decadent desserts—all served in a beloved family fish house. ✉ *7495 S.E. 98th St., South Miami,* ☎ *305/661–4237. AE, MC, V.*

## Thai

**$–$$** ✕ **Siam Lotus Room.** This aqua-color example of motel architecture can almost blind the unsuspecting driver, but inside you'll find great eating—in fact, this is one of South Florida's best Thai restaurants. Jump at the chance to sample spicy jumping squid and savory, coconut-silky *tom kar pla,* a fish soup. The curries work on many levels, as they should: aroma, taste, and sensation. For dessert, the Thai doughnut complements thick, creamy Thai iced coffee. ✉ *6388 S. Dixie Hwy., South Miami,* ☎ *305/666–8134. AE, MC, V.*

# 4 LODGING

The restored palaces of South Beach get all the ink, but there is more to Miami's hotel scene than art deco. From the dignified old resorts of Coral Gables to boutique hotels on Miami Beach, the key word is diversity, both in the hotels and in the guests they attract. Worldwide acclaim has seen to that—now the ultra-hip share the pavement with businessmen, backpackers, and families. Whether you're here for the beach or the banks, you'll find the perfect place to stay.

Updated by Matt Windsor

**AS THE NEXUS OF HAUTE HOTELS**, thanks to a building boom in the late '90s, Greater Miami has experienced the arrival of dozens of hotels and thousands of new rooms, as upscale chains and funky boutiques alike sought a slice of the magic. The established beachside grande dames are responding with a constant stream of lavish renovations. As the marketplace has become crowded with new entries, however, Miami's famously outrageous prices are holding steady or even dropping slightly—meaning a stay at even the most exclusive property is now within reason for many vacationers. There are hundreds of hotels, motels, resorts, and hostels to choose from, with prices ranging from $15 a night in a dormitory-style room to $2,000 a night or more in a penthouse suite.

When deciding where to stay, take into account the different personalities of Miami's neighborhoods. If this is a stay-up-all-night, I'm-only-going-to-be-here-once vacation, reserve a room on South Beach's Ocean Drive and expect the party atmosphere to keep you up past your bedtime. If you're here for business, a hotel downtown or in Coral Gables will put you close to the business centers. If you'd prefer access to the ocean minus the frenzy of South Beach, the grand hotels to the north, on Miami Beach's Collins Avenue and in Bal Harbour, are on the water and away from the hordes. For even greater tranquillity, check into rooms in Coconut Grove or on the quieter streets of the Art Deco District.

Although rooms are virtually always available in Miami, reservations are still essential if you have your heart set on a popular hotel during a busy time, such as the Christmas holidays or spring break. Some hotels (especially on the mainland) have adopted steady year-round prices, but most adjust their rates to reflect seasonal demand. The peak occurs in winter, with a dip in summer, and in softer seasons the prices are often more negotiable than rate cards let on. You'll find the best values between Easter and Memorial Day, which is actually a delightful time in Miami, and in September and October, the height of hurricane season.

Miami hoteliers collect roughly 12.5% for city and resort taxes. After you settle into your room, the bellhops, valet parkers, concierges, and housekeepers, all of whom you should tip, will add to your expenses. With these added costs, plus parking fees of up to $16 per evening, you can easily spend 25% more than your room rate just to sleep in Miami.

| CATEGORY | COST* |
|---|---|
| **$$$$** | over $300 |
| **$$$** | $200–$300 |
| **$$** | $110–$200 |
| **$** | under $110 |

**All prices are for a standard double room in peak season, excluding 12.5% city and resort taxes.*

## North Miami-Dade, North Miami Beach, North Miami

**$$$–$$$$** ★ **Turnberry Isle Resort & Club.** Finest of the grand resorts, even more so with the addition of a stellar spa, Turnberry is a tapestry of islands and waterways on 300 superbly landscaped acres by the bay. You'll stay at the 1920s Addison Mizner–designed Country Club Hotel on the Intracoastal Waterway. Here, oversize rooms are decorated in light woods and earth tones and have large curving terraces and hot tubs.

The marina has moorings for 117 boats; there are two Robert Trent Jones golf courses; and there's a free shuttle to the Aventura Mall. The oceanfront Ocean Club has a new playground for kids, but no longer offers accommodations. ✉ *19999 W. Country Club Dr., Aventura, Miami 33180,* ☏ *305/932–6200 or 800/327–7028,* FAX *305/933–6560,* WEB *www.turnberryisle.com. 354 rooms, 41 suites. 4 restaurants, 5 bars, in-room safes, minibars, cable TV, 2 pools, spa, steam room, 2 18-hole golf courses, 19 tennis courts, health club, racquetball, beach, dock, windsurfing, boating, helipad; no kids. AE, D, DC, MC, V.*

**$$–$$$** **Don Shula's Hotel & Golf Club.** This low-rise resort is part of Miami Lakes, a planned town about 14 mi northwest of downtown. The well-maintained golf club, opened in 1962, has a championship course, a lighted executive course, and a golf school. All club rooms are traditional English style, rich in leather and dark wood, and have balconies. The hotel, on the other hand, has a typical Florida-tropics look—light pastels and furniture of wicker and light wood. In both locations the best rooms are near the lobby for convenient access. Sixteen two-bedroom suites are geared for extended stays, with refrigerator, microwave, and VCR. ✉ *6842 Main St., Miami Lakes 33014,* ☏ *305/821–1150 or 800/247–4852,* FAX *305/820–8071,* WEB *www.donshula.com. 205 rooms, 16 suites. 2 restaurants, 2 bars, cable TV, 2 pools, sauna, steam room, 2 18-hole golf courses, 9 tennis courts, aerobics, basketball, health club, racquetball, volleyball. AE, DC, MC, V.*

**$$–$$$** **Marco Polo Ramada Plaza Beach Resort.** The Ramada's familiar name and appealing setting draw business travelers, families, and couples alike. This eclectic group can be seen around the heated pool, wading pool, and beachfront, or at the festive Tiki bar. The basement sports bar, shops, and art gallery make this resort somewhat of a small city. Of course, the hotel provides for rest, too: all rooms have two queen beds; most have full or partial ocean views; some have balconies; and a few have fully equipped kitchenettes. Clean and active (albeit miles from South Beach's action), it's worth checking into—especially for families. ✉ *19201 Collins Ave., Sunny Isles, Miami Beach 33160,* ☏ *305/932–2233 or 877/327–6363,* FAX *305/937–4139,* WEB *www.ramadaplazamiabeach.com. 350 rooms, 20 suites. Restaurant, café, cable TV, refrigerators, 2 pools, gym, beach, concierge, meeting rooms. AE, D, DC, MC, V.*

**$$–$$$** ★ **Newport Beachside Resort.** Built before the present crop of luxury towers sprang up, Newport is still one of the nicest hotels in Sunny Isles. The combination timeshare and hotel is a good place to put up Mom or Dad, when the family needs a clean, safe place to enjoy the beach and outdoor activities. The pool area is perfectly suited for enjoying the sun: there are a wading pool and a standard pool, not to mention the ocean and fishing pier—the only remaining hotel fishing pier in Miami. Back inside, the lobby is large and bright, and so are the rooms, after a remodeling that replaced all remaining standard rooms with one-bedroom suites. ✉ *16701 Collins Ave., Sunny Isles, Miami Beach 33160,* ☏ *305/949–1300 or 800/327–5476,* FAX *305/947–5873,* WEB *www.newportbeachsideresort.com. 290 suites. 4 restaurants, bar, cable TV, microwaves, refrigerators, pool, gym, beach, nightclub, shops, concierge, meeting rooms, parking (fee). AE, D, DC, MC, V.*

**$$–$$$** **Ocean Point Resort & Club.** Riding the crest of a new wave of upscale resorts in formerly tacky Sunny Isles, Ocean Point certainly plays the part of leader, with the amenities high-paying guests relish. There are Jacuzzi tubs with separate showers, in-room entertainment centers, a chichi food market downstairs, and a traditional European spa on premises. The hotel doesn't have anything particularly groundbreaking to offer, but considering the previous standards for Sunny Isles hotels, safe and reliable isn't a knock. Rooms are bright and spacious; the beach is relatively uncrowded; and the atmosphere is easy, not pompous—

## Miami Beach and North Lodging

all in all, a viable alternative to the behemoths farther south. ✉ *17375 Collins Ave., Sunny Isles, Miami Beach 33160,* ☎ *305/950–5422 or 866/623–2678,* FAX *305/940–1658,* WEB *www.oceanpointresort.com. 53 rooms, 84 1-bedroom suites, 43 2-bedroom suites, and 10 3-bedroom suites. Restaurant, bar, in-room data ports, cable TV, pool, sauna, spa, beach, dry cleaning, laundry service, concierge, business services, meeting rooms, parking (fee). AE, D, DC, MC, V.*

## Miami Beach North of 23rd Street

**$$$$** **Eden Roc Renaissance Resort & Spa.** This grand 1950s hotel designed by Morris Lapidus has always been overshadowed by its next-door neighbor and arch-rival, the larger, older Fontainebleau. But it shouldn't be. The free-flowing lines of the deco architecture impart a modern, elegant feel to the public areas, especially the terribly hip lobby bar, with its low-slung, meandering couches. South Florida's only indoor rock-climbing wall is found at the popular 55,000-square-ft Spa of Eden; and former Dolphins coach Jimmy Johnson's beachside sports bar caters to those who prefer lifting weights 16 ounces at a time. Rooms blend a touch of the '50s with informal elegance. ✉ *4525 Collins Ave., Mid-Beach, Miami Beach 33140,* ☎ *305/531–0000 or 800/327–8337,* FAX *305/674–5555,* WEB *www.renaissancehotels.com. 349 rooms. 2 restaurants, sports bar, cable TV, 2 pools, beach, spa, basketball, gym, racquetball, squash, meeting rooms. AE, MC, V.*

**$$$$** **Sheraton Bal Harbour.** Elegant without being pretentious, this Morris Lapidus–designed hotel is run by a staff that has service down to a science. The suites have marble bathrooms and Jacuzzis, and most rooms have full or partial views of the city, ocean, or Bal Harbour, and the glittering Bal Harbour shops are across the street. Other pluses include a lush oceanfront garden with waterfalls; a funky neon-laced bistro and bar; and 73,000 square ft of meeting space, all sitting on 10 acres of Atlantic coastline. Among the many kid-pleasing recreational options are a water entertainment complex and a playroom. ✉ *9701 Collins Ave., Bal Harbour, Miami Beach 33154,* ☎ *305/865–7511 or 800/999–9898,* FAX *305/864–2601,* WEB *www.sheraton.com/balharbour. 642 rooms, 52 suites. 3 restaurants, bar, cable TV, pool, wading pool, hot tub, massage, health club, windsurfing, beach, baby-sitting, meeting rooms. AE, D, DC, MC, V.*

**$$$–$$$$** ✕ **Alexander Hotel.** Amid the high-rises of the Mid-Beach district, this 16-story hotel exemplifies the elegance of Miami Beach. It has immense suites furnished with antiques and reproductions, each with a terrace that has ocean or bay views and each with a living and dining room, kitchen, and two baths. With the Aveda salon and Shula's Steak House on the second floor, you can pamper your body and appetite without leaving the property. Beware of mandatory gratuities attached to everything from valet parking to bellhops to maid service to deliveries. They can add another $100 to your stay. ✉ *5225 Collins Ave., Mid-Beach, Miami Beach 33140,* ☎ *305/865–6500 or 800/327–6121,* FAX *305/341–6554,* WEB *www.alexanderhotel.com. 74 1-bedroom suites, 67 2-bedroom suites. 3 restaurants, coffee shop, cable TV, 2 pools, hair salon, 4 hot tubs, health club, massage, sauna, spa, volleyball, beach, boating, windsurfing, baby-sitting, laundry service, concierge, meeting rooms. AE, D, DC, MC, V.*

**$$$–$$$$** ✕ **Beach House Bal Harbour.** If you've always wanted an oceanfront home but don't have the bucks to buy one, staying here is the next best thing. Cookies at the check-in desk, lollipops at turn-down, overstuffed throw pillows, and seashell collections are just a few of the homey touches in this 1956 building owned by the Rubell family (of Studio 54 fame), whose three properties (the Greenview and the Albion are the others) are all notable players on the Miami Beach hotel scene. Spacious rooms (with tiny bathrooms) are filled with Ralph Lauren furniture and Nantucket-style wainscoting. The low-key atmosphere extends to the outdoors, where there's a screened-in porch (perfect for a cool lemonade) and poolside spa. The Atlantic restaurant serves pricey but oh-so-comforting American cuisine. ✉ *9449 Collins Ave., Bal Harbour, Miami Beach 33154,* ☎ *305/535–8600 or 877/782–3557,* FAX *305/535–8601,* WEB *www.rubellhotels.com. 170 rooms, 10 suites. Restaurant, bar, cable TV, pool, spa, gym, concierge, business services. AE, DC, MC, V.*

$$–$$$$ ★ **Fontainebleau Hilton Resort and Towers.** This big, busy, and ornate grande dame just wrapped up a complete overhaul of its original building. (But even more grandiose plans are in the works, with the ongoing construction of Fontainebleau II, a new hotel–condominium complex that will remove several tennis courts but add a state-of-the-art spa.) All public areas and guest rooms have been renovated, but decor still varies wildly from room to room, ranging from 1950s to very contemporary furnishings. Adult guests enjoy free admission to the hotel's *Club Tropigala* Vegas-style floor show. The most popular spot for kids is Cookie's World, a water playground with multiple slides and jets emerging from a giant purple octopus. ✉ *4441 Collins Ave., Mid-Beach, Miami Beach 33140,* ☎ *305/538–2000 or 800/548–8886,* FAX *305/673–5351,* WEB *www.hilton.com. 1,146 rooms, 60 suites. 12 restaurants, 4 bars, cable TV, 3 pools, sauna, spa, 4 tennis courts, health club, volleyball, beach, windsurfing, boating, jet skiing, parasailing, nightclub, children's programs (ages 5–14), playground, convention center. AE, D, DC, MC, V.*

$$–$$$$ ★ **Wyndham Miami Beach Resort.** Of the great Miami Beach hotels, this 18-story modern glass tower remains a standout, as does its polished staff offering exceptional service, from helping you find the best shopping to bringing you an icy drink on the beach. The bright rooms have a tropical blue color scheme and are filled with attentive details: minirefrigerators, three layers of drapes (including blackout curtains), big closets, and bathrooms with high-end toiletries and a magnifying mirror. Two presidential suites were designed in consultation with the Secret Service, and a rooftop meeting room offers views of bay and ocean. ✉ *4833 Collins Ave., Mid-Beach, Miami Beach 33140,* ☎ *305/532–3600 or 800/203–8368,* FAX *305/534–7409,* WEB *www.wyndham.com. 378 rooms, 46 suites. 2 restaurants, 2 bars, cable TV, pool, massage, tennis court, gym, beach, meeting rooms. AE, D, DC, MC, V.*

$$$ ★ **Claridge Hotel.** A cool Mediterranean breeze in a somewhat stagnant corner of Miami Beach, the Claridge is the city's most impressive hotel renovation. The exterior has been restored to the canary-yellow glory of the 1928 original; inside, time slips back a few centuries. Rich Venetian frescoed walls are hung with Peruvian oil paintings, the floors are fashioned from volcanic ash, and the whole is supported by majestic volcanic stone columns. A Moroccan terrace overlooks the soaring inner atrium, which has a splash Jacuzzi at the far end. Rooms are a mix of Asian and European influences, with straw mats laid over wood floors, and ornate wood furniture. ✉ *3500 Collins Ave., Mid-Beach, Miami Beach 33140,* ☎ *305/604–8485 or 888/422–9111,* FAX *305/674–0881,* WEB *www.claridgefl.com. 42 rooms, 8 suites. Restaurant, in-room data ports, in-room safes, cable TV, hot tub, concierge, business services, parking (fee). AE, D, DC, MC, V.*

$$–$$$ **Bay Harbor Inn.** The inn's not on the ocean, but the tranquil Indian Creek flowing outside is sure to soothe. From your room's private porch, where you can sit with a book or drink or both, you'll have a view the village of Bal Harbour a five-minute walk away. Rooms have queen- and king-size beds and baths are large. The Bay Harbor restaurant (Is-

lands) is very nice, but so is a walk over the bridge to Surfside for a wider selection of neighborhood bars and eateries. The hotel staff is composed largely of hotel students from Johnson & Wales University, so the service is enthusiastic but not flawlessly professional. ✉ *9660 E. Bay Harbor Dr., Bal Harbour, Miami Beach, 33154,* ☎ *305/868–4141,* FAX *305/867–9094,* WEB *www.bayharborinn.com. 22 rooms, 23 suites. Restaurant, bar, cable TV, pool, exercise equipment, meeting rooms. AE, MC, V. CP.*

**$$–$$$** ★ **Indian Creek Hotel.** Not as grand as the North Beach behemoths or as hectic as the Ocean Drive lodgings, this 1936 Pueblo deco original may just be Miami's most charming and sincere lodge. Owner Marc Levin rescued the inn and filled its rooms with art deco furniture, much of it discovered in the hotel basement and put back in service. The garden rooms, however, are minimalist in design, with dark wood furniture and light green walls, in contrast to the creamy tones and plush furniture of the deco rooms. Suites have VCR–CD players and modem capabilities. The dining room has an eclectic and appetizing menu, which you can also enjoy outdoors by the lush pool and garden. Stay a while, and manager Zammy Migdal and his staff will have you feeling like family. ✉ *2727 Indian Creek Dr., Mid-Beach, Miami Beach 33140,* ☎ *305/531–2727 or 800/491–2772,* FAX *305/531–5651,* WEB *www.indiancreekhotelmb.com. 55 rooms, 6 suites. Restaurant, refrigerators, cable TV, pool, meeting rooms. AE, D, DC, MC, V.*

**$$** **The Palms South Beach.** Even though the name is partly misleading—South Beach is actually a long hike to the south—the lush grounds of the oceanfront locale do set it apart from its Mid-Beach neighbors. In remaking the former Miami Beach Ocean Resort, the current owners started with their backyard: the new pool, fountains, walkways, and all those soaring palm trees (several with hammocks strung between them) are a welcome respite from beach excesses and the traffic roaring by on Collins. There are more large palms inside, in the Great Room lounge just off the lobby, and designer Patrick Kennedy used subtle, natural hues of ivory, green, and blue for the homey, well-lit rooms. ✉ *3025 Collins Ave., Mid-Beach, Miami Beach 33140,* ☎ *305/534–0505 or 800/550–0505,* FAX *305/534–0513,* WEB *www.thepalmshotel.com. 216 rooms, 26 suites. Restaurant, 2 bars, lobby lounge, in-room data ports, in-room safes, cable TV, minibars, beach, room service, concierge. AE, D, DC, MC, V.*

**$–$$** **Days Inn North Beach Hotel.** Although the rooms and baths are small, the hotel itself is clean, and it's in a quiet, resurgent strip of Miami Beach. The natural attributes of South Beach—sun and sea—are here as well, with the big advantage of not having to fight for a parking spot or deal with creeping traffic. A good bet for families, this hotel has a game room, plus a bright breakfast room. ✉ *7450 Ocean Terr., Surfside, Miami Beach 33141,* ☎ *305/866–1631 or 888/825–6800,* FAX *305/868–4617,* WEB *www.daysinnmiamibeach.com. 92 rooms. Restaurant, bar, cable TV, pool, beach, video game room, laundry facilities. AE, D, DC, MC, V.*

**$–$$** **Ocean Surf.** With a touch more privacy than other nearby hotels, this small, privately owned art deco hotel stands in a safe, quiet, beachfront neighborhood one block east of Collins Drive. Modest in size and style, it's an affordable option if you want to get away from it all while scoring a free Continental breakfast. Rooms are generic hotel style, with doubles or queens; oceanfront rooms add a balcony "overlooking the sapphire blue waters," as the brochure says. If you don't like hotels where clerks have to break away to care for the baby in the back office, however, keep searching. ✉ *7436 Ocean Terr., Surfside, Miami Beach 33141,* ☎ *305/866–1648 or 800/555–0411,* FAX *305/866–1649,* WEB *www.oceansurf.com. 49 rooms. No-smoking rooms, cable TV, beach. AE, D, DC, MC, V. CP.*

**$–$$** **Traymore.** As you travel north on Collins from South Beach, the wall-to-wall hotels become wall-to-wall condos. Tucked between these monsters is the Traymore, an economy hotel that largely attracts Europeans. Like some other revived art deco hotels, this one seems to have lost its character during renovations: the lobby, rooms, and pool are now magnificently clean—and dull. If the accessories look familiar, you may recognize them from bargain furniture stores or other basic hotels you may have visited. There are refrigerators in oceanfront rooms. Is there a reason to stay here? There is, if you want an oceanfront hotel that won't break your budget. ✉ *2445 Collins Ave., Mid-Beach, Miami Beach 33139,* ☎ *305/534–7111 or 800/445–1512,* FAX *305/538–2632. 86 rooms, 2 suites. Restaurant, bar, cable TV, pool, beach. AE, D, DC, MC, V.*

## South Beach

**$$$$** ★ **Casa Grande.** With a lux and spicy Eastern-tinged flavor that sets it apart from the typical icy-cool minimalism found on Ocean Drive, this Chris Blackwell startup—no longer an Island Outpost property—has luxurious Balinese-inspired suites done in teak and mahogany. Expect dhurrie rugs, Indonesian fabrics and artifacts, two-poster beds with ziggurat turns, full electric kitchens with quality utensils, and large baths—practically unheard of in the Art Deco District. Insulated windows keep the noise of the Ocean Drive revelers at bay. Book well in advance for stays during peak periods. ✉ *834 Ocean Dr., South Beach 33139,* ☎ *305/672–7003 or 800/688–7678,* FAX *305/673–3669,* WEB *www.islandoutpost.com. 34 suites. Café, in-room safes, cable TV, in-room VCRs, kitchenettes, refrigerators, beach, shops, laundry service, concierge, business services, travel services. AE, D, DC, MC, V.*

**$$$$** ★ ✕ **Delano Hotel.** Visitors to the Delano typically marvel at the lobby hung with massive white, billowing drapes and yet try to act casual while watching for stars like Ben Affleck, George Clooney, and Spike Lee, all of whom have been known to stop by when in town. Fashion models and men of independent means gather beneath cabanas, pose by the infinity pool, and sniff the heady aromas wafting in from the popular Blue Door restaurant. Comprehensive executive services are offered for business travelers, and all guests have the run of a rooftop bathhouse and solarium on alternating schedules for women (morning and afternoon) and men (evening). Although the standard rooms are average-size, their stark whiteness makes them appear larger. The real appeal here is the *Alice in Wonderland*–like surrealism. ✉ *1685 Collins Ave., South Beach 33139,* ☎ *305/672–2000 or 800/555–5001,* FAX *305/532–0099. 184 rooms, 24 suites. Restaurant, bar, lobby lounge, cable TV, pool, spa, health club, beach, laundry service, concierge, business services. AE, D, DC, MC, V.*

**$$$$** **Fisher Island Club.** To reach ultraexclusive Fisher Island, you need to catch a ferry to take you and your car on a seven-minute voyage to the former estate of William Vanderbilt (which he received from Miami developer Carl Fisher in exchange for a yacht). Vanderbilt's former mansion is now the centerpiece for this resort, which, unlike some places that merely tack on the title, actually has a range of resort-style amenities, rather than just a pool and massage room. Big draws are the challenging P. B. Dye–designed 9-hole golf course; the Spa Internazionale; and 18 lighted tennis courts, hard, grass, and clay. Rooms are equally diverse in form and decor. There are suites and villas, and the cottages that surround the mansion have hot tubs. ✉ *1 Fisher Island Dr., Fisher Island 33109,* ☎ *305/535–6000 or 800/537–3708,* FAX *305/535–6003,* WEB *www.fisherisland-florida.com. 30 rooms, 27 suites, 3 cottages. 6*

Close-Up

# MIAMI'S ART DECO HOTELS

WITH APOLOGIES TO THE flamingo, Miami's most recognizable icons are the art deco hotels of South Beach. But why here? What did this city do to deserve some of the world's most beautiful and stylish buildings?

The story begins in the 1920s, when Miami Beach established itself as America's Winter Playground. Long before Las Vegas got the idea, Miami Beach sprouted hostelries resembling Venetian palaces, Spanish villages, and French châteaux. To complement the social activities of the hotels, the city provided gambling, prostitution, and bootleg whiskey. Miami became a haven for out-of-town high rollers.

In the early 1930s, drawn south by the prospect of warm beaches and luxurious tropical surroundings, middle-class tourists fueled a second boom. More hotels had to be built, but it wouldn't do for Miami to open the same type of boring, staid hotels found across America. En masse, architects decided the motif of choice would be . . . art deco.

In truth, the design was Art Moderne. For purists, the term *Moderne* was a bow to the Exposition Internationale des Arts Décoratifs et Industriels Modernes, held in Paris in 1925. Moderne offered a distinctive yet affordable design solution for the hotels, stores, clubs, and apartment buildings that would be built to accommodate the needs of a new breed of tourist.

An antidote to the gloom of the Great Depression, this look was cheerful and tidy. Along South Beach, Miami received an architectural makeover. Elaborating on the styles introduced in Paris, architects borrowed elements of American industrial design. The features of trains, ocean liners, and automobiles were stripped down to their streamlined essentials, inspiring new looks for the art deco hotels.

With a steel-and-concrete box as a foundation, architects dipped into this grab bag of styles to accessorize their hotels. Pylons, spheres, cylinders, and cubes thrust from facades and roofs. "Eyebrows," small ledges over windows, popped out to provide shade. Softening the boxy buildings' edges, designers added curved corners and wraparound windows. Sunlight, an abundant commodity in Miami Beach, was brought indoors by glass-block construction. Landscapers learned to create an illusion of coolness by planting palms and laying terrazzo floors.

A uniform style soon marked Miami's new hotels. A vertical central element raced past the roofline and into the sky to create a sense of motion. To add to the illusion that these immobile buildings were rapidly speeding objects, colorful bands known as racing stripes were painted around the corners. In keeping with the beachside setting, designers adorned hotels with nautical elements. Portholes appeared in sets of three on facades or within buildings. Images of seaweed, starfish, and rolling ocean waves were plastered, painted, or etched on walls. Some of the buildings looked as if they were ready to go to sea.

Art deco design translated the synchronized choreography of Busby Berkeley movie musicals into architecture. Ordinary travelers could now take a low-cost vacation in an oceanfront fantasy world of geometric shapes and amusing colors. All this was created not for millionaires but for regular folks, those who collected a weekly paycheck . . . who, for one brief, shining moment, could live a life of luxury.

— Gary McKechnie

*restaurants, cable TV, 5 pools, spa, golf course, 18 tennis courts, beach, concierge. AE, DC, MC, V.*

$$$$ **Marlin Hotel.** Music industry luminaries, who come to record at the on-site South Beach Studios, often stay at this mini-boutique property. Mick Jagger, U2, and Aerosmith have all passed through the doors, and beautiful young things stream into the Elite Modeling Agency office on the second floor. Every room has a completely different design, but hardwood floors, stainless steel fixtures, and muted earth tones in all create a commonality. You'll stay connected with Web TV, dual-line cordless phones, and a dedicated e-mail address. Studio suites, with rattan sitting areas, are sizable; larger suites approximate villas. For sunbathing, check out the rooftop deck. ✉ *1200 Collins Ave., South Beach 33139,* ☎ *305/604–5063 or 800/688–7678,* FAX *305/673–9609,* WEB *www.islandoutpost.com. 11 suites. Bar, in-room data ports, in-room safes, cable TV, in-room VCRs, kitchenettes. AE, D, DC, MC, V.*

$$$$ ★ **Raleigh Hotel.** Hidden behind a thick veil of greenery is one of the nicest oceanfront hotels in South Beach. Among the first Art Deco District hotels to be renovated, it has retained Victorian accents (hallway chandeliers and in-room oil paintings) to soften the 20th-century edges. Standard rooms are spacious, and the suites more so. Topping it all off is a new penthouse suite. The gorgeous fleur-de-lis pool is the focal point year-round, especially on December 31, when synchronized swimmers dive in at the stroke of midnight. Other pluses: the lobby coffee bar, a romantic restaurant (Tiger Oak Room), and the old-fashioned Martini Bar. ✉ *1775 Collins Ave., South Beach 33139,* ☎ *305/534–6300 or 800/848–1775,* FAX *305/538–8140,* WEB *www.raleighhotel.com. 111 rooms, 18 suites. Restaurant, bar, in-room data ports, in-room safes, cable TV, in-room VCRs, refrigerators, pool, massage, gym, beach, laundry service, concierge, business services, meeting rooms, parking (fee). AE, D, DC, MC, V.*

$$$$ **Ritz-Carlton South Beach.** One of three Ritz-Carltons to spring up on the Miami scene, this entry debuted in the former home of the DiLido, a cherished Art Moderne Melvin Grossman and Morris Lapidus–designed building. $100 million in renovations later, the hotel now has every amenity you'd expect from a Ritz-Carlton property, while retaining the black terrazzo floors and the lobby's grand Lapidus staircase. The beach, shopping on Lincoln Road, and the hubbub of Ocean Drive are just steps away. And if that's not enough, there's a 13,000-square-ft spa and outdoor pool. ✉ *1 Lincoln Rd., South Beach 33139,* ☎ *800/241–3333,* WEB *www.ritzcarlton.com. 375 rooms. 3 restaurants, coffee shop, lobby lounge, cable TV, room service, pool, sauna, gym, beach, concierge, business services, meeting rooms, parking (fee). AE, D, DC, MC, V.*

$$$$ **The Shore Club.** After four years of relentless buzz and maddening delays, the Shore Club debuted intent on rivaling the Delano as the hotel of choice for visiting celebrities and other trendsetters. The sprawling, low-slung design by architect David Chipperfield left plenty of space for private cabanas and a private Beach House on the sand, and a series of gardens with pergolas and hammocks separated by courtyards and reflecting pools. Rooms are fairly large but nothing especially new, style-wise, though they do add a dash of color to the blond wood furniture and stainless steel accents. The restaurant is part of the upscale Nobu chain, serving Japanese-Peruvian cuisine, and draws healthy crowds. Other healthy crowds can be found on the rooftop Sundari Spa owned by supermodel Christy Turlington. Like the Delano's Agua spa, this is a serene rooftop affair. ✉ *1901 Collins Ave., South Beach 33139,* ☎ *305/695–3100 or 877/640–9500,* FAX *305/695–3299,* WEB *www.shoreclubsb.com. 325 rooms. 3 restaurants, 2 bars, cable TV, 2 pools, spa, health club, beach, shopping, meeting rooms. AE, DC, MC, V.*

The Albion . . . . . . . . .10
Banana Bungalow . . .2
Bayliss Guest House . . . . . .20
Beacon Hotel . . . . . .43
Bel Aire . . . . . . . . . .33
Blue Moon . . . . . . . .38
Brigham Gardens . . .21
Cadet Hotel . . . . . . .11
Cardozo . . . . . . . . .23
Casa Grande . . . . . .39
Cavalier . . . . . . . . .22
Century Hotel . . . . . .46
Claremont . . . . . . . .12
The Clevelander . . . .31
Crest Hotel and Suites . . . . . . . . . . . . .8
Days Inn Convention Center . . .3
Delano Hotel . . . . . .13
Essex House . . . . . . .32
Fisher Island Club . . .48
Greenview Hotel . . . .9
The Hotel . . . . . . . . .41
Hotel Astor . . . . . . .37
Hotel Impala . . . . . .27
Hotel Nash . . . . . . . .30
Hotel Ocean . . . . . .24
Kenmore . . . . . . . . .34
Kent . . . . . . . . . . . .29
La Flora Hotel . . . . . .26
Loews Miami Beach Hotel . . . . . . .16
Marlin Hotel . . . . . . .28
Miami Beach Marriott at South Beach . . . . . . .47
Nassau Suite Hotel . . . . . . . . . . . .19
National Hotel . . . . .15
Park Central . . . . . . .44
Park Washington Hotel . . . . . . . . . . . .35
Pelican . . . . . . . . . .40
Raleigh Hotel . . . . . . .6
Richmond Hotel . . . . .7
Ritz-Carlton South Beach . . . . . . .14
Roney Palace Resort and Spa . . . . . .1
Royal Hotel . . . . . . .42
The Shore Club . . . . .4
Taft . . . . . . . . . . . . .36
The Tides . . . . . . . . .25
Townhouse . . . . . . . . .5
Villa Paradiso . . . . . .17
Wave Hotel . . . . . . .45
WinterHaven . . . . . . .18

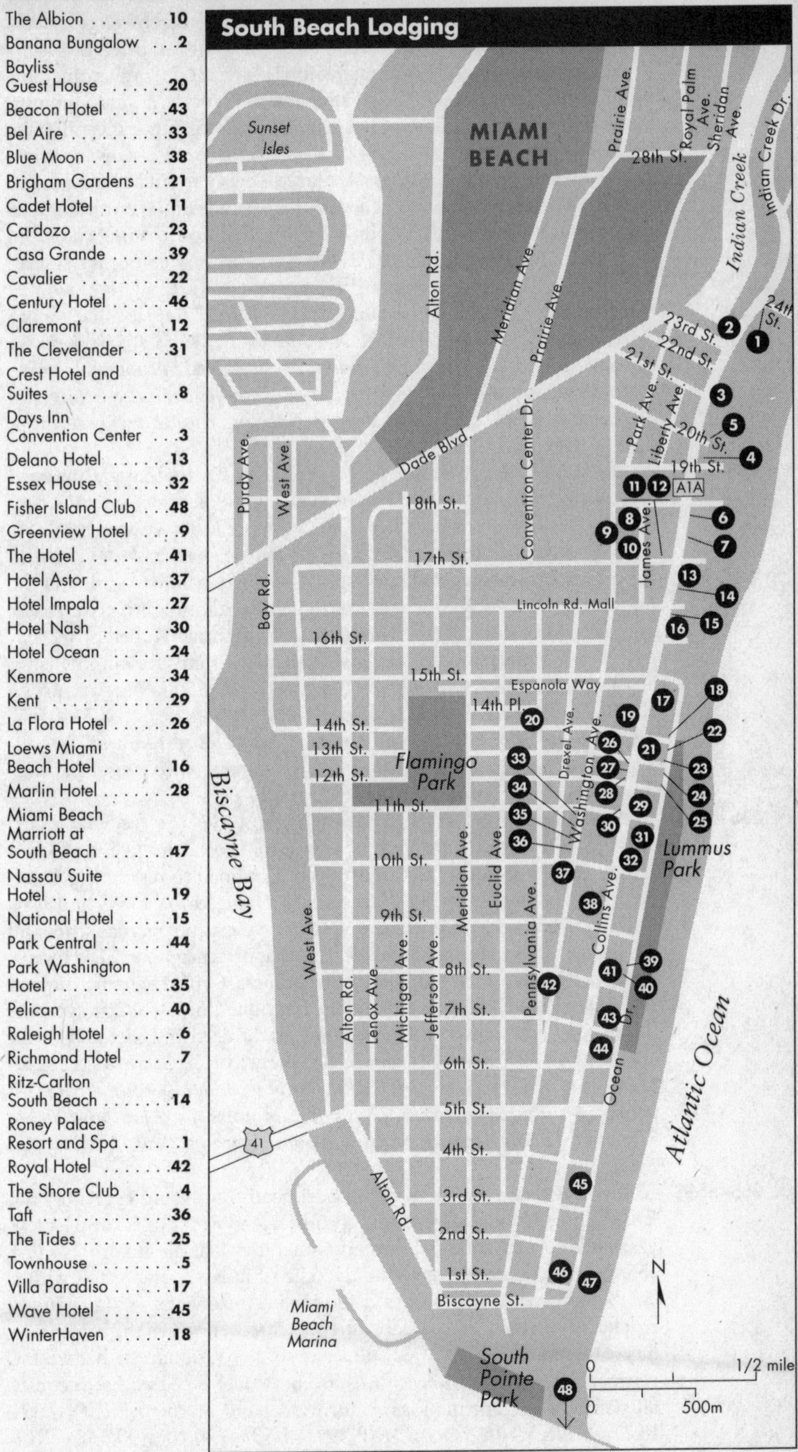

**$$$$** ★ **The Tides.** Hotelier and music magnate Chris Blackwell (formerly of Casa Grande) has put a creative twist on what can often be a sterile Miami design motif (too much white!) by introducing unique hospitality-inspiring elements into the chic and modern surroundings. Some touches are small—spyglasses in each room (since they all have big windows and face the ocean), a blackboard for messages to maids, newspapers on request. Others are large—every room has a king-size bed, capacious closets, and generous baths, the result of turning 115 rooms into 45 suites. Pretty public spaces include a reading room, an übercool dining terrace at 1220, the gorgeous contemporary restaurant. At the Olympic-size pool (the only one on Ocean Drive) women can go topless (total nudity is "undesirable"). ✉ *1220 Ocean Dr., South Beach 33139,* ☎ *305/604–5000 or 800/688–7678,* FAX *305/604–5180,* WEB *www.islandoutpost.com. 45 suites. 2 restaurants, in-room data ports, in-room safes, cable TV, minibars, pool, gym, beach, baby-sitting, dry cleaning, concierge, business services, meeting rooms, travel services. AE, D, DC, MC, V.*

**$$$–$$$$** **The Albion.** Avant-garde Boston architect Carlos Zapata updated this stylish 1939 nautical-deco building by Igor Polevitzky, and the place is full of his distinctive touches. The two-story lobby sweeps into a secluded courtyard and is framed by an indoor waterfall. A crowd of hip and friendly types makes up the clientele; they like to gather at the mezzanine-level pool, which has portholes that allow courtyard strollers an underwater view of the swimmers. As with other Rubell properties (the Beach House and the Greenview), guest rooms are minimalist in design, though filled with what you'd expect. ✉ *1650 James Ave., South Beach 33139,* ☎ *305/913–1000 or 888/665–0008,* FAX *305/674–0507,* WEB *www.rubellhotels.com. 85 rooms, 9 suites. 2 restaurants, bar, in-room data ports, cable TV, minibars, pool, gym, laundry service, concierge, meeting rooms. AE, D, DC, MC, V.*

**$$$–$$$$** ★ **Blue Moon.** It was erstwhile talk-show host Merv Griffin who joined two hotels to create Blue Moon, a place for those who like the Ocean Drive scene but quickly tire of art deco. Designed to resemble a European estate rather than a 1930s box, the Blue Moon looks and feels nothing like the other boutique hotels along the same popular strip, and the service tends to be more reliable than that of its neighbors. The rooms, while not huge, are airy and free of trendiness. Griffin has since moved on, and the Blue Moon has joined the boutique Coral Collection chain, but the hotel remains a quirky marriage of the deco and Mediterranean styles. ✉ *944 Collins Ave., South Beach 33139,* ☎ *305/673–2262 or 800/724–1623,* FAX *305/534–5399,* WEB *www.bluemoonhotel.com. 69 rooms, 6 suites. Restaurant, in-room data ports, in-room safes, cable TV, pool, laundry service, meeting rooms, parking (fee). AE, D, DC, MC, V.*

**$$$–$$$$** **Essex House.** A favorite of the European contingent, especially the British, Essex House moved into the upscale category over the past few years with a major renovation and amenities like the Il Paradiso day spa, where you can reverse the damage of a day at the beach with a combination of massages, facials, and peeling treatments. The large suites, reached by crossing a tropical courtyard, are well worth the price: each has a wet bar, king-size bed, pull-out sofa, 100-square-ft bathroom, refrigerator, and hot tub. Rooms are no slouches, either, with comfy club chairs, elegant mahogany furniture, and marble tubs. ✉ *1001 Collins Ave., South Beach 33139,* ☎ *305/534–2700 or 800/553–7739,* FAX *305/532–3827,* WEB *www.essexhotel.com. 59 rooms, 20 suites. Bar, in-room data ports, in-room safes, cable TV, in-room VCRs, pool, spa, dry cleaning, laundry service, parking (fee). AE, D, MC, V.*

**$$$–$$$$** **The Hotel.** It sounds generic, but this boutique hotel has arrived at the top of many vacation lists, primarily thanks to fashion designer Todd

Oldham, who brought the colors of the sand and the sea indoors. Individually painted tiles, pale ash desks, and mosaic-pattern rugs delight the eyes; minibars, bejeweled bathrooms with tie-dyed robes, TVs with VCRs, and stereo systems are suitable distractions in the decidedly petite, yet soundproof, rooms. Add to this soft lighting, two-person bathtubs, and products by Kiehl's and you have all the makings for a romantic tête-à-tête. The excellent restaurant Wish serves creative cuisine indoors or out. Best of all, though, is the intimate rooftop pool with spectacular views of the sea. ✉ *801 Collins Ave., South Beach 33139,* ☎ *305/531–2222 or 888/877–8434,* FAX *305/531–3222,* WEB *www.thehotelofsouthbeach.com. 48 rooms, 4 suites. Restaurant, bar, cable TV, pool, gym, concierge, business services. AE, D, DC, MC, V.*

**$$$–$$$$** **National Hotel.** The most spectacular feature of this resurrected 1939 shorefront hotel is its tropical pool—it's also Miami Beach's longest (205 ft). In daylight the pool is a perfect backdrop for the film crews that often work here. With curtains closed, poolside rooms could be generic Holiday Inn, displaying little of the creativity of other recently arrived hotels. Rooms in the main building are far more appealing and creative, however. Applause is in order for preserved pieces, such as the original chandelier and furniture in the dining room. Another notable feature is the clubby 1930s-style Press Room cigar bar and meeting room, off the lobby. ✉ *1677 Collins Ave., South Beach 33139,* ☎ *305/532–2311 or 800/327–8370,* FAX *305/534–1426,* WEB *www.nationalhotel.com. 115 rooms, 5 suites. Restaurant, bar, in-room data ports, in-room safes, minibars, no-smoking floor, pool, gym, beach, laundry service, concierge, meeting rooms, parking (fee). AE, DC, MC, V.*

**$$$–$$$$** **Roney Palace Resort and Spa.** The Roney Palace has led two lives as one of South Florida's first luxury resorts and also one of South Florida's latest reincarnates. The original Roney Palace was a Miami Beach landmark, a grande old dame of the '20s, and the luxury boom of the late '90s led to its ambitious renovation, yielding a tropically landscaped pool and possibly the largest rooms on Miami Beach. The all-suites setup means you have a choice of executive, one-bedroom, or two-bedroom suites. All are casually if not sparsely furnished with blond-wood platform beds or other lightweight materials. The huge private beach and water sports (extra) make it like a Caribbean-class resort. ✉ *2399 Collins Ave., South Beach 33139,* ☎ *305/604–1000,* FAX *305/538–7141,* WEB *www.roney-palace.com. 585 suites. 3 restaurants, 2 bars, cable TV, pool, spa, exercise equipment, beach, concierge, meeting rooms, parking (fee). AE, D, DC, MC, V.*

**$$–$$$$** **Beacon Hotel.** Terrazzo floors, whimsical furnishings, and an air of understated elegance reflect the hotel's original 1937 grand design. Art deco is in overdrive in this neighborhood, and the hotel is swept up in the energy of the district. A restaurant with sidewalk café allows you to gawk at the street life. The beach is a stone's throw away. Inside, room size is moderate and all have comfortable beds, fairly large closets, and an average-size bath. As at other hotels along this stretch, valet parking is a necessary evil since there's little room to park your own car. ✉ *720 Ocean Dr., South Beach 33139,* ☎ *305/674–8200 or 800/649–7075,* FAX *305/674–8976,* WEB *www.beacon-hotel.com. 79 rooms, 2 suites. Restaurant, bar, in-room data ports, in-room safes, cable TV, laundry service, concierge, business services, meeting rooms, parking (fee). AE, D, DC, MC, V.*

**$$–$$$$** ★ **Loews Miami Beach Hotel.** Miami Beach waited decades for a major new beachfront luxury hotel, and a few years on, this oceanfront behemoth is still at the top of the heap. Although others have been renovated, this 18-story, 800-room hotel was built from the blueprints up. Not only did Loews manage to snag 99 ft of beach, it also took over the vacant St. Moritz next door and restored it to its original 1939 art deco appearances, adding another 100 rooms to the complex. If you prefer boutique surroundings, but still want the amenities of a big resort, St. Moritz is the way to go. The resort, to give you the sense of the size, has 85,000 square ft of meeting space and an enormous ocean-view grand ballroom. Dining, too, is a pleasure, courtesy of the Argentinian-inspired Gaucho Room, Preston's South Beach Coffee Bar, and Hemisphere Lounge. ✉ *1601 Collins Ave., South Beach 33139,* ☎ *305/604–1601,* FAX *305/531–8677,* WEB *www.loewshotels.com. 740 rooms, 50 suites. 4 restaurants, 2 bars, lobby lounge, cable TV, pool, spa, beach, children's programs (ages 4–12), meeting rooms. AE, D, DC, MC, V.*

$$$ ★ **Hotel Astor.** Among the very best that South Beach has to offer, the Astor stands apart from the crowd with such quiet luxuries as thick Belgian towels and linens, down pillows, paddle fans, and a seductive pool. Guest rooms are built to recall deco ocean liner staterooms, complete with faux-portholes, and are furnished with custom-milled French furniture, Roman shades, and sleek sound and video systems. A tasteful, muted color scheme and the most comfortable king beds imaginable make for eminently restful nights, and excellent service eliminates any worries about practical matters. The Astor Place restaurant is exceptional for its cuisine, service, and setting. ✉ *956 Washington Ave., South Beach 33139,* ☎ *305/531–8081 or 800/270–4981,* FAX *305/531–3193,* WEB *www.hotelastor.com. 40 rooms. Restaurant, bar, in-room data ports, in-room safes, cable TV, minibars, room service, pool, massage, laundry service, concierge, Internet, business services, parking (fee). AE, DC, MC, V.*

$$$ ★ **Hotel Impala.** It's all very European here at the Impala, from the mineral water and orchids to the Mediterranean-style armoires, Italian fixtures, and triple-sheeted white-on-white modified Eastlake sleigh beds. Everything from wastebaskets to towels to toilet paper is of extraordinary quality. The building is a stunning tropical Mediterranean Revival in the Art Deco District and is one block from the beach. Iron, mahogany, and stone on the inside are in sync with the sporty white-trim ocher exterior and quiet courtyard. Rooms are elegant, comfortable, and complete, each with a TV/VCR/stereo and a stock of CDs and videos. The hotel does not admit children under 16. ✉ *1228 Collins Ave., South Beach 33139,* ☎ *305/673–2021 or 800/646–7252,* FAX *305/673–5984,* WEB *www.hotelimpalamiamibeach.com. 14 rooms, 3 suites. Restaurant, bar, in-room data ports, cable TV, in-room VCRs, laundry service, concierge. AE, D, DC, MC, V. CP.*

$$$ ★ **Hotel Nash.** With a kiss from Miami designer Peter Page and Laura Sheridan, manager savant, this boutique hotel dating to 1935 was awakened from a long art deco sleep. Sheridan came to Miami with Ian Schrager to open the Delano—and the Nash shows some of the same style-conscious touches, although with comforts the Delano can't offer. Perhaps it's because austerity doesn't come much into play: What is white elsewhere is sage-green and blond wood here. Clever furnishings seem lifted from the Design District: Almost-oval armoires also conceal a minibar and an ottoman doubles as rollaway seating at a low coffee-cum-Japanese table. Tiled bathrooms with rain forest shower heads are built for those who take grooming and primping seriously. (Framed floor-to-ceiling in-room mirrors serve the same purpose.) Keep your eyes peeled for Oliver Stone and fashion models, who grab up the terrace suites, and can be seen lingering at Mark's, the restaurant run by James Beard Award–winning chef Mark Militello, downstairs. ✉ *1120 Collins Ave., South Beach 33139,* ☎ *305/674–7800,* FAX *305/538–8288.* WEB *www.hotelnash.com. 52 rooms, 3 suites. Restaurant, cable TV, 3 pools, concierge. AE, D, MC, V.*

$$$ **Hotel Ocean.** If the street signs didn't read Ocean Drive, you might suspect you were whiling away the day on the Riviera. The tropical French feel is evident when you enter the shaded, bougainvillea-draped courtyard and see diners enjoying a complimentary breakfast in the hotel's brasserie. The two buildings connected by this courtyard contain a few surprises: soft beds; authentic 1930s art deco pieces; large foldout couches; clean, spacious baths; and soundproof windows ensure that rooms (which average 425 square ft each) are comfortable and quiet. ✉ *1230–38 Ocean Dr., South Beach 33139,* ☎ *305/672–2579 or 800/783–1725,* FAX *305/672–7665,* WEB *www.hotelocean.com. 4 rooms, 23 suites. Restaurant, bar, in-room data ports, in-room safes, cable TV, in-room VCRs, minibars, concierge. AE, D, DC, MC, V.*

$$$ **Miami Beach Marriott at South Beach.** Nouveau art deco flourishes conceal a new and pragmatic beach resort designed to yield as many oceanview rooms as possible. Albeit the rooms are larger than most on the beach, with a liberal helping of very un-Marriott-like tropical color that proves the mega-brand really is trying to fit in. A mini-spa, quiet beach, and reliable service make this a safe bet for business types or families who want to experience South Beach while keeping the wildest partying at a distance. ✉ *161 Ocean Dr., South Beach 33139,* ☎ *305/536–7700 or 800/228–9290,* FAX *305/536–9900,* WEB *www.miamibeachmarriott.com. 236 rooms, 7 suites. Restaurant, 2 bars, in-room data ports, in-room safes, cable TV, pool, spa, beach, laundry service, concierge, business services, meeting rooms, parking (fee). AE, D, DC, MC, V.*

$$$ **Richmond Hotel.** Even though the entrance and lobby aren't as grand as those of the neighboring Delano, the rooms here are among the most comfortable in South Beach. Chenille bedspreads, blond wood, plush sofas, and a soft 1930s floral design scheme suggest art deco without minimalism. These are rooms that make you feel at home, and wireless Internet access keep you in touch if you must. The grounds, with a large pool, half-moon hot tub, white-canvas cabanas, an eye-catching curvy stream, and adjoining curvy sidewalk, have what your place back home is probably missing. The sidewalk slices through a wide lawn and past palm trees to create a entryway to the Atlantic. ✉ *1757 Collins Ave., South Beach 33139,* ☎ *305/538–2331 or 800/327–3163,* FAX *305/531–9021,* WEB *www.richmondhotel.com. 80 rooms, 6 suites. Café, cable TV, pool, hot tub, gym, beach, laundry service, concierge, Internet. AE, D, DC, MC, V.*

$$–$$$ **Cavalier.** In any of the Island Outpost hotels (the Tides, Marlin, and Kent are the others) you can count on good service and creative surroundings. And, in most cases, you can expect to pay plenty for the privilege; but not if you get a standard room in this deco boutique that exudes a Caribbean warmth thanks to just the right pastel shades of paint. Rooms include a CD player, queen-size bed, batik fabrics, deco-style furniture, vintage black-and-white photos, and access to the pool at the Tides. Suites get an ocean view and king-size bed. And talk about location: you're right across the street from the great big Atlantic. ✉ *1320 Ocean Dr., South Beach 33139,* ☎ *305/604–5064 or 800/688–7678,* FAX *305/531–5543,* WEB *www.islandoutpost.com. 42 rooms, 3 suites. In-room safes, cable TV, in-room VCRs, minibars, business services, travel services. AE, D, DC, MC, V.*

$$–$$$ ✕ **Century Hotel.** Designed in 1939 by art deco master Henry Hohauser, the Century now garners an *InStyle* guest list. Like the Marriott across the street, it's a little south of the action, but that can be a good thing: the Century is a favorite of celebrities trying to keep a low profile. Besides, the hotel's renowned Italian restaurant, Joia, casts a heavy shadow of cool aided by a steady influx of A-listers and local glitterati. The spartan rooms are all glass and marble and hardwoods, and definitely feel

stylish, if a little remote—but that's probably the point. The Century is a good choice if you're dying to try out that newly purchased Armani wardrobe. ✉ *140 Ocean Dr., South Beach 33139,* ☎ *305/674–8855 or 888/982–3688,* FAX *305/538–5733,* WEB *www.centurysouthbeach.com. 30 rooms, 4 suites. Restaurant, in-room data ports, in-room safes, cable TV, meeting rooms. AE, DC, MC, V.*

**$$–$$$** **The Clevelander.** The first thing you'll notice about the Clevelander, if its reputation hasn't made it to your town, is the giant pool-bar, which attracts revelers for happy-hour drink specials and loud, live music every day of the week. The drinking flows into the lobby, which is part hotel and mostly sports bar. Rooms have small double beds but generous-size baths. If you need to work out, the South Beach Gym, within the hotel, extends reduced rates to guests. Because of the partying, guests must be 21, and you won't get much sleep here. Thankfully, the staff seems to be having a blast. ✉ *1020 Ocean Dr., South Beach 33139,* ☎ *305/531–3485 or 800/815–6829,* FAX *305/534–4707,* WEB *www.clevelander.com. 56 rooms. Restaurant, 6 bars, cable TV, pool, gym. AE, DC, MC, V.*

**$$–$$$** **Greenview Hotel.** This 1939 Henry Hohauser–designed art deco hotel was bought by the Rubell Family and renovated by Parisian designer Chahan Minassian (of Ralph Lauren's European Polo stores). The vibe is understated chic and seemingly straight out of a design magazine: wrought-iron scroll railings in the bi-level lobby and custom handcrafted furnishings, mid-century Modernist collectors' pieces, and pristine white upholstery ornament the simple rooms, which also have queen-size beds and large baths. The lack of on-premises amenities is tempered by the free access you have to those of the Albion, a block and a half away. ✉ *1671 Washington Ave., South Beach 33139,* ☎ *305/531–6588 or 887/782–3557,* FAX *305/531–4580,* WEB *www.rubellhotels.com. 40 rooms, 2 suites. Cable TV, laundry service, concierge, business services. AE, DC, MC, V. CP.*

**$$–$$$** **La Flora Hotel.** Design elements like the 1929 terrazzo floors and the custom-made deco furniture transport you back to Miami Beach's glory days. The lobby bar even serves classic cocktails from the 1940s. Sip them while gawking at the foot traffic on Collins Avenue, or just rest here after a relaxing day at the beach, only a block away. Rooms are decorated in pastels slightly reminiscent of an Ikea catalog, and the roomy bathrooms are done in marble. The rate includes Continental breakfast, and room service has items from the nearby Japanese and Italian restaurants. ✉ *1238 Collins Ave., South Beach 33139,* ☎ *305/531–3406 or 877/523–5672,* FAX *305/538–0850,* WEB *www.hotellaflora.com. 20 rooms, 8 suites. Cable TV, massage, gym, concierge, business services, parking (fee). AE, D, DC, MC, V. CP.*

**$$–$$$** **Nassau Suite Hotel.** For a boutique hotel one block from the beach, this airy retreat almost qualifies as a steal (by South Beach standards). The original 1937 floor plan of 50 rooms gave way to 22 spacious and smart-looking suites with king beds, fully equipped kitchens, hardwood floors, white wood blinds, and free local calls. The Nassau is in the heart of the action yet quiet enough to give you the rest you need. Note: this three-floor hotel has no elevator and no bellhop. There's also very limited parking. ✉ *1414 Collins Ave., South Beach 33139,* ☎ *305/534–2354 or 866/859–4177,* FAX *305/534–3133,* WEB *www.nassausuite.com. 22 suites. In-room data ports, cable TV, kitchenettes, concierge. AE, D, DC, MC, V.*

**$$–$$$** **Park Central.** Across from the glorious beach, this seven-story art deco hotel, painted blue, with wraparound corner windows, knows just how to stay in the forefront of the art deco revival. Many fashionistas stay here, no doubt attracted by the soothing sculpture garden and compact pool, the setting of much parading about in swimming attire. Black-and-white photos of old beach scenes, hurricanes, and familiar faces attest to its longevity, and board games in the lobby add to its charm. Rooms are decorated with Philippine mahogany furnishings—originals that have been restored. Incorporated with the property is the Imperial Hotel next door, with an additional 36 rooms. ✉ *640 Ocean Dr., South Beach 33139,* ☎ *305/538–1611 or 800/727–5236,* FAX *305/534–7520,* WEB *www.theparkcentral.com. 115 rooms, 12 suites. Restaurant, bar, in-room data ports, cable TV, refrigerators, pool, gym, laundry service, concierge, meeting rooms. AE, D, DC, MC, V.*

**$$–$$$** ★ **Pelican.** Dazzling, kitschy spaces with art deco–inspired frivolity characterize this offbeat hotel, owned by the Diesel Jeans company. Individually designed rooms, with names like Me Tarzan, You Vain, are certainly clever, but all have tiny sleeping chambers in contrast to the triple-size bathrooms with outrageous industrial piping. Amenities like in-room CD players and bath products are certainly welcome, though. The hotel's celebrity guestlist includes Yoko Ono, which figures, because room for room Pelican outweirds every place else in Miami. ✉ *826 Ocean Dr., South Beach 33139,* ☎ *305/673–3373 or 800/773–5422,* FAX *305/673–3255,* WEB *www.pelicanhotel.com. 25 rooms, 5 suites. Restaurant, bar, café, in-room safes, cable TV, in-room VCRs, refrigerators, beach, concierge, business services, parking (fee). AE, DC, MC, V.*

**$$–$$$** ★ **Townhouse.** Surely you've seen images of its white rooms accented by a red-and-white beachball? Or the glorious rooftop deck with canvas umbrellas and waterbed chaise longues? Since its arrival on the scene, this new boutique hotel designed by India Madhavi, whom Vogue called "the next best thing in the world of design," has been the site of many a fashion shoot, and the destination of many hipsters who may have otherwise headed straight for the W. Rooms are simple and streamlined, white and welcoming, although they're not everybody's definition of cozy: You get a lozenge-shape lounging "pouf" rather than a couch. But such is the price of über-modernity—although this is actually the best budget buy for the style hungry. The Penthouse suites cost that of standard rooms elsewhere. Downstairs is the Bond Street sushi bar and lounge. ✉ *150 20th St., east of Collins Ave., 33139,* ☎ *305/534–3800,* FAX *305/534—3811 or 877/534–3800.* WEB *www.townhousehotel.com. 69 rooms, 3 suites. Restaurant, lounge, cable TV, exercise equipment, laundry service. AE, D, MC, V. CP.*

**$$–$$$** **Wave Hotel.** Formerly the Lord Balfour Hotel, the Wave pulls off a difficult mix of kitsch and class that draws trendsetters. Bizarre modernist paintings and stainless-steel accents predominate in the lobby, which leads into a sedate little courtyard. Custom-made Italian furniture by Romi Ferretti, including platform beds, and funky Murano glass chandeliers adorn guest rooms, which include the requisite CD-player stereo and data ports. Wave's in-room innovation is its (eponymously memorable) wave machine next to each bed—perfect for soothing jangled nerves after an encounter with Collins Avenue's wired nightclub scene. ✉ *350 Ocean Dr., South Beach 33139,* ☎ *305/673–0401 or 800/501–0401,* FAX *305/531–9385,* WEB *www.wavehotel.com. 66 rooms. Restaurant, bar, in-room data ports, cable TV, minibars, room service. AE, D, DC, MC, V.*

**$$–$$$** ★ **WinterHaven.** "Bright" and "airy" are not words you usually associate with South Beach hotels, but this artfully restored classic is both—in spades. WinterHaven is a riot of color, from the garnet and aquamarine lobby lounge to the ginger and cream upholstery in guest rooms. Here, black-and-white photos of South Beach's former self hang over the custom-designed deco furniture that—surprise—doesn't strive to be a conversation piece. The two-story lobby and split-level mezzanine regularly play host to parties and fashion shoots, but if you take your complimentary breakfast up to the rooftop sundeck, you'll have a bird's-eye view of South Beach at dawn. ✉ *1400 Ocean Dr., South Beach 33139,* ☎ *305/531–5571 or 800/395–2322,* FAX *305/538–6387,* WEB *www.winterhavenhotelsobe.com. 71 rooms. Bar, in-room data ports, in-room safes, cable TV, concierge, parking (fee). AE, D, DC, MC, V.*

$$ **Bel Aire.** Reasonable prices (and a short walk to the beach) draw a budget-conscious crowd, but the main selling points here are the spacious rooms, a real luxury on South Beach. The suites have a sitting area, full bath with tub and shower, a stove, large refrigerator, and fully stocked kitchen. Outdoors, a winding sidewalk within the walled courtyard is quite calming, as it's immensely pleasurable to catch some rays in South Beach without worrying that passersby are ogling your spare tire. (On the other hand, if you'd rather be ogled, schedule your stay for the occasional singles weekend.) You can also enjoy the facilities of the Park Washington Resort, which includes the Park Washington, Taft, and Kenmore hotels. ✉ *1020–1050 Washington Ave., South Beach 33139,* ☎ *305/532–1930 or 888/424–1930,* FAX *305/972–4666,* WEB *www.parkwashingtonhotel.com. 18 suites. Restaurant, bar, cable TV, refrigerator, pool. AE, MC, V. CP.*

$$ **Cardozo.** Perhaps it's because this hotel is owned by Gloria and Emilio Estefan that there's such lively and loud music in the lobby. But when you're through with the check-in tango, you can retreat to a quiet and comfortable room. Leopard-print blankets and other artifacts collected on Gloria's world tours, as well as large baths with mosaic-tile sinks, and terra-cotta walls distinguish this place from the pack. Whether you opt for a standard room or a junior or deluxe suite, you'll have space to spread out. The views from oceanfront rooms are impressive (especially from Rooms 202 and 305), and all rooms have TV, VCR, and CD players. ✉ *1300 Ocean Dr., South Beach 33139,* ☎ *305/535–6500 or 800/782–6500,* FAX *305/673–8609. 44 rooms, 7 suites. Restaurant, bar, in-room safes, cable TV, in-room VCRs, minibars, beach, concierge, meeting rooms. AE, DC, MC, V.*

$$ **Crest Hotel and Suites.** Poolside Adirondack chairs, a rooftop solarium, and relative solitude make this easygoing hotel a place to consider when the R&R you desire isn't rock-and-roll. The 1939 art deco hotel is not on one of the trendy streets, yet it's only a few steps from everything worth seeing. Streamlined furniture in the lobby and rooms makes this look like a boutique hotel on the move. The simple rooms have a king- or two full-size beds, and suites include kitchenettes and microwaves. The whole place is clean as a whistle, maybe even cleaner. Two buildings are separated by a small coffee bar and an equally small pool. ✉ *1670 James Ave., South Beach 33139,* ☎ *305/531–0321 or 800/531–3880,* FAX *305/531–8180,* WEB *www.cresthotel.com. 43 rooms, 23 suites. Café, cable TV, pool, meeting rooms. AE, DC, MC, V.*

$$ **Kenmore.** Utilitarian comfort preserves the essence of 1930s art deco. The glass-block facade of the lobby invites you to a no-nonsense lodging experience, setting a tone that complements clean but smallish tropical-theme rooms with twin or king-size beds. On a very active street, the surprising privacy of the Kenmore is a strong selling point. A quiet pool (and courtyard bar) hidden behind a low wall allows you to tan in an Adirondack chair without being the subject of voyeurs. Then again, you're only a short walk from the clubs and shops of South Beach—and you get breakfast, to boot. ✉ *1020–1050 Washington Ave., South Beach 33139,* ☎ *305/532–1930 or 888/424–1930,* FAX *305/972–4666,* WEB *www.parkwashingtonresort.com. 60 rooms. Restaurant, bar, cable TV, refrigerators, pool. AE, MC, V. CP.*

$$ ★ **Kent.** There are toys in the Day-Glo–colored lobby, beanbag chairs in the rooms, and chrome ceiling fans throughout at this wackiest of the South Beach Island Outpost hotels (the Tides, Marlin, and Cavalier are the others). But the highlight of the 2001 renovation is the third-

Close-Up

# THE MEDIUM IS THE MASSAGE

**NO LONGER THE REFUGE** of dieters and effete Europeans, spas have enjoyed a whopping image boost in the last few years. By combining restful treatments, healthy (yet tasty) cuisine, and focused exercise programs, they've positioned themselves as a mind, body, and soul retreat from the stresses of everyday life. In leisure centers like Miami, no self-respecting new resort debuts without a lavish spa in place, and the competition to launch ever more exotic treatments and esoteric machinery has reached a fever pitch.

But be warned, not every spa is worthy of the name. The word is used very loosely in the Miami hotel trade, and it might refer to anything from a three-level, 30-room palace of relaxation to a spare room by the gym with a pair of massage tables. Among the big-dollar offerings, though, there is plenty of variety, depending on whether your preference is decadent pampering, unique treatments, a trendy clientele, or a good, old-fashioned sweat.

**Best place to feel like a million bucks:** To get to the ultra-posh Fisher Island Club you must take a private ferry, yacht, seaplane, or helicopter—which is an indicator of the prices that await at the Spa Internazionale. But if it's extremely personalized service you're after, this is the place. The yoga classes are very popular and include Yoga for Golf.

**Best way to unwind after a marathon meeting:** Business-oriented JW Marriott and Mandarin Oriental hotel push the stress-reducing effects of their services. JW Marriott's Spa 1111 specializes in European-style treatments, with the one-hour Muscle Aching Massage and Hydrolifting facial getting the requests. The Spa at the Mandarin Oriental mixes Asian decor and techniques with a dash of Miami flavor. The Detoxifying Sea of Senses, for example, combines skin brushing, body rubbing, and a close encounter with warmed algae fresh from the ocean.

**Best adrenaline rush:** The massive Eden Roc has all the typical spa offerings, plus a bewildering list of treatments, an oceanfront setting, and state-of-the-art fitness equipment. But what sets it apart is Mount Eden Roc, the only indoor rock climbing wall in South Florida. The ascent is challenging, even without the distraction of the blue Atlantic view.

**Best way to bring up baby:** The Pre-Natal Massage helps those in the second and third trimester fight lower back pain and water retention. Newborns aren't neglected, either: the Infant Massage rubs baby the right way, then shows parents how to try it at home.

**Best shot at rubbing shoulders with a star:** Up on the roof at the celebrity-magnet Delano is the tres-chic Agua spa. Early reservations are essential if you want to try the signature Milk and Honey body soak, or get a Manual Lift with Oxygen, which promises dramatic reshaping and firming of the face.

**Best of the new:** The long-awaited Shore Club brought along with it the Sundari Spa, owned by model Christy Turlington. It's a serene rooftop affair, with a choice of indoor treatment rooms or outside terraces. The house specialty is Asian Ayurvedic scrubs and soaks. Ritz-Carlton has debuted three hotels in Miami since 2001, and each has its own spa: a 5,000-square-ft minifacility at Coconut Grove; a 13,000-square-ft number in South Beach; and the big kahuna, a 20,000 square footer at the Ritz-Carlton, Key Biscayne. The signature treatment at that property is the Fountain of Youth Ocean Balance, where you soak away your cares while floating free in the wide Atlantic. Don't get carried away.

— Matt Windsor

floor Lucite Suite, where practically everything, from bed to desk to phones to tables, is made from translucent plastic, making it a great place to party. Sure, the rooms are on the small side, and there isn't much of a view, but the atmosphere, the pumped-up staff, and great prices make the Kent hard to beat if you're in the mood for a good time. ✉ *1131 Collins Ave., South Beach 33139,* ☎ *305/604–5000 or 800/688–7678,* FAX *305/531–0720,* WEB *www.islandoutpost.com. 52 rooms, 2 suites. In-room safes, cable TV, in-room VCRs, minibars, business services, meeting rooms, travel services. AE, D, DC, MC, V.*

**$$ ★** **Royal Hotel.** *Austin Powers* meets *2001* in this avant-garde hotel that doesn't take itself too seriously. Each room really only has two pieces of furniture: a "digital chaise lounge" and a bed, both molded white plastic contortions from designer Jordan Mozer. You can't miss the bed, with projecting wings that hold a phone and alarm clock, in the middle of the room. The headboard arcs back like a car spoiler, and doubles as a minibar, filled to your personal taste. The chaise holds a TV–Web TV and keyboard for surfing the Net. Lest all this space-age technology make the room dull, a wild shag carpet and rainbow-paisley bathrobes remind you you're here to have fun—*Yeah, baby.* ✉ *758 Washington Ave., South Beach 33139,* ☎ *305/673–9009 or 888/394–6835,* FAX *305/673–9244,* WEB *www.royalhotelsouthbeach.com. 38 rooms, 4 suites. Restaurant, in-room data ports, cable TV, laundry service, business services, meeting rooms. AE, D, DC, MC, V.*

**$–$$** **Brigham Gardens.** You may be enticed to this small hotel one block from the beach by the 100 or so species of tropical plants, fountain, and colorful birds. From the street it looks like lush urban anomaly, but things could be a little more spic and span inside—although it's no dive, either. Rooms are certainly functional and suited for budget travelers who need to dine in. Each room has a mini-refrigerator, microwave, and coffeemaker, and the one-bedroom apartments have fully equipped kitchens. Plus pets are welcome, and the mother and daughter team of Erika and Hillary Brigham will give you a 10% discount if you stay seven days or longer. ✉ *1411 Collins Ave., South Beach 33139,* ☎ *305/531–1331,* FAX *305/538–9898,* WEB *www.brighamgardens.com. 8 rooms, 12 suites. Fans, refrigerators, cable TV, laundry facilities, meeting rooms. AE, DC, MC, V.*

**$–$$** **Cadet Hotel.** Clark Gable stayed in Room 225 when he came to Miami for Army Air Corps training in the 1940s. Although this Lincoln Road district hotel doesn't have the glamour to attract stars today, it's still a clean, friendly, and perfectly placed little hotel. For a pad that's a few minutes' walk from the Jackie Gleason Theater of the Performing Arts and the convention center and two blocks from the ocean, it's about half the cost of an Ocean Drive hotel. Bright without glitz, rooms have ordinary furniture, which is mixed but not necessarily matched—nor is it crummy. Breakfast is served in the lobby or on the terrace. ✉ *1701 James Ave., South Beach 33139,* ☎ *305/672–6688 or 800/432–2338,* FAX *305/532–1676,* WEB *www.cadethotel.com. 44 rooms. Cable TV, refrigerators. AE, D, DC, MC, V. CP.*

**$–$$** **Days Inn Convention Center.** Nothing flashy and nothing trashy might be the motto. The lobby is bright and floral, with a fountain and gift shop. Rooms are standard hotel issue; deluxe rooms throw in impressive views of the ocean. If you're more concerned about your wallet than your image, this can be a good bet. Keep in mind that if you want something with character, you can find that elsewhere at these rates. Here you'll find the basic franchise dependables (including a pool)—and it's all literally seconds from the beach and the Miami Beach Cultural Center. ✉ *100 21st St., South Beach 33139,* ☎ *305/538–6631 or 800/451–3345,* FAX *305/674–0954,* WEB *www.daysinnsouthbeach.com.*

*172 rooms. Restaurant, bar, in-room safes, cable TV, refrigerators, pool, beach, laundry service, parking (fee). AE, D, DC, MC, V.*

$–$$ ★ **Taft.** The Taft's 1940s (remodeled) rooms have art deco furnishings, baths with oversize showers, and twin or king beds, so folks on a budget can still get in on the SoBe lifestyle. As part of the Park Washington Resort (which includes the Park Washington, Bel Aire, and Kenmore hotels), the Taft allows you to relax by the private pool, tip a drink at the Tiki bar or the lounge, have breakfast at the Courtyard Café, and, in general, enjoy a youth-hostel feel in a far more civilized setting. While hotels and prices go up, up, and up around it, this spot is a poor man's oasis in the heart of South Beach. ✉ *1020–1050 Washington Ave., South Beach 33139,* ☎ *305/532–1930 or 888/424–1930,* FAX *305/972–4666,* WEB *www.parkwashingtonresort.com. 30 rooms. Restaurant, bar, cable TVs with movies, in-room VCRs, refrigerators, pool. AE, MC, V. CP.*

$–$$ ★ **Villa Paradiso.** Peeking out from behind a sea of tropical foliage, quiet Villa Paradiso is a rather unassuming piece of deco architecture. But its discrete charms are evident as soon as you step through the fence into its secluded courtyard. Inside, the large rooms, which are more like apartments, have polished hardwood floors, French doors, and quirky wrought-iron furniture. Rooms are especially well suited for extended visits, with separate living and dining areas, and access to laundry facilities. Free local calls and the prospect of enjoying conversation with fellow guests on the lush patio make this a good choice and an affordable bet. ✉ *1415 Collins Ave., South Beach 33139,* ☎ *305/532–0616,* FAX *305/673–5874,* WEB *www.villaparadisohotel.com. 17 studios. In-room data ports, cable TV, kitchenettes, laundry facilities. AE, DC, MC, V.*

$ **Banana Bungalow.** This may seem like a university dormitory—indeed, some rooms have dorm-style bunk beds for about $15 a night—but the cleanliness, friendliness, and abundance of activities make this spot worth checking into, especially for hard-core student travelers. The Bungalow's social center is the large pool area, which has outdoor grills, and is surrounded by a patio bar, game room, and café. A close second is the Internet kiosk in the lobby, a must for the e-mail addicted. Some may be put off by the smell of the brackish canal nearby, but for others it's a small price to pay for a small price to stay. ✉ *2360 Collins Ave., South Beach 33139,* ☎ *305/538–1951 or 800/746–7835,* FAX *305/531–3217,* WEB *www.bananabungalow.com. 60 private rooms, 25 dorm-style rooms, all with bath. Bar, café, cable TV with video games, pool, billiards, recreation room, laundry service, Internet. MC, V. CP.*

$ **Bayliss Guest House.** At the Bayliss, rooms are abnormally large and surprisingly inexpensive. Not only are the bedrooms large, so are the kitchen, the sitting room, and bath. There are also kitchenless standard rooms available. An easy three blocks west of the ocean, the Bayliss is in a residential neighborhood that's comfortably close to—but far enough away from—the din of the Art Deco District. Can't do much better than this, if you don't mind carrying your own bags. There's very limited parking. ✉ *500–504 14th St., South Beach 33139,* ☎ *305/531–3488,* FAX *305/531–4440. 12 rooms, 7 suites. Refrigerators, cable TV, laundry facilities. AE, D, DC, MC, V.*

$ **Claremont.** If your immediate surroundings are secondary to getting a room in South Beach, consider this place. You'll get small rooms at a fair price. Rooms are small, starkly simple and offer the necessities: soft beds, private baths, and color TV—but the price is fair. Although you'll have to pay for parking, you can walk to the Lincoln Road Mall, Ocean Drive, and other South Beach attractions since they're only a few blocks away. On the downside, the rooms are slightly stuffy (bring some incense) and quite close to busy (and noisy) Collins Avenue. ✉ *1700 Collins Ave., South Beach 33139,* ☎ *305/538–*

*4661, FAX 305/538–9631. 70 rooms. Cable TV, refrigerators, parking (fee). AE, DC, MC, V.*

**$** **Park Washington Hotel.** Part of an entire block of accommodations (including the Taft, Kenmore, and Bel Air) known collectively as the Park Washington Resort, this modest hotel does 1930s art deco without going overboard. The neat and tidy rooms are middle of the road: nice and basic, with TV, ceiling fans, and powerful air-conditioning. One advantage of staying here is the size of the complex, which affords you access to a courtyard pool secluded within lush tropical vegetation. This privacy is impressive considering you're only a few feet from a busy road and a short walk to Ocean Drive. ✉ *1020–1050 Washington Ave., South Beach 33139,* ☎ *305/532–1930 or 888/424–1930,* FAX *305/972–4666,* WEB *www.parkwashingtonresort.com. 30 rooms. Restaurant, bar, cable TV, refrigerators, pool. AE, MC, V. CP.*

## Downtown Miami and West

**$$$$** ★ **Mandarin Oriental Miami.** Though it's a favorite of Wall Street tycoons and Latin American CEOs doing business with the Brickell Avenue banks, anyone who can afford to stay here won't regret it. The location is excellent, at the tip of Brickell Key in Biscayne Bay; rooms facing west have a panoramic view of the dazzling downtown skyline; those facing east overlook Miami Beach and the blue Atlantic beyond. Fanatically picky about details, the hotel stocks rooms with items like Bulova alarm clocks and gives you hand-painted room numbers on rice paper upon check-in. Rising star Michelle Bernstein runs the very popular Azul restaurant, which serves Asian/Latin cuisine and is set apart by an eye-catching waterfall and private dining area strung out at the end of a catwalk. ✉ *500 Brickell Key Dr., Brickell Key 33131,* ☎ *305/913–8288 or 866/888–6780,* FAX *305/913–8300,* WEB *www.mandarinoriental.com. 329 rooms. Restaurant, 2 bars, in-room data ports, in-room safes, cable TV, pool, spa, dry cleaning, laundry service, concierge, business services, meeting rooms, parking (fee). AE, D, DC, MC, V.*

**$$$–$$$$** **Hotel Inter-Continental Miami.** From the pool deck you don't see the ragtag street, only the clean view Miami likes best of itself: the Disney-esque Metromover, Brickell Avenue, the booming port, the beautiful bay, Bayside Marketplace, and Key Biscayne. With all the lobby's marble, it could easily look like a mausoleum, but palms and oversize wicker soften the feel. Rooms, in grays and beiges and dark chintz, may not be innovative, but they are quite comfortable. When you feel like working out, get lost amid the machines of the fifth-floor fitness center. When you feel like working in, check out the 25 meeting and conference rooms. Here you'll find big business in a big hotel. Plus big kudos are being tossed to the Indigo restaurant, which is drawing an unpredictably trendy crowd. ✉ *100 Chopin Plaza, Downtown 33131,* ☎ *305/577–1000 or 800/327–3005,* FAX *305/577–0384,* WEB *www.miami.interconti.com. 639 rooms, 33 suites. 2 restaurants, bar, cable TV, pool, health club, laundry service, business services, parking (fee). AE, D, DC, MC, V.*

**$$–$$$$** **Doral Golf Resort and Spa.** The 650-acre golf-and-tennis resort has eight beautiful, low-slung lodges along the six golf courses. Rooms, with cream-colored walls, tropical design motifs, and solid, Old Florida–style desks and chairs, open onto the green or the lush foliage of the garden, and have private balconies and terraces. Plantation shutters keep out the strong sun but invite in the Caribbean breezes. At the 148,000-square-ft spa, massages from head to foot, European facials, aroma scrubs and wraps, stress reduction, hypnotherapy, and several dozen other indulgences rejuvenate the mind, body, and soul. The

Blue Lagoon, an extravagant water park, and friendly golf instruction keep the kids busy. ✉ *4400 N.W. 87th Ave., Doral 33178,* ☎ *305/592–2000 or 800/713–6725,* FAX *305/591–4682,* WEB *www.doralresort.com. 693 rooms, 48 suites. 5 restaurants, 3 bars, cable TV, pool, spa, 5 18-hole golf courses, 11 tennis courts, basketball, health club, volleyball, fishing, pro shop, concierge, business services. AE, D, DC, MC, V.*

**$$$** ✕🏨 **Hyatt Regency Miami.** The Hyatt is well positioned to enjoy the perks of the city's late-'90s renaissance—the Miami Avenue Bridge, the Port of Miami, and AmericanAirlines Arena seemed to sprout up around it. So, if your vacation is based on boats, basketball, or business, you can't do much better. The distinctive public spaces are more colorful than businesslike, and guest rooms are done in an unusual combination of avocado, beige, and blond. Rooms also yield views of the river or port. The James L. Knight International Center is accessible without stepping outside, as is the downtown Metromover and its Metrorail connection. Superb food is available off the lobby at Japengo, where Asian dishes from six cultures are served in a slightly dark, very funky atmosphere. ✉ *400 S.E. 2nd Ave., Downtown 33131,* ☎ *305/358–1234 or 800/233–1234,* FAX *305/358–0529,* WEB *www.miami.hyatt.com. 612 rooms, 51 suites. Restaurant, 2 bars, cable TV, pool, health club, laundry service, concierge, business services, parking (fee). AE, D, DC, MC, V.*

**$$$** ✕🏨 **JW Marriott.** Grand and ornate, with service to please even the most demanding guests, the JW Marriott (named for John Willard Marriott, founder of the chain) is a bone fide upscale property masquerading as a generic business hotel, with amenities and haute cuisine to prove it. If you're a finicky eater, consider creating your own menu in consultation with a top chef in the Trapiche Room restaurant. If you're no stranger to stress, a massage therapist at Spa 1111 will work out your kinks—you can choose from a variety of massage techniques, plus body treatments and facials, including an intriguing Vitamin C treatment. ✉ *1109 Brickell Ave., Downtown 33131,* ☎ *305/374–1224 or 800/228–9290,* FAX *305/374–4211,* WEB *www.marriott.com. 300 rooms, 22 suites. 2 restaurants, 2 bars, in-room safes, cable TV, pool, spa, health club, laundry service, concierge, business services, meeting rooms, parking (fee). AE, D, DC, MC, V.*

**$$–$$$** 🏨 **Biscayne Bay Marriott.** One of the few resorts actually in downtown Miami, this 31-floor tourist-friendly waterfront property gives you easy access to Bayside Marketplace, the beaches, Coconut Grove, the Port of Miami, and AmericanAirlines Arena. Although the rooms are a bit impersonal, each has complimentary in-room coffee, satellite TV, and voice mail and data ports, and most come with a water view, as well as a spectacular glimpse of the neon-streaked Miami night sky. Jet skiing is available, as is transportation to three area golf resorts. ✉ *1633 N. Bayshore Dr., Downtown 33132,* ☎ *305/374–3900 or 800/627–7468,* FAX *305/375–0597,* WEB *www.marriott.com. 600 rooms, 18 suites. Restaurant, bar, minibars, in-room safes, cable TV, pool, hair salon, health club, laundry service, concierge, business services, meeting rooms, parking (fee). AE, D, DC, MC, V.*

**$$–$$$** ✕🏨 **Doubletree Grand Hotel Biscayne Bay.** It's an elegant waterfront option, near many of Miami's headline attractions—Port of Miami, the beaches, Bayside Marketplace, and the Seaquarium, and a short drive from Coconut Grove—rooms are rather spacious and most have a view of Biscayne Bay and the port. In-room amenities include voice mail, a coffeemaker, and other helpful items like blow-dryers. You can rent jet skis or take deep-sea fishing trips from the marina. And while you're on the water, don't hesitate to try Tony Chan's Water Club for a bite of its famous Peking Duck and those gorgeous bay views. ✉ *1717*

## Downtown Miami and West Lodging

*N. Bayshore Dr., Downtown 33132, ☎ 305/523–3300 or 800/222–8733, FAX 305/539–9228, WEB www.doubletree.com. 102 rooms, 50 suites. 3 restaurants, bar, in-room data ports, cable TV, minibars, microwaves, pool, hot tub, health club, business services, meeting rooms. AE, D, DC, MC, V.*

**$\$–\$\$\$** **Sheraton Biscayne Bay.** When you make the short drive through a grove of oak trees to the entrance, it's hard to believe that this waterfront hotel is on busy Brickell Avenue. As in most large hotels, the lobby is designed for business (as is the conference center) and has a bar, restaurant, and gift shop. But the back patio and green space take the corporate edge off. Rooms have all the accoutrements you'd expect: irons, hair dryers, voice mail. Thank management for providing self-parking (although valets are standing by). ✉ *495 Brickell Ave., Downtown 33131, ☎ 305/373–6000 or 800/284–2000, FAX 305/374–2279, WEB www.sheraton.com. 598 rooms, 14 suites. Restaurant, pool, cable TV, health club, concierge, parking (fee). AE, D, DC, MC, V.*

**$$** **Miami International Airport Hotel.** Airport hotels defeat the purpose of vacation, but if you have an early flight, you may need this option. The only hotel actually inside the concrete bunker known as MIA lets you catch a few winks while waiting for your chance to sit on the runway. If you can forget your surroundings, you'll be glad to find the restaurant and lounge. ✉ *Miami International Airport, Concourse E, 2nd floor, Airport 33159, ☎ 305/871–4100 or 800/327–1276, FAX 305/871–0800, WEB www.miahotel.com. 259 rooms, 3 suites. Restaurant, bar, cable TV, pool, gym, laundry service, concierge, meeting rooms. AE, D, DC, MC, V.*

**$$** ★ **Miami River Inn.** In five restored 1904 clapboard buildings, the only group of Miami houses left from that period, Miami River Inn dispenses attentive, personalized hospitality often lost in the gleaming deco towers of Miami Beach. The working-class neighborhood is one of Miami's safest, even if it doesn't look it. Rooms (some with tub but no shower) are filled with antiques, and many have hardwood floors. All have TVs and phones. The most popular rooms overlook the river from the second and third floors. Avoid the tiny rooms in Building D with a view of a condo. The heart of the city is a 10-minute stroll across the 1st Street Bridge. ✉ *118 S.W. South River Dr., Little Havana 33130, ☎ 305/325–0045 or 800/468–3589, FAX 305/325–9227, WEB www.miamiriverinn.com. 40 rooms, 2 with shared bath. Cable TV, pool, hot tub, laundry facilities, free parking. AE, D, DC, MC, V. CP.*

## Coconut Grove and Key Biscayne

**$$$$** ✕ **Ritz-Carlton, Key Biscayne.** One of three Ritz-Carltons in Miami, this resort is within the Grand Bay community on Key Biscayne. The 14-story oceanfront tower includes rooms, suites, and privately owned residences. You have access to a 12-court tennis center, a private beach, two heated pools, and a gourmet food market. The Ritz-Carlton health club has personal trainers and aerobics, yoga, and massage. In-room amenities (robes, slippers, toiletries, and more) anticipate your needs. Some rooms have walk-in closets and bathrooms with whirlpools. They don't call the resort's signature restaurant Aria for nothing: a tenor is on hand to belt out birthday greetings and other requests. Spanish-trained chef Jordi Valles hits a high note with his creative Mediterranean dishes. ✉ *455 Grand Bay Dr., Key Biscayne 33149, ☎ 305/365–4500 or 800/241–3333, FAX 305/365–4505, WEB www.ritzcarlton.com. 364 rooms, 38 suites. Restaurant, 2 bars, in-room data ports, cable TV, minibars, 2 pools, beach, concierge, business services, meeting rooms, parking (fee). AE, D, DC, MC, V.*

**$$$–$$$$** **Ritz-Carlton Coconut Grove.** This grand addition to Miami's hotel landscape is hard to miss. Two towers atop a small hill ensure that most of the 115 rooms have excellent views of either Biscayne Bay or the boutiques and restaurants that make this location such a hot spot. Rooms are well appointed, as you would expect in a luxury chain, with marble baths, a choice of pillows, and private balconies. A unique feature of the Ritz-Carlton chain, however, are the "technology butlers," hotel staff specially trained to resolve your computer and Internet-access problems. If those problems leave you with jangled nerves, there's a 5,000-square-ft spa on hand. ✉ *2700 Tigertail Ave., Coconut Grove 33133,* ☎ *305/644–4680 or 800/241–3333,* FAX *305/644–4681,* WEB *www.ritzcarlton.com. 88 rooms, 27 suites. Restaurant, 2 grills, cable TV, room service, pool, sauna, health club, concierge, business services, meeting rooms, parking (fee). AE, D, DC, MC, V.*

**$$$–$$$$** ★ **Sonesta Beach Resort Key Biscayne.** A great beach, stunning sea views from east-facing units, and lots of activities make this one of Miami's best and most consistent resorts. Although they're a bit dull architecturally, villas are actually three-bedroom homes with full kitchens and screened pools. The size of the property, its Olympic pool, and a range of activities make it a good family getaway, and the popular Just Us Kids program can keep the offspring creatively busy from 9 AM to 10 PM. Museum-quality modern art by prominent painters and sculptors graces public areas. The 750-ft beach, one of Florida's most gorgeous, also has a variety of recreational opportunities, including catamarans and sailing lessons. ✉ *350 Ocean Dr., Key Biscayne 33149,* ☎ *305/361–2021 or 800/766–3782,* FAX *305/361–3096,* WEB *www.sonesta.com. 284 rooms, 15 suites, 3 villas. 3 restaurants, 3 bars, snack bar, cable TV, pool, massage, steam room, 9 tennis courts, aerobics, health club, beach, windsurfing, parasailing, children's programs (ages 5–13). AE, D, DC, MC, V.*

**$$$–$$$$** ★ **Wyndham Grand Bay.** Combining the classical elegance of Greece, a stepped facade that looks vaguely Aztec, a hint of the South, and a brush of the tropical, the Grand Bay is like no other hotel in South Florida. Guest rooms are filled with superb touches, such as antique sideboards that store away house phones and televisions. But what really sets the hotel apart are the atypically spacious suite terraces—perfect for private dinners—with sweeping views of Biscayne Bay. Bice, a trendy Italian restaurant on the premises, is extremely popular. ✉ *2669 S. Bayshore Dr., Coconut Grove 33133,* ☎ *305/858–9600 or 800/327–2788,* FAX *305/859–2026,* WEB *www.wyndham.com/CoconutGrove. 125 rooms, 52 suites. Restaurant, bar, cable TV, pool, hair salon, hot tub, massage, sauna, health club, concierge, parking (fee). AE, DC, MC, V.*

**$$–$$$$** **Mayfair House.** The exclusive feel of Coconut Grove runs through the European-style luxury hotel, and is mirrored in the Tiffany windows, polished mahogany and marble accents, imported ceramics and crystal, and an impressive glass elevator. The individually furnished suites have terraces facing the street, screened by vegetation and wood latticework. Each room has a small Japanese hot tub on the balcony or a Roman tub inside, and 10 have antique pianos. A rooftop recreation area is peaceful, although the miniature lap pool is odd for such a large hotel. Head for the Mayfair Grill for hearty breakfast favorites, and Orchids for Floribbean seafood. ✉ *Streets of Mayfair, 3000 Florida Ave., Coconut Grove 33133,* ☎ *305/441–0000 or 800/433–4555,* FAX *305/447–9173,* WEB *www.mayfairhousehotel.com. 179 suites. 2 restaurants, bar, snack bar, cable TV, room service, pool, hot tub, laundry service, concierge, business services, parking (fee). AE, D, DC, MC, V.*

**$$–$$$** **Doubletree Hotel at Coconut Grove.** Along Coconut Grove's hotel row, which faces some of the best waterfront in the country, the Doubletree offers easy access to the popular Coconut Grove shops and

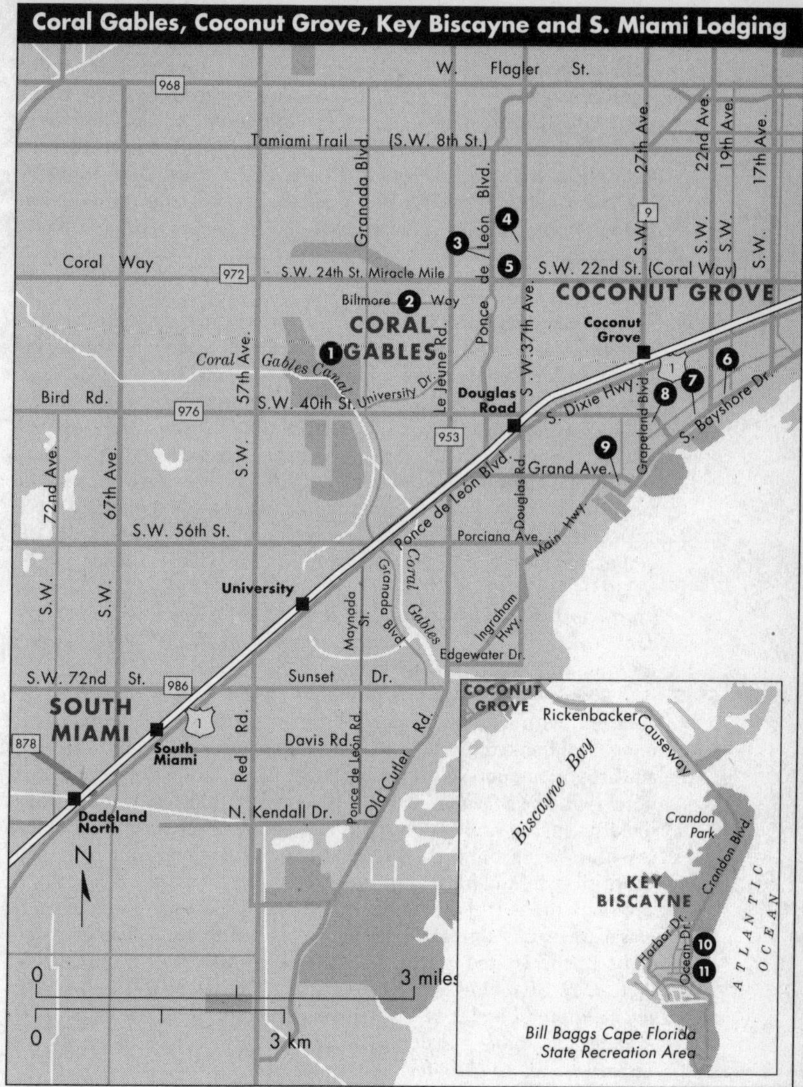


Biltmore Hotel . . . . . 1
David William Hotel . . . . . . . . . . . 2
Doubletree Hotel at Coconut Grove . . . . 6
Hotel Place St. Michel . . . . . . . . 3
Hyatt Regency Coral Gables . . . . . . 4
Mayfair House . . . . . 9
Omni Colonnade Hotel . . . . . . . . . . . 5
Ritz-Carlton Coconut Grove . . . . 8
Ritz-Carlton Key Biscayne . . . . . . . . 11
Sonesta Beach Resort Key Biscayne . . . . . 10
Wyndham Grand Bay . . . . . . . 7

restaurants, not to mention the comfort of retreating to terraced rooms open to breezes from the bay. Although the hotel may have less personality than some of its glitzier neighbors, its corporate feel is muted by the interior decor, dominated by cheerful blue and green hues, which echo the topaz water outside. ✉ *2649 S. Bayshore Dr., Coconut Grove 33133,* ☎ *305/858–2500 or 800/222–8733,* FAX *305/858–9117,* WEB *www.doubletreehotels.com. 154 rooms, 19 suites. Restaurant, 2 bars, in-room data ports, cable TV, refrigerators, minibars, pool, concierge, meeting rooms, parking (fee). AE, D, DC, MC, V.*

## Coral Gables

**$$$$** **Hyatt Regency Coral Gables.** The exterior is overtly Spanish, courtesy of tile roofs, white-frame casement windows, and pink stucco, but interior influences are more subliminally Moorish: traces in the headboard design, a stair-stepped outline at guest information, and fall browns and blonds—all this to evoke the style of the Alhambra, the 14th-century palace near Granada, Spain. As befits a business hotel, the staff is savvy and helpful, and rooms are designed as alternative offices. Still, the mood is comfortable and residential. A business center and meeting facilities are tucked to the side so vacationers don't feel they're still in the corporate world. ✉ *50 Alhambra Plaza, Coral Gables 33134,* ☎ *305/441–1234 or 800/233–1234,* FAX *305/441–0520,* WEB *www.hyatt.com. 192 rooms, 50 suites. Restaurant, lobby lounge, in-room data ports, cable TV, pool, sauna, steam room, health club, business services, meeting rooms, parking (fee). AE, D, DC, MC, V.*

**$$$–$$$$** ★ **Biltmore Hotel.** Miami's grand boom-time hotel recaptures a bygone era, with its semicircular drive and formal facade, grand swimming pool flanked by a colonnaded walkway, and period furnishings and artwork indoors. Now owned by the city of Coral Gables, the 1926 hotel rises like a sienna-color wedding cake in the heart of a residential district. The vaulted lobby has hand-painted rafters on a twinkling sky-blue background. Large guest rooms are done in a restrained Moorish style, and for slightly more than the average rate ($2,550) you can book the Everglades Suite—Bill Clinton's favorite room when he was in town. La Palme D'Or is quite simply one of the best French restaurants in the United States. ✉ *1200 Anastasia Ave., Coral Gables 33134,* ☎ *305/445–1926 or 800/727–1926,* FAX *305/913–3159,* WEB *www.biltmorehotel.com. 237 rooms, 38 suites. Restaurant, bar, lobby lounge, café, cable TV, pool, sauna, spa, 18-hole golf course, 10 tennis courts, health club, meeting rooms. AE, D, DC, MC, V.*

**$$–$$$** **Omni Colonnade Hotel.** Clearly built for business, the oversize rooms come in 26 floor plans and several styles, each with a sitting area, built-in armoires, and traditional mahogany furnishings. Meeting rooms are in abundance, newspapers are delivered to your door, and 24-hour room service is ready when you're working 'round the clock. The pool, on a 10th-floor terrace, looks south toward Biscayne Bay. Ask for a room with a private balcony. Although you can't miss the 13-story towers of this hotel, office, and shopping complex from the street, on display throughout the hotel are photos, paintings, and other heirlooms of the Merrick family, which founded the "City Beautiful." ✉ *180 Aragon Ave., Coral Gables 33134,* ☎ *305/441–2600 or 800/843–6664,* FAX *305/445–3929,* WEB *www.omnihotels.com. 135 rooms, 22 suites. Restaurant, bar, room service, in-room data ports, in-room fax, cable TV, pool, 2 saunas, gym, meeting rooms. AE, D, DC, MC, V.*

**$$** **David William Hotel.** Surrounded by leafy foliage in a green spot of downtown Coral Gables, this workmanlike structure sits in the shadow of the Biltmore, literally and figuratively. About a half mile from the ornate structure with which it shares management, the David William pales in comparison—but only if looks count. Lodgings are more than comfortable, with full kitchens in suites and a refrigerator and microwave in standard rooms. Best of all, you can use the services and facilities at the Biltmore, including the fitness center and spa, golf course, tennis courts, and the magnificent Palme d'Or restaurant. ✉ *700 Biltmore Way, Coral Gables 33134,* ☎ *305/445–7821 or 800/757–8073,* FAX *305/913–1933,* WEB *www.davidwilliamhotel.com. 70 rooms, 33 suites. Restaurant, bar, in-room data ports, in-room fax, cable TV, pool, health club, baby-sitting, dry cleaning, business services, meeting rooms. AE, D, DC, MC, V.*

**$$** ★ **Hotel Place St. Michel.** Built in 1926, the historic and intimate inn is kept filled with the scent of fresh flowers, circulated by paddle fans. Art Nouveau chandeliers suspended from vaulted ceilings light the public areas. Each guest room has its own dimensions, personality, and antiques imported from England, Scotland, and France, although plusher beds would be a welcome improvement. Dinner at the superb Restaurant St. Michel is a must, but there is now a more casual bar and dining area behind the lobby, better suited for quiet breakfasts or late night aperitifs. The inn is within easy walking distance of Miracle Mile. ✉ *162 Alcazar Ave., Coral Gables 33134,* ☎ *305/444–1666 or 800/848–4683,* FAX *305/529–0074,* WEB *www.hotelplacestmichel.com. 24 rooms, 3 suites. Restaurant, bar, cable TV, laundry service, parking (fee). AE, DC, MC, V. CP.*

# 5 NIGHTLIFE AND THE ARTS

Fueled by the South Beach club boom, heated up by Latin and Caribbean influences, shot with a heavy dose of New York chic, and seasoned by salty sea breezes—there's a nightlife here like no other. Greater Miami is more than party central. With a solid foundation in classical arts institutions and plenty of cutting-edge arts groups, this young, multicultural city promises to mature into a world class cultural destination that also just so happens to be a whole lot of fun.

Updated by Gretchen Schmidt

**GREATER MIAMI'S POTENT CULTURAL MIX** keeps its pulse pounding with nonstop nightlife. When sultry, humid nights, the huge full moon rising out of the ocean, and fragrant night-blooming jasmine intoxicate the senses, who can resist Cuban salsa, Jamaican reggae, and Dominican merengue, with some disco and hip-hop thrown in for good measure? When this place throws a party, hips shake, fingers snap, bodies touch. It's no wonder many clubs are still rocking at 5 AM.

The reputation of Miami and Miami Beach as playgrounds for the hip and famous is well deserved, making the cities' nightlife some of the best on the planet. But if you're in search of finer cultural fare, you face more of a challenge. The museums aren't as easy to find as the beaches. Theaters don't advertise as widely as nightclubs. And the art houses that show foreign films and independents are tucked away in nooks and crannies of the city. All that's starting to change, however; so you have your pick of entertainment here night and day. Whether you're interested in dancing 'til dawn to the hottest DJs or catching the newest work by Latin artists in exile, you'll want to head to a newsstand first.

## FINDING OUT WHAT'S GOING ON

The ***Miami Herald*** (www.herald.com) is a good source for information on what to do in town. The "Weekend" section, included in the Friday edition, has an annotated guide to on everything from plays and galleries to concerts and nightclubs. The "Ticket" column of this section details the week's entertainment highlights. You can also pick up the Herald's free weekly tabloid, *The Street,* at newstands and bookstores for a list of local happenings. Providing even more detailed information is ***Miami New Times*** (www.miaminewtimes.com), the city's largest free alternative newspaper, published each Thursday. It lists nightclubs, concerts, and special events; reviews plays and movies; and provides in-depth coverage of the local music scene. "Night & Day" is a rundown of the week's cultural highlights.

Two upscale fashion and lifestyle magazines, ***Channels*** and ***Ocean Drive,*** squeeze club, bar, restaurant, and events listings in with fashion spreads, reviews, and personality profiles. Paparazzi photos of local party people and celebrities give you a taste of Greater Miami nightlife before you even put on your black going-out ensemble.

In South Beach various independent newspapers devote themselves to the area's huge nightlife scene. ***Wire*** (www.thewireonline.com), the longest running of these, is published on Thursday and is distributed free at many clubs, restaurants, and retail establishments in South Beach and the Miami Design District. It includes a directory of nightclubs and restaurants, amusing columns on local politics, and information on gay venues.

The Spanish-language ***El Nuevo Herald,*** published by the *Miami Herald,* has extensive information on Spanish-language arts and entertainment, including dining reviews, concert previews, nightclub highlights, and more. **Spanish-language radio,** primarily on the AM dial, is also a good source of information about arts events. Tune in to WXDJ (95.7 FM), Amor (105.7 FM), or Radio Mambi (710 AM).

Much news of upcoming events is disseminated through flyers tucked onto windshields or left for pickup at restaurants, clubs, and stores. They're technically illegal to distribute, but they're mighty useful. And if you're a beachgoer, chances are that as you lie in the sun, you'll be approached by kids handing out cards announcing the DJs and acts appearing in the clubs that night.

# THE ARTS

If the arts are what make cities like New York, London, Tokyo, Buenos Aires, and Paris great, then Miami and Miami Beach are not great cities—not quite yet. But seeds of greatness, sown decades ago, have sprouted strong and true. Greater Miami, perceived by some as a comely lightweight in the arts, is undergoing a cultural renaissance about which other cities only dream.

Many Miamians are heaving a sigh of relief as their hometown at long last shrugs off its reputation as a cultural backwater. Led by an expanding roster of up-and-coming collecting museums and performing groups, the arts scene in Greater Miami is coming into its own. In recent years nonprofit cultural organizations have grown dramatically in number, from 110 to 750 in the last 20 years, including the internationally known Miami City Ballet and the New World Symphony. But to savor the area's vibrant cultural diversity, don't overlook the smaller, lesser-known arts groups. Performances from dance companies such as La Rosa Flamenco Ballet and the smooth Freddick Bratcher & Company, Afro-Haitian drumming and dance from the Performing Arts Network, and works from the Bridge Theater's Hispanic and Hispanic-American authors are as Miamian as yucca and plantains.

Larger venues regularly attract international talent such as contemporary dance and theater troupes and touring Broadway shows. The winter season especially brings traveling art exhibits to local museums and gallery walks to Coral Gables and South Beach, as well as occasional special events to the Design District, a cluster of galleries and interior design showrooms just north of downtown. And there are any number of cultural festivals throughout the year.

Thanks to the Art in Public Places program, you've probably already been exposed to large-scale installations: the sound- and color-charged 180-ft *Harmonic Runway* at Miami International Airport's Concourse A, or Michele Oka Doner's bronze and mother-of-pearl marine life in the terrazzo walkway in the same concourse. In Miami Beach, you can't miss the exuberantly painted shuttle buses cruising down Washington Avenue, or monumental outdoor sculptures like Claes Oldenburg and Coosje van Bruggen's *Dropped Bowl with Scattered Slices and Peels,* at downtown's Government Center. Major new cultural projects under way are the restoration of the 85-year-old Lyric Theater in Overtown, home to famous jazz artists in the 1930s and '40s, and a $10 million art museum at Florida International University. New on the scene is the Cultural Campus, a two-square-block arts complex housing offices, performing space, rehearsal studios for the Miami City Ballet, and a new library, all adjacent to the recently renovated Bass Museum, in Miami Beach. And after years of delay, ground was finally broken on the Performing Arts Center complex, due to open in 2004.

There have been missteps and setbacks: the city's sole (and beloved) classical music radio station was abruptly replaced with techno-dance programming; funding squabbles threaten such venerable venues as the 75-year-old Coconut Grove Playhouse; and politics periodically disrupt appearances from Cuban musicians or cause major events, such as the Latin Grammys, to find a friendlier host city. But forward thinkers see enough in the works to envision a Miami that can fully express its multicultural uniqueness in limitless forms. So arts junkies, never fear—Miami is on its way.

## Film

Greater Miami is a popular destination for filmmakers, who have used it as a location for movies ranging from the Elvis Presley classic *Clambake* to the 1983 crime flick *Scarface* to the gross-out comedy *There's Something About Mary.* It's also full of choices for filmgoers, who can see first-run foreign and independent films at an ever-expanding list of film festivals.

Those interested in moving images, including video and television work, should stop at the **Wolfson Media Center** (✉ 300 N.E. 2nd Ave., Downtown Miami, ☎ 305/375–1505), on the downtown campus of Miami-Dade Community College. The center houses a collection of rare videos, including TV images of the Cuban Missile Crisis, John F. Kennedy's visit to Miami, and the 1968 Republican Convention, which it displays in special screening programs. The center also sponsors bus tours of Miami neighborhoods, during which you can watch video from earlier time periods to learn how development has changed the face of the city.

### Film Festivals

Walk the red carpet in Miami. Although festival passes can cost plenty, most individual screenings are only $10.The most high profile of the lot is the FIU–**Miami Film Festival** (☎ 305/348–5555, WEB www.miamifilmfestival.com), which unspools each January–February with 50 screenings of Hollywood and international biggies at downtown's historic Gusman Center for the Performing Arts (✉ 174 E. Flagler St.), South Beach's Colony Theater (✉ 1040 Lincoln Rd.), the Regal South Beach Cinema (✉ 1100 Lincoln Rd.), and free big screen showings right on the beach. In December Florida International University sponsors the **Jewish Film Festival** (☎ 305/576–4030), which presents screenings of new work as well as workshops and panel discussions with filmmakers in several Miami Beach locations. In March, the **Miami Latin Film Festival** (☎ 305/279–1809, WEB www.hispanicfilm.com) presents French, Italian, and Portuguese movies along with exhibition of Spanish and Latin American movies. During the last week of April and first week of May, the **Miami Gay and Lesbian Film Festival** (☎ 305/534–9924, WEB www.miamigaylesbianfilm.com) hosts screenings and events at the Colony Theater and at other nearby venues. Each May, South Beach hosts the **Brazilian Film Festival** (☎ 305/899–8998, WEB www.brazilianfilmfestival.com), which unveils on a huge outdoor movie screen built on the beach especially for the occasion.

### Film Houses and Cinemas

As in any major U.S. city, you can see Hollywood releases and some foreign and independent films at the many neighborhood multiplexes in Miami and Miami Beach. Most mainstream cinemas are in suburban shopping centers, such as Dolphin Mall in West Dade, Shops at Sunset Place in South Miami, and Loehmann's Fashion Island in Aventura. Out-of-the-ordinary venues include the striking glass-walled Regal South Beach Cinema on Lincoln Road, and the sleek, renovated Mercury Theatre in Little Haiti.

**Absinthe House Cinematheque.** Art films are the draw at this theater in the heart of Coral Gables. The snack bar is a cozy lounge with a plush sofa, artwork, and artsy magazines. ✉ *235 Alcazar Ave., Coral Gables,* ☎ *305/446–7144.*

**Bill Cosford Cinema.** Run by the School of Communication at the University of Miami, this first-run motion picture theater has Florida premieres, film favorites, foreign and independent American films, presentations by visiting filmmakers, and mini-festivals. ✉ *University* *of Miami campus, Memorial Building, Coral Gables,* ☎ *305/284–4861,* WEB *www.miami.edu.*

**Cocowalk 18.** Popular with teens on weekends, this theater at Coconut Grove's busy mall shows first-run movies and occasionally foreign films. ✉ *Cocowalk, 3015 Grand Ave., at Virginia St., Coconut Grove,* ☎ *305/448–7075.*

**IMAX.** See dazzling, giant screen and 3-D movies at this big, comfortable theater. ✉ *Shops at Sunset Place, 5701 Sunset Dr., at S.W. 57th Ave., South Miami,* ☎ *305/663–4629,* WEB *www.imax.com/miami.*

**Mercury Theatre.** In Miami's upper east side, you can see first-run foreign and American independent films, classic film revivals, and documentaries on a big screen. ✉ *5580 N.E. 4th Court, at N.E. 55 St., Little Haiti,* ☎ *305/759–8809,*

**Regal South Beach Cinema.** Purists were not pleased when this huge glass-walled building went up at the end of Lincoln Road, but its mix of first run movies and independent foreign films made it a welcome addition for South Beach movie lovers. You can order good food—sandwiches, salads, muffins—from the second floor café, and it will be delivered to your seat. ✉ *1100 Lincoln Rd., at Alton Rd., South Beach, Miami Beach,* ☎ *305/674–6766.*

**Tower Theater.** Originally built in 1926, this was the first Miami cinema to show films with Spanish subtitles. Miami historian Arva Moore Parks described the Little Havana landmark as "the Plymouth Rock for Cuban people," because it was such an important cultural center for exiles in the 1960s. A new cinema and arts complex hosts subtitled Spanish-language films and performances. ✉ *1508 S.W. 8th St., at 15th Ave., Little Havana Miami,* ☎ *305/644–3307.*

## Fine Arts

### Art Galleries

Greater Miami's young visual arts community took a major leap in international status when the prestigious annual art fair Art Basel announced its debut in Miami Beach for December 2001. When the events of September 11, 2001, caused the Swiss art fair to postpone the event for one year, area galleries didn't throw in the towel. Instead, they went ahead with exhibits and events planned to coincide with the fair, drawing crowds of locals and out-of-towners in the process.

South Florida artists are enjoying an unprecedented popularity and local galleries, many of which showcase important Latin American artists, are also growing in recognition. One of the art gallery hot spots is Lincoln Road, South Beach's colorful pedestrian mall, which hosts a **Gallery Walk** on the second Saturday of each month, where you can stroll from gallery to gallery and enjoy food and wine along with the artwork. **Second Thursdays** celebrates the arts with free access to museum and gallery exhibits throughout Miami Beach. Venues normally closed at night are included; some host special events, like meet-the-artist wine and cheese receptions, and one-time performances. In Coral Gables, the stylish **Gallery Nights** are held the first Friday evening of every month, and a free shuttle bus takes you between galleries. Another impressive collection of galleries is in Miami's Design District, north of downtown. Check newspaper listings for events in this always intriguing area.

If you like to watch artists at work, check out the Bakehouse Art Complex in the Design District, and ArtCenter–South Florida, in three locations on Lincoln Road. During the week many area galleries are open by appointment only, so be sure to call ahead.

SOUTH BEACH

**ArtCenter–South Florida.** More than a gallery, this 60,000-square-ft campus includes 52 artists' studios, exhibition galleries, and art education classrooms. The 800 Lincoln Road Gallery presents month-long exhibits by resident and outside artists. This is one of the galleries that ignited South Beach's resurrection, and it's a good place to see works in progress: the studios are open to the public. ✉ *Main studio: 924 Lincoln Rd., South Beach,* ⏲ *Daily 11–11; gallery annexes:* ✉ *800 Lincoln Rd., South Beach,* ⏲ *Mon.–Thurs. 1–10, Fri.–Sun. 11–11;* ✉ *810 Lincoln Rd., South Beach,* ☎ *305/674–8278,* WEB *www.artcentersf.org.* ⏲ *Mon.–Thurs. 1–10, Fri.–Sun. 11–11.*

**Bettcher Gallery.** This contemporary art gallery promotes the achievement and evolution of emerging, mid-career, and established artists from around the world. ✉ *919 Collins Ave., South Beach,* ☎ *305/534–8533,* WEB *www.bettchergallery.com;* ✉ *5582–3 N.E. 4 Court, Miami,* ☎ *305/758–7556,* ⏲ *Sun.–Thurs. noon–7, Fri.–Sat. noon–10.*

**Britto Central.** Romero Britto's colorful and playful pop art has become a ubiquitous part of the South Florida landscape, encompassing murals, billboards, sculpture, even neckties and scarves. ✉ *818 Lincoln Rd., South Beach,* ☎ *305/531–8821,* WEB *www.britto.com.* ⏲ *Wed.–Sat. 11–11, Sun. noon–9.*

DOWNTOWN MIAMI AND DESIGN DISTRICT

**Bakehouse Art Complex.** You can watch visual and performance artists at work at this former 1920s bakery. In addition to the working studios, public galleries offer juried exhibitions, workshops, and classes; some of the artists work with the public schools. Renowned Miami outsider artist Purvis Young exhibits here, as do Caribbean artists. Free shows are hosted in the performance space. ✉ *561 N.W. 32nd St., Design District,* ☎ *305/576–2828.* ⏲ *Call for schedule weekdays 10–4.*

**Barbara Gillman Gallery.** A pioneer in discovering and exhibiting Florida artists, Barbara Gillman also shows contemporary American and Latin American painting, sculpture, ceramics, works on paper, mixed media, and photography, including jazz photography and prints. ✉ *5582 NE 4 Ct., Downtown, Miami,* ☎ *305/759–9155.* ⏲ *Mon.–Thurs. noon–7, Fri.–Sat. noon–9.*

**Haitian Art Factory.** Here you'll find colorful paintings, sculpture, sequined ceremonial voodoo flags representing saints and deities, and other forms of folk art by Haitian artists. Check newspaper listings for special exhibitions. ✉ *835 N.E. 79th St., Little Haiti,* ☎ *305/758–6939.* ⏲ *Mon.–Thurs. 10–5, Fri. 10–4, Sat. 10–2.*

**Wallflower Gallery.** Sip green tea while perusing works by Miami artists in this unpretentious downtown place—or come listen to Haitian dance and music performances, appearances by local bands, and poetry readings. ✉ *10 N.E. 3rd St., Downtown, Miami,* ☎ *305/579–0069,* WEB *www.wallflowergallery.com.* ⏲ *Tue.–Fri. 10–8.*

CORAL GABLES AND KEY BISCAYNE

**Artspace–Virginia Miller Galleries.** This venerable contemporary gallery, one of Miami's oldest, has changing exhibits of paintings, drawings, and sculpture, specializing in Latin American, Cuban, European, and American artists. ✉ *169 Madeira Ave., Coral Gables,* ☎ *305/444–4493,* WEB *www.virginiamiller.com.* ⏲ *Weekdays 11–6.*

**Fredric Snitzer Gallery.** In a warehouse district, with a space that lends itself to large scale installations, this gallery represents such contemporary artists from the United States and Latin America as Purvis Young and Naomi Fisher, and Miami-based artists such as José Bedia.

✉ *3078 S.W. 38th Court, Coral Gables,* ☎ *305/448–8976,* WEB *www.snitzer.com.* ⏲ *Tues.–Sat. 11–5.*

**Gary Nader Fine Art.** Established by one of the world's top Latin American art dealers, this gallery exhibits works by such masters as Fernando Botero, Wifredo Lam, and Rufino Tamayo. ✉ *3306 Ponce de León Blvd., Coral Gables,* ☎ *305/442–0256,* WEB *www.garynader.com.* ⏲ *Weekdays 11–6.*

**Meza Fine Art.** Relax in a café that has live and DJ music, poetry readings and performance art, and contemporary artworks for sale. ✉ *275 Giralda Ave., Coral Gables,* ☎ *305/461–2723.* ⏲ *Mon.–Sat. 10–11.*

**Studio Gallery Napp.** German artist Gudrun Napp exhibits her own colorful works and those of Florida artists. ✉ *260 Crandon Blvd., Suite 18, Key Biscayne,* ☎ *305/365–3690.* ⏲ *Tues.–Fri. 11–3.*

## Art Museums and Collections

Greater Miami's art museums parallel the fast track that the area's cultural scene is moving on: they're growing, upgrading, and gaining national and international respect. Whether relative newcomers, like the unique Wolfsonian–FIU, or established venues that get a major makeover, like the Bass Museum of Art, these important facilities are attracting attention from locals and visitors alike. Add to that Greater Miami's ever-increasing art-related annual events, such as Art Deco Weekend, Art Miami, Miami Modernism, the Beaux Arts Festival, and, yes, even the Coconut Grove Arts Festival, and it's no wonder that Greater Miami is becoming a big league member of the culture club.

**Art Museum at Florida International University.** Being affiliated with the Smithsonian means the FIU museum has access to that institution's huge collection of art and artifacts and is a major cultural institution. Known especially for its Latin-American and 20th-century American art, it's also home to ArtPark at FIU, an outdoor sculpture park with works from the Martin Z. Margulies sculpture collection, including pieces by Alexander Calder and Isamu Noguchi. Permanent collections include paintings by such major 20th-century figures as Hans Hofmann, Rufino Tamayo, and Cundo Bermudez; an extensive collection of American prints from the 1960s, including Andy Warhol and Roy Lichtenstein; pieces by Haitian fine artists; and Haitian and Brazilian folk art. ✉ *FIU campus, S.W. 107th Ave. at S.W. 8th St., West Miami-Dade, Miami,* ☎ *305/348–2890,* WEB *www.artmuseumatfiu.org.* 🎟 *Free.* ⏲ *Mon. 10–9, Tue.–Fri. 10–5, weekends noon–4.*

**Bass Museum of Art.** Open again following a lengthy facelift and ongoing expansion, this provocative and growing museum on the northern fringes of South Beach (on land given to the city by Miami Beach founder John Collins) has substantial exhibition space, a café, and a courtyard. Its expansion is part of a two-square-block Miami Beach Cultural Campus, which also houses the Miami City Ballet. Although its permanent collection includes an Albrecht Dürer and a Peter Paul Rubens, the Bass is most notable for visits by cutting-edge traveling exhibits of contemporary art, such as the recent *Liza Lou II* show, a young California artist whose room-size installations are done entirely with beads. ✉ *2121 Park Ave., South Beach, Miami Beach,* ☎ *305/673–7530,* WEB *www.bassmuseum.org.* 🎟 *$6.* ⏲ *Tues., Thurs.–Sat. 10–5, Sun. 11–5, second Thurs. of month 10–9.*

**Historical Museum of Southern Florida.** Many kid-friendly exhibits here say "Please touch," including a player piano, an authentic trolley car from 1920s Miami, Victorian dress-up clothes, and living maps that let you "walk across the world" while experiencing the cultures that have influenced South Florida's history. Try a family overnight adventure—the museum calls them "camp-ins"—that's designed to let both parents and kids go behind the scenes. ✉ *Miami-Dade Cultural Center, 101 W. Flagler St., Downtown Miami,* ☎ *305/375–1492,* WEB *www.historical-museum.org.* 🎫 *$5.* 🕑 *Mon.–Sat. 10–5, Thurs. 10–9, Sun. noon–5.*

**Latin American Art Museum.** For a small storefront museum, it has an extensive collection of works by Cuban and Latin American artists, with an emphasis on emerging artists and a special dedication to women artists. The museum participates in Little Havana's Cultural Fridays on the last Friday of every month. ✉ *2206 S.W. 8th St., Little Havana Miami,* ☎ *305/644–1127,* WEB *www.latinoweb.com/museo.* 🎫 *Free.* 🕑 *Tue.–Fri. 11–5, Sat. 11–4.*

**Lowe Art Museum.** The museum's permanent collection includes art from the European Renaissance and Baroque periods, as well as pre-Colombian pieces and works by Latin-American and American artists. In 1999 it acquired the collection of the Cuban Museum of the Americas, which includes 300 works by Cuban artists in exile. *Catalyst: 50 Years of Collecting at the Lowe* celebrates the golden anniversary of this museum, the county's first visual arts museum. Each January the Lowe sponsors the Beaux Arts Festival in Coral Gables, one of the area's largest outdoor art markets. ✉ *University of Miami, 1301 Stanford Dr., Coral Gables,* ☎ *305/284–3603,* WEB *www.lowemuseum.org.* 🎫 *$5.* 🕑 *Tue.–Wed., Fri.–Sat. 10–5, Thurs. 12–7, Sun. 12–5.*

**Miami Art Museum.** Along with the main library and the Historical Museum of Southern Florida, this component of downtown's Miami-Dade Cultural Center is one of Miami-Dade County's largest museums. It exhibits contemporary art of the western hemisphere with a focus on works from the 1940s to the present. In addition to the 80 works in the permanent collection, the museum has provocative works by artists including Frank Stella, James Rosenquist, and Robert Rauschenberg. This is no stuffy space: the second Saturday of the month is free for families. Interactive programs designed by the museum's education department make fine art fun for kids and activities usually incorporate current work on display. ✉ *Miami-Dade Cultural Center, 101 W. Flagler St., Downtown, Miami,* ☎ *305/375–3000,* WEB *www.miamiartmuseum.org.* 🎫 *$5.* 🕑 *Tues.–Fri. 10–5, weekends noon–5.*

**Museum of Contemporary Art (MoCA).** Known for its provocative exhibitions, and its 1996 building and grounds designed by Charles Gwathmey, MoCA presents eight to ten shows each year. Its collection of 20th-century American and European works reaches for the cutting edge. Permanent pieces include works from such artists as Louise Nevelson, Julian Schnabel, Dennis Oppenheim, and Anna Gaskell. Programs range from classic cinema to jazz and to lectures by contemporary artists. Tuesday is pay what you can. ✉ *770 N.E. 125th St., North Miami,* ☎ *305/893–6211,* WEB *www.mocanomi.org.* 🎫 *$5.* 🕑 *Tues.–Sat. 11–5, Sun. noon–5.*

**Rubell Family Collection.** In a huge warehouse in the Design District, the family that owns South Beach's Albion and Greenview hotels and Bal Harbour's Beach House displays their collection of conceptual art, photography, sculpture, and paintings by contemporary names such as Julian Schnabel, José Bedia, Cindy Sherman, Jean Michael Basquiat, Charles Ray, Takashi Murakami, and Jeff Koons. It's currently one of the country's leading private contemporary art collections and is expanding to a second location. ✉ *95 N.W. 29th St., Design District,* ☎ *305/573–6090.* 🎫 *Free.* 🕑 *Thurs.–Sat. 11–4 and by appointment.*

**Sanford L. Ziff Jewish Museum of Florida: Home of MOSAIC.** The permanent exhibit in this restored art deco synagogue, entitled *MOSAIC: Jewish Life in Florida,* documents the long and rich history and culture of the Jewish residents of South Florida from 1763 until the present. Temporary exhibits focus on Jewish art and history. ✉ *301 Washington Ave., South Beach, Miami Beach,* ☎ *305/672–5044,* WEB *www.jewishmuseum.com.* 🎫 *$5.* ⏲ *Tues.–Sun. 10–5.*

**Spanish Cultural Center.** Exhibitions of work by Spanish and Latin-American artists celebrate Miami's Hispanic past, present, and future as well as the cultures of Spanish-speaking countries. Recent exhibits have included photography from Mexico and paintings from Spain. ✉ *800 Douglas Rd., Suite 170, Coral Gables,* ☎ *305/448–9677.* 🎫 *Free.* ⏲ *Mon.–Fri. 10–3.*

★ **Vizcaya Museum and Gardens.** Once the winter residence of Miami pioneer James Deering, this Coconut Grove mansion on Biscayne Bay has 34 rooms decorated in rococo, baroque, neoclassical, and Italian renaissance styles. In essence, Deering and his architect created a lavish 16th-century Italian country villa and complementary manicured grounds in Miami. A small café overlooks the swimming pool. ✉ *3251 S. Miami Ave., Coconut Grove Miami,* ☎ *305/250–9133,* WEB *www.vizcayamuseum.com.* 🎫 *$10.* ⏲ *Daily 9:30–5; gardens 9:30–5:30.*

★ **Wolfsonian–FIU.** Thousands of artifacts of the applied, decorative, and commercial arts of the 19th and 20th centuries are on display at this stylish museum of modern art and design. Collected from around the world by Wometco heir Mitchell Wolfson Jr., the pieces occupy an elegant former storage facility. The Wolfsonian's collection is concerned with the power of propaganda in art, and its exhibitions accentuate the ideological role of design in industrialization, consumerism, and politics. It regularly mounts exhibitions on European and American art and design, including World's Fairs and architecture, British Arts and Crafts, and glorious German graphic design. The museum is administered by Florida International University. ✉ *1001 Washington Ave., South Beach, Miami Beach,* ☎ *305/531–1001,* WEB *www.wolfsonian.fiu.edu.* 🎫 *$5.* ⏲ *Mon., Tues., Fri., and Sat. 11–6, Thurs., 11–9, Sun. noon–5.*

## Performing Arts

In addition to the several large performing arts venues it already enjoys, the City of Miami has plans to unite its most distinguished performing arts institutions in a permanent residence, the **Performing Arts Center of Greater Miami,** which is slated for completion in 2004. Incorporating the art deco Sears Tower, the monumental complex will house a symphony concert hall, ballet–opera house, and stageless black-box studio theater in a complex near the AmericanAirlines Arena, on Biscayne Boulevard. Boosters hope it will transform the long-derelict Omni-Venetia District into a dazzling, pedestrian-friendly destination. And dazzle it will: Argentine architect Cesar Pelli's expansive plans will give patrons spectacular views of the nearby bay, the downtown skyline, and the inland landscape.

### GETTING TICKETS

To order tickets for performing arts events by telephone, call **Ticketmaster** (☎ 305/358–5885) or contact the venue directly.

### PERFORMING ARTS VENUES

**AmericanAirlines Arena.** Home to the NBA Miami Heat and the WNBA Miami Sol, this sleek bayfront arena also hosts concerts, ice shows, circuses, and other events. ✉ *601 Biscayne Blvd., Downtown, Miami,* ☎ *786/777–1000.*

**Colony Theater.** Once a commercial movie theater, the Colony has become a 465-seat city-owned performing arts center featuring dance, drama, music, and experimental cinema. ✉ *1040 Lincoln Rd., South Beach, Miami Beach,* ☎ *305/674–1026.*

★ **Gusman Center for the Performing Arts.** If you have the opportunity to attend a concert, ballet, movie, or touring stage production here, do so. The colorful box office kiosk and Olympia Theater marquee out front whet your appetite for what's inside this 1,739-seat downtown landmark—a stunningly beautiful and fanciful hall, with twinkling stars and rolling clouds on the ceiling and Roman-style statues guarding the wings. The Gusman's showcase event is the annual Miami Film Festival. ✉ *174 E. Flagler St., Downtown, Miami,* ☎ *305/372–0925.*

**Gusman Concert Hall.** Not to be confused with the ornate Gusman Center, this modern, spacious 600-seat facility on the University of Miami campus is the site of concerts by UM School of Music student groups, guest artists, and the annual Festival Miami concert series. ✉ *University of Miami, 1314 Miller Dr., Coral Gables,* ☎ *305/284–6477.*

**Jackie Gleason Theater of the Performing Arts.** With 2,700 seats, this is the premier auditorium on Miami Beach and the site from which the rotund comedian broadcast his popular TV shows in the 1960s. Named for Gleason after his death, it offers an assortment of professional, community, and student theater, with productions including all types of musicals, comedies, and dramas. Each year the auditorium hosts five or six major touring productions and the popular Broadway Series of avant-garde fare, familiar shows, and headliners. Performing artists such as David Copperfield, the *Stomp* troupe, and Liza Minnelli perform here when they're in town, and the hall is the site of many classical and pop concerts. ✉ *1700 Washington Ave., South Beach, Miami Beach,* ☎ *305/673–7300.*

**James L. Knight Center.** You can catch musical events, concerts (particularly popular Latin groups), and other musical events in this 5,000 seat riverfront venue. *400 S.E. 2nd Ave., Downtown,* ☎ *305/372–4633.*

**Miami-Dade County Auditorium.** Good sight lines, acceptable acoustics, and 2,498 comfortable seats satisfy patrons despite the auditorium's rather outdated design. Opera, concerts, and touring musicals are usually on the schedule, as well as the city's annual Christmas pageant, an imaginative mix of traditional and tropical elements. ✉ *2901 W. Flagler St., Little Havana,* ☎ *305/545–3395.*

**Miccosukee Resort and Convention Center.** Nationally televised World Championship Boxing, big name entertainers, and late night salsa and merengue dance parties are presented in the 2,000-seat Sports and Entertainment Dome at this resort and casino, on the edge of the Everglades, west of Miami. ✉ *500 S.W. 177 Ave., West Miami-Dade, Miami,* ☎ *305/925–2555,* WEB *www.miccosukee.com.*

## Classical Music

Despite what you may hear blaring from boom boxes and car radios, Greater Miami is not all salsa and hip-hop. There's a solid tradition of classical music, led by performances by such well-respected institutions as the Fort Lauderdale-based **Florida Philharmonic** (☎ 954/561–2997, WEB www.floridaphilharmonic.org), the Florida Grand Opera, and the New World Symphony. Churches and synagogues sponsor classical music series with internationally known performers. **Coral Gables Congregational Church** (☎ 305/448–7421, WEB www.coralgablescongregational.org) serves up jazz, blues, classical, and even barbershop quartets during its popular Summer Concert Series at this acoustically excellent church. **Temple Beth Am** (☎ 305/667–6667) hosts the Children's Concert Series, including music, song, and dance, and the Adults' Concert Series with classical artists.

**Concert Association of Florida.** Directed by Judy Drucker, this not-for-profit organization is celebrating its fourth decade as the South's largest presenter of classical arts, music, and dance. Performers such as Luciano Pavarotti, José Carreras, Cecilia Bartoli, Isaac Stern, Yo-Yo Ma, Mikhail Baryshnikov, the Alvin Ailey American Dance Theater, Van Cliburn, and the New York Philharmonic have all come to various venues in Miami thanks to this group. ✉ *555 17th St., South Beach,* ☎ *305/532–3491,* WEB *www.concertfla.org.*

**Friends of Chamber Music.** At the acoustically perfect Gusman Concert Hall, the Friends present an annual series of seven chamber concerts by internationally known guest ensembles, such as the Emerson, Guarneri, Tokyo, and Talich quartets. ✉ *169 E. Flagler St., Suite 1619, Downtown, Miami,* ☎ *305/372–2975.*

**New World Symphony.** One of Miami's most valued cultural institutions, the New World is known as "America's training orchestra" because its musicians are recent graduates of the best music schools nationwide. They perform a largely modern repertory here for three years before going on to more established orchestras around the country. Under the direction of conductor Michael Tilson Thomas, the New World has become a widely acclaimed, artistically dazzling group that has toured extensively in its 16 seasons so far. From October through May, performances take place in its home venue, the landmark art deco **Lincoln Theater.** Once a major movie palace, the theater was renovated in 1989 to become Miami Beach's loveliest and most acoustically perfect auditorium. The symphony's concerts are broadcast live via speaker (and sometimes video) over the Lincoln Road Mall. Who would have thought you could rollerblade outdoors to live classical music? It's a beautiful way to spend a Saturday evening or Sunday afternoon. ✉ *555 Lincoln Rd., South Beach, Miami Beach,* ☎ *305/673–3331 or 305/673–3330,* WEB *www.nws.org.*

## Dance

You get a very clear picture of Greater Miami's very global nature by looking at its dance world: Cuba, Africa, Spain, India, Brazil, the Middle East, the Caribbean, and other cultures are all represented here, either through local dance groups or visiting performers. A good example of Miami's dance and diversity can be experienced at the annual **Florida Dance Festival** (New World School of the Arts, 25 N.E. 2nd St., Downtown, ☎ 305/674–3350, WEB www.fldance.org), held two weeks in June.Cutting-edge national and international performers also regularly visit Miami Beach's Jackie Gleason Theater of the Performing Arts, Colony Theater, and the Gusman Center downtown.

**Black Door.** South Florida's first contemporary African-American dance company brings together dancers from Jamaican, Haitian, Cuban, Trinidadian, Native American, and African-American heritages for performances at the Colony Theater and elsewhere. *No phone,* WEB *www.tigertail.org.*

**Freddick Bratcher and Company.** Catch this longtime company's modern, jazz, and spiritual moves at the Colony Theater. ☎ *305/448–2021.*

**Giovanni Luquini and Dancers.** The dance theater of Brazilian-born Giovanni Luquini has been lauded by critics for its innovation and excitement. Featured in local festivals and national tours outside of South

Florida, the dancers perform at the Colony Theater and the Lincoln Theatre. ☎ *305/604–9765.*

**Hanan Dance Cooperative (HDC).** HDC produces Arabic dance and music shows, often in collaboration with local artists in such disciplines as fashion, Afro-Cuban dance, and poetry. The Middle Eastern dance cooperative also has workshops and classes at FIU and the Miami Light Project. ☎ *305/738–4349.*

**Ifé-Ilé Afro-Cuban Dance and Music Ensemble.** This organization presents traditional Afro-Cuban dance and music at various venues such as the Colony Theater and **Miami-Dade Community College Wolfson Campus** (✉ 300 N.E. 2nd Ave., Downtown, Miami, ☎ 305/237–3010). ✉ *Afro-Cuban Center, 4545 N.W. 7th St., Suite 13, Miami,* ☎ *305/476–0388.*

**Iroko Dance and Performance Center.** The center presents Haitian and Afro-Cuban dance performances and workshops in an intimate studio space. Drumming classes are also available. ✉ *2100 Washington Ave., South Beach, Miami Beach,* ☎ *305/604–9141.*

**La Rosa Flamenco Theater.** Spreading the art form of flamenco since 1985, this group presents company dancers and international guests at performances and workshops throughout the year, many at the Colony Theater. ☎ *305/672–0552.*

**Maximum Dance Company.** Pushing the boundaries of modern ballet, this contemporary ballet troupe, with artistic directors Yanis Pikieris and David Palmer, has a new home at the historic Gusman Center for the Performing Arts. ✉ *174 E. Flagler St., Downtown, Miami,* ☎ *305/259–9775.*

**Miami City Ballet.** Miami's preeminent classical troupe and America's fastest-growing dance company has risen rapidly to international prominence in its relatively short existence. Since 1986, when one-time New York City Ballet principal Edward Villella became artist director, the ballet has become a world-class ensemble. As Florida's first major, fully professional, resident ballet company, the troupe re-creates the Balanchine repertoire and introduces works of its own during its September–March season. Villella also hosts children's works-in-progress programs. In January 2000 the ballet moved into a new home, part of the two-square-block Miami Beach Cultural Campus. ✉ *2200 Liberty Ave., South Beach, Miami Beach,* ☎ *305/929–7000,* WEB *www.miamicityballet.org.*

**Miami-Dade Community College Cultural Affairs Office.** Along with Miami Light Project, with whom it sometimes collaborates, this organization is one of two important presenters of dance in Miami. Operating out of its office at the community college, the group brings in national and international dance troupes for performances at the Colony Theater and the Gusman Center downtown. ✉ *300 N.E. 2nd Ave., Suite 1467, Downtown, Miami,* ☎ *305/237–3010.*

**Miami Light Project (MLP).** The MLP presents cutting-edge national and international dance and music groups, with performances at Miami Beach's Colony Theater and the Gusman Center downtown. It commissions new works each year (*Radio Mambo: Culture Clash Invades Miami* is one that went on to critical and popular acclaim around the country); artists such as Laurie Anderson, Robert Wilson, Philip Glass, and longtime Cuban musicians Los Fakires have been on the bill. The Project's annual Here and Now Festival, in February, showcases local talent in the Light Box, the performance space adjacent to the MLP offices. ✉ *3000 Biscayne Blvd., Downtown, Miami,* ☎ *305/576–4350,* WEB *www.miamilightproject.com.*

**Momentum Dance Company.** One of the oldest contemporary dance companies in the southeastern United States, this company gives more than 50 annual performances at various locations, including concert performances and children's programs. ☎ *305/858–7002.*

**Performing Arts Network.** A hub for multicultural arts activities, the Network gives workshops and performances in various dance traditions, including Egyptian, Israeli, flamenco, salsa, jazz, ballet, and modern. ✉ *13126 W. Dixie Hwy., North Miami,* ☎ *305/899–7730.*

## Opera

You may think of merengue more often than *Manon* when South Florida comes to mind, but Miami and Miami Beach have a burgeoning opera audience. The entire city turned out in 1995 to hear Pavarotti's open-air sundown performance on Miami Beach and again when the Three Tenors visited Pro Player stadium in 1997. And for purists, the city does have a reputable opera company.

**Florida Grand Opera.** The 13th-largest opera company in the United States, South Florida's leading opera company has been turning out world-class productions since 1941. It now presents five or six productions each year in the Miami-Dade County Auditorium, featuring the Florida Philharmonic Orchestra from Ft. Lauderdale. The series brings such luminaries as Placido Domingo and Luciano Pavarotti to Miami; in fact, Pavarotti made his American debut with the company in 1965, in *Lucia di Lammermoor.* The usually traditional European fare is sung in its original language, with English subtitles projected above the stage. ✉ *1200 Coral Way, The Roads, Miami,* ☎ *305/854–1643,* WEB *www.fgo.org.*

## Theater

British and American classics, original works by local playwrights, and Spanish-language plays are common to Miami's theater scene. A number of small avant-garde theater companies in South Beach and Coral Gables host original works. Children's theater also abounds, with regular series at the Actors' Playhouse at the Miracle Theater in Coral Gables.

**The Acorns Civic Theatre.** Acorns mounts both community and professional theater productions in its unpretentious South Beach locale. ✉ *2100 Washington Ave., South Beach,* ☎ *305/673–7730.*

**Actors' Playhouse at the Miracle Theater.** This professional company presents musicals, comedies, and dramas year-round in Coral Gables' beautifully restored 600-seat Miracle Theater. More intimate productions as well as musical theater for younger audiences take place in the 300-seat Children's Balcony Theater. ✉ *280 Miracle Mile, Coral Gables,* ☎ *305/444–9293,* WEB *www.actorsplayhouse.org.*

**City Theatre.** Catch local talent at the City Theatre company's very popular Summer Shorts Festival—short plays, that is—held at the University of Miami in June. Locals are encouraged to wear their shorts, too. ✉ *Jerry Herman Ring Theater, 1380 Miller Dr., Coral Gables,* ☎ *305/365–5400,* WEB *www.citytheatre.com.*

**Coconut Grove Playhouse.** Built in 1926 as a movie theater, the Playhouse is now a serious regional theater owned by the state of Florida. It started presenting live theater in 1956, with the American debut of *Waiting for Godot,* starring Bert Lahr and Tom Ewell. In the main theater and cabaret-style Encore Room of the Spanish rococo–style Grove fixture, audiences enjoy tried-and-true Broadway plays and musicals as well as experimental productions. ✉ *3500 Main Hwy., Coconut Grove,* ☎ *305/442–4000 or 305/442–2662,* WEB *www.cgplayhouse.com.*

**GableStage.** Professional performers stage modern classics and contemporary theater by American and British playwrights. The company is moving from its Biltmore Hotel venue at the end of the 2003 season. ✉ *1200 Anastasia Ave., Coral Gables,* ☎ *305/446–1116,* WEB *www.gablestage.org.*

**Juggerknot Theatre Company.** Experimental and avant garde pieces attract a younger crowd looking for something edgy and new. The company performs at Drama 101 and other venues. ✉ *6789 Biscayne Blvd., Miami,* ☎ *305/448–0569.*

**Lyric Theater.** Once one of the major centers of entertainment for the African-American community, the Lyric showcased more than 150 performers including Aretha Franklin, Count Basie, Sam Cooke, B.B. King, Ella Fitzgerald, and the Ink Spots. This newly restored theater is now the anchor site of the Historic Overtown Folklife Village. ✉ *819 N.W. 2nd Ave., Overtown, Miami,* ☎ *305/358–1146.*

**Miami Shores Theater.** Once a Paramount movie palace, this building now houses a lively and talented theater organization whose productions include lost classics and rarely done gems from the past four decades. ✉ *9806 N.E. 2nd Ave., Miami Shores,* ☎ *305/751–0562.*

**New Theatre.** The company has relocated to a 104-seat theater, where it mounts contemporary and classical plays, with an emphasis on new works and imaginative staging. ✉ *4120 Laguna St., Coral Gables,* ☎ *305/443–5909,* WEB *www.new-theatre.org.*

**Jerry Herman Ring Theater.** The University of Miami has a lively theater department with a program that's often just as ambitious as its professional counterparts (Broadway legend Jerry Herman is the drama school's most successful alumnus). The university's Department of Theatre Arts venue seats 311 and is where students stage four to six productions a year. ✉ *1380 Miller Dr., Coral Gables,* ☎ *305/284–3355.*

### SPANISH-LANGUAGE THEATER

At any given time about 20 Spanish theater companies are staging light comedy, puppetry, vaudeville, bawdy farces, and political satire. Some of the companies participate in annual festivals. To find out what's happening, read the Spanish newspapers or the *Miami Herald*'s "Weekend" section. When you call for tickets or information, be prepared for a conversation in Spanish—few box-office personnel speak English.

**Las Mascaras.** Cuban sex farces and Saturday comedies are on the bill at this lively Little Havana theater. ✉ *2833 N.W. 7th St., Little Havana, Miami,* ☎ *305/642–0358.*

**Teatro Avante.** The city's most successful crossover theater, with works that cater to the tastes of its mostly middle-aged Cuban-American audiences, provides supertitles for non-Spanish-speakers. Each summer Teatro Avante sponsors the Hispanic Theatre Festival, during which international directors, playwrights, and actors converge on Miami, often presenting the most provocative stagings around, all in Spanish, English, and Portuguese, and attracting a multicultural audience to various Greater Miami venues. ✉ *235 Alcazar Ave., Coral Gables,* ☎ *305/445–8877,* WEB *www.teatroavante.com.*

**Teatro de Bellas Artes.** Audiences fill this 255-seat theater on Calle Ocho for Spanish plays and musicals staged throughout the year. Midnight musical follies, concerts, and female-impersonator acts are also part of the lineup. ✉ *2173 S.W. 8th St., Little Havana, Miami,* ☎ *305/325-0515.*

### Theater and Music for Children

**Actor's Playhouse Children's Theater.** After the show, at this popular children's musical theater you can speak with the cast and pose with them for pictures. ✉ *Miracle Theater, 280 Miracle Mile, Coral Gables,* ☎ *305/444-9293,* WEB *www.actorsplayhouse.org.*

**Sunday Afternoons of Music for Children.** Presented by Temple Beth Am, this series has child-friendly concerts at the University of Miami's Gusman Concert Hall. Concerts have included UM's Jazz Vocal Ensemble singing *Rhythm in My Nursery Rhymes* and the Miami City Ballet School performing *Something to Dance About.* ☎ *305/667-6667.*

**Young People's Concert Series.** Produced by the New World Symphony this program puts a new twist on the petting-zoo concept: here kids can handle the musical instruments they've heard in performance. A recent concert featured music inspired by Dr. Seuss, such as *Green Eggs and Ham* and *Gertrude McFuzz,* conducted by the composer Rob Kapilow. ✉ *541 Lincoln Rd., South Beach,* ☎ *305/673-3330,* WEB *www.nws.org.*

## NIGHTLIFE

On weekend nights—and on weeknights in high season—the level of activity in popular Miami and Miami Beach neighborhoods can be exhilarating or maddening, depending on your perspective, as partiers spill into the streets and traffic grinds to a stop. Parking is a challenge in areas with lots of bars and clubs. If you do find a metered space on the street, you'll need plenty of quarters. Parking lots and garages (especially at complexes such as Bayside and CocoWalk) are an easier but potentially more expensive option than street parking. In South Beach, don't even think about driving from club to club; park in one of the municipal lots and take the Electrowave shuttle that makes a loop along key streets. Once you've found a place for your car, do your club crawling on foot: the major nightlife neighborhoods are safe and compact.

How to get past the velvet ropes at the hottest South Beach nightspots? First, if you're staying at a hotel, use the concierge. Decide which clubs you want to check out (consult *Ocean Drive* magazine celebrity pages if you want to be among the glitterati), and the concierge will fax your name to the clubs in order for you to be put on the guest list. This means much easier access and usually no cover charge (which can be $20 or so) if you arrive before midnight. Guest list or no guest list, follow these pointers: make sure there are more women than men in your group. Dress up—casual chic is the dress code. For men this means no sneakers, no shorts, no sleeveless vests, and no shirts unbuttoned past the top button. For women provocative and seductive is fine; overly revealing is not. Black is always right. At the door: don't name-drop—no one takes it seriously. Don't be pushy while trying to get the doorman's attention. Wait 'til you make eye contact, then be cool and easygoing. If you decide to tip him (which most bouncers don't expect), be discreet and pleasant, not big-bucks obnoxious—a $10 or $20 bill quietly passed will be appreciated, however. With the right dress and the right attitude, you'll be on the dance floor rubbing shoulders with South Beach's finest clubbers in no time.

## South Beach Nightlife and the Arts

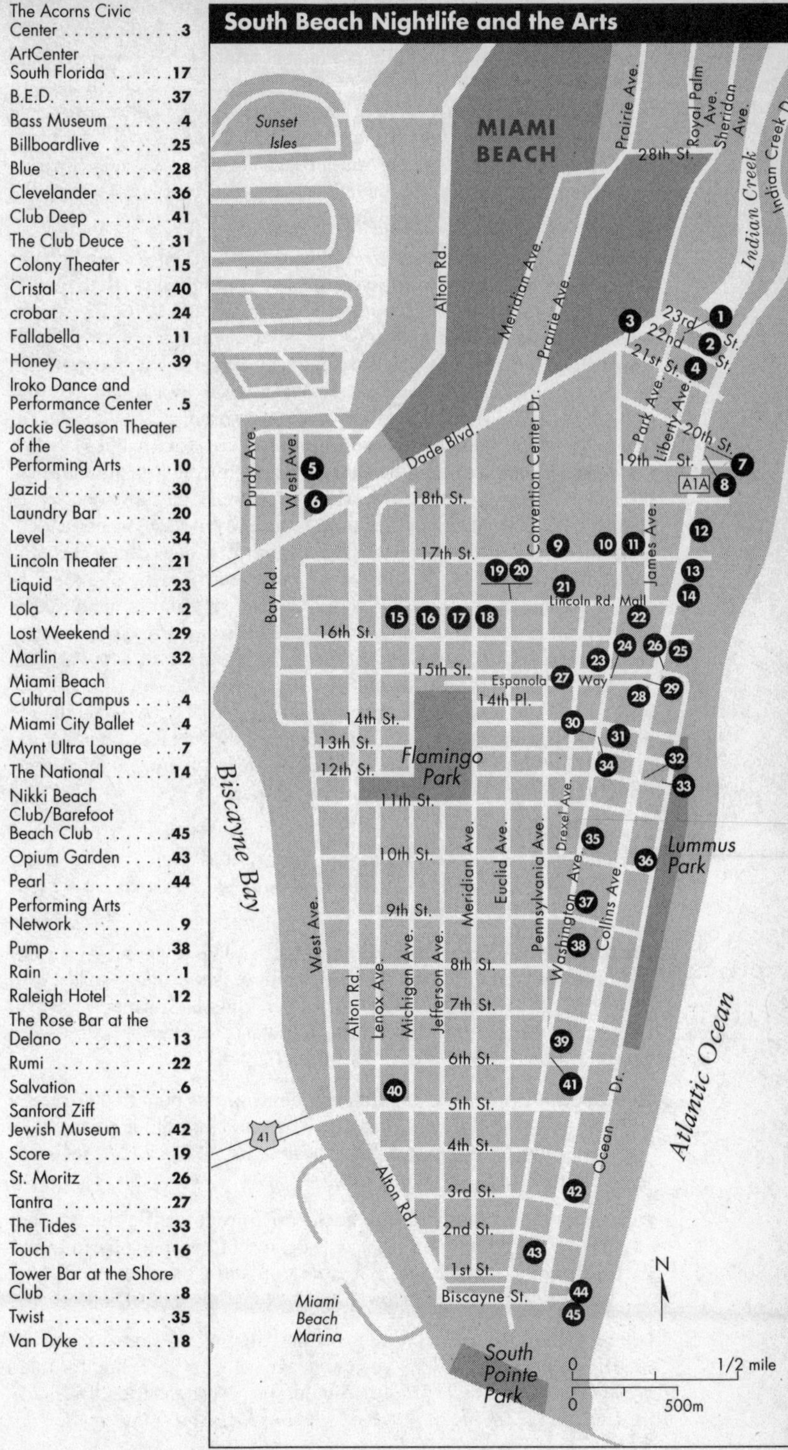


The Acorns Civic Center . . . . . . . . . . . . 3
ArtCenter South Florida . . . . . . 17
B.E.D. . . . . . . . . . . . 37
Bass Museum . . . . . . . 4
Billboardlive . . . . . . . 25
Blue . . . . . . . . . . . 28
Clevelander . . . . . . . 36
Club Deep . . . . . . . . 41
The Club Deuce . . . . 31
Colony Theater . . . . . 15
Cristal . . . . . . . . . . 40
crobar . . . . . . . . . . 24
Fallabella . . . . . . . . . 11
Honey . . . . . . . . . . 39
Iroko Dance and Performance Center . . 5
Jackie Gleason Theater of the Performing Arts . . . . 10
Jazid . . . . . . . . . . . 30
Laundry Bar . . . . . . . 20
Level . . . . . . . . . . . 34
Lincoln Theater . . . . . 21
Liquid . . . . . . . . . . 23
Lola . . . . . . . . . . . 2
Lost Weekend . . . . . . 29
Marlin . . . . . . . . . . 32
Miami Beach Cultural Campus . . . . . 4
Miami City Ballet . . . . 4
Mynt Ultra Lounge . . . 7
The National . . . . . . 14
Nikki Beach Club/Barefoot Beach Club . . . . . . 45
Opium Garden . . . . . 43
Pearl . . . . . . . . . . . 44
Performing Arts Network . . . . . . . . . . 9
Pump . . . . . . . . . . . 38
Rain . . . . . . . . . . . . 1
Raleigh Hotel . . . . . . 12
The Rose Bar at the Delano . . . . . . . . . 13
Rumi . . . . . . . . . . . 22
Salvation . . . . . . . . . 6
Sanford Ziff Jewish Museum . . . . 42
Score . . . . . . . . . . . 19
St. Moritz . . . . . . . . 26
Tantra . . . . . . . . . . 27
The Tides . . . . . . . . 33
Touch . . . . . . . . . . . 16
Tower Bar at the Shore Club . . . . . . . . . . . . 8
Twist . . . . . . . . . . . 35
Van Dyke . . . . . . . . . 18

## Bars and Lounges

One of Greater Miami's most popular pursuits is bar hopping. Bars range from intimate enclaves to showy see-and-be-seen lounges to loud, raucous frat parties. There's a decidedly New York flair to some of the newer lounges, which are increasingly catering to the Manhattan party crowd who escape to South Beach for long weekends. If you're looking for a relatively unfrenetic evening, your best bet is one of the chic hotel bars on Collins Avenue.

If getting to the newest place is your priority, however, you might want consider the more high-profile restaurant-cum-nightclubs that are definitely the establishments *du jour* in South Beach. **B.E.D.** (✉ 929 Washington Ave., South Beach, ☎ 305/532–9070), which innocently stands for beverages, entertainment, and dining, also offers king pillow-strewn beds in place of tables. **Pearl** (✉ 1 Ocean Dr., South Beach, ☎ 305/673–1575) is an airy space lab of white and orange bathed in lavender light. It overlooks the ocean and is next door to Nikki Beach Club—the food's not bad either. **Rumi** (✉ 330 Lincoln Rd., South Beach, ☎ 305/672–4353), named after the 13th-century Persian poet, serves eclectic cuisine amid Moroccan furnishings and tapestries in rich chocolate, burgundy and red, before shedding its Zen-like calm to become a club. **Tantra** (✉ 1445 Pennsylvania Ave., South Beach, ☎ 305/672–4765), with its grass floor lobby and aphrodisiac dinner menu, takes sensory enhancement a step further when it transforms into a nightclub on Friday and Saturday, and hosts its popular Goddess Party on Monday nights. Tropical **Touch** (✉ 910 Lincoln Rd., South Beach, ☎ 305/532–8003) is so hip that even jaded New Yorkers will feel they're getting something new—a restaurant where lingering is not merely permissible, but *de rigueur.* And remember, you're in Miami—mojitos, martinis, and margaritas are the drinks of choice.

### South Beach

**Blue.** Electric Blue is laid back and chic and has been know to draw high-profile celebs such as Dennis Rodman. ✉ *222 Espanola Way, at 6th St., South Beach,* ☎ *305/534–1009.*

**The Clevelander.** Wanna meet other tourists? This always busy indoor sports bar and outdoor patio with live bands draws a college-style crowd that keeps its eye on the game or on the bikini-clad throng on Ocean Drive. It's the main draw at the hotel of the same name. ✉ *1020 Ocean Dr., at 10th St., South Beach,* ☎ *305/531–3485.*

**Club Deuce.** Although it's completely unglam, this pool hall attracts a colorful crowd of clubbers, locals, celebs—and just about anyone else. Locals consider it the best spot for a cheap drink. ✉ *222 14 St., at Collins Ave., South Beach,* ☎ *305/531–6200.*

**Fallabella.** Long and sleek with back-to-nature futuristic chic, the bar at the groovy Albion hotel is a serene getaway from mad Ocean Drive. ✉ *1650 James Ave., between Washington and Collins Aves., at 16th St., South Beach,* ☎ *305/913–1000.*

**Laundry Bar.** Do your laundry while listening to house music or quaffing a drink at the bar (you can leave your dry cleaning, too). It's mostly gay (with a ladies' night), but definitely straight-friendly. ✉ *721 N. Lincoln La., 1 block north of Lincoln Rd., South Beach,* ☎ *305/531–7700.*

**Lola.** Low-key and industrial, with pool tables and a 120-ft bar, this lounge is popular with locals, who are avoiding attitude, and celebs, who are avoiding the spotlight. A DJ plays funk, eclectic '80s and '90s music, and old and new rock. ✉ *247 23rd St., South Beach,* ☎ *305/695–8697,* WEB *www.lolabar.com.*

**Lost Weekend.** Players at this pool hall are serious about their pastime, so it's hard to get a table on weekends. The full bar, which has 150 kinds of beers, draws an eclectic crowd, from yuppies to drag queens to slumming celebs like Lenny Kravitz and the guys in Hootie and the Blowfish. ✉ *218 Espanola Way, at Collins Ave., between 14th and 15th Sts., South Beach,* ☎ *305/672–1707.*

**Marlin.** It's the Austin Powers look here—fuchsia and orange pillows and cushions and mirrors everywhere. Deejays spin a different type of music every night for the 25-to-40 crowd. ✉ *1200 Collins Ave., at 12th St., South Beach,* ☎ *305/605–5000.*

**Mynt Ultra Lounge.** The name of this upscale lounge is meant to be taken literally—not only are the walls bathed in soft green shades, but an aromatherapy system pumps out different fresh scents, including mint. Celebs like Enrique Iglesias, Angie Everhart, and Queen Latifah have cooled down here. ✉ *1921 Collins Ave., at 19th St., South Beach,* ☎ *786/276–6132.*

★ **The National.** Don't miss a drink at the hotel's nifty wooden bar, one of many elements original to the 1939 building, which give it such a sense of its era that you'd expect to see Ginger Rogers and Fred Astaire hoofing it along the polished lobby floor. The adjoining Martini Room has a great collection of cigar and old airline stickers and vintage Bacardi ads on the walls. There's live jazz most nights. Don't forget to take a peek at the pool. ✉ *1677 Collins Ave., at 17th St., South Beach,* ☎ *305/532–2311.*

**Rain.** Happily on the fringes of South Beach, this new indoor–outdoor lounge, with its color-changing glass ceiling, eschews attitude, instead focusing on music by high-energy lounge DJs. ✉ *323 23rd St., at Collins Ave., South Beach,* ☎ *305/674–7947.*

**Raleigh Hotel.** In this art deco hotel there's a small, classy martini bar that's worth a visit. ✉ *1775 Collins Ave., at 18th St., South Beach,* ☎ *305/534–6300.*

★ **Rose Bar at the Delano.** The airy lobby lounge at South Beach's trendiest hotel manages to look dramatic but not cold, with long gauzy curtains and huge white pillars separating conversation nooks (this is where Ricky Martin shot the video for "La Vida Loca"). A pool table brings the austerity down to earth. There's also a poolside bar with intimate waterside cabanas. ✉ *1685 Collins Ave., at 16th St., South Beach,* ☎ *305/672–2000.*

**St. Moritz.** Although the mismatched, chain-hotel look of the main building and bar is uninviting, the adjoining St. Moritz is a restored art deco hotel with a delightful piano bar, the Gaucho Room. The oversize animal-print chairs are an ideal place to settle in and enjoy a tequila martini, visit the olive bar, and listen to live jazz. ✉ *1601 Collins Ave., at 16th St., South Beach,* ☎ *305/604–1601.*

**The Tides.** For South Beach fabulousness, belly up to the glass-top bar for martinis and piano jazz in the cream-and-white lobby of this way-hip hotel. ✉ *1220 Ocean Dr., at 12th St., South Beach,* ☎ *305/604–5000.*

**Tower Bar at the Shore Club.** This luxurious bar is at the top of the 21-story tower that makes up part of the long-awaited Shore Club. With solid teak floors, white leather-cushion banquettes, and green silk walls, this is a sophisticated place to unwind with a vintage tequila after dining. The **Nobu Lounge** next to the Shore Club has Japanese martinis and sake for those waiting to dine at Nobu. ✉ *1901 Collins Ave., at 19th St., South Beach,* ☎ *305/695–3100.*

## Downtown Miami and Little Havana

**Bayside Marketplace.** A shamelessly touristy retail and entertainment complex filled with stores and restaurants that you'll find in any big American city is somehow one of Florida's most-visited attractions. You can hop a disco boat for a midnight cruise, visit a daiquiri kiosk, or hang out at **Hard Rock Cafe** (☎ 305/377–3110), which you can locate by looking for the enormous guitar at the entrance. ✉ *401 Biscayne Blvd., at N.E. 4th St., Downtown,* ☎ *305/577–3344.*

**Hardaway's Firehouse Four.** This renovated firehouse turns into a sizzling nightspot for the mid-30s to 40s set, with different nights to suit all tastes: jazz, gothic, gay, hip-hop. ✉ *1000 S. Miami Ave., at S.E. 10th St., Brickell Village,* ☎ *305/371–3473.*

**M-Bar.** At the lobby bar of the impeccably elegant Mandarin Oriental hotel, you can choose from 250 martinis. Pick one and gaze out over Biscayne Bay. ✉ *500 Brickell Key Dr., Brickell Key,,* ☎ *305/913–8288.*

**Tobacco Road.** Opened in 1912, this classic holds Miami's oldest liquor license: No. 0001! Upstairs, in a space that was occupied by a speakeasy during Prohibition, local and national blues bands perform nightly. There's excellent bar food, a dinner menu, and a selection of single-malt Scotches, bourbons, and cigars. This is the hangout of grizzled journalists, bohemians en route to or from nowhere, and club kids seeking a way station before the real parties begin. ✉ *626 S. Miami Ave., at S.E. 7th St., Miami,* ☎ *305/374–1198.*

## Coconut Grove

**CocoWalk.** One of Miami's touristy shopping-and-eating complexes, CocoWalk is sweltering in the summertime and packed in the wintertime. In short, it's very popular. **Fat Tuesday** (☎ 305/441–2992) is a typical touristy place, serving sickly sweet concoctions like 190 Octane (190-proof alcohol), Swampwater (also 190 proof), Banana Banshees (banana liqueur, cream, and vodka), and Long Island Iced Tea. ✉ *3015 Grand Ave., at McFarlane Rd.,* ☎ *305/444–0777.*

**Iguana Cantina.** Popular with the 25- to 40-year-old professional crowd, it has a little bit of everything: live Top 40 music, and the Babalu Bar, with live bands playing salsa, merengue, and top Latin hits. ✉ *Streets of Mayfair, 2911 Grand Ave., at Mary St.,* ☎ *305/443–3300.*

**Monty's in the Grove.** The outdoor bar here has Caribbean flair, thanks especially to live calypso and island music. It's very kid-friendly on weekends days, when Mom and Dad can kick back and enjoy a beer and the raw bar while the youngsters dance to live music. Evenings bring a DJ and reggae music. ✉ *2550 S. Bayshore Dr., at Aviation Ave.,* ☎ *305/858–1431.*

**Orchid Lounge.** The quirky furniture and such fanciful details as feathered lampshades characterize the bar. You can sip a fine cognac or choose from the extensive wine list and listen to live jazz, presented nightly. ✉ *Mayfair House Hotel, 3000 Florida Ave., at Virginia St.,* ☎ *305/441–0000.*

**Sandbar Grill.** This rowdy sports bar replaced the venerable Hungry Sailor, bringing with it lots of varieties of beer and tequila, and plenty of TV sets. The kitchen serves Southern California–Mexican snacks, such as fish tacos, 'til 2 AM. ✉ *3064 Grand Ave., at Main Hwy.,* ☎ *305/444–5270.*

**Taurus Ale & Grill.** A Grove institution, the Taurus has survived a few rocky years, but still has steaks and such, and—thankfully—the same casual indoor–outdoor bar, attracting a colorful crowd of eccentric Grove-ites and friendly over-30 locals. Good local bands play rock and oldies Friday–Saturday. ✉ *3540 Main Hwy., at Charles Ave.,* ☎ *305/648–1525.*

**Wyndham Grand Bay.** With striped white pine and cherry floors, oversize bar stools, and pastel murals, this hotel bar serves up lots of European chic—and no wonder, it adjoins the elegant Northern Italian Bice restaurant. There's live jazz Wednesday through Saturday, and sushi or Italian appetizers during Happy Hour (Wednesday at 5:30). ✉ *2669 S. Bayshore Dr., at 27th Ave.,* ☎ *305/858–9600.*

## Coral Gables

Stodgy Coral Gables? Not any more. This affluent suburb is undergoing a metamorphosis as its demographic changes from wealthy older folks to stylish younger professionals, and formerly uptight city officials loosen the reins to allow street festivals and sidewalk dining and drinking venues, adding a spirited outdoors dimension to its nightlife. The Gables will never have the sex appeal of South Beach or the high energy of the Grove, but it's increasingly popular with locals—young and old—who like its safe, tree-lined streets and easy parking.

**Alcazaba.** This dress-up nightclub at the Hyatt Regency has retro disco dancing, salsa, and merengue on Wednesday and Saturday nights. ✉ *50 Alhambra Plaza, at Douglas Rd.,* ☎ *305/569–4614.*

**Bar at Ponce and Giralda.** One of the oldest bars in South Florida, the old Hofbrau has been reincarnated and now serves up no-nonsense, live homegrown rock-and-roll and a nontouristy vibe. ✉ *172 Giralda Ave., at Ponce de León Blvd.,* ☎ *305/442–2730.*

**Biltmore Hotel.** This magnificent hotel's intimate and elegant bar attracts over-40 professionals and executives. ✉ *1200 Anastasia Ave., at De Soto Blvd.,* ☎ *305/445–1926.*

**Doc Dammer's Saloon.** At the Omni Colonnade Hotel, this sedate bar draws an older, sophisticated crowd for live jazz. ✉ *180 Aragon Ave., at Ponce de León Blvd.,* ☎ *305/441–2600.*

**The Globe.** The centerpiece of Coral Gables' new emphasis on nightlife draws crowds of twentysomethings who spill into the street for live jazz Wednesday through Saturday and a bistro-style menu nightly. Outdoor tables and an art-heavy, upscale interior are comfortable, if you can find space to squeeze in. ✉ *377 Alhambra Circle, at Le Jeune Rd.,* ☎ *305/445–3555.*

**JohnMartin's.** The cozy upscale Irish pub hosts an Irish cabaret on Saturday night, with live contemporary and traditional music—sometimes by an Irish band—storytelling, and dancers. ✉ *258 Miracle Mile, at Ponce de León Blvd.,* ☎ *305/445–3777.*

**Meza Fine Art gallerycafe.** One of the few places in the Gables with live entertainment nightly, Meza combines art, dining, music with storytelling, folklore recitals, and such. ✉ *275 Giralda, at Salzedo,* ☎ *305/461–2723.*

**Stuart's Bar-Lounge.** Inside the charming 1926 Hotel Place St. Michel, this bar is favored by locals. Its style is beveled mirrors, mahogany paneling, French posters, pictures of old Coral Gables, and Art Nouveau lighting. ✉ *162 Alcazar Ave., at Ponce de León Blvd.,* ☎ *305/444–1666.*

**Titanic Brewery & Restaurant.** Noisy but cheerful, this new nightspot attracts University of Miami students and upscale locals for live jazz and blues. ✉ *5813 Ponce de León Blvd., at San Amaro Dr.,* ☎ *305/ 667–2537.*

## Cabaret, Comedy, and Supper Clubs

If you're in the mood for scantily clad showgirls and feathered headdresses, you can still find the kind of song-and-dance extravaganzas that were produced by every major Miami Beach hotel in the 1950s. Modern-day offerings include flamenco shows, salsa dancing, and comedy clubs.

**Casa Panza.** The visionary Madrileñan owners of this Little Havana restaurant have energized the neighborhood with a recent expansion. At twice-weekly celebrations honoring *La Virgen del Rocío* (the patron saint of a province in Andalusia), the room is darkened and diners are handed lighted candles and sheet music. Everyone readily joins in the singing, making for a truly enjoyable evening. There is flamenco dancing on Tuesday, Thursday, Friday, and Saturday, and flamenco classes on Monday. ✉ *1620 S.W. 8th St., at 16th Ave., Little Havana, Miami,* ☎ *305/643–5343.*

**Cafe Nostalgia at the Forge.** Relocated from its tiny Little Havana abode to its new home next to the elegant Forge Restaurant, this place captures the look and sound of Cuba in the 1940s. The evening begins with old black-and-white Cuban films and heats up as the 10-piece house band plays salsa and Cuban standards. Of course, cigars are part of the scene. ✉ *432 Arthur Godfrey Rd., at Sheridan Ave., Mid-Beach, Miami Beach,* ☎ *305/604–9895.*

**Club Tropigala.** Once the La Ronde Room, where Frank Sinatra crooned for a crowd decked out in mink stoles and pinky rings, the Fontainebleau Hilton's nightspot is now a tropical jungle, with leaves dangling from the ceiling and orchids, banana leaves, and cascading waterfalls throughout. It's as close as you'll get to a Vegas-style revue. With such stars as Julio Iglesias, Ricky Martin, and José Feliciano, Hispanic luminaries Albita and Julio Sabala, and a band that plays standards and Latin music for dancing, Club Tropigala brings back the old glamour of Miami Beach. Hotel guests receive complimentary admission, and reservations are suggested. ✉ *4441 Collins Ave., at 44th St., Miami Beach,* ☎ *305/ 672–7469.* 🎟 *$20.*

**Hoy Como Ayer.** This tiny cabaret, adorned with Cuban artwork, is best known for Fuácata on Thursdays, where a DJ mixes old Cuban standards with hip-hop and is accompanied by a live drummer for a unique fusion experience. Other evenings include Spanish theater, live Latin salsa and jazz. ✉ *2212 S.W. 8th St., at S.W. 22 Ave., Little Havana, Miami,* ☎ *305/541–2631.*

**Improv Comedy Club.** This long-standing comedy club hosts nationally touring comics nightly. Comedy club faithfuls will recognize Margaret Cho and George Wallace, and everyone knows Damon Wayans and Chris Rock, both of whom have taken the stage here. Urban Comedy Showcase is held Tuesday and Wednesday, with an open mike part of the evening on Wednesday. A full menu is available. ✉ *Streets of Mayfair, 3390 Mary St., at Grand Ave., Coconut Grove, Miami,* ☎ *305/441–8200.* 🎟 *$10–$32.* ⏲ *Shows Tues. 8, 10:30, Wed.–Thurs. 8:30, Fri. 8:30 and 10:45, Sat. 7:45, 10, midnight, and Sun. 8:30.*

**Lombardi's.** You can watch Flamenco dance performances on Sunday night, or shake it salsa-style or merengue on Friday, Saturday, and Sun-

Close-Up

# SALSA, MIAMI STYLE

**WHILE MANY VISIT MIAMI** to soak up some sun, others come here for something far hotter—the steamy salsa clubs. From Latin nights at hotel bars and spicy salsa-only nightclubs in Miami Beach, to ranch-like settings inland, far from the glittering lights, that attract hordes of hard-core *salseros* (salsa dancers), Miami's vibrant salsa clubs are a terrific nightlife experience, if only to watch or be watched.

Miami's salsa, called *Rueda* or Casino-style salsa, is unique. Debbie Ohanian—a Miami transplant who started one of the city's foremost salsa clubs, Starfish—describes it as a sort of choreographed line dancing, like a Latin square dance, that started in Cuba's social clubs in the 1950s. Traditionally there are 180 different turns that people learn, and there's a caller. Unlike some other forms of salsa, there's not a lot of eye contact, and, also like a square dance, partners are exchanged. At many clubs, where a Casino Rueda typically begins the evening, the circles of dancers get so large, smaller circles form within. Having over 100 people in a Rueda is typical for Miami.

Beginners can get an overview of the salsa experience at www.salsaweb.com. You'll find out about the differences in big-city styles of salsa, from L.A.-style, to New York, to Miami, and everything else you wanted to know about this passion, from music to moves to movies.

Salsa novices should consider a salsa lesson, which are offered by several Miami nightclubs before the crowds turn out. Some lessons are free, while others are part of the cover charge. **Alcazaba** (✉ 50 Alhambra Plaza, Coral Gables, ☎ 305/569–4614) in the Hyatt Regency Coral Gables has basic salsa lessons on Saturday. **Bermuda Bar** (✉ 3509 N.E. 163rd St., at N.E. 35th Ave., N. Miami Beach, ☎ 305/945–0196) in North Miami Beach gives salsa lessons on Thursday night. Gloria and Emilio Estefan's restaurant, **Bongos Cuban Cafe** (☎ 786/777–2100) at the AmericanAirlines Arena, turns into a Latin-flavored dance club on Friday and Saturday nights, with lessons on Thursday. Several nights a week, **Cafe Nostalgia at the Forge** (✉ 432 Arthur Godfrey Rd., Mid-Beach, Miami Beach, ☎ 305/695–8555) has live music for Latin dancing. **Club Mystique** (☎ 305/265–3900) in the Hilton Miami Airport, has free salsa lessons on Thursday. Other clubs may offer special salsa nights; check the weekly free *New Times* listings for details.

Ready to try out your salsa skills? Get out on the floor and don't be shy to ask someone better than you to dance. (Just ask if they wouldn't mind showing you a couple turns if you're still new at it.) In addition to the clubs with classes, there are other nightspots with salsa nights (call first). Perhaps the most authentic salsa experience in Miami can be had at **La Covacha** (✉ 10730 N.W. 25th St., at 107th Ave., West Miami-Dade, Miami, ☎ 305/594–3717), an open-air dance hall in West Miami-Dade County where you can hear not only salsa, but merengue, samba, soca, and Spanish-flavored rock. La Covacha attracts the young and old, Hispanics and Anglos, beginning dancers and seasoned salseros. Coconut Grove's **Club 609** (✉ 3338 Virginia St., ☎ 305/444–6096) does salsa on Saturdays. Saturday night is salsa night at **Miami Park Plaza Hotel** (✉ 7707 N.W. 103rd St., Hialeah Gardens, ☎ 305/825–1000). **Señor Frog's** (✉ 3480 Main Hwy., Coconut Grove, ☎ 305/448–0999; ✉ 616 Collins Ave., South Beach, ☎ 305/673–5262) sheds its Mexican restaurant mode on Saturday and becomes a hot Latin music nightspot.

day nights. ✉ *Bayside Marketplace, 401 Biscayne Blvd., at N.E. 4th St., Downtown, Miami,* ☎ *305/381–9580.*

## Dance Clubs

### Miami Beach and North

**Bermuda Bar & Grille.** The DJ here plays *loud* dance music into the wee hours of the morning. Male bartenders wear knee-length kilts, while female bartenders are in matching minis; however, the crowd dresses stylish island casual to match the atmosphere. In the big indoor tropical forest there are booths you can hide in, seven bars, and three pool tables. Draft beer is served in yard glasses and frosted mugs. The place is closed Monday and Tuesday. ✉ *3509 N.E. 163rd St., at N.E. 35th Ave., North Miami Beach,* ☎ *305/945–0196.*

**Jimmy'z at Cuba Club.** Adjacent to the Forge steak house, this is as upscale a club as Miami Beach can offer, a VIP lounge indeed. That doesn't mean the party doesn't get bacchanalian at times, especially on Wednesday. Any night, though, you'll see power suits with young things draped on either arm grooving to contemporary international music. ✉ *432 41st St., at Pine Tree Dr., Mid-Beach, Miami Beach,* ☎ *305/604–9798.*

### Miami

**Club Space.** Want 24-hour partying? Here's the place. Created from four downtown warehouses, Space has three dance rooms, an outdoor patio, a New York industrial look, and a 24-hour liquor license. It's open on weekends only, and you'll need to look good to be allowed past the velvet ropes. ✉ *142 N.E. 11th St., Downtown, Miami,* ☎ *305/375–0001.*

### South Beach

**Billboardlive.** When you enter, a multicolored fixture on the ceiling illuminates multicolored beams projecting onto a mirror, creating an infinite cage of lights that sets the stage for a dazzling experience. You'll find world class DJs here. Besides the dance floors, the four floors of high energy entertainment include a performance stage, restaurants, bars, private rooms, and a skybox. ✉ *1501 Collins Ave., at 15th St.,* ☎ *305/538–2251,* WEB *www.billboardlive.com.*

**Club Deep.** Dance atop a 2,000-gallon aquarium at this steamy disco. ✉ *621 Washington Ave., at 6th St.,* ☎ *305/532–1509.*

**Cristal.** Live Latin music, hip-hop, R&B, and reggae get the crowd moving here. ✉ *1045 5th St., between Lenox and Michigan Aves.,* ☎ *305/604–2582.*

**crobar.** Sophisticated and fun, this South Beach branch of the popular Chicago club combines sleek architecture in the form of massive sculptured monuments (think *Blade Runner*); performance art, such as angels swooping down on bungee cords; and state-of-the-art light and sound systems to dazzle the senses. Gwyneth Paltrow, Lennox Lewis, and Vanilla Ice have already checked it out. It's housed in the historic Cameo Theater, which is, unfortunately, carpeted. ✉ *1445 Washington Ave., at 14th St.,* ☎ *305/531–5027.*

**Honey.** This newcomer's soft lighting, cozy couches and chaise longues, and low-down music go down as smoothly as their trademark honey-dipped apples. ✉ *645 Washington Ave., 6th St.,* ☎ *305/604–8222.*

**Jazid.** Thanks to a new and modern interior design job, Jazid is now a sultry and candlelighted standout on the strip; the music is jazz, with blues and R&B. ✉ *1342 Washington Ave., at 13th St.,* ☎ *305/673–9372.*

**Level.** Looking for Studio 54-type energy? Level's four dance floors total 40,000 square ft. There are six VIP areas, five rooms, and lots of, um, levels. ✉ *1235 Washington Ave., at 12th St.,* ☎ *305/532–1525.*

**Liquid.** Familiar name, new owners, different location—Liquid is back, bringing with it the vibe that made it one of the most enduring A-list clubs in the '90s. And Fat Black Pussycat—with rare groove, funk, and R&B—returns on Fridays. ✉ *1532 Washington Ave., at 15th St.,* ☎ *305/531–9411,* WEB *www.liquidnightclub.com.*

★ **Nikki Beach Club and Barefoot Beach Club.** With its swell on-the-beach location, the full-service Nikki Beach Club has become a favorite pretty-people and celeb hangout. Teepees and hammocks on the sand, dance floors both under the stars and inside, and beach parties make this a true South Beach experience. ✉ *1 Ocean Dr., at 1st St.,* ☎ *305/538–1231.*

**Opium Garden.** Enter the Asian temple, and behold a lush waterfall, lots of candles, dragons, and tapestries. Casually chic twenty- and thirtysomethings go for the exotic intrigue of the popular nightspot and dance to house music and hip-hop. ✉ *136 Collins Ave., at 1st St.,* ☎ *305/674–8360.*

## Evening Cruises

Miami's waterfront location means there's no shortage of water-oriented activities, even at night. Several evening cruises depart from **Bayside Marketplace,** in downtown Miami, offering different styles of entertainment to different crowds, and another cruise departs from **Dinner Key,** off Bayshore Drive in Coconut Grove. Gambling cruisers must be at least 21 years old. Get there in plenty of time to buy tickets and board. For gambling on land, head to the **Miccosukee Resort and Convention Center** (500 S.W. 177 Ave., West Miami-Dade, ☎ 305/925–2555).

***Casino Princesa.*** Right next to the Hard Rock Cafe, you can embark on a gambling cruise to nowhere. ✉ *315 Biscayne Blvd., south of Bayside Marketplace, Downtown Miami,* ☎ *305/379–5825,* WEB *www.casinoprincesa.com.* 🎫 *$5.95.* ⏲ *Daily 12:30 PM and 7:30 PM; late-night cruises Sat.–Sun. 1 AM–6 AM.*

***Celebration.*** A sightseeing boat by day becomes a party boat by night, cruising the bay and blasting music. ✉ *401 Biscayne Blvd., at Bayside Marketplace, Downtown Miami,* ☎ *305/373–7001.* 🎫 *$10–$12.* ⏲ *Fri.–Sun. 9, 11 PM.*

**Full Moon Cruise.** If you're in town when the moon is full, make reservations for an evening on the Miami Sailing Club's 56-ft *Malu Kai.* The combination of a spectacular moonrise, dazzling skyline, and gentle sea breeze is unforgettable, making the drinks and snacks all the more enjoyable. ✉ *Dinner Key Marina, 3400 Pan American Dr., at Bayshore Dr. and S.W. 27th Ave., Coconut Grove,* ☎ *305/858–1130.* 🎫 *$50 per person, $90 per couple.* ⏲ *Call for exact sailing dates and times.*

***Heritage.*** This stately vessel offers sedate one- and two-hour sunset and skyline cruises. ✉ *401 Biscayne Blvd., south of Bayside band stage, Downtown Miami,* ☎ *305/442–9697.* 🎫 *$10–$15.* ⏲ *Weekdays 6:30; weekends 6:30, 8, 9, 10, 11.*

***Island Queen.*** When the sun goes down, this sightseeing boat lights up with neon and plies Biscayne Bay while you dance to salsa and reggae.

Trips depart on the hour. ✉ *401 Biscayne Blvd., at Bayside Marketplace, Downtown, Miami,* ☎ *305/379–5119.* 💵 *$14.* ⏲ *Daily 11–7.*

## Gay Nightlife

Aside from a few bars and lounges on the mainland, Greater Miami's gay action centers on the dance clubs in South Beach. That tiny strip of sand rivals New York and San Francisco as a hub of gay nightlife, if not in the number of clubs then in the intensity of the partying. The neighborhood's large gay population, plus the generally tolerant attitudes of the hip straights who live and visit here, encourages gay-friendliness at most South Beach venues that are not specifically gay, such that you'll have many options from which to choose. In fact many mixed clubs, like crobar, have one or two gay nights. Laundry Bar has a mixed scene, which also hosts a gay night, including one for the ladies. Generally gay life in Miami is overwhelmingly male-oriented, and lesbians, although welcome everywhere, will find themselves in the minority. To find out what's going on, pick up the South Beach club rags, ***Outlook*** and ***Hotspots,*** widely available as the weekend approaches, or the alternative weekly ***Wire*** (www.thewireonline).

### Bars and Lounges

**Cactus Nightclub.** In the northern reaches of downtown, this is the place to head if you don't want to stay up 'til 4 AM to get some nightlife in. Special events include drag nights, male strippers, and a very popular Noche Latina on Saturday. ✉ *2041 Biscayne Blvd., at 20th St., Downtown, Miami,* ☎ *305/438–0662.*

### Dance Clubs

**crobar.** Steamy club windows on Monday nights are due to the fantastically popular Back Door Bamby night, with go-go girls and boys. Keep in mind the carpeted dance floor—your lug soles will resist movement. ✉ *1445 Washington Ave., at 14th St., South Beach,* ☎ *305/531–5027.*

**Ozone.** One of the most popular men's dance clubs on the mainland, this South Miami multilevel dance complex attracts Latin and Anglo patrons in their 20s and 30s. Pool tables and other games offer an alternative to elbow bending. ✉ *6620 Red Rd., 1 block off U.S. 1, South Miami,* ☎ *305/667–2888.*

**Pump.** This afterhours club gets going at 3 AM, so you can party for breakfast. ✉ *841 Washington Ave., at 8th St., Miami Beach, South Beach,* ☎ *305/538–7867.*

**Score.** This popular Lincoln Road hangout draws a good-looking, largely younger crowd. There's loud dance music and an outdoor patio perfect for people-watching. The Sunday tea dance is packed, with a DJ spinning old disco tunes and progressive music. ✉ *727 Lincoln Rd., at Euclid Ave., South Beach,* ☎ *305/535–1111.*

**Twist.** This longtime hot spot and local favorite with two levels, an outdoor patio, and a game room is crowded from 8 PM on, especially on Monday, Thursday (2-for-1), and Friday nights. ✉ *1057 Washington Ave., at 10th St., South Beach,* ☎ *305/538–9478.*

## Live Music

**Churchill's Hideaway.** Never mind its off-the-beaten path location in Little Haiti—one of Miami's oldest rock clubs is the place for hard-driving live rock and, occasionally, national acts. ✉ *5501 N.E. 2nd Ave., at 55th St., Little Haiti, Miami,* ☎ *305/757–1807.*

**La Covacha.** This spot west of the airport has strayed a bit from its Latin roots by playing disco and non-Latin music. For the best in salsa, merengue, and Spanish pop, head here on a Friday night. ✉ *10730 N.W. 25th St., at 107th Ave., West Miami-Dade,* ☎ *305/594–3717.*

**Luna Star Cafe.** Yearning for the pre-electric '60s? Then head here and listen to folk and acoustic music, blues and jazz, with a little storytelling thrown in. There's a full menu, plus exotic coffees, beers, ales, ciders, and fruit-and-spice beverages to complete the folksy experience. ✉ *775 N.E. 125th St., at 7 Ave., North Miami,* ☎ *305/892–8522.*

**Satchmo Blues Bar & Grill.** Coral Gables' hot blues venue is packing in the crowds, especially on weekend nights. Local and national talent, a spacious and sleek layout with a great long bar, and tasty Cajun treats make Satchmo a must-visit for blues lovers. ✉ *60 Merrick Way, at Aragon Ave., Coral Gables,* ☎ *305/774–1883.*

**Van Dyke Café.** More restaurant than jazz club, this News Café spin-off hosts live jazz (or crooning Brazilian songstresses) on the second floor seven nights a week. Its location on South Beach's Lincoln Road Mall makes it a great spot to take a break during an evening shopping excursion or to stop for a drink after dinner. ✉ *846 Lincoln Rd., at Euclid Ave., South Beach,* ☎ *305/534–3600.*

# 6 OUTDOOR ACTIVITIES AND SPORTS

Greater Miami beaches, almost too numerous to mention, offer everything from jogging along oceanfront paths in Surfside to bathing with your dog on Virginia Key. Then there's diving on the nation's only living coral reef; windsurfing in a warm, shallow bay; canoeing past manatees in mangrove-shrouded tunnels; or angling for sailfish on the edge of the Gulf Stream. Add world-class golf and tennis resorts and championship professional teams to the mix, and you've got one action-packed destination.

SUN, SAND, AND CRYSTAL-CLEAR WATER mixed with an almost nonexistent winter and a cosmopolitan clientele make Miami and Miami Beach ideal for year-round sports and recreation. Water sports are hardly the whole picture. Greater Miami has championship golf and tennis courses, miles of bike trails along placid canals and through subtropical forests, and skater-friendly concrete paths under the elevated Metrorail. And it's hard to find a city with as many championship teams. The Miami Dolphins, the only NFL team to have ever played a perfect season, regularly make the playoffs, as do the NBA Heat. In major-league baseball, the Florida Marlins won the World Series after only five seasons, and are negotiating for a new downtown Miami stadium. On the intercollegiate level, the Miami Hurricanes, the alma mater of Warren Sapp, Edgerrin James, and Vinnie Testaverde, are top-10 contenders, with five national football championships since 1983. They have a new coach, Larry Coker, since Butch Davis defected to the NFL after months of saying he wouldn't.

By Kathy Foster

# BEACHES

Almost every side street in Miami Beach dead-ends at the ocean. Sandy shores also stretch along the southern side of the Rickenbacker Causeway to Key Biscayne, where you'll find two more popular beaches. Greater Miami is best known for its ocean beaches, but there's freshwater swimming here, too, in pools and lakes. Below are just a few highlights for the get-wet set.

## Miami Beach and North

You'll find plenty of parking and plenty of people at **Haulover Beach Park,** a county park. Tunnels leading from the beach to the lots are less than pristine, but folks still head here for swimming under the watchful gaze of lifeguards. The beach is nice for those who want to get to the water without a long march across hot sand, and at the north end of the shore, a rare clothing-optional beach lures people who want to tan every nook and cranny. There are facilities for barbecues, tennis, or volleyball, plus showers for rinsing off after a day in the sun and surf. Or check out the kite rentals, charter fishing excursions, and a par-3, 9-hole golf course. ✉ *10800 Collins Ave., north of Bal Harbour, North Miami Beach,* ☎ *305/947–3525.* 🎫 *$4 per car.* ⏲ *Daily dawn–dusk.*

A natural setting beckons at **North Shore Park Open Space** from 79th to 87th streets on Collins Avenue, Miami Beach. North Shore has a saltwater beach, and plenty of picnic tables, rest rooms, and healthy dunes. An exercise trail, concrete walkways, a playground, and lifeguards compromise or enhance the otherwise natural scene, depending on your point of view. You can park at a meter or in one of the pay lots across Collins Avenue. ✉ *7901 Collins Ave., south of Surfside, Miami Beach,* ☎ *305/993–2032.* 🎫 *$1 per person.* ⏲ *Daily 7–6.*

Across the Intracoastal Waterway from Haulover is **Oleta River State Recreation Area,** a thousand acres of subtropical beauty along Biscayne Bay. Swim in the calm bay waters and bicycle, canoe, and bask among egrets, manatees, bald eagles, and fiddler crabs. Highlights include picnic pavilions, five on the Intracoastal and two adjacent to a manmade swimming beach; a playground for tots; a mangrove island accessible only by boat; mountain bike trails; and primitive but air-conditioned cabins ($40 per night, reservations required) for those who wish to tackle the trails at night. ✉ *3400 N.E. 163rd St., North Miami*

*Beach,* ☎ *305/919–1846.* 🎟 *$1 on foot or bike, $4 per car with up to 8 people, $1 each additional.* ⊙ *Daily 8* AM*–sunset.*

*Parlez-vous français?* If you do, you'll feel quite comfortable at **Surfside Beach.** This stretch of beach is filled with the many French Canadians who spend the winter here. ✉ *Collins Ave. between 88th and 96th Sts., Surfside, Miami Beach.*

## South Beach

The **beach on Ocean Drive from 1st to 22nd streets**—primarily the 10-block stretch from 5th to 15th streets—is one of the most talked-about beachfronts in America. The beach is wide, white, and bathed by warm aquamarine waves. Separating the sand from the traffic of Ocean Drive is palm-fringed Lummus Park, with its volleyball nets and chickee huts for shade. The beach also has some of the funkiest lifeguard stands you'll ever see, pop stars shooting music videos, and visitors from all over the world. Popular with gays is the beach at **12th Street.** Because much of South Beach has an adult flavor—women are often casually topless, many families prefer the beach's quieter southern reaches, especially **3rd Street Beach** (✉ Ocean Dr. and 3rd St., South Beach). Unless you're parking south of 3rd Street, metered spaces near the waterfront are rarely empty. Instead, opt for a public garage and walk; you'll have lots of fun people-watching, too. ☎ *305/673–7714.*

You can't swim at **South Pointe Park,** but you can walk or bicycle out on 50-yard Sunshine Pier, which adjoins the 1-mi-long jetty at the mouth of Government Cut. It's a great place to fish or watch huge cruise ships pass. No bait or tackle is available in the park. Facilities include two observation towers, rest rooms, and volleyball courts. ✉ *1 Washington Ave., South Beach.*

## Key Biscayne and Virginia Key

Beyond Key Biscayne's commercial district, at the southern tip of the island, is **Bill Baggs Cape Florida State Recreation Area,** a natural oasis with great beaches, sea grass–studded dunes, blue-green waters, and plenty of native plants and trees. The 410-acre park has a restored lighthouse, 18 picnic shelters, and two cafés that serve beer and wine and meals that range from hot dogs to lobster. A stroll or bike ride along paths and boardwalks provides wonderful views of the bay and Miami's skyline. Also on site are bicycle, skate, kayak, and people-powered water-bike rentals, plus a playground and fishing platforms. ✉ *1200 S. Crandon Blvd., Key Biscayne,* ☎ *305/361–5811 or 305/361–8779.* 🎟 *$4 per vehicle with up to 8 people, $1 per person on bicycle, bus, motorbike, or foot.* ⊙ *Daily 8–sunset, lighthouse tours Thurs.–Mon. 9:30 and 12:30.*

The 3½-mi-long beach at **Crandon Park** has been rated among the top 10 in North America by the University of Maryland's esteemed Dr. Beach. The sand is soft, there's a great view of the Atlantic, and parking is inexpensive and plentiful. On busy days be prepared for a long hike from your car to the beach. There are bathrooms, outdoor showers, plenty of picnic tables and concession stands, and a restored carousel (open weekends 10–5, until 7 PM in summer, admission $1). Marine-theme play sculptures, a dolphin-shape spray fountain, and an old-fashioned outdoor roller rink draw kids to the beachfront playground. Skates rent for $5 an hour. At the park's north end is the just-completed $4 million **Marjory Stoneman Douglas Nature Center** (☎ 305/361–6767). ✉ *4000 Crandon Blvd., Key Biscayne,* ☎ *305/361–5421.* 🎟 *$4 per vehicle.* ⊙ *Daily 8–dusk.*

Just after crossing the causeway onto Virginia Key, you'll see a long strip of bay front popular with windsurfers and sailboaters, called **Hobie Beach** after the Hobie Cats that set sail from the shore. It's also the only Miami-area beach that allows dogs. Nearby rest rooms and a great view of the curving shoreline make this an ideal place to park and have your own tailgate party. ✉ *South side of Rickenbacker Causeway, Virginia Key,* ☎ *305/361–1281.* *Expressway toll $1 per vehicle.* *Daily dawn–dusk.*

## Coral Gables

Among the estates along historic Old Cutler Road, in an area few visitors realize is part of Coral Gables, is **Matheson Hammock Park.** Named for the type of characteristically Floridian ecosystem found here (not for a preponderance of hammocks swinging from trees), Miami-Dade County's oldest park is one of its most appealing, with a bathing beach separated by a narrow walking path from peaceful Biscayne Bay. Even the parking lot is on the bay. The beach's slowly sloping shore is ideal for children. The park has plenty of lush walking and bike trails, picnic tables under towering trees, changing facilities, showers and bathrooms, plus a seafood restaurant. ✉ *9610 Old Cutler Rd., Coral Gables,* ☎ *305/665–5475.* *$4 per car.* *Daily 6–sunset.*

## Kendall

**Larry and Penny Thompson Park,** a Miami secret, is a laid-back and beautiful 243-acre county park with a 35-acre freshwater lake, white-sand beach, water slide, and concession stand. ✉ *12451 S.W. 184th St., take Exit 13S on Florida's Turnpike–Rte. 821, go 1 mi west, South Miami,* ☎ *305/232–1049.* *$2 lake, $3 beach and waterslide.* *Memorial Day–Labor Day, daily 10–6.*

# PARTICIPANT SPORTS

## Ballooning

**Balloonport of Coconut Grove** offers an aerial view of Miami-Dade, from the Atlantic Ocean to the Everglades. Because of South Florida's unusual wind patterns, balloon flights take place in early morning. Owner Don Kaplan gives his passengers a 5:30 AM wake-up call, setting up a meeting spot along U.S. 1 south of Miami. From there the launch site is determined by the wind. Time spent in flight is about an hour, and a champagne toast celebrates the landing. Balloons hold from two to seven passengers. ✉ *Box 1211, Miami, 33233,* ☎ *305/858–2719.* *$150 per person. Reservations essential.*

## Bicycling

Perfect weather and flat terrain make Miami-Dade County a popular place for cyclists. Add a free color-coded map that points out streets best suited for bicycles, rated from best to worst, and it's even better. Also available are printouts listing parks with multiuse paths and information about local bike clubs. The map is available from bike shops and also from the **Miami-Dade County Bicycle Coordinator** (✉ Metropolitan Planning Organization, 111 N.W. 1st St., Suite 910, Miami 33128, ☎ 305/375–1647), whose purpose is to share with you the glories of bicycling in South Florida. There's some especially good cycling to be had in South Miami-Dade.

Hook up with local riders through **Aventura Riders** (☎ 305/937–4463). Casual rides of about 18 mi follow different routes each week starting at 10 AM Sunday at the Waterway Shops, at Aventura at Northeast 207th Street east of Biscayne Boulevard (U.S. 1). Information on dozens of monthly group rides is available from the **Everglades Bicycle Club** (☎ 305/598–3998). For a free map of the 10 mi of traffic-free bike trails on Key Biscayne, stop by **Mangrove Cycles** (✉ 260 Crandon Blvd., Key Biscayne, ☎ 305/361–5555), which also rents bikes for $7 for two hours or $10 per day. Another rental option is the **Miami Beach Bicycle Center** (✉ 601 5th St., Miami Beach, ☎ 305/674–0150), which rents for $20 per day or $5 per hour. Tours of the Deco District are given once a month.

Riders who want to take it easy can visit **Bill Baggs Cape Florida State Recreation Area,** where you can pedal into the park and follow the paved, speed-controlled road to the beach, picnic areas, or lighthouse. If you arrive by car, park near the lighthouse and catch the paved path that meanders for 2 mi along Biscayne Bay and through the tropical hardwoods.

The Old Cutler Trail, a popular leisurely bike ride, leads 2 mi south from Cocoplum Circle (at the end of Sunset Drive in Coral Gables) to Matheson Hammock Park and Fairchild Tropical Garden. You can turn into **Matheson Hammock Park** (✉ 9610 Old Cutler Rd., Coral Gables, ☎ 305/665–5475) and take a bike path a mile through the mangroves to Biscayne Bay. You'll feel as if you've discovered South Florida before the Spanish conquistadors arrived.

There aren't any mountains within 500 mi of Miami, but **Oleta River State Recreation Area** (☎ 305/919–1846) does have challenging dirt trails with hills and views of Biscayne Bay for experienced all-terrain bikers. Several miles of new trails were added for technical riding and speed. Still under construction is a teeter-totter bridge and an elevated boardwalk over an area that floods in rainy season. Admission is $1 for bicyclists.

## Fitness Classes and Gyms

Miami is like L.A. in the sense that gym culture is, well, culture, so you won't have a hard time finding a place to workout, especially in South Beach. **Club Body Tech** (✉ 1253 Washington Ave., between 12th and 13th Sts., South Beach, ☎ 305/674–8222) is for the already fit and buff. But what did you expect? You're in Miami. Day passes are $14, and the gym's equipment is worth it. **Crunch Fitness** (✉ 1259 Washington Ave., South Beach, ☎ 305/674–8222 or 305/674–0247 for class schedule), the leader in forward-thinking classes and gym fashion, will sell you a day pass for about $20 or a 3-day one for $50, which is good for most classes, equipment, and weights.

## Fishing

In Greater Miami, before there was fashion, there was fishing. Deep-sea fishing is still a major draw, and anglers drop a line for sailfish, kingfish, dolphin, snapper, wahoo, grouper, and tuna. Small charter boats cost $450–$500 for a half day and provide everything but food and drinks. If you're on a budget, you might be better off paying around $30 for passage on a larger fishing boat—rarely are they filled to capacity. Most charters have a 50–50 plan, which allows you to take (or sell) half your catch while they do the same. Just don't let anyone sell you an individual fishing license; a blanket license for the boat should cover all passengers.

**Crandon Park Marina.** Crandon Park has earned an international reputation for its knowledgeable charter-boat captains and good catches.

Heading out to the edge of the Gulf Stream (about 3 to 4 mi), you're sure to wind up with something on your line (sailfish are catch-and-release). ✉ *4000 Crandon Blvd., Key Biscayne,* ☎ *305/361-1281.* 🎟 *6-passenger boats $750 full day, $500 half day (5 hrs).*

**Haulover Beach Park.** Plenty of ocean-fishing charters depart from Haulover Beach Park, including **Blue Waters Sportfishing Charters** (☎ 305/944-4531, 🎟 6-passenger boats, $750 full day, $450 half day), the **Kelley Fleet** (☎ 305/945-3801, 🎟 65- or 85-ft party boats, $29 per person), ***Therapy IV*** (☎ 305/945-1578, 🎟 6-passenger boat, $90 per person), and about 10 others. ✉ *Haulover Beach Park, 10800 Collins Ave., north of Bal Harbour, North Miami Beach,* ☎ *305/947-3525.* 🎟 *$4 per car.* ⏲ *Daily dawn-dusk.*

**Miami Beach Marina.** Charters from here include the two-boat **Reward Fleet** (☎ 305/372-9470). Rates run $30 per person including bait, rod, reel, and tackle; $15 for kids. ✉ *MacArthur Causeway, 300 Alton Rd., Miami Beach,* ☎ *305/673-6000.*

**Key Biscayne.** If you want to take out a boat to fish in the bay, the **Key Biscayne Boat Rentals** rents six-passenger, 21-ft open Fisherman motorboats for $120 for two hours, $195 for a half day, and $275 for a day. ✉ *3301 Rickenbacker Causeway, Virginia Key,* ☎ *305/361-7368.*

## Golf

Greater Miami has more than 30 private and public courses. Costs at most courses are higher on weekends and in season, but you can save by playing on weekdays and after 1 or 3 PM, depending on the course—call ahead to find out when afternoon-twilight rates go into effect. To get a **"Golfer's Guide for South Florida,"** which includes information on most courses in Miami and surrounding areas, call ☎ 800/864-6101. The cost is $3.

The 18-hole, par-71 championship **Biltmore Golf Course,** known for its scenic layout, has been restored to its original Donald Ross design, circa 1925. Greens fees range from $29 to $55 in season, and the gorgeous hotel makes a great backdrop. ✉ *1210 Anastasia Ave., Coral Gables,* ☎ *305/460-5364.* 🎟 *Optional cart $21.*

The **California Golf Club** has an 18-hole, par-72 course, with a tight front nine and three of the area's toughest finishing holes. A round of 18 holes will set you back between $30 and $50, cart included. ✉ *20898 San Simeon Way, North Miami Beach,* ☎ *305/651-3590.* 🎟 *Cart required, $18.*

Overlooking the bay, the **Crandon Golf Course,** formerly the Links at Key Biscayne, is a top-rated 18-hole, par-72 public course in a beautiful tropical setting. Expect to pay around $131 for a round in winter, $52 in summer, cart included. After 3, the winter rate drops to $36. The Royal Caribbean Classic is held here. ✉ *6700 Crandon Blvd., Key Biscayne,* ☎ *305/361-9129.*

**Don Shula's Hotel & Golf Club,** in northern Miami, has one of the longest championship courses in Miami (7,055 yards, par-72), a lighted par-3 course, and a golf school, and it hosts more than 100 tournaments a year. Weekdays you can play the championship course for $100, $140 on weekends; golf carts are included. The lighted par-3 course is $12 weekdays, $15 weekends, and $15 for an optional cart. ✉ *7601 Miami Lakes Dr., off Rte. 826, Miami Lakes,* ☎ *305/820-8106.*

Among its six courses and many annual tournaments, the **Doral Golf Resort and Spa,** just west of Miami proper, is best known for the par-

72 Blue Monster course and the annual Genuity Championship, with $2 million in prize money. Fees range from $195 to $275. Carts are not required, but there's no discount for walking. ✉ *4400 N.W. 87th Ave., off Rte. 826, Doral, Miami,* ☎ *305/592–2000 or 800/713–6725.*

For a casual family outing or for beginners, the 9-hole, par-3 **Haulover Golf Course** is right on the Intracoastal Waterway at the north end of Miami Beach. The longest hole on this walking course is 120 yards; greens fees are only $6, less on weekdays for senior citizens. ✉ *Haulover Beach Park, 10800 Collins Ave., north of Bal Harbour, North Miami Beach,* ☎ *305/940–6719.*

**Normandy Shores Golf Course,** on its own little bay-side island between South Beach and Surfside, is good for senior citizens, with some modest slopes and average distances; it's par-71. The $55 per-person fee includes cart. ✉ *2401 Biarritz Dr., Isle of Normandy, Miami Beach,* ☎ *305/868–6502.*

**Turnberry Isle Resort & Club** has 36 holes designed by Robert Trent Jones Sr., but only hotel guests can play them. Par is 70 on the North Course and 72 on the South. Fees, including a mandatory cart, range from $121 to $145. Proper golf shoes are required. ✉ *19999 W. Country Club Dr., Aventura,* ☎ *305/933–6929.*

## In-Line Skating

Miami Beach's ocean vistas, wide sidewalks, and flat terrain make it a perfect locale for in-line skating. And don't the locals know it. Very popular is the **Lincoln Road Mall** from Washington Avenue to Alton Road; many of the pedestrian mall's restaurants let you keep your skates on and eat inside. For a great view of the Art Deco District and action on South Beach, skate along the sidewalk on the east side of **Ocean Drive** from 5th to 14th streets. In South Miami, an often-traversed concrete path winds **under the elevated Metrorail** from Vizcaya Station (across U.S. 1 from the Miami Museum of Science) to Red Road at U.S. 1 (across from the Shops at Sunset Place). You don't have to bring your own; a number of in-line skate shops offer rentals that include protective gear.

**Fritz's Skate and Bike Shop** (✉ 730 Lincoln Rd., South Beach, ☎ 305/532–1954) charges $8 an hour, $15 overnight (6 PM–noon), or $4, 10–10). **Skate 2000** (✉ 9525 S. Dixie Hwy., Pinecrest, ☎ 305/665–6770) has rates as low as $10 a day.

## Jogging

There are numerous places to run in Miami, but the routes recommended below are considered among the safest and most scenic. **Foot Works** (✉ 5724 Sunset Dr., South Miami, ☎ 305/667–9322), a running-shoe store that sponsors races and organizes marathon training, is a great source of information. The **Miami Runners Club** (✉ 8720 N. Kendall Dr., Suite 206, Miami, ☎ 305/227–1500) has information on running-related matters, such as routes and races.

The beachside **Bal Harbour** jogging path begins at the southern boundary of town, where it connects with the Surfside path. Mostly made of hard-packed sand and gravel at this point, the path turns into paved brick behind the Sheraton Bal Harbour. This jogging trail, which runs between the hotels and the ocean, will take you about 2 mi, ending at the Haulover Cut passageway between the Intracoastal Waterway and the Atlantic Ocean, a popular fishing spot.

In **Coconut Grove** follow the pedestrian-bicycle path on South Bayshore Drive, cutting over the causeway to Key Biscayne for a longer run and a chance to jog uphill on the two wide bridges linking the key to the mainland. **Coral Gables** has a jogging path around the Riviera Country Club golf course, south of the Biltmore Country Club. From the south shore of the Miami River in **downtown Miami,** you can run south along the sidewalks of Brickell Avenue, turn left on 8th Street and right on Brickell Bay Drive, and continue along the bay to Southeast 15th Street.

In **South Beach** good running options are Bay Road, parallel to Alton Road, or the Ocean Drive sidewalk across the street from the art deco hotels and outdoor cafés. And, of course, you can run right along the Atlantic on the beach. One good route is to follow the ramp down to the beach at 21st Street, then jog south along the hard-packed sand all the way to South Pointe Park, at the southernmost tip of Miami Beach. There you can get a great view of Government Cut, the passageway that cargo and cruise ships take as they leave the Port of Miami and head out toward the Bahamas or the Caribbean. You also get a close-up view of the ultra-chic, multimillion-dollar condos on Fisher Island, on the far side of Government Cut.

**Surfside,** north of Miami Beach, has brilliant ocean vistas. You can park your car on any side street near 87th Street and Collins Avenue and walk onto the sand. Climb the rise to the path that looks like a levee. This elevated hard-packed, sand-and-gravel trail, which runs between the condos and hotels and the beach from 87th to 96th streets, gives you a clear view of the ocean. Another plus is that it's off-limits to skaters and bikers.

## Tennis

Miami-Dade has more than a dozen tennis centers and nearly 500 public courts open to visitors; nonresidents are charged an hourly fee. Some courts take reservations on weekdays.

**Biltmore Tennis Center** has 10 hard courts and a view of the beautiful Biltmore Hotel. ✉ *1150 Anastasia Ave., Coral Gables,* ☎ *305/460–5360.* 🎫 *Day rate $4.50, night rate $5.50, per person per hr.* ⏲ *Weekdays 7 AM–10 PM, weekends 7–8.*

Very popular with locals, **Flamingo Tennis Center** has 19 clay courts smack dab in the middle of Miami Beach. You can't get much closer to the action. ✉ *1000 12th St., South Beach,* ☎ *305/673–7761.* 🎫 *Day rate $2.67, night rate $3.20, per person per hr.* ⏲ *Weekdays 8 AM–9 PM, weekends 8–8.*

**North Shore Tennis Center,** part of Miami Beach's North Shore Park, has nine lighted courts, six clay, and three hard courts. Two additional hard courts are for daytime use only. ✉ *350 73rd St., at Harding Ave., near Isle of Normandy, Miami Beach,* ☎ *305/993–2022.* 🎫 *Day rate $2.66, night rate $3.20, per person per hr.* ⏲ *Weekdays 8 AM–9 PM, weekends 8–7.*

The 30-acre **Tennis Center at Crandon Park** is one of America's best. Included are 2 grass, 8 clay, and 17 hard courts. Reservations are required for night play. The only time courts are closed to the public is during the NASDAQ-100 Open. ✉ *7300 Crandon Blvd., Key Biscayne,* ☎ *305/365–2300.* 🎫 *Laykold courts: day rate $3, night rate $5, per person per hr. Clay and grass courts: $6 per person per hr day rate.* ⏲ *Daily 8 AM–9 PM.*

## Water Sports

Whatever your aquatic pleasure, Greater Miami can fulfill it. As if the Atlantic Ocean and Biscayne Bay were not enough, rivers, lagoons, canals, and lakes abound. One-stop equipment shopping can be had at **Water Play** (✉ 2220 Coral Way, at S.W. 22nd Ave., Coral Gables, ☎ 305/860–0888). The store sells gear for kayaking, windsurfing, sailing, and skiing—and can direct you to vendors that organize excursions.

## Canoeing and Kayaking

Looking at Miami's skyscrapers, it's hard to remember the outback is so close. Canoe-friendly canals crisscross the city, leading from urban areas to parks or to Biscayne Bay.

Canoes and kayaks are perfect for **Oleta River State Recreation Area,** an unexpected natural watersource in the middle of a bustling commercial district, near Intercoastal Mall—although it rents paddle boats, too. Rentals come with a map showing the various mangrove channels splitting off the Intracoastal Waterway. Allow about an hour to paddle the canals, where you'll spot wading herons, crabs scuttling among the hairy mangrove roots, and maybe a lumbering manatee. ✉ *3400 N.E. 163rd St., North Miami Beach, North Miami,* ☎ *305/919–1846.* *$1 on foot or bike; $4 per vehicle with up to 8 people, $1 each additional; canoes $12 per hr, $30 half-day, $35 day, $45 overnight; kayaks $12 per hr, $20 half-day, $25 day, $30 overnight.* ⏲ *Daily 8 AM–dusk.*

On Key Biscayne, and Windsurfer Beach to be exact, **Sailboards Miami** (✉ 1 Rickenbacker Causeway, Key Biscayne, ☎ 305/361–7245), ⅓ mi past the causeway toll plaza, rents kayaks for $13 per hour for a single, $18 for a double. Right on the bay, **Shake-A-Leg** (✉ 2600 S. Bayshore Dr., Coconut Grove, ☎ 305/858–5550), a nonprofit organization for the physically and mentally disabled and for youth at risk, also rents kayaks to the general public for $10 an hour, $30 for four hours; doubles $15 per hour, $45 for four hours.

You can rent and launch a kayak at **Bill Baggs Cape Florida State Recreation Area** (✉ 1200 S. Crandon Blvd., Key Biscayne, ☎ 305/361–5811 or 305/361–8779). **Matheson Hammock Park** (✉ 9610 Old Cutler Rd., Coral Gables, ☎ 305/665–5475) has a launch site but no rentals.

A favorite **South Miami put-in spot** for a bring-your-own canoe or kayak is just beyond the locks on the east side of Red Road, south of South Miami and near the former site of the original Parrot Jungle & Gardens (✉ 11000 S.W. 57th Ave., at S.W. 112th St., Pinecrest, South Miami). From here it's an easy paddle to Biscayne Bay. Parrot Jungle & Gardens moved to Watson Island in 2003.

To get away from it all, take a canoe or kayak to **Black Point Park** (✉ 24775 S.W. 87th Ave., north of the 79th St. Causeway Bascule Bridge, Cutler Ridge, ☎ 305/258–4092). The put-in spot is past the picnic pavilion. Within 100 yards you'll come to a lagoon; immediately to the east is Biscayne Bay; to the north is a waterway filled with mangrove hammocks to explore.

## Diving and Snorkeling

Diving and snorkeling on the off-shore coral wrecks and reefs on a calm day can be comparable to the Caribbean. Chances are excellent you'll come face to face with a flood of tropical fish. One option is to find Fowey, Triumph, Long, and Emerald reefs in 10- to 15-ft dives that are perfect for snorkelers and beginning divers. On the edge of the continental shelf a little more than 3 mi out, these reefs are just ¼ mi away from depths greater than 100 ft. Another option is to paddle around the tangled prop roots of the mangrove trees that line the coast, peering at the fish, crabs, and other creatures hiding there.

It's a bit of a drive, but the best diving and definitely the best snorkeling to be had in Miami-Dade is on the incredible living coral reefs in **Biscayne National Park,** in the rural southeast corner of the county.

Perhaps the area's most unusual diving options are the **artificial reefs.** Since 1981, Miami-Dade County's Department of Environmental Resources Management (DERM) has sunk tons of limestone boulders and a water tower, army tanks, a 727 jet, and almost 200 boats of all descriptions to create a "wreckreational" habitat where divers can swim with yellow tang, barracudas, nurse sharks, snapper, eels, and grouper. Most dive shops sell a book listing the location of these wrecks. Information on wreck diving can be obtained from the Miami Beach Chamber of Commerce. (✉ 1920 Meridian Ave., South Beach, Miami Beach, ☎ 305/672–1270).

**Bubbles Dive Center** (✉ 2671 S.W. 27th Ave., at Unity Blvd., Miami, ☎ 305/856–0565), an all-purpose dive shop with PADI affiliation, runs night and wreck dives right in the center of it all. Its boat, *Divers Dream,* berths at Watson Island Marina on Watson Island off I–395. From the full-service **Crandon Park Marina** (✉ 4000 Crandon Blvd., Key Biscayne, ☎ 305/361–1281), you can also embark on scuba dives. **Divers Paradise of Key Biscayne** (✉ 4000 Crandon Blvd., Key Biscayne, ☎ 305/361–3483) has a complete dive shop and diving-charter service next to the Crandon Park Marina, including equipment rental and scuba instruction with PADI affiliation. The PADI-affiliated **Diving Locker** (✉ 223 Sunny Isles Blvd., Sunny Isles North Miami Beach, ☎ 305/947–6025) sells, services, and repairs scuba equipment, plus it has three-day and three-week international certification courses as well as more advanced certifications. The three-day accelerated course for beginners is $350. Wreck and reef sites are reached aboard fast and comfortable six-passenger dive boats.

## Pool

The 825,000-gallon **Venetian Pool,** fed by artesian wells, is so unique it's on the National Register of Historic Places. The picturesque pool design and lush landscaping place it head-and-shoulders over typical public pools, and a snack bar, lockers, showers, and free parking make an afternoon here pleasant and convenient. Children must be at least 38″ tall or three years old. ✉ *2701 De Soto Blvd., Coral Gables,* ☎ *305/460–5356.* 🎟 *$5–$8, free parking across De Soto Blvd.* ⏲ *June–Aug., weekdays 11–7:30, weekends 10–4:30; Sept.–Oct. and Apr.–May, Tues.–Fri. 11–5:30, weekends 10–4:30; Nov.–Mar., Tues.–Sun. 10–4:30.*

## Sailing and Yachting

Boating, whether on sailboats, power boats, or luxury yachts, is a passion in greater Miami. The Intracoastal Waterway, wide and sheltered Biscayne Bay, and the Atlantic Ocean provide ample opportunities for fun aboard all types of watercraft.

### MARINAS

Named for an island where early settlers had picnics, **Dinner Key Marina** is Greater Miami's largest, with nearly 600 moorings slips at nine piers. There's space for transients and a boat ramp. ✉ *3400 Pan American Dr., Coconut Grove,* ☎ *305/579–6980.*

**Haulover Marine Center,** which has a bait-and-tackle shop and a 24-hour marine gas station, is low on glamour but high on service. ✉ *15000 Collins Ave., north of Bal Harbour, North Miami Beach,* ☎ *305/945–3934.*

Near the Art Deco District, **Miami Beach Marina** (✉ MacArthur Causeway, 300 Alton Rd., Miami Beach, ☎ 305/673–6000) has about every marine facility imaginable—restaurants, charters, boat and vehicle rentals, a complete marine-hardware store, a dive shop, excursion vendors, a large grocery store, a fuel dock, concierge services, and 400 slips accommodating vessels of up to 190 ft. There's also a U.S. Customs clearing station and a charter service, Florida Yacht Charters.

One of the busiest marinas in Coconut Grove is **Monty's Marina,** handy if you've brought your own vessel but otherwise of little interest to visitors. ✉ *2640 S. Bayshore Dr., Coconut Grove,* ☎ *305/854–7997.*

RENTALS AND CHARTERS

You can rent power boats 20- to 34-ft in length through **Club Nautico,** a national power boat rental company. Half- to full-day rentals range from $229 to $1,250. You may want to consider buying a club membership; it'll cost a bundle at first, but you'll save about 60% on all your future rentals. ✉ *2560 Bayshore Dr., Coconut Grove,* ☎ *305/858–6258;* ✉ *5420 Crandon Blvd., Key Biscayne,* ☎ *305/361–9217.*

Whether you're looking to be on the water for a few hours or a few days, **Cruzan Yacht Charters** is a good choice for renting manned or unmanned sailboats and motor yachts. If you plan to captain the boat yourself, expect a three- to four-hour checkout cruise and at least a $400 daily rate (three-day minimum). ✉ *3375 Pan American Dr., Coconut Grove,* ☎ *305/858–2822 or 800/628–0785.*

Although **Matheson Hammock Park** (✉ 9610 Old Cutler Rd., Coral Gables, ☎ 305/665–5475) has no charter services, it does have 252 slips and boat ramps. **Castle Harbor** (☎ 305/665–4994, WEB www.castleharbor.com), in operation since 1949, rents sailboats for those with U.S. Sailing certification and classes for those without. When you're ready to rent, take your pick of a 22-ft Capri ($190 per day) or a 23-ft Ensign (about $130 per day).

The family-owned, **Florida Yacht Charters** (✉ MacArthur Causeway, 300 Alton Rd., Miami Beach, ☎ 305/532–8600 or 800/537–0050), at the full-service Miami Beach Marina, will give you the requisite checkout cruise and paperwork, then you can take off for the Keys or the Bahamas on a catamaran, sailboat, or motor yacht. Charts, lessons, and captains are available if needed.

## Wave Runners

Vendors on Miami Beach and Virginia Key rent gas-powered Wave Runners, known also as jet skis, by the hour (a minimum age of 18 or 19 often applies). Rates are about $60–$80. If you call in advance, Super Jet Bike can arrange wave-runner excursions off Fisher Island, Key Biscayne, or Star Island.

➤ WAVE RUNNER VENDORS: **Key Biscayne Boat Rentals** (✉ 3301 Rickenbacker Causeway, Virginia Key, ☎ 305/361–7368). **Super Jet Bike** (✉ near 2nd St. and Ocean Dr., South Beach, ☎ 305/318–9268).

## Windsurfing

Windsurfing is more popular than ever in Miami Beach. The best spots are at **1st Street** (north of the Government Cut jetty) and at **21st Street**; you can also windsurf around 3rd, 10th, and 14th streets. The safest and most popular windsurfing area in city waters is south of town at **Hobie Beach** (✉ south side of Rickenbacker Causeway, Virginia Key).

The friendly folks at **Sailboards Miami** (✉ 1 Rickenbacker Causeway, Key Biscayne, ☎ 305/361–7245), ⅓ mi past the causeway toll plaza, rent equipment and say they teach more windsurfers each year than anyone in the United States. Rentals average $20 for one hour, $38 for two hours, and $150 for 10 hours. They promise to teach anyone to windsurf within two hours—for $69.

## Yoga

**Miami YogaShala** (✉ 747 4th St., at Meridian Ave., South Beach, ☎ 305/538–4059, WEB www.miamiyoga.com) has basic and ashtanga classes daily (guided ashtanga is recommended for all levels), many taught by notable yogi Fred Busch ($14). **Synergy Center for Yoga and the Healing Arts** (✉ 435 Española Way, at Drexel Ave., South Beach, ☎ 305/ 538–7073, FAX 305/538–1244, WEB www.synergyyoga.org) has a range of courses offered daily ($14)—one of which is offered on the beach and only costs $5 (bring a towel)—plus specialty workshops and body work treatments.

# SPECTATOR SPORTS

In addition to contacting the venues directly, you can get tickets to major sporting events from **Ticketmaster** (☎ 305/358–5885).

## Auto Racing

**Hialeah Speedway** holds stock-car races on a ⅓-mi asphalt oval in a 5,000-seat stadium. Don't be fooled: the enthusiasm of the local drivers makes this as exciting as Winston Cup races. Five divisions of cars run weekly. The Marion Edwards, Jr., Memorial Race, for late-model cars, is held in December. The speedway is on U.S. 27, ¼ mi east of the Palmetto Expressway (Route 826). ✉ *3300 W. Okeechobee Rd., Hialeah,* ☎ *305/821–6644.* *$10, special events $15.* *Sat., gates open at 5 PM, races 7–11. Closed mid-Dec.–late Jan.*

For Winston Cup events, head south to the **Homestead–Miami Speedway,** which brought the NASCAR Winston Cup Series to South Florida for the first time with the 1999 Penzoil 400. The Winston Cup race highlights the speedway schedule and is held annually on the second Sunday in November in conjunction with the Miami 300, part of the NASCAR Busch series. The racing facility, built in 1995, is also home to the Infiniti Grand Prix of Miami (March 2003), and Indy car racing. Other major races include the Grand Am Sports Car Event in spring and a NASCAR Craftsmen Truck Series in fall. From Miami take Florida's Turnpike (Route 821) south to Exit 6, at Southwest 137th Avenue. ✉ *1 Speedway Blvd., Homestead,* ☎ *305/230–7223.* *Weekdays 9–5.* *Prices vary according to event.*

## Baseball

The **Florida Marlins** (☎ 305/626–7400, WEB www.marlins.mlb.com) won the 1997 World Series in only their fifth season. Although the team was split up afterward, its sale to John W. Henry in 1999, the energy of young new players, and the possibility of a new rainproof stadium renewed excitement of fans. But difficulty in finding a new stadium has since put the team's future in doubt. The season runs from April to the beginning of October; for now, the team plays at **Pro Player Stadium,** 16 mi northwest of downtown. (✉ 2267 N.W. 199th St., Lake Lucerne, Miami, ☎ 305/626–7426, WEB www.pro-player-stadium.com. $4–$55, parking $9).

To watch a national championship team, catch the **Miami Hurricanes** at Mark Light Stadium. The team, coached by Jim Morris, has advanced to the NCAA College World Series in seven of his eight series at Miami, including the 2001 national championship, a title they have won four times. ✉ *University of Miami campus, corner of San Amaro Dr. and Ponce De León, Coral Gables,* ☎ *305/284–2263 or 800/462–2637,* WEB *www.miamihurricanes.com.* *$5–$15, parking free.*

## Basketball

The **Miami Heat,** four-time defending NBA Atlantic Division champs (1996–97 through 1999–2000), play at the 19,600-seat, waterfront AmericanAirlines Arena. The state-of-the-art venue has indoor fireworks, restaurants, a wide patio overlooking Biscayne Bay, and a special-effect scoreboard that resembles a metallic sea anemone with tentacles holding wide-screen TVs. During Heat games, when the 1,100 underground parking spaces are reserved for season ticket holders, you can park at Bayside, at metered spaces along Biscayne Boulevard, or in lots on side streets, where prices range from $5 two blocks from the arena to $25 across the street (a limited number of disabled spaces are available on-site for nonseason ticket holders for $25). Better yet take the Metromover to the Park West or Freedom Tower station. Home games are held November through April. ✉ *AmericanAirlines Arena, 601 Biscayne Blvd., Downtown, Miami,* ☎ *786/777–4328; 800/462–2849 ticket hot line,* WEB *www.nba.com/heat.* 🎟 *$10–$180.*

The WNBA **Miami Sol** is gearing up for its fourth season. Made up of professional female athletes including Olympic medalist, Sandy Brondello, and NCAA center, Ruth Riley, who led Notre Dame to its first national title victory in 2001. The team plays a 32-game season June through August at AmericanAirlines Arena. They're coached by Ron Rothstein, the first head coach for the Miami Heat. ✉ *AmericanAirlines Arena, 601 Biscayne Blvd., Downtown, Miami,* ☎ *786/777–4765 (4SOL),* WEB *www.wnba.com/sol.* 🎟 *$6–$52.*

After years of trying to gain recognition in a city accustomed to championship teams, the **University of Miami Hurricanes** (☎ 305/284–2263 or 800/462–2263, WEB www.hurricanesports.com) basketball team has finally hit the big time. Reborn in the mid-'80s after a two-decade hiatus, the team, part of the Big East Conference, won the Big East regular season title for 2000 and advanced to the Sweet Sixteen in the NCAA Basketball Tournament. Now coached by Perry Clark, the Hurricanes have been NCAA top 25 contenders for the last four years. The new Ryder Center opens for the 2002–2003 season and seats 7,000 fans on the UM campus in Coral Gables. In the meantime, the Hurricanes play home games during the November–March season at downtown's Ryder Center (✉ 1 Dauer Dr., Coral Gables, ☎ 305/530–4400. 🎟 $15–$20, parking $5–$7.50).

## Dog Racing

**Flagler Greyhound Track** has dog races during its June–November season and a poker room that's open when the track is running. Closed-circuit TV brings harness-racing action here as well. The track is five minutes east of Miami International Airport, off Dolphin Expressway (Route 836) and Douglas Road (N.W. 37th Avenue). ✉ *401 N.W. 38th Ct., Little Havana, Miami,* ☎ *305/649–3000.* 🎟 *Free for grandstand and clubhouse, parking free–$3.* ⏲ *Racing Mon.–Sun. 8:05 PM, Tues., Thurs., and Sat. 1:05 PM.*

## Football

Consistently ranked as one of the top teams in the NFL, the **Miami Dolphins** (☎ 305/620–2578), under new head coach Dave Wannstedt, are continuing the winning tradition. Year in and year out, the Dolphins have one of the largest average attendance figures in the league. Fans may be secretly hoping to see a repeat of the 1972 perfect season, when the team, led by legendary coach Don Shula, compiled a 17–0 record (a record that still stands). September through January, on home game days, the Metro Miami-Dade Transit Agency runs buses to **Pro Player Stadium,** 16 mi northwest of downtown. (✉ 2267 N.W. 199th St., Lake Lucerne, Miami, ☎ 305/626–7426. 🎫 $20–$140, parking $20).

Also worth checking out is the **University of Miami Hurricanes** (☎ 305/284–2263 or 800/462–2637, WEB www.hurricanesports.com) football team. A powerhouse within the Big East Conference, the team is regularly a top-10 contender, with five national football championships since 1983. An undefeated season included a climactic win at the 2001 Rose Bowl. During the September–November season, the home-team advantage is measured in decibels, as about 45,000 fans literally rock the stadium when the team is on a roll. They play their home games at venerable **Orange Bowl Stadium** (✉ 1145 N.W. 11th St., Downtown, Miami, ☎ 305/575–5240. 🎫 $30–$40, parking $15–$20).

## Golf

The week of festivities planned around the PGA's **Genuity Open** (☎ 305/820–8106) brings hoards of pro-golf aficionados to the Doral Golf Resort and Spa (4400 N.W. 87th Ave., Doral) in late February and early March.

The **Royal Caribbean Classic** (☎ 305/374–6180), held at the Crandon Golf Course (4000 Crandon Blvd., Key Biscayne), kicks off the Senior PGA tour each winter; dates for 2003 are January 27–February 2.

## Horse Racing

The glass-enclosed, air-conditioned **Calder Race Course** has an unusually extended season, from late May to early January, though it's a good idea to call the track for specific dates. Calder and Gulf Stream Park rotate their race dates, so be sure to check with each park to see where the horses are running. Each year between November and early January Calder holds the Tropical Park Derby for three-year-olds. The track is on the Miami-Dade–Broward County line near I–95 and the Hallandale Beach Boulevard exit, ¾ mi from Pro Player Stadium. ✉ *21001 N.W. 27th Ave., Lake Lucerne, Miami,* ☎ *305/625–1311.* 🎫 *$2, clubhouse $4, parking $1–$5.* ⏲ *Gates open at 11, racing 12:30–5.*

**Gulfstream Park,** north of the Miami-Dade County line, usually has the January through March race dates; it hosted the 1999 Breeder's Cup; the track's premiere race is the Florida Derby. ✉ *21301 Biscayne Blvd. (U.S. 1), between Ives Dairy Rd. and Hallandale Beach Blvd., Hallandale,* ☎ *954/454–7000.* 🎫 *$3, clubhouse $5, parking free.* ⏲ *Wed.–Mon. post time 1 PM.*

## Jai Alai

Don't know what it is? Visit the **Miami Jai Alai Fronton** to learn about this game invented in the Basque region of northern Spain. Jai alai is perhaps the world's fastest game: jai alai balls, called *pelotas,* have been clocked at speeds exceeding 170 mph. The game is played in a 176-ft-long court, and players literally climb the walls to catch the ball in a *cesta* (a woven basket), which has an attached glove. You can place your wager on the team you think will win or on the order in which you think the teams will finish. The Miami fronton was built in 1926, a mile east of the airport, and is America's oldest. Thirteen games (14 on Friday and Saturday) are held daily except Tuesday—some singles, some doubles. ✉ *3500 N.W. 37th Ave., Miami,* ☎ *305/633–6400.* 🎫 *$1, reserved seats $2, Courtview Club $5.* ⏲ *Mon., Wed.–Sat, noon–5, Wed., Fri., Sat., 7–midnight, Sun. 1–6.*

## Tennis

Each spring the **NASDAQ-100 Open** (formerly the Ericsson Open; ☎ 305/442–3367) is held for 12 days at the Tennis Center at Crandon Park (✉ 7300 Crandon Blvd., Key Biscayne, ☎ 305/365–2300). The pro tournament is the world's fifth largest in attendance, prize money, and player draw. With more than $6 million in prize money, you will see top players such as Pete Sampras, Andre Agassi, Gustavo Kuerten, Venus and Sabrina Williams, and Martina Hingis compete in a 14,000-seat stadium. Admission is $10–$45 per day; junior tickets (ages 14 and under) start at $5.

# 7 SHOPPING

Shoppers come from all over the world to explore Miami's decor and design shops, and chichi outdoor shopping malls—and to take advantage of some excellent deals on local specialties such as cigars rolled by highly trained Cuban experts, bright and distinctive Haitian art, and fashions that run the gamut from custom-made guayaberas—the natty four-pocket dress shirts favored by Latin men—to the heights of haute couture, all while soaking up the sun.

Updated by Karen Schlesinger

**MIAMI TEEMS WITH SOPHISTICATED SHOPPING** malls whose wares beckon to thousands of shoppers daily, and the bustling avenues of its commercial neighborhoods that glitter with storefronts of name-brand retailers from Armani to Zegna. Bal Harbour Shops, the ultimate shopping mall, is anchored by Neiman Marcus and Saks Fifth Avenue and overflows with high-end merchandise from Escada, Chanel, Prada, Cartier, Fendi, Gucci, and dozens of other exclusive shops. Collins Avenue in South Beach satisfies all kinds of fashion appetites, whether for Banana Republic, Theory, or Nike. One block over on Washington are a handful of trend-conscious shops like Versace Jean Couture and Betsey Johnson and flashy club wear stores. The discriminating Design District is where many top name designers hold shop when they are not rehabbing the latest South Beach hotel.

But this is also a city of tiny boutiques tucked away in side streets—such as South Miami's Red, Bird, and Sunset roads intersection—and where outdoor markets tout unusual and delicious wares. Bring your wallet and choose from a wide variety of booty that is downright rare anywhere but here. Stroll through Spanish-speaking neighborhoods where shops sell clothing, cigars, and other goods from all over Latin America. At an open-air flea market stall, score an antique glass shaped like a palm tree and fill it with some fresh Jamaican ginger beer from the table next door. Or stop by your hotel gift shop and snap up an alligator magnet for your refrigerator, an ashtray made of seashells, or a bag of gumballs shaped like Florida oranges. Who can resist?

## Malls

People fly to Miami from all over the world just to shop, and the malls are high on their list of spending spots. Stop off at one or two of these climate-controlled temples to consumerism, many of which double as mega entertainment centers, and you'll understand what makes Miami such a vibrant shopping destination.

**Aventura Mall.** With more than 250 shops you could spend a day here meandering through Macy's, Lord & Taylor, JCPenney, Sears, Burdines, Bloomingdale's alone, and then a spend an evening at the 24-screen multiplex theater with inclined stadium seating. Its smaller stores—Anika for cutting-edge designer fashions, Coach for luxury leather goods—are alluring, too. ✉ *19501 Biscayne Blvd., Aventura,* ☎ *305/935–1110,* WEB *www.shopaventuramall.com.*

★ **Bal Harbour Shops.** Local and international shoppers flock to this swank collection of 100 high-end shops, boutiques, and department stores, which include such names as Christian Dior, Gucci, Hermès, Salvatore Ferragamo, Tiffany, and Valentino. Newest shops include Lalique, Valentino, Louis Vuitton Global Store. Expected on the scene are Rive Gauche (Yves St. Laurent), a Gianfranco Ferre Jeans boutique, and a new shop for Dolce & Gabanna. Restaurants and cafés, in tropical garden settings, overflow with style-conscious diners. ✉ *9700 Collins Ave., Bal Harbour,* ☎ *305/866–0311,* WEB *www.balharbourshops.com.*

**Bayside Marketplace.** This 16-acre shopping complex overlooking Biscayne Bay has 100 specialty shops, a concert pavilion, tour-boat docks, a food court, outdoor cafés, Latin steakhouses, seafood restaurants, and a Hard Rock Cafe. It's open late (until 10 during the week and 11 on Friday and Saturday), and its restaurants stay open even later. ✉ *401 Biscayne Blvd., Downtown, Miami,* ☎ *305/577–3344,* WEB *www.baysidemarketplace.com.*

**CocoWalk.** It's got three floors containing nearly 40 chain and specialty shops (Coco Paris, Victoria's Secret, and Express, among others), blending the bustle of a mall with the breatheability of an open-air venue. Newest to the mall are full-size Gap stores (Gap, Gap Body, Gap Baby, and Gap Kids). Hanging out and people-watching is somewhat of a pastime here. The stores stay open almost as late as the popular restaurants and clubs. Plus, there's a 16-screen movie theater. ✉ *3015 Grand Ave., Coconut Grove,* ☎ *305/444–0777,* WEB *www.cocowalk.com.*

**Dadeland Mall.** The oldest retail mall in the county also feels like the biggest and busiest. Retailers include Saks Fifth Avenue, JCPenney, Lord & Taylor, Florida's largest Burdines department store, plus more than 175 specialty stores and 17 restaurants. It's on the south side of town, and close to the Metrorail station. ✉ *7535 N. Kendall Dr., Kendall,* ☎ *305/665–6226,* WEB *www.simon.com.*

**Dolphin Mall.** The Dolphin Mall has more than 200 outlet, dining, and entertainment venues, many of which are new to the area, including Hilo Hattie's, Mario Hernandez, Quicksilver, and the terrific knock-off store Forever XXI. Major anchors include Linens 'N Things, Marshalls Megastore, Off 5th Saks Fifth Avenue Outlet, and Old Navy. A 400,000-square-ft entertainment center includes Dave & Busters and a 28-screen cinema. The mall also has an enormous 850-seat food court and daily tourist-only shuttle service. Need more? Miami International Mall is next door (✉ 1455 N.W. 107th Ave.). ✉ *11401 N.W. 12th St., West Dade,* ☎ *305/365–7446,* WEB *www.dolphinmall.com.*

**The Falls Shopping Center.** Taking its name from the waterfalls and lagoons inside, this upscale, open-air mall on the city's south side has Macy's and Bloomingdale's, 100 specialty stores, restaurants, a 12-theater multiplex, and a butterfly garden. Shop highlights are Tupelo Honey, for casual cotton clothing; the Discovery Channel Store, with science and nature-theme merchandise; and Restoration Hardware, a source for retro chic housewares. ✉ *8888 S.W. 136th St., at U.S. 1, South Miami,* ☎ *305/255–4570,* WEB *www.shopthefalls.com.*

**Loehmann's Fashion Island.** Although it's clearly anchored by Loehmann's, the nationwide retailer of off-price designer fashions, this specialty mall also has a few other biggies, including Rochester Big & Tall and a Barnes & Noble bookstore. You can also grab a bite at one of 11 restaurants, lounges, and snack shops. ✉ *18701 Biscayne Blvd., Aventura,* ☎ *no phone.*

**Main Street.** From cobblestone sidewalks to fountains and vintage-looking street lamps, Main Street was designed to resemble a picturesque small town. This shopping and restaurant promenade is home to Victoria's Secret, Gap, and a number of small boutiques, along with such eateries as Tony Roma's, shula's steak 2, and El Novillo, a Nicaraguan steak house. Main Street also hosts a number of annual festivals and events. ✉ *15255 Bull Run Rd., Miami Lakes,* ☎ *305/817–4198.*

**Sawgrass Mills.** This massive outlet mall is actually north of Miami in western Broward County, but it's definitely worth a stop. Over a mile long, Sawgrass has more than 300 manufacturer and retail outlet stores, name-brand discounters, specialty stores, pushcarts, and kiosks. Choices include Off 5th Saks Fifth Avenue Outlet, the Clearance Center from Neiman Marcus, Spiegel Outlet Store, and many more. Two huge food courts, plus nine restaurants, a 23-screen cinema, and a GameWorks fun zone offer a break from shopping. ✉ *12801 W. Sunrise Blvd., Fort Lauderdale, Sunrise,* ☎ *954/846–2300,* WEB *www.sawgrassmillsmall.com.*

## Greater Miami Shopping

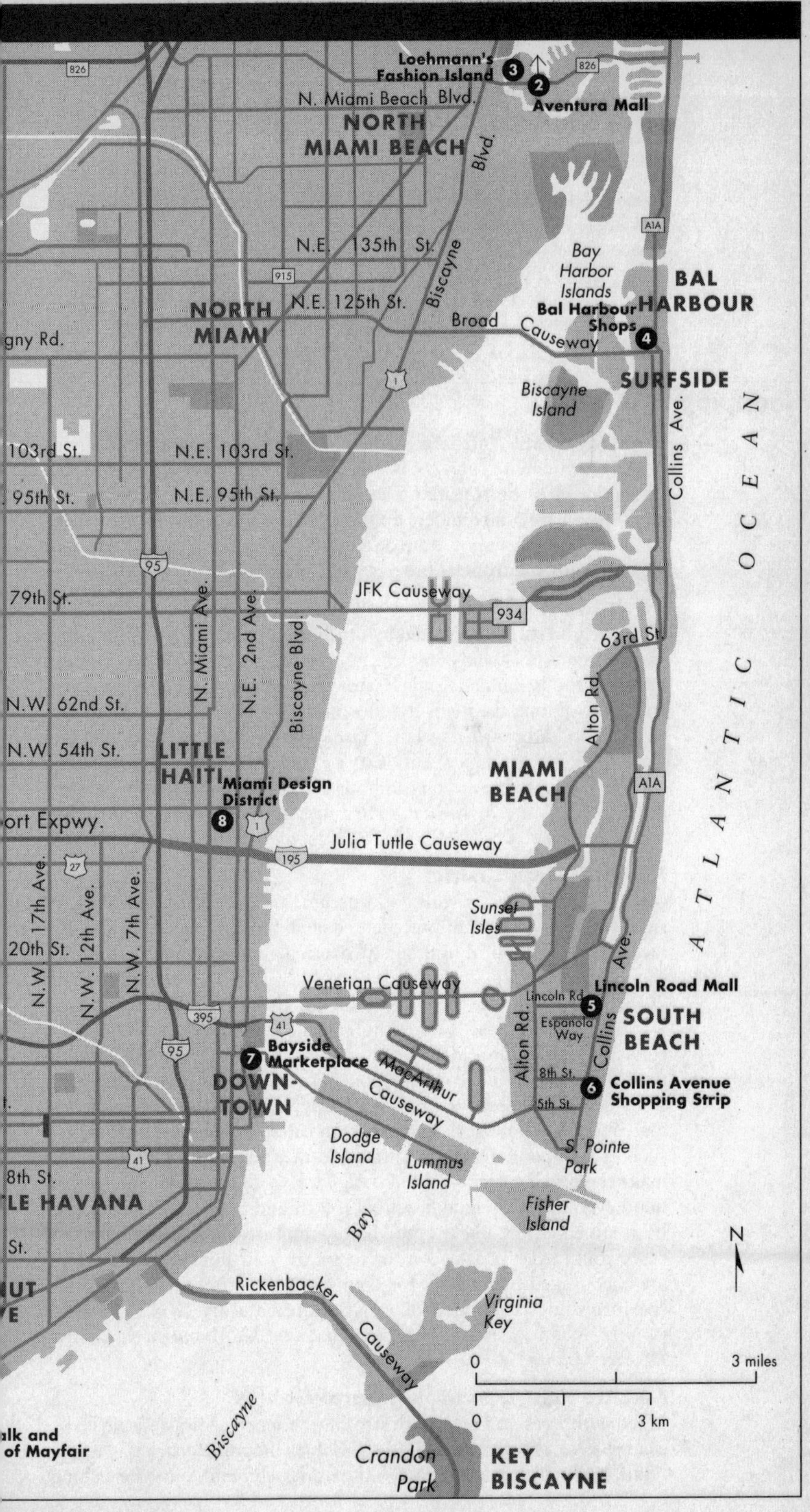

Loehmann's Fashion Island
Aventura Mall
N. Miami Beach Blvd.
NORTH MIAMI BEACH
Biscayne Blvd.
N.E. 135th St.
N.E. 125th St.
NORTH MIAMI
Bay Harbor Islands
BAL HARBOUR
Bal Harbour Shops
Broad Causeway
Biscayne Island
SURFSIDE
Collins Ave.
ATLANTIC OCEAN
N.E. 103rd St.
N.E. 95th St.
103rd St.
95th St.
79th St.
JFK Causeway
63rd St.
Alton Rd.
N. Miami Ave.
N.E. 2nd Ave.
Biscayne Blvd.
N.W. 62nd St.
N.W. 54th St.
LITTLE HAITI
Miami Design District
MIAMI BEACH
Julia Tuttle Causeway
Sunset Isles
N.W. 17th Ave.
N.W. 12th Ave.
N.W. 7th Ave.
20th St.
Venetian Causeway
Lincoln Road Mall
Lincoln Rd.
Espanola Way
SOUTH BEACH
Bayside Marketplace
MacArthur Causeway
DOWNTOWN
8th St.
5th St.
Collins Avenue Shopping Strip
Dodge Island
Lummus Island
S. Pointe Park
Fisher Island
8th St.
LE HAVANA
Bay
Rickenbacker Causeway
Virginia Key
0
3 miles
3 km
Biscayne
Crandon Park
KEY BISCAYNE
N

**Shops at Sunset Place.** A huge banyan tree spreads its tendrils in front of an entrance to this giant pastel bunker, containing FAO Schwarz, NikeTown, A/X Armani Exchange, Virgin Megastore, and four dozen others. Entertainment includes a 24-screen cinema, an IMAX theater, and a GameWorks arcade of state-of-the-art electronic games. ✉ *5701 Sunset Dr., U.S. 1 and Red Rd., South Miami,* ☎ *305/663–4222,* WEB *www.simon.com.*

**Streets of Mayfair.** This open-air complex of promenades, balconies, and sidewalk cafés bustles both day and night, thanks to its Coconut Grove setting and its popular tenants—News Café, Limited, Borders Books Music Cafe, and a few dozen other shops and restaurants. An improv comedy club, martini lounge, and all-night dance clubs are also here. ✉ *2911 Grand Ave., Coconut Grove,* ☎ *305/448–1700,* WEB *www.streetsofmayfair.com.*

## Shopping Districts

If you're over the climate-controlled slickness of shopping malls and can't face one more food-court "meal," you've got choices in Miami. Head out into the sunshine and shop the streets of Miami, where you'll find big-name retailers and local boutiques alike. Take a break at a sidewalk café, to power up on some Cuban coffee or fresh-squeezed OJ and enjoy the tropical breezes.

### Downtown Miami

Nearly 1,000 stores, anchored by Burdines, Marshalls, Dress for Less, and La Época (a Havana import), line the streets of downtown Miami. Sporting goods, cameras and electronics, beauty products, and housewares are among the items for sale in this commercial hub. With the Seybold Building as its flagship, a large jewelry district is second in the United States only to New York City's Diamond District. Hourly parking lots are available or you can hop on Metrorail or Metromover for downtown. ✉ *Biscayne Blvd. to 3rd Ave. and S.E. 1st St. to N.E. 3rd St., Downtown,* ☎ *305/379–7070,* WEB *www.downtownmiami.net.*

### Miami Design District

Miami is synonymous with good design, and its visitor-friendly Design District is a rather unprecedented melding of public space and the rather exclusive world of design. Covering a few city blocks, the Design District, at N.E. 2nd Avenue and N.E. 40th Street, has more than 200 showrooms and galleries—look for the yellow Buick building with the painted cameos of mythological Latin figures on Second Avenue marking the entrance. What's unique is that showrooms here are typically the beat of decorators alone, but the Miami Design District's showrooms are open to the public, occupy windowed street-level buildings, and many double as art galleries or cafés. Visitor-friendly touches, such as an indoor river in Tui Pranich and art exhibits in Holly Hunt, make the once austere world of design less forbidding—the neighborhood even has its own high school (of art and design, of course) and hosts street parties, like for the Miami Film Festival. Although in most cases you'll need your decorator to secure your purchases, browsers are encouraged to consider for themselves the array of rather exclusive furnishings, decorative objects, antiques, and art. ✉ *N.E. 36th St. to N.E. 41st St. between N.E. 2nd Ave. and N. Miami Ave., Design District Miami.*

### Miracle Mile–Downtown Coral Gables

Lined with trees and busy with strolling shoppers, Miracle Mile is the centerpiece of the downtown Coral Gables shopping district, which is home to men's and women's boutiques, jewelry and home furnishing stores, and a host of exclusive couturiers and bridal shops. More than 30 first-rate restaurants offer everything from French to Indian cuisine, while unique art galleries and the Actors' Playhouse give the area a cultural flair. ✉ *Douglas Rd. to LeJeune Rd. and Aragon Ave. to Andalusia Ave., Coral Gables,* ☎ *305/569–0311,* WEB *www.shopcoralgables.com.*

### South Beach–Lincoln Road Mall

This eight-block-long pedestrian mall has more than 150 shops, 20-plus art galleries and nightclubs, about 50 restaurants and cafés, and is home to the Colony Theatre. Tiffany & Co. was one of the first of the exclusive boutiques here. Today an 18-screen movie theater anchors the west end of the street, which is where most of the worthwhile shops are; the far east end is mostly discount and electronic shops. Sure, there's a Pottery Barn, a Gap, and a Williams-Sonoma, but the emphasis is on emporiums with unique personalities like En Avance, Neo Scarpa Accessories, and Été. Do like the locals, and meander along The Road day or night, and stop for a refreshment at one of the top-flight bistros and open-air eateries. ✉ *Lincoln Rd. between Alton Rd. and Washington Ave., South Beach,* ☎ *305/672–1270.*

### South Beach–Collins Avenue

Give your plastic a workout on Gianni Versace's old stomping grounds, just south of Lincoln Road. Among the high-profile tenants on this densely packed two-square-block stretch of Collins Avenue between 6th and 8th streets are Club Monaco, Quicksilver, Intermix, Kenneth Cole, Laundry Industry, and A/X Armani Exchange. Wilke-Rodriguez sells upscale men's fashions by homegrown Miami designer Eddie Rodriguez. Sprinkled amid the upscale vendors are hair salons, spas, cafés, and familiar stores including Gap, Urban Outfitters, and Banana Republic. Be sure to head over one street east and west to catch the shopping on Ocean Drive and Washington Avenue. ✉ *Collins Ave. between 6th and 8th Sts., South Beach.*

## Specialty Stores

Beyond the shopping malls and the big-name retailers, Greater Miami has all manner of merchandise to tempt even the casual browser. For consumers on a mission to find certain items—art deco antiques or cigars, for instance—the city streets burst with a rewarding collection of specialty shops.

### Antiques

**Alhambra Antiques Center** (✉ 2850 Salzedo St., Coral Gables, ☎ 305/446–1688) houses the collections of four antiques dealers that sell high-quality decorative pieces from Europe.

**American Salvage** (✉ 7001 N.W. 27th Ave., northwest of downtown, Miami, ☎ 305/691–7001) is off the beaten path, but is the place to rescue less-than-perfect art deco furniture such as 1930s armoires, bookshelves, and kitchenware at bargain prices.

**Architectural Antiques** (✉ 2500 S.W. 28th La., Coconut Grove, ☎ 305/285–1330) carries large and eclectic items—railroad crossing signs, statues, English roadsters—in a cluttered setting that makes shopping an adventure.

**Artisan Antiques** (✉ 110 N.E. 40th St., Design District, Miami, ☎ 305/573–5619) purveys china, crystal, mirrors, and armoires from the French art deco period, but an assortment of 1930s radiator covers, which can double as funky sideboards, are what's really neat here.

**Leah's Gallery** (✉ 191 N.E. 40th St., Design District, Miami, ☎ 305/573–9700) is four floors of wonderful 19th-century statuary and sculpture, park benches, mannequins, stained-glass doors and panels, and a gigantic carved-wood Victorian birdcage, to name a few.

**Senzatempo** (✉ 1655 Meridian Ave., Miami Beach, ☎ 305/534–5588) has a unique collection of vintage home accessories by European and American designers of the 1930s through the 1970s, including electric fans, klieg lights, and chrome furniture.

**Valerio Antiques** (✉ 250 Valencia Ave., Coral Gables, ☎ 305/448–6779) is a store with fine French art deco furniture, bronze sculptures, and original art glass by Gallé and Loetz among others.

## Beauty

**Aveda** (✉ 932 Lincoln Rd., South Beach, ☎ 305/531–9580) brings its line of cosmetics to Lincoln Road Mall. It's a good place to stock up on deliciously scented shampoos and conditioners for your tresses, as well as skin cream.

**Brownes & Co.** (✉ 841 Lincoln Rd., South Beach, ☎ 305/532–8703, WEB www.brownesbeauty.com) provides luxurious products to those who appreciate them the most. Cosmetics include Molton Brown, Body & Soul, Le Clerc, and others. It also sells herbal remedies and upscale hair and body products from Bumble and Bumble. Try to resist something from the immense collection of scented European soaps in all sizes and colors. A popular in-house salon, **Some Like It Hot** (☎ 305/538–7544), offers some of the best waxing in town.

**The Fragrance Shop** (✉ 612 Lincoln Rd., South Beach, ☎ 305/535–0037) carries more than 800 perfume oils, including those that mimic famous brands, in a setting that resembles an 18th-century apothecary. The staff will customize a unique blend for you or sell you a hand-blown perfume bottle made by one of many international artisans.

**Guerlain Shop at Loews** (✉ Loews hotel, 1601 Collins Ave., South Beach, ☎ 305/604–1601) is modeled after its 1930s-era hotel-shop predecessors: the entire boutique is devoted to Guerlain perfumes and other Guerlain products.

**Histoire de Parfums** (✉ 531 Lincoln Rd., South Beach, ☎ 305/534–7500) is not just a perfume store, it's also a museum. Toiletries from the 18th and 19th centuries are displayed in this well-appointed shop that also sells original perfumes named after George Sand, Colette, Mata Hari, and others.

**Sephora** (✉ 721 Collins Ave., South Beach, ☎ 305/532–0904) is a makeup, skin care and fragrance emporium. Find Bliss, Calvin Klein, Clinique, Hardy Candy, Nars, Shu Uemura, and Stila among the masses of beauty products organized alphabetically.

## Books

### ENGLISH-LANGUAGE BOOKS

**Barnes & Noble** (✉ 152 Miracle Mile, Coral Gables, ☎ 305/446–4152; ✉ 18711 N.E. Biscayne Blvd., Loehmann's Fashion Island, Aventura, ☎ 305/935–9770), like others in the superstore chain, encourages customers to pick a book off the shelf and lounge on a couch. A well-stocked magazine and international news rack and an espresso bar–café make it even easier to while away a rainy morning here.

**Books & Books, Inc.** (✉ 265 Aragon Ave., Coral Gables, ☎ 305/442–4408; ✉ 933 Lincoln Rd., South Beach, ☎ 305/532–3222), Greater Miami's only independent English-language bookshops, specialize in contemporary and classical literature as well as in books on the arts, architecture, Florida, and Cuba. At the newer Coral Gables location you can lounge at the café, browse the photography gallery, or sit in the courtyard and flip through magazines. It also hosts poetry readings the last Friday of every month, and both stores host terrific regular author readings.

**Borders** (✉ 3390 Mary St., Coconut Grove, ☎ 305/447–1655; ✉ 19925 Biscayne Blvd., Aventura, ☎ 305/935–0027; ✉ 9205 S. Dixie Hwy., Pinecrest, ☎ 305/665–8800; ✉ 8811 S.W. 107th Ave., Kendall, ☎ 305/271–7457) carries more than 2,000 periodicals in 10 languages from 15 countries, in addition to books, CDs, and videos.

**Eutopia Books** (✉ 1627 Jefferson Ave., Miami Beach, ☎ 305/532–8680) is the rare Miami area store that sells rare books. In addition to an impressive collection of vintage art books, you'll find early 20th-century children's classics.

**Kafka's** (✉ 1464 Washington Ave., South Beach, ☎ 305/673–9669), a bookstore and café with character, sells previously owned books and has a good selection of used art books and literature. In addition, the shop carries a terrific selection of obscure and familiar periodicals and has computers for word processing and Internet access for a fee.

**Murder on Miami Beach** (✉ 16850 Collins Ave., Sunny Isles, ☎ 305/956–7770) is not as sinister as it sounds. The store specializes in mysteries, with an impressive selection of books by Miami authors. They also stock new, used, and antiquarian books along with mystery games and puzzles. Ask for a gift basket containing a teapot and English-detective novels.

**Super Heroes Unlimited** (✉ 1788 N.E. 163rd St., North Miami Beach, ☎ 305/940–9539) beckons to comic-book readers looking for monthly refills of *Spawn* and *X-Men* and tempts with an enviable selection of Japanese *animé*.

#### SPANISH-LANGUAGE BOOKS

**Downtown Book Center** (✉ 247 S.E. 1st St., Downtown Miami, ☎ 305/377–9939) sells novels by leading Central and South American authors, as well as Spanish-language maps, and computer manuals.

**La Moderna Poesia** (✉ 5246 S.W. 8th St., Little Havana Miami, ☎ 305/446–9899), with more than 100,000 titles, is the region's largest and most complete source for *los libros en español*. There's also a second, smaller location (✉ 3870 E. 4th Ave., Hialeah, ☎ 305/556–7717).

**Libreria Distribuidoroa Universal** (✉ 3090 S.W. 8th St., Little Havana Miami, ☎ 305/642–3234) is a favorite of book lovers who want Cuban flavor in their reading material. You'll also find Latin American and Caribbean reference books and literature here, too.

**Pierre Books** (✉ Biscayne Harbor Shops, 18185 Biscayne Blvd., Aventura, ☎ 305/792–0766) is a pleasant place to browse for and buy books in Spanish, French, or Portuguese. This store happily accommodates special orders of foreign-language titles.

### Children's Books, Clothing, and Toys

**Afro-In Books and Things** (✉ 5575 N.W. 7th Ave., Miami, ☎ 305/756–6107) specializes in books by African-American writers for children and teen readers—although it has an impressive section of books for adults, too.

**Al Bon Marché** (✉ 5800 S.W. 40th St., Miami, ☎ 305/668–4522) imports heirloom quality, special occasion children's clothing for infants to six years old. Smock detailing and delicate, intricate handwork are the boutique's specialties.

**F.A.O. Schwarz** (✉ Bal Harbour Shops, 9700 Collins Ave., Bal Harbour, ☎ 305/865–2361; ✉ Aventura Mall, 19501 Biscayne Blvd., Aventura, ☎ 305/692–9200; ✉ Shops at Sunset Place, 5701 Sunset Dr., South Miami, ☎ 305/668–2300), the ultimate toy store, has three area locations.

**Gap Kids** (✉ Bayside Marketplace, 401 Biscayne Blvd., Downtown, Miami, ☎ 305/539–9334, WEB www.gapkids.com) carries casual sportswear for the discriminating youngster, ages two years and up. (Baby Gap is for children up to 24 months.) With more than 10 Gap Kids in town, you can find one in most malls and shopping districts.

**La Canastilla Cubana** (✉ 1300 W. 49th St., Hialeah, ☎ 305/557–5505), the stork's basket in English, carries children's toys and specializes in elegant furnishings and designer clothing for new arrivals.

**Peekaboo** (✉ 6807 Main St., Miami Lakes, ☎ 305/556–6910) carries educational toys for kids and has an exceptional collection of European clothing for infants to teens.

## Cigars

**Bill's Pipe & Tobacco** (✉ 2309 Ponce de León Blvd., Coral Gables, ☎ 305/444–1764) has everything for the smoker, including a wide selection of pipes and pipe tobacco, cigars, accessories, and gifts.

**Condal & Peñamil** (✉ 741 Lincoln Rd., South Beach, ☎ 305/604–9690) is a cigar shop and café where you can get boxes of cigars with personalized labels. Name a dozen after yourself or your new kid.

**El Credito Cigars** (✉ 1106 S.W. 8th St., Little Havana, Miami, ☎ 305/858–4162), in the heart of Little Havana, employs rows of workers at wooden benches. They rip, cut, and wrap giant tobacco leaves, and press the cigars in vises. Dedicated smokers find their way here to pick up a $90 bundle or to peruse the *gigantes, supremos,* panatelas, and Churchills available in natural or *maduro* wrappers.

**Harriels Tobacco Shoppe** (✉ 11401 S. Dixie Hwy., Kendall, ☎ 305/252–9010, WEB www.harriels.com) caters to the serious smoker with a vast selection of premium cigars, imported cigarettes, and decorative pipes.

**Macabi Cigars** (✉ 3473 S.W. 8th St., Little Havana, Miami, ☎ 305/446–2606) carries cigars, cigars, and more cigars, including premium and house brands. Humidors and other accessories are also available.

**Yucky's Tobacco & Emporium** (✉ 3418 Main Hwy., Coconut Grove, ☎ 305/444–4997), a popular store with University of Miami students, stocks smoking paraphernalia, including water pipes, incense, and things that glow in the dark.

## Clothing for Men and Women

**Banana Republic** (✉ 1100 Lincoln Rd., South Beach, ☎ 305/534–4706, WEB www.bananarepublic.com), with its dependable, grown-up styles, is in a former bank—dressing rooms are in the bank's old vault and cashiers in the old teller stations. This two-story space also showcases the season's latest work-or-play fashions for men and women, all with that slightly trendy yet sophisticated Gap-enterprise touch.

**BASE** (✉ 939 Lincoln Rd., South Beach, ☎ 305/531–4982) is a cute shop with hanging Chinese paper lanterns, patchwork carpet floor, and a bamboo mural CD station. Stop here for men's and women's eclectic clothing, shoes, and accessories that mix Japanese design with Caribbean-inspired materials. The often-present house label designer may help select your wardrobe's newest addition.

**Chroma** (✉ 920 Lincoln Rd., South Beach, ☎ 305/695–8808) is where fashionistas go for Barbara Bui, Catherine Malandrino, and Mint, and clothing and accessories by up-and-coming designers.

**Intermix** (✉ 634 Collins Ave., South Beach, ☎ 305/531–5950) is a modern New York boutique with the variety of a department store. You'll find fancy dresses, stylish shoes, slinky accessories, and trendy looks by sassy, mid-price designers like Daryl K and Katayone Adeli.

**J. Bolado Clothiers** (✉ 336 Miracle Mile, Coral Gables, ☎ 305/448–2507) has been in the neighborhood for more than 30 years. This family-owned men's store carries classic styles from imported and domestic designers. With three generations of tailors on premise, the house specialties are made-to-measure suits and custom shirts.

**Kristine Michael** (✉ 7271 S.W. 57th Ave., South Miami, ☎ 305/665–7717) is a local fashion institution with suburban moms and University of Miami students. The store's hip and up-to-the-minute selection of pieces from Theory, Alberta Ferretti, Chaiken, Kors, and William B. stands out from the national retailers across the street at Shops of Sunset Place.

**Sylvia Tcherassi** (✉ 3403 Main Hwy., Coconut Grove, ☎ 305/447–4540), the Colombian designer's signature boutique, features feminine and frilly dresses and separates accented with chiffon, tulle and sequins.

**Mynaya** (✉ 5580 N.E. 4th Ct., Miami, ☎ 305/758–5155) shares a garden courtyard with neighbor Soyka's restaurant. The owner's dog lounges around this store furnished with imported fashion accessories and home knickknacks. Shopping here is like browsing in a world traveler's closet filled with beautiful souvenirs from each port of call.

**Nicole Miller** (✉ 656 Collins Ave., South Beach, ☎ 305/535–2200) showcases the spunky New York designer's distinctive fashions, including boxers and ties for him and handbags and shoes for her.

**Polo Ralph Lauren** (✉ Bal Harbour Shops, 9700 Collins Ave., Bal Harbour, ☎ 305/861–2059) has a complete selection of Polo for Men and Ralph Lauren for women, along with accessories and a few items from the Home Collection, including frames and fragrances.

**Scoop** (✉ Shore Club Hotel, 1901 Collins Ave., South Beach, ☎ 305/695–3297), the New York shop for pretty young things, has a small but spaciously arranged Miami outpost (thankfully!), which carries all the Helmut Lang, Marc Jacobs, and hip-slung Earl and Seven Jeans that you'll need to make it through a club's velvet rope.

**Seize sur Vingt** (✉ 203 11th St., South Beach, ☎ 305/695–1779) is known for its gorgeous custom-tailored and ready-to-wear men's clothes. The modern dress shirt, made from your choice of exquisite Egyptian cotton patterns, is the shop's specialty.

### SHOES

**Giroux** (✉ 638 Collins Ave., South Beach, ☎ 305/672–3015) carries some men's and women's shoes by American, Spanish, and house-label designers. But the highlight of the selection is the Italian shoe company by brothers Goffredo Fantini and Enrico Fantini, who design independent men's lines and collaborate on their women's shoe collection, Materia Prima.

**Koko & Palenki** (✉ CocoWalk, 3015 Grand Ave., Coconut Grove, ☎ 305/444–1772) is where Grovers go for a well-edited selection of trendy shoes by Calvin Klein, Casadei, Charles David, Stuart Weitzman, Via Spiga, and others. Handbags, belts, and men's shoes add to the selection. Koko & Palenki also has stores in Aventura and Dadeland Malls.

**Neo Scarpa** (✉ 817 Lincoln Rd., South Beach, ☎ 305/535–5633) carries each season's must-have men's and women's shoes—Dolce & Gabbana, Giuseppe Zanotti, Miu Miu, and Sigerson Morrison top the charts. If you're looking for Prada, they staff will send you across the road to their sister store.

**Santini Mavardi** (✉ 935 Washington Ave., South Beach, ☎ 305/538–6229) is where celebs stop for custom made shoes and a matching outfit. Platform sandals with feather accents, Lucite stilettos with rhinestones, and wood wedge heels with lace-up leather straps round out this ultra-sexy shoe selection.

### SWIMWEAR

It's particularly easy to find swimwear in South Beach, so if your hometown search leaves you suitless, trunkless, or generally empty handed, have no fear, you'll find one here.

**Absolutely Suitable** (✉ 1560 Collins Ave., South Beach, ☎ 305/604–5281) carries women's and men's swimwear and accessories for lounging poolside. The salespeople will put you in a suit that fits just right and dress you from sunhat to flip-flop.

**Everything But Water** (✉ Aventura Mall, 19501 Biscayne Blvd., Aventura, ☎ 305/932–7207) lives up to its name, selling everything for the water (except the water itself). The complete line of women's swimwear, includes one- and two-piece suits and tankinis (tank tops with bikini or high-top bottoms) and there are always a few pieces for men.

**X-Isle** (✉ 437 Washington Ave., South Beach, ☎ 305/673–5900) is a local's surfshop that has been riding the wave on Miami Beach more than 10 years. Packed with gear, clothing, and swimwear for guys and gals, this store also stocks wake, surf, and skateboards.

### VINTAGE CLOTHING

**Anonymous** (✉ 3300 Rice St., Coconut Grove, ☎ 305/443–4331) sells consignment items by top designers at pre-owned prices, including Chanel suits and Fendi bags.

**Fly Boutique** (✉ 650 Lincoln Rd., South Beach, ☎ 305/604–8508) is where South Beach hipsters flock for the latest arrival of used clothing. At this resale boutique, '80s glam designer pieces fly out at a premium price, but vintage camisoles and Levi's corduroys are still a resale deal.

**Miami Twice** (✉ 6562 S.W. 40th St., Miami, ☎ 305/666–0127) has fabulous vintage clothes and accessories from the last three decades. After all, everyone needs a leisure suit or platform shoes. Check out the vintage home collectibles and furniture, too.

**Vintage Soul** (✉ 1235 Alton Rd., Miami Beach, ☎ 305/538–2644) is a shabby-chic style house in which rooms teem with vintage clothing and gotta-have-it furnishings. Be sure to look up—the eclectic lanterns are also for sale.

## Essentials

**Central Hardware** (✉ 545 41st St., Miami Beach, ☎ 305/531–0836) is less a hardware store than a place to outfit your apartment, efficiency, or hotel room with nondisposable items ranging from corkscrews to coolers.

**Compass Market** (✉ 860 Ocean Dr., South Beach, ☎ 305/673–2906) crams wall-to-wall merchandise into a cute and cozy basement shop (whose somewhat confusing entrance is on 9th Street). The market stocks all the staples you'll need, from sandals, souvenirs, cigars, and deli items to umbrellas, newspapers, wine, and champagne. If they don't have it, you probably don't really need it!

## Food

**Epicure Market** (✉ 1656 Alton Rd., Miami Beach, ☎ 305/672–1861) is one of Miami's most cherished establishments. Pick up jars of homemade chicken noodle or green pea soup or some of the exquisite (if pricey) produce. The bakery has a scrumptious array of cookies, cakes, and breads made daily, or you can wander down aisles full of imported chocolate and local celebrities.

**Oak Feed Natural Food Market** (✉ Oak Ave. and Mary St., Coconut Grove, ☎ 305/448–7595), in a new location, peddles more than grains and granola. Nearly everything you'd need to live a preservative-free existence is here—baking mixes, teas, and environmentally friendly household products. There's even a veggie lunch counter.

## Furniture

**Addison House** (✉ 5201 N.W. 77th Ave., West Dade Miami, ☎ 305/640–2400) is an outlet for a wide variety of traditional name-brand furniture from North Carolina, a premier furniture-producing region.

**Eclectic Elements** (✉ 2227 Coral Way, Coral Gables, ☎ 305/285–0899) carries a playful collection of very Miami modern and retro furniture, mirrors, and clocks that would have pleased the Jetsons.

**Ethan Allen Home Interiors** (✉ Sunniland Shopping Center, 11825 S. Dixie Hwy., Pinecrest, ☎ 305/235–7200) caters to traditionalists looking for American reproductions, and to recent college grads trying to reproduce the Nick@Nite look of the living rooms on their favorite TV shows.

**Inspiration Furniture** (✉ 3025 N.E. 163rd St., North Miami Beach, ☎ 305/944–8080) sells contemporary Scandinavian-design furniture that goes beyond the basics of blond wood.

**Luminaire** (✉ 2331 Ponce de León Blvd., Coral Gables, ☎ 305/448–7367) is Miami's leading purveyor of contemporary furniture, with pieces from more than 100 manufacturers and 200 designers, including European manufacturers such as Cassina and Interlubke.

**Raphia** (✉ 1008 Lincoln Rd., South Beach, ☎ 305/532–9700) sells wicker, raffia, and wood furniture from Indonesia and the Philippines, as well as teak furniture from India.

## Gifts and Souvenirs

**Art Deco District Welcome Center** (✉ 1001 Ocean Dr., South Beach, ☎ 305/531–3484) hawks the finest in Miami-inspired kitsch, from flamingo salt-and-pepper shakers to alligator-shape ashtrays, along with books and posters celebrating the Art Deco District and its revival.

**Britto Central** (✉ 818 Lincoln Rd., South Beach, ☎ 305/531–8821) is both a gallery and working studio, with posters, prints, ties, and other objects featuring the vibrant graphic designs of the Brazilian artist and Miami resident, Romero Britto.

**Indies Company** (✉ 101 W. Flagler St., Downtown Miami, ☎ 305/375–1492), the gift shop of the Historical Museum of Southern Florida, is dedicated to the proposition that Miami is more than just art deco. You'll find books on South Florida as well as interesting artifacts of Miami's history, including some inexpensive reproductions.

**Le Chocolatier** (✉ 1840 N.E. 164th St., North Miami Beach, ☎ 305/944–3020, WEB www.lechocolatier.com) tempts the palate with hand-dipped and molded chocolate creations, used to create gift baskets and other gift items, or eaten on the spot. You can linger to watch chocolate being made through a glass partition.

**Pink Palm** (✉ 737 Lincoln Rd., South Beach, ☎ 305/538–8373) flaunts a sometimes racy, sometimes funny, and sometimes beautiful selection of sophisticated greeting cards, gifts, and souvenirs.

**Wick** (✉ 1624 Alton Rd., Miami Beach, ☎ 305/538–7949) moved into Spiaggia, its home furnishing sister store, but there's still plenty for wax addicts and browsers alike. Light up your life with giant tabletop candles, tiny tapers, and novelty candles in every shape imaginable.

**Wolfsonian Museum Gift Shop** (✉ 1001 Washington Ave., South Beach, ☎ 305/531–1001 or 305/535–2680) sells books on design and architecture, small objects from the world of Alessi and other kitchenware geniuses, as well as posters and reproductions from the museum's collection of objects from the 1930s.

## Home Furnishings

If you're serious about decor, you and your decorator should head straight to the Design District.

**Cookworks** (✉ Bal Harbour Shops, 9700 Collins Ave., Bal Harbour, ☎ 305/861–5005) accesses your inner Martha Stewart with a fabulous array of kitchen items, including table linens, plates and utensils, small appliances and gadgets, gourmet foods and wines, cookbooks and gift items. Most of the merchandise is direct from France or Italy.

**Details** (✉ 1711 Alton Rd., Miami Beach, ☎ 305/531–1325) has amusing home accessories, offbeat knickknacks, coffee tables, mirrors, and more. The sofas summon you to sit on them and consider just how good your home would look with one—or two.

**Fabric Depot** (✉ 10175 S. Dixie Hwy., Pinecrest, ☎ 305/666–0177) has a huge selection of fabrics at discount prices, everything from silks and chenilles to velvets, damasks, and outdoor fabrics. If home decorating is your hobby, you could spend hours pouring over the trimmings alone.

**Oriental Rugs International** (✉ 131 N.E. 40th St., Design District Miami, ☎ 305/576–0880) sells antique and contemporary rugs from Persia and Europe.

**World Resources** (✉ 56 N.E. 40th St., Design District Miami, ☎ 305/576–8799) stocks Indonesian, Indian, and Asian imports, from vases and tea chests to ornate canopy beds.

## Jewelry

**Beverlee Kagan** (✉ 5831 Sunset Dr., South Miami, ☎ 305/663–1937) specializes in vintage and antique jewelry, including art deco–era bangles, bracelets, and cuff links.

**Bulgari** (✉ Bal Harbour Shops, 9700 Collins Ave., Bal Harbour, ☎ 305/861–8898) jewelry, watches, silver, and luxury perfumes are known the world over. If you're looking for a gift that will impress, from a silk scarf or tie, to a leather accessory, this is the place.

**Gray & Sons Jewelers** (✉ 9595 Harding Ave., Surfside, ☎ 305/865–0999, WEB www.grayandsons.com) offers fine new and pre-owned watches and estate jewelry, with more than 35 brands to choose from.

**Holden** (✉ 608 Lincoln Rd., South Beach, ☎ 305/672–1527) carries reproductions of period timepieces, as well as funky retro-looking modern watches.

**Me & Ro** (✉ Shore Club Hotel, 1901 Collins Ave., South Beach, ☎ 305/672–3566) is a trendy New-York based jewelry shop run by Michele Quan and Robin Renzi (Mi & Ro?). These unique designs, primarily crafted from silver, gold, and semi-precious stones, have a celebrity clientele that reads like a who's who.

**Morays Jewelers** (✉ 50 N.E. 2nd Ave., Downtown Miami, ☎ 305/374–0739) has been a downtown mainstay for more than 50 years. An authorized dealer of more than 30 top-quality Swiss watch brands, they also offer an array of jewelry and gift items.

**Starck Design** (✉ 704 Lincoln Rd., South Beach, ☎ 305/674–7656) stocks German-designed jewelry and watches, including stainless steel and titanium pieces.

## Lighting

Lighting, like home decor and good design, is important in Miami. These stores sell to the customer, and the Design District showrooms sell to your decorator.

**Benson Lighting and Fans** (✉ 12955 S.W. 87th Ave., South Miami, ☎ 305/235–5841) is the place to go if you're hoping to give your home a tropical makeover, complete with classic ceiling fans.

**Farrey's** (✉ 1850 N.E. 146th St., North Miami, ☎ 305/947–5451; ✉ 4101 Ponce De Leon Blvd., Coral Gables, ☎ 305/445–2244) is a giant warehouse of lighting fixtures. Check out the selection of nautical-deco fixtures for inside and outside the house.

**Lunatika** (✉ 900 Lincoln Rd., South Beach, ☎ 305/534–8585) lights up South Beach with funky, creative chandeliers, wall sconces, and table lamps.

**Twery's Imports and Antiques** (✉ 160 N.E. 40th St., Design District, Miami, ☎ 305/576–0564) is sure to have the antique chandelier you want, whether your taste runs to Victorian or deco.

## Music

**Blue Note Records** (✉ 16401 N.E. 15th Ave., North Miami Beach, ☎ 305/940–3394) is the place for rare oldies and vinyl rarities, as well as the latest discs from contemporary artists. A sister store, **Blue Note Jazz** (✉ 2299 N.E. 164th St., North Miami Beach, ☎ 305/354–4563), caters to jazz fans.

**Do-Re-Mi Music Center** (✉ 1829 SW 8th St., Little Havana, ☎ 305/541–3374) satisfies shoppers who want to go home with their suitcases full of salsa or other Latin dance music.

**MARS Music** (✉ 12115 Biscayne Blvd., North Miami, ☎ 305/893–0191; ✉ Dolphin Mall, 11421 N.W. 12th St., West Dade, ☎ 786/331–9688) calls itself "the musician's planet" because it stocks supplies from guitar strings and drumsticks to amps and keyboards. A keyboard room, DJ demo room, and drum–percussion room let you sample the merchandise before buying.

**Spec's Music** (✉ 501 Collins Ave., South Beach, ☎ 305/534–3667) has 15 locations in Greater Miami. The South Beach supermarket-size store has new releases of rock, hip-hop, jazz, R&B, Spanish-language titles, and world music. Spec's across from the University of Miami (✉ 1570 S. Dixie Hwy.) and in North Miami (✉ 12415 Biscayne Blvd.) also have extensive selections.

## New Age

**Maya Hatcha** (✉ 3058 Grand Ave., Coconut Grove, ☎ 305/443-9040) has feng shui crystals, candles, Indian and Native American jewelry, and imported clothing.

**Mystical Aamulet Network** (✉ 7360 S.W. 24th St., Miami, ☎ 305/265-2228) serves the Wiccan, pagan, and metaphysical communities. Visitors can pick up books on witchcraft, as well as amulets, tarot cards, crystals, and jewelry.

**9th Chakra** (✉ 811 Lincoln Rd., South Beach, ☎ 305/538–0671) offers inspirational books (in English and Spanish), crystals, jewelry, feng shui products, candles, essential oils, and music to meditate by.

## Odds and Ends

**Condom USA** (✉ 3066 Grand Ave., Coconut Grove, ☎ 305/445-7729) sells condoms by the gross, sexually oriented games, and other titillating objects. If you're easily offended, stay away, but if you're easily aroused, stay the night (or at least until closing—2 AM on Friday and Saturday, midnight the rest of the week).

**Funky*Sexy.Com** (✉ 637 Lincoln Rd., South Beach, ☎ 305/532-2649) carries costumelike club gear for eccentric party goers. Don't be scared off by the window displays, among the hot pink wigs inside are fun accessories for normal folks.

**Gotta Have It! Collectibles** (✉ 4231 S.W. 71st Ave., Miami, ☎ 305/446–5757) caters to autograph hounds with its signed team jerseys, canceled checks from the estate of Marilyn Monroe, Beatles album jackets, and Jack Nicklaus scorecards. If they don't have the autograph you desire, they'll track one down.

**La Casa de los Trucos** (✉ 1343 S.W. 8th St., Little Havana, Miami, ☎ 305/858–5029) is a popular magic store that first opened in Cuba in the 1930s; the exiled owners reopened it here in the 1970s. When they're in, the owners perform for you.

**Oceans of Notions** (✉ 10990 Biscayne Blvd., North Miami, ☎ 305/893–3194) is a no-frills notions store with fabric, thread, leather cord, beads, and boas for do-it-yourself fashion projects.

**Phat** (✉ 843 Washington Ave., South Beach, ☎ 305/604–8090) pumps out the club music at deafening decibels as it targets young club goers looking for body-piercing accessories, tobacco-related accoutrements, and fashions for guys, gals, and those in between.

**Yarn Studio** (✉ 940 Lincoln Road, South Beach, ☎ 305/531–1050) is a second-floor studio overflowing with yarn for all your knitting needs. Lessons are available for the knitting novice.

## Only in Miami

**Botanica Nena** (✉ 902 N.W. 27th Ave., Miami, ☎ 305/649–8078) is the largest and most complete *botanica* (a store specializing in the occult) in Miami, stocking roots, herbs, seashells, candles, incense, and potions of all sorts.

**Dog Bar** (✉ 723 N. Lincoln La., South Beach, ☎ 305/532–5654), just north of Lincoln Road's main drag, caters to enthusiastic animal owners who simply must have that perfect leopard-skin pet bed.

**El Aguila Vidente (The Seeing Eagle)** (✉ 1122 S.W. 8th St., Little Havana, ☎ 305/854–4086) is dedicated to the practice of the Afro-Cuban religion Santería. The shop does not welcome gawkers. Among the merchandise are herbs, potions, and ceramic figures of saints—some of them 8–10 ft tall and bejeweled, costing in the thousands.

**La Casa de las Guayaberas** (✉ 5840 S.W. 8th St., Miami, ☎ 305/266–9683) sells custom-made guayaberas, the natty four-pocket dress shirts favored by Latin men. Hundreds are also available off the rack.

**Orchids** (✉ 2662 S. Dixie Hwy., Coconut Grove, ☎ 305/665–3278) will satisfy your yen for the mysteriously beautiful varieties: orchids, bromeliads, and bonsai.

**Sinbad's Bird House** (✉ 7201 Bird Rd., Miami, ☎ 305/262–6077) has the perfect address for a purveyor of chirping, chattering, fluttering critters. Find everything you need to care for Polly right here.

**Snakes at Sunset** (✉ 9761 Sunset Dr., South Miami, ☎ 305/757–6253) will sell you friendly snakes, spiders, lizards, and amphibians to bring that special touch of warmth to your home.

### Sporting Goods

**Bikes to Go** (✉ 6600 S.W. 80th St., Miami, ☎ 305/666–7702) puts you on wheels and sells products that protect you from the hazards of biking.

**Miami Fantasias** (✉ 78 E. Flagler St., Downtown, Miami, ☎ 305/358–5801) has a convenient downtown location for those headed to the reefs. Stock up on flippers, masks, and other snorkel and scuba gear.

**Miami Golf Discount Superstore** (✉ 111 N.E. 1st St., 2nd floor, Downtown, Miami, ☎ 800/718–8006, WEB www.miamigolfdiscount.com) has 10,000 square ft of golf equipment, including clubs, balls, shoes, and clothing. A practice net lets you test your swing.

**Power Sports** (✉ 17777 N.W. 2nd Ave., North Miami Beach, ☎ 305/651–4999) appeals to the oceangoing fast crowd with brand-name jet skis.

**Ride** (✉ 711 Washington Ave., South Beach, ☎ 305/673–3307) will help you zip around South Beach on your very own motorized Italjet, Aprillia, Kymco, or Moskito scooter. Buy one along with accessories and apparel—or rent one while you're in town.

## Outdoor Markets

Pass the mangos! Greater Miami's farmers markets and flea markets take advantage of the region's balmy weather and tropical delights to lure shoppers to open-air stalls filled with produce and collectibles.

**Coconut Grove Farmers Market.** The most organic of Miami's outdoor markets specializes in a mouthwatering array of local produce as well as ready-to-eat goodies such as cashew butter, homemade salad dressings, and fruit pies. ✉ *Grand Ave. 1 block west of MacDonald Ave., S.W. 32nd Ave., Coconut Grove,* ☎ *305/444–7270.* ⏲ *Sat. 8–2.*

★ **Española Way Market.** This market has been a city favorite since its debut in the heart of South Beach in 1995. Along a two-block stretch of balconied Mediterranean-style storefronts, the road closes to traffic and vendors set up tables on the wide sidewalks as street musicians beat out Latin rhythms. You might find silver jewelry, antique lanterns, orchids, leather jackets, cheap watches, imports from India and Guatemala, or antique Venetian painted beads. Scattered among the merchandise, food vendors sell tasty but inexpensive Latin snacks and drinks. Park along a side street. ✉ *Española Way between Drexel and Washington Aves., South Beach,* ☎ *305/672–1270.* ⏲ *Sun. noon–9.*

**Farmers Market at Merrick Park.** Some 25 local produce growers and plant vendors sell herbs, fruits, fresh-squeezed juices, chutneys, cakes, and muffins here. Regular events include gardening workshops, children's activities, and cooking demonstrations offered by Coral Gables' master chefs. ✉ *Le Jeune Rd., S.W. 42nd Ave., and Biltmore Way, Coral Gables,* ☎ *305/460–5311.* ⏲ *Mid-Jan.–late Mar., Sat. 8–1.*

**Flagler Dog Track Flea Market.** Planners must have had a laugh when they decided to set up a flea market at a dog track. But the bargains here are incredible and multicultural. More than 500 vendors sell secondhand items, books, clothes, shoes, toys, antiques, furniture, tools, housewares, and objects defying description—the stuff that makes flea markets so much fun. You can sample Cuban, Caribbean, and American food and buy fresh produce from farmers. The track is five minutes east of Miami International Airport, off Dolphin Expressway (State Road 836) and Douglas Road (N.W. 37th Avenue). ✉ *401 N.W. 38th Ct., Miami,* ☎ *305/649–3000.* ⏲ *Weekends 8–4.*

**Lincoln Road Farmers Market.** Though it still has all the familiar trappings of a farmers market, this is quickly becoming a must-visit event for antiques collectors interested in modern and Moderne furniture and home accessories. It brings about 15 local produce and bakery vendors to the Lincoln Road Mall and often features plant workshops, art sales, and children's activities. This is a good place to pick up live orchids, too. ✉ *Lincoln Rd. between Meridian and Euclid Aves., South Beach,* ☎ *305/672–1270.* ⏲ *Sun. 9–6.*

**Lincoln Road Outdoor Antique and Collectibles Market.** An eclectic variety of goods should satisfy post-Impressionists, deco-holics, Edwardians, Bauhausers, Gothic, and '50s junkies. ✉ *Lincoln Rd. and Alton Rd., Miami Beach,* ☎ *305/672–1270.* ⏲ *Oct.–May, 2nd and 4th Sun. 10–5.*

**Opa-Locka–Hialeah Flea Market.** With 1,200 dealers, this is one of the largest and liveliest outdoor markets in South Florida. It's open seven days a week, but weekends are best. Expect to find everything from cast-off junk to new and used books and toys and vintage fabrics; some vendors will barter for goods. A separate building houses a food court, where southern specialties such as pork chops and fried chicken vie for your attention with Cuban and Chinese food. ✉ *12705 N.W. 47th Ave., Hialeah,* ☎ *305/688–0500.* ⏲ *Daily 7–7.*

# 8 PORTRAITS OF MIAMI AND MIAMI BEACH

# MAGIC CITY

Magic City. City of the Future. City of Dreams. Gateway to the Caribbean. Capital of South America. The New New York. These names and scores more have been coined for a city that clings to a strip of ancient coral sea-bottom heaved up eons ago between the Gulf Stream and the Everglades. Known on the map and in the news as Miami, it was originally an Indian settlement, then an agricultural community purveying some odd root called "coontie," a backwater and a port for pirates and ship-scuttlers. Later, the 1920s boomtown was erased by a scourge called hurricane and entered a period of sleepy tourism. Those "Moon over Miami" days gave rise by the 1950s to an East Coast version of Las Vegas.

Things picked up some more in the 1960s, when Miami became a second home for thousands of Cubans fleeing Fidel, and the city served as the staging area for the ill-fated Bay of Pigs invasion. That stormy decade went out with a bang, with protests in Miami Beach and race riots in Liberty City sparked by the presidential nomination of Richard Nixon at the 1968 Republican National Convention. The 1970s were the glory days of the hometown football team, the Dolphins, and then the 1980s kicked off with the Mariel boatlift of political refugees and purged prisoners from Cuba to South Florida. An explosion of immigration from South America, Latin America, and the Caribbean and, of course, the explosion of *Miami Vice* on television rounded out the decade. Enter the 1990s and more home teams—the Heat and Marlins and Panthers. South Beach was reborn as "SoBe," crammed with more models, more movie and fashion shoots, more art deco hotels, more outdoor cafés, and more retro fashion per square ft than anyplace else on Earth.

In a little more than 100 years of boom and bust, crime and punishment, high times and low, Miami has endured it all. Here, human cycles wax and wane like the tides that have lapped the shores of Biscayne Bay from the days long before time was invented.

Which brings us to the true source of the world's endless fascination with Miami: its natural beauty. Flora and fauna in exotic profusion, and beaches brushed by temperate breezes from an Atlantic riding high outside a sheltering reef, make it a paradise and a wellspring of living poetry: palm, hibiscus, bougainvillea. Anhinga, osprey, gull. Manatee, snapper, bonefish, grouper. Coral reef and hardwood hammock. Mangrove, banyan, and the fabled Dade County pine, so dense, the story goes, it takes two men to carry those two-by-fours. Mango, guava, litchi nut, grapefruit. Alligator and flamingo. Orange, lemon, lime.

Miami is a pleasure dome, but it is also a working city, a place of constant beginnings and renewal, a place where anything can happen—and often does. It is, as it always has been, a city of dreams. The late poet Richard Hugo once told a gathering of students that he had always lived on the edge in his profession and lifestyle, just as he had always lived on the edge of the continent, on one coast or another. "It's the perfect place for the writer," he said. "Out there on the edge, looking in, where you're able to observe things more clearly."

Hugo would have loved Miami, city on the edge, on the frontier; gateway between North and South, portal to the Caribbean, entry point for seekers of the American Dream. Contemporary commentators as diverse as Joan Didion (*Miami*), David Rieff (*Going to Miami*), and T. D. Allman (*Miami: City of the Future*) have agreed that the very future of the nation can be glimpsed from the vantage point of this city. As New York served as bellwether for a changing America at the beginning of the 20th century and Los Angeles did at midcentury, so Miami serves at the end of one century and the beginning of the next. Hugo would have loved the intellectual energy of it all, as wave after wave of new, revitalizing culture sweeps ashore. Miami is not a melting pot, but rather a rich stew, dizzying in its complexity.

A Miami commuter, stalled in an unaccountable traffic jam, stares in wonder as a young, bare-chested man races down the center line of a busy multilane boulevard, holding aloft a Nicaraguan flag the size of a small billboard. Buoyant strains of music trail in the young man's wake. There's a flatbed truck stopped in the intersection ahead, a troupe of musicians up there, blaring Latin rhythms at maximum volume, a cheering crowd gathered around. Nicaragua has just defeated Colombia in soccer, someone explains to the stalled commuter. Just an exhibition match in the Orange Bowl, a few miles away, but it's a big victory anyway, and normal life will have to wait a few minutes here in Miami. The stalled commuter reflects that, as reasons for being stuck in traffic go, this one is, at the very least, remarkable.

There's a certain chaos to life in a city of some 2 million that contains a full-blown colony of so many Latin American and Caribbean expatriates. But what a panoply of variety comes with the chaos: shops, markets, restaurants, consulates, and even ethnic driving schools devoted to serving a newly arrived populace. Within a 20-minute driving radius, places like these offer the old-timer (someone who's lived in Miami for more than a decade) a taste of another, and then another, culture. Some people might pick a place to live or to visit because it's all of a piece—no surprises, every warp and weave of the cultural fabric an indistinguishable part of the whole. Comfortable perhaps, and reassuring, but they won't find it in Miami.

Hugo would have treasured Miami's everyday poetry: the sights, sounds, smells, and tastes—and the touch of the Gulf Stream breeze. There might be millions of bodies milling about the metropolis, but there's always an avenue of escape. Live a lifetime in Miami, and the possibilities only multiply. Calm bay waters for sailing or for puttering about the shallows in a john boat with a pole and some bait shrimp, prospecting for mangrove snapper. Find a friend or a willing captain for a high-powered cruise to Hemingway's beloved great blue Gulf Stream, where the fins and the swords of the great game fish still cross—all just a half hour out.

Say you're a country kid at heart, yearning for a fix of rustic—if that's the case, you head south. Fortify yourself with a breakfast of *huevos rancheros* at a modest South Miami-Dade storefront run by a Mexican family that came over to work the sprawling vegetable fields covering that part of Miami-Dade County. Another few miles south, you find yourself covering terrain as vast, unspoiled, and awesome as the African veldt. No lions lurking in the unpopulated "river of grass" that is Everglades National Park, of course, but don't tell your imagination that. Besides, once you get to Flamingo—the end of the road—and stare out over those boundless tidal flats at the thousands of meandering pink creatures that give the place its name, you'll forget about the lions anyway.

Locals like to make this trip in winter. For one thing, the mosquitoes are in hibernation. For another, you can stop off on the way home for a fresh-picked-strawberry shake and some home-baked goods at the stand an enterprising Amish family maintains every season, a place tucked alongside a country road as remote and Rockwellian as a Pennsylvania lane.

Another mood might send a person into Miami's heart, say, for lunch on bustling Calle Ocho—Southwest 8th Street—the main thoroughfare of Little Havana. Although Little Havana might now be more properly called Little Latin America, there are still any number of Cuban restaurants where veteran waitresses will guide the uninitiated toward *ropa vieja,* fried pork or grouper chunks, a chicken breast braised in lime juice, and some black beans and rice and diced onion to go with that, of course. To wash it down, maybe have a Hautey cerveza or two, now that the once-celebrated Cuban beer is again being produced, now stateside. Come to Little Havana in the evening and you can combine dinner with a visit to a club for a Rio-style revue or a knockout solo performance. Whether you watch Cuban chanteuse Albita belting out a tune or high-kicking beauties in Carmen Miranda getups, you'll swear you've slipped through a warp into another life and time. But it's really Miami, and there are still another three dozen cuisines and cultures to go.

No misunderstanding why Miami has been called America's Casablanca. In the same way bits of every Mediterranean culture found their way to that North African port, so has every Latin and Caribbean culture left its mark on modern-day Miami. Much as Casablanca did, Miami mixes the elegant and the raffish, the sophisticated and the casual. At one of the scores of sidewalk cafés on South Beach sidewalks, a pair of leggy models in bikini tops and cutoffs rollerblade up to a table, chatting in German. They plop down next to a group of suited businessmen hammering out the possibilities—in rapid-fire Spanish—of a convention hotel on the vacant property just over there, at the end of Ocean Drive, where barely a decade ago one might have snapped up a run-down pensioner's hostel for the price of an upscale automobile.

A**T THE EDGE**, there is always action, and there is the heat that comes with it. Where a decade ago there was only one professional sports team in South Florida, suddenly there are four, and it's no accident that the basketball club is named for that amalgam of climatological factors and plain old frictional force known as heat.

Of course, to some, being "on the edge" leads to edginess, what with all those cultures colliding and sometimes sending off sparks. Nothing like a session of the Miami-Dade County government for a lesson in pluralism, for example. This friction has captured the attention of a certain group of artists.

In the 1920s, the writers went off to Paris. In the late 1950s, the poets hung out in North Beach and Berkeley, the novelists took New York, and the most interesting among them were known as the Beats. Now, as a new century begins—apparently these things cycle every 40 years or so—there's another literary center and another group of writers scribbling away there: genus, *Miami*; species, *mystery writer.*

There's little doubt that Miami supports more crime, thriller, and mystery writers per capita than just about any other city in the country. There's Carl Hiaasen, James W. Hall, Edna Buchanan, Paul Levine, Barbara Parker, James Grippando, Carolina Garcia Aguilera, Vicki Hendricks, and Cherokee Paul MacDonald, not to mention yours truly. Elmore Leonard spends half the year down this way and sets about the same amount of his work in these parts. Although, sadly, John D. MacDonald, who gave us Travis McGee, and Charley Willeford, who gave us Hoke Moseley, have left us, and Doug Fairbairn (*Shoot, Street Eight*) is no longer writing, their work is still in print and swells the oeuvre significantly.

Not too long ago, *Tropic* magazine commissioned a spoof, a serialized mystery novel jestingly titled *Naked Came the Manatee,* to be penned in weekly installments by members of the Miami mystery crew. Within days, and long before the first word saw newsprint, three major publishing houses heard of the venture and entered into a bidding war that escalated well into the six figures, this for the rights to reprint within hard covers what is essentially an extended joke.

How to explain it? As James W. Hall likes to say, Miami history can be divided into three periods: 1) before *Miami Vice,* 2) during *Miami Vice,* and 3) after *Miami Vice.* It's not only a good joke, it is incisive commentary on what is going on here. The 1980s television series ("*Saturday Night Fever* on a Donzi ," as one wag dubbed it) not only revolutionized American television, it's ingrained in our consciousness, worldwide and forevermore, the idea that danger, double-dealing, and flash flourish in Miami. The impact of *Miami Vice* is more than an accident of television programming. Viewers and readers are captivated by the beauty here, to be sure, as they are by the irony and the tragedy of violence in such paradise. And the attraction of Miami crime fiction, whether in print, on film, or on television, goes deeper.

Miami has become the American city of the future, the focal frontier town where immigrants stream in to settle, clash, and clamor up against all the interests that have been established before them. It is, above all, a city on the edge, where everything is up for grabs, where nothing has yet been decided, where the conflicts and the comminglings presage that which is to come for America as a whole.

South Florida's beauty represents paradise. Its open portals signify promise. The attendant and seemingly inescapable violence portends the difficulties faced by a nation that has been living on the quick since the first days of the republic. But the flip side is the sense of possibility that's palpable in the Miami air. There's a freshness here, a sense that no group's firmly in charge, that one person's dreams are as good as anyone else's, and just as likely to come true. In Miami. On the edge.

— *Les Standiford*

Les Standiford, one of Miami's crew of crime novelists, is the author of nine books, including *Presidential Deal, Black Mountain,* and *Miami: City of Dreams.*

# BOOKS AND VIDEOS

## Books

### Fiction

Steamy nights, sultry breezes, palm-dotted beaches, the heady whiff of frangipani in the air—all this idyllic setting needs is some seedy characters, a femme (or homme) fatale and a hard-boiled detective. South Florida's colorful scenery, both natural and human, is the canvas used by a whole posse of detective, mystery, and crime writers.

Interestingly, some of the finest fiction writers come from the *Miami Herald,* the city's top-notch daily newspaper. At the top of the list is Carl Hiaasen, who brilliantly skewers the pack of corrupt politicians, big-business phonies, land developers, and tourism interests every week in his *Herald* column. But it is his satirical fiction that manages to encompass everything that makes up Florida, for better and for worse. Populated by con artists, plastic surgeons, crooked cops, rednecks, bass fishermen, strippers, the Mafia, theme-park developers, backwoods hermits, and lottery winners, Hiaasen's hilarious novels will tell you all you need to know about South Florida. Read *Lucky You, Stormy Weather, Tourist Season, Skin Tight, Double Whammy, Native Tongue, Sick Puppy,* and *Strip Tease,* and you will be educated and entertained.

Pulitzer Prize–winner Edna Buchanan's two nonfiction books, *The Corpse Had a Familiar Face* and *Never Let Them See You Cry,* related the unbelievable and absolutely true crime stories she covered as a *Miami Herald* reporter. She later turned to fiction with a series of mysteries featuring Britt Montero, a Cuban-American reporter, including *Margin of Error*; *Contents Under Pressure*; *Miami, It's Murder*; and *Suitable for Framing.*

Other Miami-based mysteries are Paul Levine's Jake Lassiter series, featuring a pro football player turned lawyer, including *Night Vision* and *False Dawn*; Elmore Leonard's Palm Beach–based *Maximum Bob*; Les Standiford's *Deal on Ice,* featuring contractor-sleuth John Deal; and Charles Willeford's *Miami Blues,* with his lead character, Miami cop Hoke Mosely. James W. Hall's *Body Language* is a thriller set in Miami about a police photographer. Also located in Miami is *The Informant,* James M. Grippando's thriller about an FBI hunt for a serial killer. Author Peter Matthiessen's *Killing Mister Watson* is a novel about a real-life entrepreneur in the turn-of-the-20th-century Everglades.

The country's most gleefully sophomoric humor columnist, Dave Barry, is on staff at the *Miami Herald,* and his many weekly columns and books deal with living in South Florida. One of his latest is *Dave Barry Turns 50.*

For a peek into Cuban-American society, check out Christina Garcia's *The Agüero Sisters,* the story of two long-estranged Cuban sisters, one in Cuba, the other in Florida. *Miami Herald* columnist Ana Veciana-Suarez chronicles the lives of three generations of Cuban-American women in *The Chin Kiss King.* Although they are not set in South Florida, the novels of young Haitian author Edwidge Danticat—*Breath, Eyes, Memory*; *The Farming of Bones: A Novel*; and *Krik? Krak!*—offer insight into Haitian life and culture.

### Nonfiction

A good introduction to greater Miami is *Miami, the Magic City,* by historian Arva Moore Parks, one of the best-known chroniclers of local lore. Full of photographs and illustrations, this coffee-table book provides a fact-filled overview of the city's history from the time it was inhabited by human beings thousands of years ago. Also check out the well-documented *Miami Beach: A History,* by Howard Kleinberg. *The Life and Times of a Deco Dowager: The Edison Hotel* relays the art deco past of one of Ocean Drive's grand dames.

Pictures tell photogenic greater Miami's story well. With 400 color photos, *Miami: Hot and Cool,* by Laura Cerwinske, takes a sophisticated look at Miami as the capital of American chic. *Miami,* by Santi Visalli, is one of a series of large-format photographic books on great American cities. Another good coffee-table book is *Miami: City of Dreams,* by Les Standiford and photographer Alan S. Maltz.

As an environmental hero, the late environmentalist Marjory Stoneman Douglas's name adorns Miami-Dade County streets, a school, and a nature center. Her classic *The Everglades: River of Grass* is a must-read for those interested in capturing the essence of those unique wetlands. Landscape photographer Clyde Butcher, whose Big Cypress Gallery is on Tamiami Trail in Ochopee, shows breathtaking Florida scenes from deep in the wilderness in *Clyde Butcher, Portfolio I: Florida Landscapes.*

How Miami deals with its unique cultural diversity and influx of immigrants has been a hot topic for social observation, leading to a number of thoughtful books on the topic. *City on the Edge: The Transformation of Miami,* by Alejandro Portes documents the development of Miami's ethnic communities. Other titles include T. D. Allman's *Miami, City of the Future*; David Rieff's *Going to Miami: Exiles, Tourists and Refugees in the New America*; and Joan Didion's *Miami,* an exploration of the influential Cuban community.

The chronicles of South Beach's Art Deco District are told by one of the key players in the preservation movement, the late Barbara Baer Capitman, in *Deco Delights: Preserving the Beauty* and *Joy of Miami Beach Architecture.* For more deco pick up *Tropical Deco: The Architecture and Design of Old Miami Beach,* by Laura Cerwinske and David Kaminsky, photographer.

A good way to whet your appetite for South Florida's distinctive cuisine—dubbed Floribbean or New World by foodies—is to check out *Mmmmiami: Tempting Tropical Tastes for Home Cooks Everywhere,* by cooking teacher Carole Kotkin and *Miami Herald* food editor Kathy Martin. Their recipes reflect Miami's tropical cuisine with strong Caribbean influences. Another good choice is Steven Raichlen's *Miami Spice: The New Florida Cuisine,* with 200 recipes that use native ingredients to capture the convergence of Latin, Caribbean, and Cuban cultures.

## Film and Video

Greater Miami's ever-growing film business is visible as movie, fashion, and music video shoots take over the streets of South Beach, locations such as the Venetian Pool, or lush lots in Coconut Grove. Locals have come to take the street closings and detours in stride, but celebrity sightings are duly reported the next day in the *Miami Herald.*

Certainly Greater Miami's moviemaking industry has increased in stature since 1967, when Elvis Presley's *Clambake* was shot here (despite the appearance of mountains in some of the Miami scenes), and 1972, when Linda Lovelace's infamous *Deep Throat* gained notoriety. Recent movies at least partially filmed in South Florida include *Random Hearts,* with Harrison Ford; *Primary Colors,* with John Travolta and Emma Thompson; *Donnie Brasco,* with Johnny Depp and Anne Heche; *The Birdcage,* with Robin Williams and Nathan Lane; *Up Close and Personal,* with Robert Redford and Michelle Pfeiffer; and *Wrestling Ernest Hemingway,* with Robert Duvall and Shirley MacLaine.

The blockbuster gross-out comedy *There's Something About Mary,* with Cameron Diaz and Ben Stiller, was filmed at several South Florida locations. So was Jim Carrey's popular *Ace Ventura: Pet Detective. True Lies,* one of James Cameron's pre-*Titanic* megaeffects extravaganzas, captivated downtown Miami for days during filming of a helicopter mounted on a highrise. Key scenes for critical dud *The Specialist,* with sometime Miami resident Sylvester Stallone and Sharon Stone, were shot at the Biltmore in Coral Gables.

Other films—panned by critics but sometimes providing escapist fun—include *Wild Things,* with Kevin Bacon and Neve Campbell; *Big City Blues,* with Burt Reynolds and Vivian Wu; *Fair Game,* with William Baldwin and Cindy Crawford; *Blood and Wine,* with Jack Nicholson and Jennifer Lopez; and the unfortunate film version of Carl Hiaasen's very funny novel *Strip Tease,* starring Demi Moore and Burt Reynolds.

# INDEX

### Icons and Symbols

★ Our special recommendations
✕ Restaurant
🏨 Lodging establishment
✕🏨 Lodging establishment whose restaurant warrants a special trip
Good for kids (rubber duck)
☞ Sends you to another section of the guide for more information
✉ Address
☎ Telephone number
⏲ Opening and closing times
Admission prices

Numbers in white and black circles ③ ❸ that appear on the maps, in the margins, and within the tours correspond to one another.

## A



## B



## C